A History of
ARABIC LITERATURE

BY

CLÉMENT HUART

DARF PUBLISHERS LIMITED
LONDON
1987

FIRST PUBLISHED 1903

NEW IMPRESSION 1987

ISBN 1 85077 178 2

Printed and bound in Great Britain
by A. Wheaton & Co. Ltd., Exeter, Devon

EDITORIAL PREFACE

THIS volume has been written at my invitation for this series of Short Historics of the Literatures of the World, and has been translated from the author's manuscript by Lady Mary Loyd.

Professor Clément Huart, who is one of the most distinguished and most widely accomplished of living Orientalists, was born in 1854. He is among the many eminent Eastern scholars who have proceeded from the École des Langues Orientales Vivantes, and it is his rare distinction to have proceeded, from the first, at equal steps along the investigation of Arabic, Persian, Turkish, and Romaic literatures. He was early attached to the service of the French Foreign Office, and exercised for several years the functions of chancellor at the French Consulate at Damascus. He was ultimately called to Constantinople, originally as dragoman to the French Embassy, then as Consul. In 1890 he was sent to Asia Minor to make a report on the Arabic epigraphy of that province, and he has made similar investigations in Syria. He was recalled to Paris to fill the responsible office of secretary-interpreter for Oriental languages to the French Government. The publications of Professor Huart are numerous, and are known to all Eastern scholars.

I have to thank Professor Huart for the kindness with which he has adapted his extraordinary stores of information to the scope of the volumes of the present series. As the system of literation used for the Arabic language in France is quite different from that employed by English scholars, it was necessary to transpose Professor Huart's spelling of proper names, and this task has been performed for me by Mr. Reynold A. Nicholson, late Fellow of Trinity College, Cambridge, and now Lecturer in Persian to that University.

EDMUND GOSSE.

January 1903.

CONTENTS

ERRATA

Page 29, line 3, *for* 'Nadhîr' *read* 'Naḍîr.'

, 61, „ 13, *after* 'Lûṭ' *insert* 'ibn Yaḥyâ.'

„ 140, „ 25, *for* 'al-Mustanîr' *read* 'al-Musta'mir.'

„ 155, „ 10, *for* 'Caliph' *read* 'Caliph 'Alî.'

„ 169, „ 4 from foot, *for* 'al-Afḍal' read 'al-'Âdil.'

„ 302, „ 22, *after* 'court' *insert* 'of Mas'ûd, son.'

A HISTORY OF

ARABIC LITERATURE

CHAPTER I

THE CLIMATE AND THE RACE—ORIGINS OF ARABIC POETRY—ITS PRIMITIVE FORMS

RANGE after range of grey serrated mountain peaks; southward, again, huge plains, stretching to endless horizons, and strewn with blackish pebbles; and, last of all, the sandy Desert, tinged with red, its rolling drifts blown hither and thither by the winds, to the unceasing terror of the traveller: such are the regions which part Arabia from the rest of the earth, and which made it for so long a time a land of mystery. On every other side, the sea. The Red Sea, with its depths peopled with myriad madrepores, its dangerous reefs just hidden beneath the surface of the waters. The Indian Ocean, with its periodical monsoons, and its wild hurricanes raging over the open. The Persian Gulf, whose wavelets die on the alluvia of two great historic rivers—Euphrates and Tigris. In the centre of the Peninsula, tall, bare mountains rise once more. About their feet, where water springs are found, stand towns, with palm groves clus-

tering round them. On the sea coast are many ports, where ships embark the produce of the country—dates, coffee, gums, and balsams, while some small quantities of European exports are landed in exchange.

From time immemorial, the nomad Arabs, owners of great flocks and herds, have wandered to and fro upon this territory, moving their camps of black camel's hair-cloth tents whithersoever the grass grows or a tiny rill of water tinkles; journeying from one point to another on single-humped camels—the only steed the nature of the country will permit—in endless caravans, which sometimes become warlike expeditions.

What is this nation, which at one moment of its history leapt up before the world in sudden and amazing fortune, overthrowing the great Persian Empire of the Sâsânians, and defeating the Roman Legions of the Lower Empire? One burst of enthusiasm—it was but a flash—sent forth these men (who had done naught, hitherto, but quarrel over a good camping-ground, or fight to avenge some wrong) to conquer the whole world. But the Bedouin fell back ere long into his primitive way of life. Lovingly has he clung to the native ignorance, which he never would cast off. As for the town-bred Arab, intercourse with Syrian and Chaldean merchants, before the days of Islam, and with the pilgrims who have gathered to venerate the Sacred Temple of Mecca, the Ka'ba and its Black Stone, ever since the times of Mahomet the Prophet, has done something, it may be—but little enough—towards his civilisation, and those vices which are the virtues of the primitive man—cunning, greed, suspicion, cruelty—reign unchecked, even to this day, in the hearts of the dwellers in these inaccessible towns.

The Arab of the Desert is a man of courage, at all events. His adventurous mode of life makes bravery indispensable. A perpetual traveller, he wanders to and fro seeking the necessary water-supply for his encampment, and the scanty herbage without which his flocks cannot exist. For a lengthened period his camel was his only steed. This animal is the only one mentioned in the Bible and the ancient classics. The introduction of the horse—we know not the exact period—provided fresh food for his moral qualities. The Arab became an excellent horseman; and, from the fourth century of our era, Saracen cavalry makes its appearance. The Thamûdites, an Arab tribe, numbered fighting men who brandished lances, and rode that pachyderm whose conquest was held by Buffon to be a noble thing. Often two warriors bestrode the same dromedary, as in those squadrons which General Bonaparte sent out to scout the Desert. When the scene of combat was reached, one rider would descend, and mount the charger he had led, barebacked, to the spot. Dressed in the coat of mail borrowed from the Persians, helmet on head, and waving the long bamboo lance which ships had brought up the Persian Gulf from India to Al-Khaṭṭ, these horsemen charged and then fled, ready to charge down again upon the enemy who should advance in their pursuit. This was war: but the Bedouin was a robber too, a bandit, a brigand. The *Ghazw*—the *Razzia*, as the French say, borrowing an Algerian expression—is, indeed, a primitive form of the struggle for existence, but, to us civilised folk, it is an act of brigandage—flocks and herds driven off, women and children carried away into slavery, and now and again a general massacre. The poetry of these same brigands is by no means the

least charming among that which has come down to us from the old days.

Whence did this people spring? By language and ethnological conformation, it certainly belongs to the great Semite group, which is scattered over the whole of hither Asia. The Peninsula may possibly have been populated by a migration of tribes from the lower Babylonian plains. Yet its traditions betray some cross breeding with African races. At a very early period the slave-trade had carried negroes to Arabian soil. It is a curious fact that the Arabs themselves ascribe pure Arab blood to the Yemen populations, whom we know to be allied by race and dialect with the Ethiopians; and accept as a more recent source of their own nationality, a Semite emigration, led by Ishmael, son of Abraham and Hagar, or the issue of his marriage with a daughter of Yemen. Be that as it may, it was the struggle between the descendants of Qaḥṭân, King of Sheba, and the children of ʿAdnân, of the house of Ishmael, and the wars of the tribes connected with them, whose migrations led them hither and thither across the mountains and over the wide sand wastes, which evoked the poetic genius of Arabia.

The long caravan-marches across the monotonous deserts, when the camel's steady swing bends the rider's body almost double, turning the unaccustomed traveller sick and giddy, soon taught the Arab to sing rhymes. He even noted, very soon, that as he hurried the pace of his recitation the long string of camels would raise their heads and step out with quickened pace. This creature, stupid and vindictive though it be, is sensitive, to some extent, to music, or, at all events, to rhythm. Its four heavy steps gave the metre, and the

alternations of long and short syllables in the spoken language the successive pulsations of the said metre. This was the *ḥidâ*, the song of the leading camel-driver of the caravan. And here we have the origin of the prosodic metre, unconsciously invented by the native genius of the Bedouin, springing from the necessities of the life in which his monotonous existence dragged itself out, for which the theorists of a later date formulated laws. We know that the idea of Khalîl's prosody came to him from hearing the hammers of the workmen in the bazaars ringing on their anvils with alternate cadenced strokes. Until the wise grammarian made this fruitful discovery, the Arabs had produced poetry with no knowledge of its rules, beyond their own innate feeling for poetic rhythm.

Here, then, we see the Arab singing his way along his lengthy journeys, and weaving poems which celebrated a few restricted subjects—the image of the best beloved, the remnants of a forsaken camp, or the struggles of some bloody feud. Not that his memories of the frays in which he had fought, the pillaged caravans, the quarrels over a spring of water, the contentions about stolen camels, had ever stirred an epic feeling in him. That wondrous appanage of the Indo-European races, their power of translating historic or legendary events into mighty poems, teeming with grandiose pictures, whose superhuman heroes are types of an ideal for ever sought and never realised, has no existence in the brain of the peoples speaking the Semitic tongues. The breath comes shorter, but it is none the less mighty for that; and though its expression of thought may be concise, its effect on the human mind has been considerable, since from this inspiration have sprung the

religious prose-poems which had their birth in Jerusalem and Mecca.

It was from the Desert, then, that Arab poetry was to come ; for the towns were too much preoccupied with commercial matters to give literature any chance of growth. Southwards, the Ḥimyarite populations, living on those trade routes which, from the most ancient times, had connected Egypt with India by the sea highway, had founded cities which grouped themselves into States—amongst them that of Sheba, whose legendary Queen figures amongst the great folk who journeyed to salute the glory of the children of Israel, the son of mighty David, the wise King Solomon, and the existence of which, in the first centuries of the Christian era, is proved by monuments now in ruins, in Yemen and Ḥaḍramaut, and by inscriptions in Ḥimyaric characters, surveyed by J. Halévy and Glaser. Northwards, Syrian civilisation had early reached the Arabian oases, and brought Syrian gods with it, as at Taimâ. On the frontiers of the Roman Empire, and on those of the Persian Empire of the Arsacids and Sâsânians, little States had grown up—the princes of Ghassân, to the west of the Syrian Desert, the princes of Ḥîra, not far from the Euphrates, ruled small kingdoms, centres of civilisation which shed their brightness farther than one would have thought. At Ḥîra, notably, where a mixed population drawn from divers countries had settled, the ʿIbâds, former slaves, who had been freed, and remained clients of the reigning tribes, practised mercantile pursuits, and travelled about Arabia, whither they carried the wines grown on the banks of the great river and ripened in their own cellars. These ʿIbâds were Christians, and we shall shortly see that it was these wine

merchants who, when they sold the Bedouins the enchanting beverage their own oases did not supply, brought in ideas of Christianity as well, and made proselytes such as would hardly have been expected, seeing the nature of the gospel they set out to preach.

The most ancient remnants of this primitive Arab poetry are fragments of poems relating to the *Hijâ*—satire—to which a superstitious feeling was attached, and a magic power ascribed. The poet—properly speaking, the sage, *Shâ'ir*, a sort of soothsayer—was called on to compose these satires, which passed from lip to lip amongst tribes of a common origin, and were swiftly answered by other satires, sprung from the brain of the poet of the tribal adversaries.

Nothing now remains of the songs improvised—according to a former Prefect of Constantinople, St. Nîlus, who turned hermit about A.D. 400—by the Sinai Arabs, when they reached a spring after a long journey. Sozomen, a Greek author, who wrote an ecclesiastical history in the fifth century, reports that in A.D. 372 Mania or Mavia, Queen of the Saracens, defeated the Roman troops in Palestine and Phœnicia, and that the memory of this victory was preserved by the Arabs in their popular songs. Human remembrance, unless set down on brick, or stone, or paper, is a very short-lived thing, and the memory of bygone days soon fades away. We must not wonder, then, that the most ancient of the Arab poems only go back to the sixth century of our era, when Nabatean travellers brought the Estrangelo alphabet from Syria, and applied it to the Arab tongue—an attempt of this kind may be noted in the bilingual inscription of Ḥarrân.

It was to the Jinns, the mischievous rather than

wicked spirits which inhabit solitary places, that the ancient poet ascribed his inspiration; and the Jinn breathed into him the idea of bantering the tribal enemy, always with the underlying thought that the biting satire, repeated in the various camps, might work the foe some harm, might cast a spell upon him, as our own magicians of the Middle Ages used to say. The poet was the wise man, the learned in magic processes, the tribal oracle, inspired by the Jinn. It was at the order of the old poet Zuhair ibn Janâb that the encampment was moved, or set up, at whatever time and place he deemed best. On his advice wars were made, and when the booty was divided he was given his share, the portion of the bravest. Satire was his weapon, wounding, tormenting, like the sharpest blade, driving the peoples to fall upon each other. But at the same time it was an incantation, threatening the foe, seeking to harm him by stirring up the malevolent deities of the Desert, cursing him, dooming him to ruin and destruction, by the use of the fetish word known to the sage, the *shâʿir*, and to him alone. Unfortunately no text of any of these satires has come down to us. But we can easily imagine the subjects on which they turn, by a reference to Balaam's famous curse.

The *Hijâ* had special rites connected with it, such as the anointing of the hair on one side of the head, and the wearing of one sandal only, and the trailing of the mantle on the ground. The formulas were first of all pronounced in rhymed prose, *sajʿ*; this was replaced by the metre called *rajaz*, a sort of very simple chant, two long syllables, followed by a short, and then another long: from that time Arab poetry had an actual existence, although this, according to native feeling, is not a

true prosodic metre. But the Arabs have at all events preserved its memory as being their primitive metre, from which all the rest have proceeded—all, at least, used by the Desert poets. For, as time went on, town life, and the influence of music and the dance, led to the invention of other rhythms.

CHAPTER II

PRE-ISLAMIC POETRY

THE most ancient pre-Islamic poems are those forming the collection of the seven *mu'allaqât*—literally "the suspended," a name given them at a much later date by Ḥammâd-al-Râwiya, and on which is founded the absolutely untrue legend that these pieces, written with golden ink, were hung up in the famous Temple at Mecca, in the Ka'ba. The name was merely intended as an allusion to the place of honour they hold on the Arabian Parnassus, even as a chandelier may be suspended in the midst of an apartment, or rather as a necklace may be worn hanging about the neck—for they were also called *al-Sumûṭ*, "the necklaces of pearls." The poets whose masterpieces have received the honour of being thus grouped together are Imru'u'l-Qais, Ṭarafa, Zuhair, Labîd, 'Amr ibn Kulthûm, 'Antara, and Al-Ḥârith ibn Ḥilliza (according to some, the two last poets are Nâbigha and A'shâ). At this epoch, the *qaṣîda* had already reached its definite form. According to the ancient rules quoted by Ibn Qutaiba, the author of a *qaṣîda* must begin by a reference to the forsaken camping-grounds. Next he must lament, and pray his comrades to halt, while he calls up the memory of the dwellers who had departed in search of other encampments and fresh water-springs. Then he begins to touch on love-matters,

bewailing the tortures to which his passion puts him, and thus attracting interest and attention to himself. He recounts his hard and toilsome journeying in the Desert, dwells on the lean condition of his steed, which he lauds and describes; and finally, with the object of obtaining those proofs of generosity which were the bard's expected meed and sole support, he winds up with a panegyric of the Prince or Governor in whose presence the poem is recited.

This last rule is, of course, not applicable in the case of the poet whose works are believed to be the most ancient of the Seven, and whom fate had placed from birth upon a throne. IMRU'U'L-QAIS Ḥunduj, the wandering king, came of a southern race, the Kinda. His ancestors had built up a principality in Najd. His father, Ḥujr, a severe man, desiring to punish his son for the amorous passion which possessed him, sent him away to act as shepherd to his flocks. Ḥujr lost his life in the revolt of the Beni-Asad, and the poet began a career of adventure, living the life of a dethroned king, seeking means to re-establish his father's power, which he never recovered. He took refuge at last with Samuel, Prince of Taimâ, who owned the Castle of Ablaq, and professed the Jewish faith. Towards the year 530, the Roman Emperor Justinian, who had thought of utilising his services against the Persians, then threatening his frontiers, granted Imru'u'l-Qais leave, at the request of the Prince of Ghassân, who held the Syrian frontier for the Romans, to wait on him. He journeyed by post (horse-post and camel-post) to Constantinople, and sojourned there a long time, expecting a place, which was slow in coming, from the Emperor, already an aging man. He was appointed Phylarch of

Palestine, and was making his way back to the Desert, when he died at Ancyra, poisoned by the Emperor's order, and, as the legend runs, by a garment of honour —a robe of Nessus which covered his body with ulcers, as punishment for the seduction of a royal lady. Mahomet held him to be the best of all the poets, and their chief; and according to tradition, he was the first to make fixed rules for poetic composition. When the messengers came to tell him of his father's death, he was drinking wine and throwing the dice. He went on with his game, and not till it was finished did he cry: "I will touch neither wine nor woman till I have slain a hundred men of the Beni-Asad, and shorn the forelocks, as a trophy, from the heads of another hundred!" He was a bold spirit, and did not hesitate to cast the three arrows of fate at the idol called Dhû'l-Khalaṣa, in the town of Tabâla, because destiny forbade him to pursue his vengeance for his father's death.

With the poet-king we must mention, as a creator of the *qaṣîda*, Muhalhil, whose surname has generally been translated "the subtle poet," but it seems more probably to have been a nickname given him on account of his having used the expression *halhaltu*, in one of his lines, to denote "I made an echo." Only a very small number of his verses are extant.

Nâbigha Dhubyânî, who belonged to a tribe from the neighbourhood of Mecca, was a town-dweller. We find him at Ḥîra—a half-Persian, half-Arab city—during the reigns of the Kings Al-Mundhir III. and Al-Mundhir IV. This town became a literary centre whence poetry radiated all over the Peninsula. The successor of the last-named King, Nu'mân Abû Qâbûs, grew angry with the poet, who had used too great freedom in some lines

written to flatter the Queen. The exile departed to Damascus, to princes who were the rivals of the rulers of Ḥîra, and clients of the Court of Constantinople, the Ghassânids. He was right well received by 'Amr ibn Ḥârith, but, after that prince's death, he returned to Ḥîra and was taken back into favour. When his patron died, he withdrew from the court of the usurper imposed on the State by the conquering Persians, returned to his own tribe, and there died, very shortly before Mahomet's preaching set Arabia aflame. Nâbigha was a courtier-poet. He boasted that he kept his compositions for princes, but he made superb use of the liberal gifts his flatteries won him. He was at every feast, but he spent his money royally.

In contrast, we have a true Desert poet, 'ANTARA, son of Shaddâd, whose name was later to serve the popular story-tellers of the Romance of 'Antar as the incarnate type of the virtues ascribed to the wandering paladins of the heathen tribes. The hero of the tribe of 'Abs was a mulatto, the son of an Abyssinian slave, and his lower lip was split. His personal bravery won him reputation as a warrior, and advanced him from his state of slavery to the position of Shaddâd's acknowledged son. He took part in the terrible war arising out of the rivalry between the stallion Dâḥis and the mare Ghabrâ. Treachery alone prevented the famous courser from winning the race, and in his vengeance, Qais, chief of the tribe of 'Abs, waged bitter war against his enemies. 'Antara was the rhapsodist of these long fights. He sang the battle of Al-Farûq, at which the prowess of the Absites saved their women from slavery. He had sworn he would never leave his enemy in peace "as long as they waved a lance." 'Antara perished while fighting against

the tribe of Ṭai. He had grown old, and his youthful activity had forsaken him. He is said to have fallen from his horse, and to have been unable to regain his feet in time. His death was the signal for peace, and the end of the long-drawn hostilities. In spite of the tribe's desire to avenge its hero and its bard, a compensation of a hundred camels was accepted for the murder of one of its scions, and the poets celebrated the close of the long struggle. ʿAntara sang the praises of ʿAbla, his mistress, but a good fight was always the favourite subject of his lay. He it was who said, "We whirled as the millstone whirls on its axis, while our swords smashed upon the fighters' skulls."

Another court-poet was ṬARAFA, whose name was ʿAmr ibn al-ʿAbd. He formed one of the circle about a king of Ḥîra, ʿAmr, the son of Hind. His uncle, Mutalammis, was called Jarîr, the son of ʿAbdal-Masîḥ (or, according to Ibn Qutaiba, of ʿAbdal-ʿUzzâ). He was surnamed Mutalammis, "he who seeks earnestly," because he had spoken, in a celebrated line, of the blue fly that pries everywhere. His sister Khirniq was also a writer of verse. Ṭarafa, who was of a thoughtless and ungrateful turn, made game of his uncle, who had used an improper expression in one of his lines. "Thy tongue will be thy ruin," quoth the uncle. The nephew ventured to make game of the king himself, who, to get rid of him, bethought him of sending him with his uncle Mutalammis on a mission to the Governor of Baḥrain. The uncle opened his own letter of credentials, and discovered that the king therein commanded the governor to put him to death. Thinking his nephew's letter contained the same order, he counselled him to open it. But Ṭarafa would not break the king's seal. The uncle

took fright, and fled into Syria. Ṭarafa continued his journey, and was buried alive as soon as he reached Baḥrain. It is curious to note that his poetry gives more proof of judgment than did his behaviour. He is almost the only one of the ancient poets in whose work we find some signs of meditation, maxims, or apophthegms. All his fellows are carried away by the exuberance of their own eager but childish nature.

ZUHAIR ibn Abî Sulmâ, of the tribe of Muzaina, is, with Imru'u'l-Qais and Nâbigha Dhubyânî, one of the three great poets of the Arab tribes. It is hard to say which is to be preferred, but all critics agree in placing them far above the rest. Zuhair came of a family possessing the poetic gift. His father-in-law, Aus ibn Ḥajar, his sisters Sulmâ and Al-Khansâ, and his son, Ka'b, the panegyrist of Mahomet, all made themselves reputations. He had the moralist's temperament; his verses were marked by seriousness, by a sententious and didactic tendency. He cared little for praise, which does not ensure immortality, and especially he shunned untruthful praise. He would not borrow lines from other poets to insert them amongst his own, or use words difficult to understand. Such is the opinion expressed concerning him by the Caliph 'Umar, who specially admired Zuhair's careful avoidance of anything "ḥûshî," that is to say, unintelligible, in his language. There is a story—but probably a mere legend, like so many handed down from those ancient times—that when Zuhair was a hundred years old, he met the prophet Mahomet, who prayed God to protect him from the *jinn* that inspired his poetic effusions. The poet, who was a warrior, suddenly forsook his tribe, in consequence of some injustice done him in a division of booty,

took refuge with the tribe of Ghaṭafân, and there remained. He sang the peaceful outcome of the long war of Dâḥis.

Harim, his patron, had vowed to give him gifts on every occasion, whether he sang his praises, or sought a favour, or even made him a sign of salutation. Zuhair, ashamed of receiving slaves or horses in this fashion, made it a rule, when he met Harim in any gathering, to greet every one save him. These are scruples peculiar to the Desert, manners of a certain noble harshness. In later years Harim's descendants were to say, "The praise is noble indeed, but so also were our gifts!" And the answer was to come, "Your gifts have vanished, but his poems live on. They are robes of honour which Time cannot decay."

His reputation was that of a high-born and wealthy man, of gentle manners, and remarkable for his scrupulous piety. His verses are preferred because they show superior beauty, and the least exiguity in thought; they convey the largest number of ideas in the fewest words, their expressions of praise are the most excessive, and they contain the largest number of proverbs. To Al-Khansâ fell the melancholy duty of pronouncing the funeral oration over her brother.

'ALQAMA ibn 'Abada, surnamed Al-Faḥl, was of the race of Tamîm. He addressed a poem to Al-Ḥârith ibn Jabala, Prince of Ghassân, in gratitude for his release of some prisoners, the poet's compatriots. The story of his rivalry with Imru'u'l-Qais is a mere legend. His comparison of the camel-mare which was bearing him across the desert with a fleeing ostrich, is famous. He describes the huge, long-legged bird leaving its nest to search for food, feeding quietly on the bitter seeds borne by the bushes growing in the sands,

and then, as it remembers its forsaken eggs, setting off running on its long, bare, black shanks. Elsewhere he gives a striking picture of the whitened skeletons of the camels dead of weariness upon the sands, the skin, dried and shrivelled by the sun, all blackened, and still clinging, here and there, to the pale bones.

The *Mu'allaqât* are not the only ancient poems preserved to us. There are also the *Dîwâns* (collections of poems arranged according to the alphabetical order of the rhyme) of the six poets, brought together by the grammarian Al-Aṣma'î, preserved in a revised form —which we owe to the learned Spanish Arab, Yûsuf al-A'lam of Santa Maria, who lived in the eleventh century—and published by Ahlwardt; the poems known as *Mufaḍḍaliyyât*, so called after Al-Mufaḍḍal al-Ḍabbî, who collected them into one volume for his pupil, Prince Al-Mahdî, in the eighth century—a beginning of the publication of these was made by Thorbecke; the *Jamharat Ash'âr al-'Arab* (collection of Bedouin poetry), compiled under a fictitious name, but quoted as early as the eleventh century, by Ibn Rashîq, and printed at Bûlâq; the *Ḥamâsa*, or collection of warlike deeds, of Abû Tammâm, published by Freytag, and translated into German by F. Rückert; a work of the same name and kind, compiled at the same period (ninth century), by Al-Buḥturî, a single manuscript copy of which is at Leyden; the *Akhbâr al-Luṣûṣ* (stories of brigands) by the grammarian Sukkarî, a fragment of which has been published by Wright; and the great *Kitâb al-aghânî* (Book of Songs) of Abû'l-Faraj 'Alî al-Iṣfahânî, published at the Bûlâq printing-press in twenty volumes, to which M. Brünnow has added a twenty-first, from manuscripts discovered in European

libraries. This huge literary compilation is our most valuable source as to everything regarding the circumstances amidst which the poets of the first centuries of Arab literature lived their lives and composed their works. In addition to these texts we should mention the poems of the Hudhailites—the tribe of Hudhail which dwelt to the south-east of Mecca, and which has left us poetry both of pre-Islamic and Moslem times, which has been collected by Sukkarî, and studied and partially translated by Kosegarten, Abicht, and Wellhausen.

Side by side with the six poets thus grouped together by their admiring commentators, we find many warriors, singing their own exploits and their loves. Thâbit ibn Jâbir al-Fahmi was surnamed TA'ABBAṬA-SHARRAN (one who carries evil under his arm), because he was seen one day carrying a knife under his armpit. Like ʻAntara, he was a mulatto, like him, he was a wandering paladin, and if he has not attained a like celebrity, it is because no popular romance carried his name to distant lands.

There is a tale that he brought a ram back with him out of the desert, and that this ram was really a *Ghoul*, a female *jinn;* and another that he brought his mother back a sack full of vipers. These are mere explanations, made up at a later date, of his strange nickname. He was a robber; he could run down the very gazelles. In his poems, he mentions his adventures with the ghouls, and how he saw them, with their two eyes set in the middle of a hideous head, like a cat's, their split-up tongues and misshapen legs, looking like roasted dogs wrapped in a rough fustian garment. Abû Wahb, a man of Thaqîf, who was a coward in spite of his inches, met the famous runner one day, when he himself was wearing a handsome cloak. He inquired how it was

that he could overcome every one, though he was short and slight and stunted. "It is my name," replied the brigand. "When I meet a man, I say 'I am Ta'abbaṭa-Sharran,' then his courage melts away, and he gives me whatever I demand." The questioner proposed that he should buy the other's name, the price to be the gorgeous cloak, and the right to bear the surname Abû Wahb; the bargain was struck, and the purchaser gave up his new garment, receiving rags and tatters in exchange. But the poet went from tribe to tribe, singing, "Though we may have exchanged names, who will give Abû Wahb my patience in adversity, my indomitable courage in the face of all misfortunes?" He was fertile in cunning artifice, and his sense of hearing was singularly delicate. One night he warned his camp companions that the foe was near at hand, and when they inquired on what he founded this opinion, he replied, "I hear men's hearts beating, here, under my feet." Are those fine lines in the Ḥamâsa, on the death of the poet's kinsmen, his work? "On the road below Salʿ a slain man lies, whose blood shall not be shed without due vengeance!" Some Arab critics have ascribed them to Khalaf al-Aḥmar.

The comrade of Ta'abbaṭa-Sharran's adventures, SHANFARÂ, "the man with thick lips," a very hard-featured personage, was one of those celebrated runners whom a horse at full gallop could not outstrip. Hence the famous proverb, "A swifter runner than Shanfarâ."

During a war with the Beni-Salâmân, he swore to kill a hundred men, and kept his oath as follows. Every time he came across a man of the tribe, he shot an arrow and struck him in the eye. In this fashion he piled up ninety-nine victims. The tribe of

the Beni-Salâmân set about ridding itself of this troublesome enemy. Usaid, son of Jâbir, one of his rivals in fleetness, lay in wait for him, and caught him one night when he had gone down into a gorge to slake his thirst. Thus he perished; but, the legend tells us, one of his foes, passing later where his skull lay on the ground, gave it a kick. A splinter of bone ran into his foot, making a wound of which he died; and so the full tale of victims was accomplished, and the vow was kept. Shanfarâ, if we may believe his lines preserved in the Ḥamâsa, had himself requested that he might lie unburied. "Bury me not! for you are forbidden to perform this duty for me. But thou, O Hyena, shalt rejoice when they carry off my head (and in my head the most of me resides)." Ta'abbaṭa-Sharran pronounced his funeral oration in verse.

He is famous for his great ode, the *Lâmiyyat al-ʿArab*, or poem rhyming in *l*, of which Silvestre de Sacy and Fresnel have given us fine translations. Doubt has been felt as to whether the famous poem was really written by Shanfarâ, and it has been pointed out that the ancient Arab philologists were not aware of its existence. But if Shanfarâ was not the author, it is certainly the work of some one who was thoroughly acquainted with Arab life in ancient times, and who felt the inspiration of the wild sons of the desert stirring within him. In this case it can have been written by no other than Khalaf al-Aḥmar.

Besides the name of ʿAntara, the tribe of ʿAbs may cite with pride that of ʿURWA IBN AL-WARD; he was, in fact, considered more as a poet, and ʿAntara more as a hero. His father, whose praises ʿAntara sang, had fought in the war of Dâḥis. He himself, like all his

fellows, was a warrior. He was called "*ʿUrwa of the Needy*," because he had gathered a troop of poor plunderers, whose needs he supplied when they came in empty-handed from a foray. He sang of them: "May God cast shame upon the poor man, when, wrapped in the darkness of the night, he crawls along the soft earth, fumbling among the skinned camels. But how noble-looking is the poor man when his cheek is reddened by the flame of fire borrowed from his neighbour, which casts light upon him! If he meet death, it is a glorious death. If he gain riches, he has made himself worthy of them!" He had carried off a young girl named Salma, given her her freedom, and married her. Ten years later, her family bought her back, snatching ʿUrwa's consent in a moment of drunkenness. Salma left him, extolling his generosity and valour; but she had never learnt to endure being treated as a slave by the women of his tribe. His liberality knew no bounds. "As for me, I would cut up my body to feed my guests, and I am content to drink pure water." He has been compared with the famous Ḥâtim, of the tribe of Ṭai.

DHÛ'L-AṢBAʿ AL-ʿADWÂNÎ, whose proper name was Ḥurthân ibn al-Ḥârith, owed his surname of "the man with the finger," to the fact that one of his fingers had withered as the result of a viper's bite. The tribe of Adwân, to which he belonged, was powerful on account of its numerous fighting men, of the fame of ʿÂmir, son of Ẓarib, who was accepted by every Arab of Qais blood as his *Ḥakam*, or supreme arbiter, and of its peculiar prerogative, that of haranguing the pilgrims on their return from Mecca, and granting them leave to rejoin their tribes. This prosperity died away, as a result of internecine quarrels, and it was the downfall of his tribe

which inspired the elegies of Dhû'l-Aṣba'. "The props of the tribe of 'Adwân were like unto serpents crawling on the ground. They strove to rise one higher than the other, and all they reached was emptiness." He reached a very advanced age; and his four sons-in-law, fearing he might fall into dotage, endeavoured to prevent him from dissipating his fortune; but he made answer to them: "If you assert that I have grown old, know ye that I have never been held to be a burden, nor a being of dulness or imbecility. Wherefore then do ye so slander me?" And in another piece of verse: "Marvel not, Umâma, at these happenings. Fortune and Fate have overwhelmed us!" Umâma was his daughter, herself a poetess, who mourned with him the decay of the power of 'Adwân. "They have passed a goblet round; woe to those who have drunk! They have perished, they have sought refuge in the desert!" In the counsels given to his son Usaid (the lion-cub), he sets forth a noble ideal for the Arab warrior. "Use thy goods nobly; make thyself the brother of all generous men, whenever thou findest means of entering into brotherhood with them. However wide the distance, never forget the debt thou owest thy brother, and the poor. Rush into battle where the most intrepid of heroes shuns the charge, and when thou art summoned on an important matter, take all the burden of it on thee."

QUTBA IBN AUS AL-ḤÂDIRA fell out with Zabbân ibn Sayyâr, and there was an exchange of satires between the two. It was Zabbân who surnamed him Al-Ḥâdira (the thick, the squat), and the nickname stuck to him. "One would think you were a woman, with big shoulders and thin flanks!" It was when they had been out hunting

together. Zabbân drew aside, in the evening, to roast the game. Then Ḥâdira called out: "You forsake your comrade, you think of nothing but your own jaws out there in the darkness!" Nettled by the speech, Zabbân shot back the line, in which he compared him to a "big-shouldered woman," and so the duel went on.

ʿAbîd ibn al-Abraṣ, of the tribe of Asad, dwelt at the court of Ḥîra, and held habitual intercourse with Nâbigha Dhubyânî. He is said to have been put to death, at an advanced age, by King Mundhir, the son of Mâ'ul-samâ, sacrificed on the tomb of two of the king's former friends, whom he had caused to be buried alive, in a fit of rage. The king had sworn to slay the first person who entered his presence on the second day of annual mourning he had voluntarily imposed on himself, and to feed the ravens with his blood. The poet pleaded for leave to drink himself drunk before he died. This barbarous custom held sway until the king was touched by the nobility of a certain Ḥanẓala, of the tribe of Ṭai, who, having asked a respite, and promised to return, came back in time to fulfil his promise and save his surety, who was just about to suffer in his stead. After that incident, Mundhir abolished all bloody sacrifices. ʿAbîd was a poor man, with no possessions of his own. One day he was leading the flocks belonging to his sister Mâwiyya to the well, when he was driven away by a man who struck him on the forehead. The poor wretch turned him about, crestfallen, and fell asleep under some shady trees. He rose from that slumber a poet. A genius had come to him in his sleep, and laid a poetic charm between his lips.

Famous everywhere for his unbounded generosity is Ḥâtim, of the tribe of Ṭai. When the "deaf month"

(Rajab), observed by the pagans of Muḍar, began, he killed ten camels a day, and fed his guests. The poets, Al-Ḥuṭai'a and Bishr ibn Abî Khâzim, were both partakers of his hospitality. He had lost his father in early youth, and was brought up by his grandfather, Sa'd ibn al-Ḥashraj, on whom he played the sorry trick of presenting the herd of camels he had been sent out to keep, as a gift to a passing caravan of poets. His ambition to be considered the most generous of men had led him into this piece of extravagance. His grandfather could not forgive the prank. He struck his tents and left Ḥâtim alone, with the slave girl he had given him, his mare and her foal. Then it was that Ḥâtim spoke the splendid lines: "I suffered not when Sa'd and his family departed, leaving me lonely in my home, parted from all my kin. By squandering my fortune I have won swift glory, just as War is baring her hideous twisted fangs." Ḥâtim's tomb was set round with stones, standing facing each other, like mourners. Hither came Abû'l-Khaibarî, calling upon the dead man, and praying him to provide a feast. Next morning he found his camel-mare slaughtered and his comrades feasting on her flesh. Shortly afterwards Ḥâtim's son came to him, saying his father had appeared to him in a dream, and charged him to replace the camel he had been forced to slaughter to keep up his reputation for hospitality. And there were many more. Laqîṭ ibn Ya'mur, of the tribe of Iyâd, which haunted the wide Mesopotamian plains, composed a long ode, warning his fellow-tribesmen of the ambushes prepared by the Persian King, Chosroes, who was resolved to clear the banks of the Euphrates of these marauders; but they would not believe their poet's warnings, and were all surprised and put to the sword. Aus ibn

Ḥajar, of the tribe of Tamîm, belonged to the far-off province of Baḥrain. He was a wandering bard, who travelled through Northern Arabia and the countries watered by the Euphrates, whither the court of Ḥîra attracted him. His verses, mere fragments of which remain to us, are full of descriptions of hunting and warlike episodes of every kind. During one of his journeys he was thrown from his camel and broke both his legs. He was tended by Fuḍâla ibn Kilda, who came and pitched his tent on the very spot where the poet lay, and by his daughter Ḥalîma, and, in his gratitude, dedicated poems to them, which we still possess.

An interesting historical figure is that of UMAYYA, son of Abû'l-Ṣalt, a Meccan, born at Ṭâ'if, "who had read the books and practised the doctrines of the Jewish Christians," and who, nevertheless, remained a pagan till he died, in 630, eight years after the Hegira. Towards the year 572, either he or his father had been one of a deputation sent by the Quraishites to wait on the King of Yemen, Saif ibn Dhî Yazan, and had offered him congratulations in verse on his victory over the Abyssinians. The subjects of Umayya's poetry, as a rule, were religious, and drawn from the common source of Jewish and Christian ideas. He may be looked on as a precursor of Mahomet. In one of his poems he called the Day of Judgment "the day of mutual disappointment," *yaum al-takhâbun*, an expression which has passed into the text of the Koran (chap. 64). He applied strange names to the Deity, such as had never fallen on Arab ears before. Sometimes *siltît*, "the emperor"; sometimes, again, *taghrûr*, "the crown-bearer" (Persian, *taka-barâ*). He wore a hair shirt to mortify his flesh. In his poems he refers to the Old Testament prophets,

and to the *Ḥanîfs*, an Arab sect which held the tenets of Abraham's faith, and was the cradle of Islamism. He forbade the use of wine, and did not believe in idols. The Moslems asserted that he would fain have been chosen by God to be His prophet, and that on this account he was jealous of Mahomet, against whom he was still composing satires in 624.

The real name of AL-A'SHÂ was Maimûn ibn Qais. He was born in the distant land of Yamâma, south of Najd, which lies along the great trackless desert of Dahnâ. His tomb was to be seen there, in the village of Manfûḥa. With his eulogies, for which he took his fee, he fared all through Arabia, from Ḥaḍramaut to Ḥîra, near the Euphrates. His mocking verses made him the terror of his foes. He was a monotheist, and believed in the Resurrection and the Last Judgment. His opinions had felt the influence of his Christian associates, whether of the 'Ibâds of Ḥîra, who sold him wine, or of his friend the Bishop of Najrân in Yemen. His verse is praised for the variety of its metre, and the art of its panegyric and its satire. His descriptions of wine and of the wild ass are much quoted. The ode in which he sang the Prophet Mahomet's mission is famous all over the East. His father, Qais, had been surnamed *Qatîl al-jû'* (dead of hunger) because, when he entered a cave for the sake of shade, a rock slipped down the mountain and closed the orifice, so that he could not get out, and was starved to death.

The son takes front rank among the Arab poets. Silvestre de Sacy held him a worthy equal of the authors of the Mu'allaqât, and the Arabs, when reckoning up their best pre-Islamic poets, likened him to Imru'u'l-Qais, Nâbigha, and Zuhair. His verses sing the praise

of Huraira, his beloved, a black slave. She had a beautiful voice, and her master made her sing for his delight. He went every year to the fair at ʿUkâẓ, and was enabled, by the praises he addressed to a certain Muhallek, a poor man, in gratitude for his hospitality, to assist him in finding husbands for his eight daughters. Once when he was returning from the fair, laden with gifts, and feared he might be robbed by the Beni-ʿÂmir, through whose territory he had to pass, he begged ʿAlqama, son of ʿUlâtha, to protect him. ʿAlqama undertook to defend him from men and jinns. Al-Aʿshâ inquired if he would promise to defend him from death as well, a request which ʿAlqama refused. But ʿÂmir, the son of Ṭufail, promised to protect him from death itself. "How so?" asked Aʿshâ. "If death comes to thee whilst thou art under my protection," answered ʿÂmir, "I will pay thy kinsfolk the fine which is the price of blood." This reply satisfied Aʿshâ, but not his original and now ousted protector, who cried: "If I had known what he was asking me, I would have granted his desire."

Amongst the town poets we must mention QAIS, son of Al-Khaṭîm, who lived at Yathrib, a town later called Medina, which name it bears at the present day. He made himself famous by his avenging pursuit of the murderers of his father and grandfather, and by the war he thus caused between the Aus and Khazraj tribes. He was a handsome man, with eye-brows that met, great black eyes, red lips, and dazzlingly white teeth. Ḥassân ibn Thâbit had counselled the poetess Al-Khansâ to direct her satires against Qais. "I never attack a person I have never seen," she answered. One day she went to see him, and found

him lying on the floor of a room. She stirred him with her foot until he rose, and then made him step backwards and forwards, till Qais exclaimed : "One would think she was examining a slave before she buys him in the market!" Then he lay down and went to sleep again. "Never will I attack such a man as that!" said Al-Khansâ. He died in battle of an arrow wound.

The custom of mourning over the dead, and the trade of professional female mourners, gave birth to the elegy in praise of the dead (*marthiya*), the composition of which, like the performance of this portion of the obsequies, was confided to women only. Such poems open with a description of the feelings of the bereaved, and the tears the mourner is unable to control. They go on to detail the virtues of the defunct, and the poignant regret the loss of such an individuality must cause. These eulogies are for the most part based on the chief virtues of the pagan Arab, valour and generosity. Last of all comes the appeal for vengeance. AL-KHANSÂ won fame by her elegies in this style. Her name was Tumâḍir. The surname by which she is known signifies "The wild cow with a crushed muzzle." She was first married to Mirdâs, the son of Abû ʿÂmir, and secondly, after his death, to ʿAbdallah, the son of ʿAbd al-ʿUzzâ. She sang the memories of her two brothers, Muʿâwiya and Ṣakhr, the younger of whom, himself a poet, was killed in a foray.

JEWISH AND CHRISTIAN POETS

In the towns in the north of Ḥijâz there dwelt Jews, who may possibly have left Palestine during the wars of Titus and Hadrian. But local tradition asserts that

they came into the country soon after the death of Moses, and that at the time of the Roman Conquest, the Quraiẓa, Hadal, and Nadhîr tribes joined their co-religionists. These colonies formed a nucleus of religious propaganda, and Arab tribes associated themselves with them. Their religion was the only thing they had preserved. Their language had become purely Arab. Like other nomads, they began to chant verses, and the greatest of their poets was SAMAUAL (Samuel), the grandson of ʽÂdiyâ. He was a rich nobleman, who dwelt in the castle of Ablaq, called "the unique," close to the town of Taimâ. This castle had been built by his grandfather, who had digged a well within it. The Arabs came there, and held a market. Samaual is famous for his fidelity to his sworn oath, which led him to sacrifice his own son for Imru'ul-Qais. The poet-king, fallen from his high estate, had taken refuge with Samaual, and besought him to recommend him to the Kings of Ghassân, who might interest the Roman Emperor of Constantinople in his cause. He was given a guide to conduct him into Syria. When Al-Ḥârith ibn Ẓâlim, sent by Al-Mundhir to seize the treasure confided by Imru'ul-Qais to Samaual's care, laid siege to the castle, he seized the person of the Jewish prince's son, as he was hunting in the neighbourhood. "I will never give up the money which has been confided to my care," said the faithful guardian, and his cruel enemy caused the youth's body to be cut in two, across the middle. Then Samaual sang : "I have faithfully kept the breastplates of the Kindite. . . . I was faithful, where so many are traitors."

Amongst Samaual's co-religionists we may cite AL-RABÎʽ, son of Abû'l-Ḥuqaiq, who fought valiantly at the

head of his tribe at Buʿâth, and whose sons were fierce opponents of the Prophet. He strove with Nâbigha in that poetic pastime in which the first poet spoke a hemistich, and the second had to complete both sense and rhyme with another, delivered impromptu.

Christianity, like Judaism, had made proselytes in Arabia. Syria, whither the Northern Arabs were continually leading caravans, was full of churches and convents; in Mesopotamia the whole population was Christian. The Princes of Ghassân, at Damascus, professed the faith, and the Lakhmites, at Ḥîra, adopted it likewise. The verses of such a poet as Umayya ibn Abî'l-Ṣalt, who, though not himself a Christian, propagated, under the desert tents, views drawn from Jewish-Christian books, had done much to spread these ideas about Arabia.

In the town of Ḥîra, peopled by a mixture of Aramean and Arab elements, the ʿIbâds formed the very groundwork of the primitive population, side by side with the Arabs of the Tanûkh tribe, half Bedouin, half husbandmen, who had seized the country, and the *Aḥlâf*, dependants or clients, who had taken refuge in the city from every corner of Arabia. Now these ʿIbâds were Christians. Together with a few Jews, they had monopolised the wine trade of the Euphrates valley, and carried their wares across the deserts to the Arabs, all hard drinkers, in their towns and camps. ʿAntara tells us of one desert hero who drank so deep that he "lowered the wine merchants' flags"—an allusion to their habit of hoisting a flag over their tents when they had wine to sell, and lowering it when the supply was exhausted. The religious ideas of the poet Al-Aʿshâ had already felt the influence of his talks with these wine merchants, who

brought the "good news" with them. Among these Christians, who were probably the first to apply the characters of the Syrian alphabet to the Arab tongue, were several poets, of whom the most celebrated was 'ADÎ IBN ZAID. He came of an ancient family, holding a high position in the city of Ḥîra. His father had been brought up at Ctesiphon, at the court of the Persian Sâsânians. During the interregnum between the kings Nu'mân I. and Al-Mundhir, he was chosen governor of Ḥîra. He continued in this office under the last-named king. 'Adî, like his father, received his education in Persia. He was favoured by the king of kings, was sent on an embassy to Constantinople, and passed through Damascus, where his first poem was written. When he returned, his father was dead. But the poet loathed official trammels. He preferred to remain free and independent, oscillating betwixt Ḥîra and Ctesiphon, and singing the praises of good wine. He helped to set Nu'mân, son of Al-Mundhir, upon the throne, but the Beni-Marînâ, whose candidate was ousted, vowed his destruction. They accused him of having spoken disparagingly of the monarch, who partly owed his crown to him; the king tempted him within his boundaries, and then cast him into prison. The King of Persia would have taken up his cause, but when his envoy reached Ḥîra, he found the poet murdered in his dungeon. 'Adî ibn Zaid's Bacchic verses were later to be the joy of the Omeyyad Caliph, Walîd II.

PROSE

None of the prose of those ancient times has come down to us. It was not written, and was, indeed, not

reckoned of sufficient importance to merit such an honour. The researches of the Arab philologists give us some idea of what this very primitive stage of literature must have been like. There were evening tales (*samar*) told under the nomads' tents, stories which were already being carried from town to town by the professional story-tellers, such as Naḍr ibn Ḥârith, of Mecca, who had learnt the fine legends of the ancient Persian kings at Ḥîra, and by them gained a fame which at one moment counterbalanced that Mahomet owed to the Koran stories, drawn from the Bible. The battle of Bedr put an end to this dangerous competition. There were also the legendary and not at all trustworthy recitals of the Arab *Days*—tales of the great desert battles; proverbs, collected at a later date by philologists, and founded on forgotten incidents, frequently incomprehensible, and explained by purely imaginary comments and allocutions, whose makers flattered themselves they would impress the minds of their fellow-creatures. All these go to make up the elements of a literary art of which we possess no written specimen, but which was eventually to undergo a great development.

CHAPTER III

THE KORAN

BORN of a poor and lightly esteemed family, MAHOMET (or MOḤAMMED), who had begun life by travelling with caravans from Mecca into Syria, had acquired a fortune by his marriage with Khadîja. In his days, two religious sects, distinct from the believers in Judaism and Christianity, the growth of which we have already noticed, had taken root in Arabian soil. One of these was the Rakûsiyya, the other the Ḥanîfs. The first was undoubtedly descended from the Mandaïtes, or Christian disciples of St. John Baptist, known in the Middle Ages under the name of Ṣâbians, and of whom a community still exists in Lower Mesopotamia. They were Ebionites, who venerated the Forerunner, and were the predecessors of the Gnostic movement. The Ḥanîfs were Essenians, who fancied themselves to be practising, under the name of the faith of Abraham, a kind of Judaism purified of all ritual observances, and which did not involve any perusal of the sacred writings. It was in the bosom of this sect of the Ḥanîfs that Islamism came into existence. Mahomet himself used to say that he was a Ḥanîf, like those known at Mecca, Ṭâ'if, and Yathrib. Ḥanîf stands for monotheist, a hater of idolatry; and when Mahomet began to preach, the men of Mecca told him he had turned Ṣâbian. These Ḥanîfs carried

about a book called the *Ṣuḥuf*, or scrolls, of Abraham. A few years previous to the Prophet's mission, a missionary of the sect appeared in the Ḥijâz, preached the monotheism of Abraham, and found some followers. In later days Mahomet declared these scrolls to be forgeries. Now, were they really a book, as Sprenger believed, or must we accept the title as a vague one, possibly describing the Israelitish Bible? However that may be, the Christian followers of St. John Baptist and the Ḥanîfs had prepared the way, amid all the polytheism of the Arabian Peninsula, for the success of the preacher of the monotheism of Islam.

As for the Jews—who lived in the chief cities, and had converted certain tribal chieftains to their faith—and the Syrians and Mesopotamian Christians—whose propaganda had found a singularly useful supporter in such a poet as Umayya ibn Abî'l-Ṣalt, who told the Bible stories in the Bedouin camps—their influence cannot be denied.

The Koran was revealed in bits and scraps, and the condition in which we have received it gives us but a faint conception of the manner of its composition. For when it was finally edited, under Caliph 'Uthmân, the chapters or *sûras* were, with the exception of the first, placed in order according to their length—a purely artificial arrangement.

Mahomet, the Koran tells us, was inspired by the Holy Ghost, whom he held to be an angel, and whom he called, in later chapters, written at Medina, by the name of the Archangel Gabriel, which he pronounced Jabrîl. During the fits of ecstasy in which the inspiration came to him, he believed he beheld the archangel's face, and when he was asked what he was like, he always men-

tioned a young man of the tribe of Kalb, named Diḥya ibn Khalîfa. The revelation was always imparted in small instalments, only one verse, or a few together, at a time. When the revelation ceased, Mahomet called one of his secretaries, generally 'Abdallah ibn Sa'd ibn Abî Sarḥ, to write the words from his dictation, and had the newly written sheet inserted at such or such a place.

The word *sûra* is Hebrew. It signifies a row of stones in a wall, and thus, by analogy, a line of writing —Koran means reading. *Furqân*, another name given to the book, means (in Semitic languages other than the Arabic) "liberation, deliverance" of the "revelation."

The style of the Koran differs very much according to the periods of the Prophet's life at which the revelation was received. Its principal characteristic is that it is altogether written in rhymed prose. This is strongly apparent in the earlier *sûras*, which have very short verses, and is only marked in the longer chapters inspired at Medina by the terminal *pause* of each verse, which rhymes assonantly with the other pauses. It must further be borne in mind that the present arrangement of the chapters is quite artificial. The manner in which the book was compiled is well known. The Prophet's hearers had begun by trusting their memories to retain the words of the revelations they had received from him. Later, those who could write traced them in ancient characters on palm-leaves, on tanned hides, or on dry bones. When the Prophet died, and his followers perceived that the hour of the Last Judgment seemed to grow farther and farther off (for the first Moslems, like the first Christians, believed that the days were accomplished, and that the great Resurrection was upon them), that civil wars and frontier raids were increasing, and

that death was sweeping away numbers of those who knew all the Koran, or part of it, by heart, fear fell on them lest the Word of God should be utterly lost, and all the scattered fragments were brought together. Zaid ibn Thâbit, Mahomet's disciple, was charged by Abû Bekr, the first Caliph, to collect all that could be discovered of the sacred text, and form it into one volume. The chapters were then arranged without any regard to historical sequence, simply according to their length. First came the longest, preceded by the *Fâtiḥa*, or short chapter of seven verses which opens the book, and then the shorter ones. Now these short ones are the oldest. They were revealed at Mecca, before the emigration, while the long ones placed at the beginning of the book belong for the most part to the period when the Prophet, then Head of the army and the State, was at Medina, in command of the troops who were soon to place him in possession of the religious capital of Islam. This edition of Zaid's may be considered the final one, for the revision of twenty years later affected details of language and grammar, rather than the general arrangement of the text.

The style of the Koran is not, and hardly could be, uniform. Its expression of thought is purely Semitic, and is closely allied with that long series of documents emanating from Hebraic sources, which begin with the ancient verses of the Tôrâ, pass through all the prophetic inspiration that gravitated round Jerusalem, and so descend to the Gospels. The sentences are cut up into verses, very short verses at first, then very long. The rhymed prose is marked by the alliterations at the close of each verse. The chapters fall into two great classes, according as they were produced at Mecca or

Medina. The first belongs to the preaching period, before the emigration. The second came after the Hegira.

At the outset the expression is curt, because the inspiration is powerful, the adjuration is pathetic. God speaks, and the man falls out of sight. Here Mahomet appears as the Prophet. He has not yet become the statesman, the legislator, who calls a new state of society to life. His object is not to give his fellow-countrymen a code of laws, but to teach them to worship the true God. There is no mention of ritual nor any reference to social laws. Mahomet calls on his hearers to believe the evidence of their own apperception of the universe. He bids them admire the marvels of nature, the stars, the moon, the sun, "all of them signs of God's power, if you will understand them"; or else he recounts the misfortunes which have befallen past generations who would not hearken to the prophets —legends which are a mixture of the Rabbinic fables with old national traditions concerning the vanished tribes of 'Âd and Thamûd.

In the oldest of the Meccan *sûras*, the sentences have a rhythmic connection, although there is no regular metre; prosodic forms occur but very seldom, and only in short passages. The expression of thought is very succinct, and generally exceedingly vague and incomplete. But the address is bold and passionate. One feels that the Prophet is straining every nerve to convince the careless that his mission is genuine. His vehemence of expression is apparent even athwart the dull pall cast over it by translation into our analytic tongues. There is as much of the poet as of the preacher in him, as Stanley Lane-Poole accurately remarks. His

great argument, in his exhortations to do right and fear God, is the Day of Judgment; and the believers' reward, which he holds up glittering before their eyes, is the hope of Paradise. "When the heavens part, when the stars are scattered, when the waters of the seas are mingled, when the tombs are overthrown, then shall each soul behold its deeds, from first to last. . . . The just shall dwell in bliss, but the faithless shall be in hell." His imprecations against his foes are frightful, but it must not be forgotten that throughout the Koran it is God who speaks, while the Prophet merely transmits the revelation. The fierce feelings of the desert Arab are frankly unveiled, without a touch of hypocrisy to hide their cruelty. Mahomet's curse upon his uncle, Abû Lahab, is famous. "May the two hands of Abû Lahab perish, and may he perish himself likewise!"

In a second category of the Mecca chapters, the adjurations "by the sun and its brightness, by the moon when it follows close upon it, by the sky and Him who built it," have almost disappeared. The formula "by the Koran!" takes their place. The address opens with the declaration, "This is the revelation of God," and, so that there may be no doubt as to whence the words spoken by the Prophet proceed, he prefixes to them the divine order, in the word "Say!" The history of the ancient Hebrew prophets, obtained from the Jewish Haggada, through his verbal intercourse with Jewish acquaintances, is the chief proof of his mission put forward by Mahomet. Small wonder that the history, coming in so indirect a fashion, should be incorrect and full of legends.

A third period, that of argument, is marked by the more prosaic nature of the language used. The only

novel feature is the Prophet's answer to the "wicked and adulterous generation" that presumes to demand a miracle in proof of the truth of his mission. Miracles, he says, are everywhere about us. "Wherefore ask for a miracle when the whole of nature is a miracle? I am only sent to warn you!" A special mention should also be made of all the verses in which the name applied to the Deity is "al-Raḥmân" (the Merciful), the name borne by the pagan divinity of certain tribes.

The second part of the Koran comprises the four-and-twenty chapters written during the ten years spent at Medina after the flight. Enthusiasm is less fierce; the preacher is giving place to the lawgiver, the statesman. He teaches, he explains. His object is no longer to subjugate and to convince. The ideas of his followers are formed. They believe, and the swelling multitude of his disciples forces his unbelieving foes to the conviction that they will soon have to reckon with his growing power. The style loses its poetic character. It becomes a lengthy prose, with constant repetitions, intended to drive certain simple ideas into even the most obtuse of brains. The sermons, which opened during the Meccan period with the formula "O men!" now begin "O ye who believe!" or, when the preacher speaks to his enemies, "O Jews!" or even "O hypocrites!" The general style is heavy and diffuse; the verses are very long. The chapters are made up of fragmentary harangues and detached sentences; yet from time to time passages of a truly wonderful beauty and nobility of thought and expression occur. The principles of the religious, civil, and penal code of the newly formed society are nearly all contained in the three longest chapters—the second, fourth, and fifth—

which form almost a tenth part of the whole of the sacred volume.

The text of the Koran was certainly not brought together during the Prophet's lifetime. Only four of his disciples, Ubayy ibn Ka'b, Mu'âdh ibn Jabal, Zaid ibn Thâbit, and Abû Zaid Anṣârî, had gathered more or less complete collections of its words. The struggle with Musailima, the false prophet, had cost the lives of many of the chosen depositaries of the original text, when Abû Bekr, impelled by 'Umar, who had seen the end of many of these precious witnesses, ordered that every written text to be discovered should be collected, and confided this task to Zaid, who had acted as Mahomet's secretary. 'Umar, who supervised this edition, would only accept written passages supported by the declaration of two witnesses. Thus many fragments of the revelation, for which this twofold testimony could not be adduced, were not incorporated, though they may well have been authentic. This gave the Shî'ites ground for affirming, in later days, that the Sunnite text was incomplete, and that everything relating to the providential mission of 'Alî and his family had been expunged therefrom. The edition bore no official character—a proof of this lies in the fact that, when 'Umar died, it became the property of his daughter, Ḥafṣa.

During the wars in Armenia and Âdharbaijân, the soldiers from 'Irâq wrangled with those from Syria over the way in which the Koran should be read. Ḥudhaifa, their leader, laid the question before Caliph 'Uthmân, who commanded Zaid ibn Thâbit and some other Quraishites to draw up an authoritative text. They collected all the existing copies, but acknowledged that of Abû Bekr, preserved by Ḥafṣa, as their true basis,

and when the work was finished, ʿUthmân had all the others done away with, except Abû Bekr's, which itself was shortly afterwards destroyed by Marwân, Governor of Medina. All the copies of the Koran now scattered over the Moslem world, therefore, without exception, are reproductions of ʿUthmân's edition.

Mahomet, who had no love for heathen poets, and was always afraid his followers might forsake him and go back to the rhythmic chants to which their cradles had been rocked, sought out bards to sing his own praises. One of the poems of LABÎD is included in the Muʿallaqât. He belonged to a prominent family of the Beni-Jaʿfar. His father, Rabîʿa, had earned by his generosity the sobriquet of "Rabîʿa of the needy." Born about 560, he lived to a great age, till the beginning of the Caliphate of Muʿâwîya, towards 661. Legend asserts him to have been a hundred and forty-five years old when he died. He heard the Mecca sermons, and was not a whit impressed by them. When Mahomet had retired to Medina, Labîd's uncle, ʿÂmir, whose prowess had earned him the surname of "Champion of the lance," fell sick, and sent his nephew to consult the Prophet as to his case. Labîd then heard the Koran recited, and these recitals, delivered with all the gravity and earnestness of conviction, made the deepest impression upon his mind. The passage which worked his final acceptance of the new faith is actually quoted :—

"These are they who have bought error with the coin of truth, but their bargain has brought them no profit, they have not continued in the right way. They are like unto a man who has kindled a fire. When the fire has cast its light on all that is about it, and God has suddenly quenched it, leaving men in dark-

ness, they can see nothing at all. Deaf, dumb, blind, they are not able to retrace their steps. They are like unto those who, when a great cloud heavy with darkness and thunder and lightning comes down from heaven, are filled with the fear of death, and stop their ears with their fingers to shut out the noise of the thunder, while the Lord hems in the infidels on every side. The thunderbolt well nigh blinds them. When the lightning flashes they walk by its light. When it leaves them in darkness, they stop short. If God so willed it, He would take sight and hearing from them, for He is all-powerful. O men! worship your Lord, who has created you and those who came before you. Mayhap you will fear Him."

After his uncle's death Labîd went with a deputation of his tribe to Medina, and was there publicly converted. Once a Moslem, he cared no more for his poems, and never mentioned them of his own will. What he specially valued in the new order of things was the social organisation which he saw taking the place of the penury, the frays, and life of general rapine, which had hitherto been the lot of the nomad Arabs. He thought it an admirable thing that there should be "a public force established to protect men from each other, institutions out of which a servant bearing wallets brings support to those who need it, and a public treasury which pays each man the salary which is his due." This gives a vivid idea of the state of the Peninsula before the Prophet's time.

Labîd had a brother, Arbad, who was killed by lightning while on his way back from Medina, whither he had journeyed, it is said, in the hope of taking the Prophet by surprise and killing him. His sudden death was attri-

buted to the vengeance of heaven. The poet mourned long for his brother. He composed sad elegies about him, in which he sang of the emptiness of life. "Man is but a little flame. A little while after it has risen into the air, it turns to ashes." Before he died, he desired his two daughters to mourn him for one year. "Do not tear your faces nor shave off your hair. Say rather: 'Our father was a man who never forsook a comrade, nor betrayed the trust of a friend.' Repeat these words till one year has gone by, and then go in peace. For he who has mourned a whole year through, has fulfilled his duty, and deserves no reproach."

But for ḤASSÂN IBN THÂBIT was reserved the glory of acting as the Prophet's panegyrist, and singing his glories. He was born at Medina, visited Ḥîra and Damascus in his younger days, and finally attached himself to Mahomet as his court-poet, whose duty it was to reply to the bards accompanying the deputations sent by the different tribes to make their submission. Beside the great heathen models, Ḥassân strikes us as colourless, and his style as very bald. But the subject of his work has ensured him undying renown amongst the Moslems. KA'B IBN ZUHAIR, son of the poet of the Mu'allaqa, had begun by scoffing at the new Prophet. The conversion of the Muzaina tribe, of which he was a member, and even that of his brother Bujair, only increased the bitterness of his jests. This was displeasing to the Prophet, and threatened to be an ultimate source of danger to him, on account of the hold exercised by poets over the Bedouin mind. He decreed this poet's death. It was not easy to escape the execution of the terrible fiat. But Ka'b succeeded in doing so in very skilful fashion. The encomiums he showered on the

victorious leader were so agreeable to him that he presented their author with his own cloak (*burda*), a gift that established the verse-maker's reputation, and for which he expressed his gratitude in a poem, known by its two opening words "*Bânat Suʿâd* . . . ," which has been read and admired all over the Moslem East.

Celebrity has been won by the elegies, full of deep feeling, in which MUTAMMIM IBN NUWAIRA mourned the tragic fate of his brother Mâlik. Mâlik was chief of the Yarbûʿ, a branch of the Tamîm tribe. He had embraced the Moslem faith, and had been appointed a tax collector. After the Prophet's death, when the Arabs ceased to feel the heavy hand which had kept them silent, he, with others, rebelled against Caliph Abû Bekr, the Prophet's successor, and endeavoured to cast off an authority they thought oppressive. My readers are aware that this movement was speedily put down by the Caliph's generals; Mâlik was defeated, surrendered to Khâlid, and, Moslem though he was, paid for his rebellion with his life.

ABÛ MIḤJAN waited till the Thaqîf tribe, to which he belonged, had been convinced by armed force of the truth of the Prophet's mission before he himself became a Moslem. But one of his heathen errors he always retained—an immoderate love of wine. This earned him some term of imprisonment at the hands of the leaders of the new religion, who allowed no trifling on the point. Finding him incorrigible, Caliph ʿUmar sent him away, at last, to the Abyssinian frontier, where he shortly died. He was a brave warrior, as he proved in the Persian war, at the battle of Qâdisiyya. We only possess some fragments of his Bacchic verse.

Jarwal ibn Aus had been surnamed the Dwarf, AL-

ḤUṬAI'A. He was one of the masters of satire. A wandering troubadour, going from tribe to tribe, dwelling sometimes with the Beni-ʿAbs, sometimes with other communities, he lived on the gifts bestowed on him by the rich and powerful, either to reward his panegyrics, or because they dreaded his bitter attacks. His talent in this direction stirred up such hot anger wherever he was that he was considered a dangerous man, whom Caliph ʿUmar was obliged to put in prison in the interest of public safety and the general peace. Other poets, like ABÛ DHU'AIB of the Hudhailite tribe, had taken service in the conquering army. He accompanied ʿAbdallah ibn Saʿd into Northern Africa, and was deputed by that general to announce the taking of Carthage to the Caliph ʿUthmân. He suffered the misfortune of seeing his five sons swept away by the plague in Egypt, and devoted an elegy to this sad memory.

With ABÛ'L-ASWAD AL-DU'ALÎ we forsake the desert, for he was a town-dweller, a well-known citizen of Bassora, remarkable for the political part he played in connection with the Caliph ʿAlî, whose partisan he was; he fought at his side through that long battle of Ṣiffîn, which was the prelude to the misfortunes of the ʿAlids. To him is ascribed the invention of the Arabic grammar, and this has brought him a certain renown, which casts a reflected gleam on his poetry, itself somewhat mediocre in quality. Critics regard the origin of the poems ascribed to Abû Ṭâlib, Mahomet's uncle, as doubtful, and are still more convinced of this as regards those bearing the name of the Caliph ʿAlî. The Shîʿite tendencies of these last quickly convinced students that they were composed, at some uncertain time, to serve the interests of the ʿAlids.

CHAPTER IV

THE OMEYYAD DYNASTY

THE successful revolt of Mu'âwiya and the final disappearance of the Medina Caliphate, whereby the capital of the new Empire was removed from the Arabian deserts to Damascus, a locality naturally inheriting an ancient Greco-Syrian civilisation, robbed the nomad tribes of their predominant position, and conferred it on the dwellers in towns. In literary matters, we find the poets of this second period still sacrificing, in clumsy imitation, on the altar of the *Qaṣîda*, the ancient Bedouin ode. But we find, at the same time, an ample harvest of occasional poems, inspired by all the unexpected incidents of the political life of the new Empire. 'UMAR IBN ABÎ RABÎ'A was of the tribe of Quraish, to which Mahomet belonged, but which had not hitherto produced any poet. His father was a merchant, who had been sent by the Prophet to rule one of the southern provinces of the Peninsula, a duty which he performed till the death of 'Umar, and it may be even under Caliph 'Uthmân. He finally returned to his native country, and there the youthful poet grew to manhood. He never left the town till his death, except when he was taken, as a prisoner, to Damascus, and did not play any part in the wars waged by the Moslems on the frontiers of their growing Empire. A rich man and an idle,

he found opportunities of extolling the charms of many fair ladies, two princesses of the reigning house amongst them. His love affairs brought him into bad odour with the Caliph of Damascus, ʿUmar II., who had him bound with chains and brought into his presence, together with his friend Al-Aḥwaṣ. Al-Aḥwaṣ was banished to the Isle of Dahlak, in the Red Sea, and ʿUmar ibn Abî Rabîʿa was forced to take an oath to forswear his art, an oath he probably found it easy enough to keep, seeing he had already reached his seventieth year. He died, indeed, soon after, about the year 719, possibly by shipwreck, but this fact is not well established. His poems, set to music, and popularised by professional singers, made their way all over the Arab world.

In his turn, ABDALLAH IBN QAIS AL-RUQAYYÂT distinguished himself by the share he took in the attempts of ʿAbdallah ibn Zubair to obtain the Caliphate. He accompanied ʿAbdallah's brother, Muṣʿab, to ʿIrâq, of which country he had just been appointed governor, bore him company in the disastrous battle in which Muṣʿab lost his life (690), hid himself for a year after it, and then returned to Medina. Caliph ʿAbdal-Malik pardoned him, but did not give him back the pension he had formerly enjoyed. Amongst other poets belonging to Medina at this period, we may mention Qais ibn Dharîḥ, foster-brother to Ḥusain, ʿAlî's unhappy son, martyred at Kerbelâ, who loved a certain Lubnâ, and made her name so famous by his verse that in later days every poem in which the name of Lubnâ figured was ascribed to him. The same thing happened in the case of the celebrated Majnûn, the madman of the tribe of Beni-ʿÂmir, whose real name was Qais ibn Mulawwaḥ. His passion for

the lovely Lailâ had crazed his brain, and his adventures served the Persian poets as subjects with which to embroider the canvas of their mystic poems. Jamîl ibn ʿAbdallah loved Buthaina, even as Kuthayyir loved Azza the Bedouin. The last-named poet belonged to the Shîʿite sect of the Kaisaniyya, in spite of which he was well received at Damascus by ʿAbdal-Malik. Within the walls of the city also dwelt at that time a singer, of Persian origin, named Jonas (Yûnus), and surnamed Kâtib (the secretary), who had learnt music from Suraij ibn Muḥriz and Al-Gharîd. Caliph Walîd, the son of Yazîd, brought him from Syria when he ascended the throne in 742. This singer was an author too, and wrote a Book of Songs which was the original model of the famous *Kitâb al-aghânî* of Abû'l-Faraj al-Iṣfahânî.

In the person of AL-AKHṬAL, the Omeyyads found the special bard of their brave deeds. He was a Christian, of the tribe of Taghlib, which had originally belonged to Najd, but was then settled in Mesopotamia. His name was Ghiyâth. Akhṭal means, "one whose ears are flabby and hang down." Was the poet really afflicted with a blemish of this kind? If so, his enemies would not have failed to mock at it, and they never did so. Other authorities aver that the word should be taken to mean "chatterer," a signification it does also possess.

While quite young, Al-Akhṭal attacked the reputation of Kaʿb ibn Juʿail, a member of his own tribe, and the recognised poet of the nation, and the two waged a war of epigrams. He lost his mother, Lailâ, at an early age, and had to endure persecution from a cruel step-mother, who set him laborious tasks, and sent him out to herd the goats: he avenged himself by tricking her out of a

jar of milk and some dried fruit. Al-Akhṭal's religion was one of purely formal and external observances. He wore a cross on his breast, and kept it there even within the Omeyyad Palace at Damascus, when the favour of the princes of that family called him thither. He occasionally endured somewhat severe penances, as when the priest of his tribe took him by the beard and trounced him. Caliph ʿAbdal-Malik, though he cared little for religion, tried to convert him to the Moslem faith. "I consent," quoth the poet, "if I am allowed to drink wine and exempted from fasting in Ramaḍân!" and he wrote the lines: "Never will I go braying like an ass, 'Come to prayers,' but I will go on drinking the kindly liquor, and prostrating myself when the sun rises." The last line is interesting, because it shows that the ancient primitive Christian habit of gathering themselves together and turning towards the rising sun was still in force amongst the Arabs of the Taghlib tribe, in the eighth century.

Kaʿb ibn Juʿail bore Al-Akhṭal no malice on account of his epigrams, for he it was who recommended him to Yazîd, son of Muʿâwiya, when he was seeking a poet to compose diatribes, which were to be diffused about the deserts, and carried by the singers through all the towns of the Peninsula, thus serving the political ends of the Omeyyads, and withdrawing the affections of the populace from the Ansârs, men of Medina who had been the Prophet's first defenders. Yazîd's protection saved him from the spites stirred by his violent language.

A subject of frequent argument at the Omeyyad Court was the relative merits of the three poets, Akhṭal, Ferazdaq, and Jarîr. The princes would amuse themselves by making their courtiers pronounce an opinion, and the courtiers, who dreaded the vengeance of the two poets

who must be passed over if the palm was awarded to the third, would get out of the difficulty by taking refuge in generalities. "Jarîr draws water from a well," said one; "Ferazdaq hews out of the rock; as for Akhṭal, he excels in eulogy and in heroic verse."

In later days, under the 'Abbâsids, when passions had cooled, grammarians ended by preferring Akhṭal, because his verses were more finished and correct, and because he had been able to produce the largest number of poems of a certain length which are irreproachable, from beginning to end, both in subject and in form. The qualities most valued in his work are fulness of afflatus and purity of expression. We are told nothing as to the loftiness of his inspiration. But one famous line, which Hârûn al-Rashîd loved to recall, proves the nobility of the moral sentiments he enunciated. It occurs in his ode addressed to the Caliph 'Abdal-Malik, in which, speaking of the Omeyyads, he says: "Terrible in their rage if they are withstood, they are the most clement of men when victory is won."

While Akhṭal's fame was spreading over Mesopotamia and Syria, the renown of the two other poets, Jarîr and Ferazdaq, was growing in 'Irâq.

FERAZDAQ was a pious and fervent Moslem, entirely devoted to the Prophet's family, and with it all a cynic, a libertine, whose sport it was to attack women's honour, who made vile use of the terror his ribald verse inspired, while he himself was a mean coward, more timorous than a sparrow, spiteful and vindictive. Such was the shabby nature of this great poet. His name was Hammâm, and he belonged to the tribe of Tamîm. He was born at Bassora towards 641. Caliph 'Alî advised him to learn the Koran instead of running after poetry, and the young

man is said to have fastened chains to his own feet until he got the sacred lines by heart. But his father's death soon brought back all his poetic instincts. The hatred of the Beni-Nahshal drove him into exile. He betook himself to Kûfa and Medina, where he was kindly treated by Sa'îd ibn al-ʿÂṣ. His imprudent boast, in one of his poems, that he had entered the precincts of a harem by means of a rope-ladder, stirred the rage of the worthy pharisees of Medina. He was banished by Marwân, and would have settled at Mecca if the death of his enemy Ziyâd, Governor of ʿIrâq, had not made it possible for him to rejoin his tribe. His adventures with his cousin Nawâr (whom he married, who sought to divorce him, and who could find no one to bear witness for her before the judge, so great was the dread of the poet's satires, who took refuge with ʿAbdallah ibn Zubair, the Medina pretender, and at last obtained her husband's consent to a separation) have, like his strife with his adversary Jarîr, been the subject of many poems.

He died of a skin disease, contracted during a desert journey, towards the year 728. He was a determined supporter of the rights of the ʿAlids, and the verses in which he acclaimed Zain al-ʿÂbidîn, ʿAlî's grandson, brought him to a dungeon. Ferazdaq was then a man of seventy. But satire is his special field, and it must be acknowledged that in it he knew no limit, whether of decency or honour; and further, that he was constantly and immoderately guilty of a sin with which Arab writers are frequently charged—that of shamelessly stealing lines from his neighbours' compositions. He was a plagiarist, forcing his competitors to leave him in possession of lines that took his fancy, and below which he wrote his own name.

Born in the Ḥijâz, KUTHAYYIR was famous for his eccentricities. He was a partisan of the 'Alids, and professed the most extreme religious views. His absurd affectations had won him the surname of "Antichrist." He was very short, too, which gave food for the scoffers' jeers. There was a joke—it was Akhṭal who first retailed it—that, when he moved from the Ḥijâz into Syria, he had been starved and numbed by the—relative—chilliness of the last-named country.

But JARÎR, of Yamâma, in the south of Najd, was the popular favourite. He, too, was of the tribe of Tamîm. He dwelt in 'Irâq, and had opportunities of extolling Al-Ḥajjâj, the terrible governor of that province, at whose severity all men trembled. But the favour of the Omeyyad princes was not bestowed on him ; Akhṭal had prejudiced 'Abdal-Malik against him. He had to wait till Umar II. ascended the throne before seeing himself preferred before his rivals. He was a mighty fighter, and his life was spent in poetic tournaments. The most famous of these was that with Ferazdaq, who was backed by Akhṭal. 'Ubaid, who was called "the camel-herd," because he had written five lines describing these creatures, the nomad's inseparable comrades, had sided with Ferazdaq. Jarîr could not forgive him, and poured sarcasms upon him till he drove him out of Bassora, and turned the anger of his own tribe against him. Jarîr and Ferazdaq died in the same year, 728. The first-named poet had returned to his own tribe, the Yamama, towards the end of his life.

At the same period, Ghailân ibn 'Uqba, surnamed DHÛ'L-RUMMA, was carrying on, though with lowered vitality, the tradition of the desert poets. Ferazdaq complained that he was too fond, like the ancient

authors, of descriptions of forsaken encampments, of camels, and the bird called *qaṭâ*. He himself, indeed, admitted that his comparisons might go on for ever. Nevertheless, his poems were long held in high admiration by the philologists, more especially, perhaps, on account of the uncommon words occurring in them.

Beside these poets who carried on the classic tradition of the long rhythmic recitations, we find the simplest of prosodic metres, the *rajaz*, suddenly springing into considerable importance, and rising as high as its fellows in the popular estimation. The *rajaz*, despised by the heathens, looked on as a sort of cadenced prose, only fit, at its best, for improvisations, had been softened and transformed by Al-Aghlab ibn ʿUmar ibn ʿUbaida, who fell fighting gallantly at the Battle of Nehâwend in 641, and reached its full development in the work of Abû Najm al-Faḍl ibn Qudâma al-ʿIjlî, the friend of the Caliph Hishâm, Al-ʿAjjâj, and his son Ru'ba.

The funeral elegies written by a woman, LAILÂ AL-AKHYALIYYA, are famous, more especially those devoted to the memory of Tauba ibn al-Ḥumayyir, who loved her, and suffered the anguish of seeing her married by her father to a stranger, a mean and jealous fellow, who beat her. The story goes that one night, sick of ill treatment, she called an unknown guest who had joined the tribe at nightfall ; that he came, under cover of the darkness, struck the husband three or four hearty blows across the shoulders with a stick, and departed, the poetess having prevented his further interference in the domestic broil. He went away unrecognised, and was never seen again. Lailâ saved her friend from many ambushes prepared for him by jealous rivals. He was

true to her till his death, which took place in an intertribal quarrel in 704. The celebrity won by these touching compositions encouraged their authoress to persevere. She paid visits to princely courts, waited on Caliph 'Abdal-Malik, and on the Governor of 'Irâq, Al-Ḥajjâj, to whom she offered eulogies. She died in 707, while on her way to visit her cousin, Qutaiba ibn Muslim, the Moslem general then governing the province of Khurâsân. Al-Khansâ is the only Arab poetess who can be considered her superior. She was a tall woman with great black eyes. Lailâ waged a war of epigrams with Nâbigha al-Ja'dî, who hotly answered her, concerning the attacks of a certain Sawâr ibn Aufâ, called Ibn al-Ḥayâ, after his mother, who had spoken evil in his verses of the tribe of Azd. Nâbigha had replied, and all this happened at Ispahan. The verses circulated through the desert, and the censured tribes threatened an appeal to the Governor of Medina, or even to the Caliph.

Amongst the desert poets who were Christians must be mentioned 'Abdallah ibn al-Mukhâriq, called the Nâbigha of the Beni-Shaibân, who swore by the Gospels, the monks, and all the usual Christian oaths. He was fond of leaving his Syrian steppes to recite his well-paid eulogies in the presence of the Caliphs at Damascus. 'Abdal-Malik and Walîd were his patrons. Hishâm, on the contrary, could not endure him, and kept him at a distance. The poem beginning "Mine eyes have shed tears . . . at the sight of the traces left at Ḥafîr . . . dying away in solitude . . . sorrowful like the verses of the Psalms," long maintained its popularity. 'Umair ibn Shuyaim, of the tribe of Taghlib, and nephew to Al-Akhṭal, was another Christian, but he eventually turned

Moslem. He was called Al-Quṭâmî, the Sparrow-hawk, on account of a simile which he had rendered famous, and also Ṣarî' al-Ghawânî—the victim of the fair—an expression of his own invention, and on which Muslim in later days conferred celebrity. He died in 728.

Beside these poets we must also place A'SHÂ HAMDÂN, a Koran-reader and lawyer, belonging to Kûfa, who forsook his legal studies to declaim poetry, and fought against the heathens of Dailam, among the mountains south-west of the Caspian Sea. He fell into their hands as a prisoner of war, was saved by the love of a young girl of that country, and took up the cause of 'Abdal-Raḥmân ibn al-Ash'ath, who had ventured to proclaim the deposition of 'Abdal-Malik, and whom some held to be the Qaḥṭânid expected by the Moslems as a precursor of the Last Judgment, but who was vanquished by Al-Ḥajjâj in 702. The poet shared his leader's sad fate. Herded with a crowd of other prisoners, he was put to death by the terrible Governor of 'Irâq, who could not forgive the imprudent attacks he had made on him in his poems. Aḥmad al-Naṣîbî, with whom he had entered into bonds of brotherhood, after the fashion of the desert Arabs, was a musician, who sang the lines written by his friend.

Al-Ḥajjâj had a sister, Zainab, who was beloved by Numairî of Ṭâ'if, a writer of erotic stanzas. But the governor thought the poet's praise compromised the reputation of his family, and Numairî had to seek refuge with the Caliph of Damascus. Zainab, who had been sent to the same city at the time of Al-Ash'ath's revolt, died there of an accident—a fall from her mule. Numairî found consolation in singing elegies over her tomb.

The Moslem Conquest had given a huge ascendency to the Arab tongue, and literary efforts by men whose native language was not Arabic were already beginning to appear. It would be impossible, were it only on account of his surname, *Al-A'jam*, not to recognise the Persian origin of ZIYÂD IBN SULAIMÂN, who was "client" of an Arab tribe (by client must be understood either a freed slave or a man who voluntarily lived under the ægis of a patronage which raised him above the singular humiliations which were the lot, at that period, of a vanquished foe, even of one who had embraced the Moslem faith) dwelling at Persepolis, was born, according to some, at Ispahan, and died in Khurâsân in 689. His funeral eulogium of Muhallab ibn Abî Ṣufra won universal praise. "Tell the caravans that valour and generosity have been buried at Merv, in the clearest fashion." His poetic talent rose above an inconvenient impediment in his speech. He was accused of pronouncing like a peasant. He could not articulate the letter *Ain*—the peculiar onomatopœia of the Arab tongue, which reproduces the grunt of the camel as it is being loaded—pronounced the *ṣâd* or emphatic *ṣ* wrong, and could not produce the guttural *ḥ* at all.

Another Persian who became an Arab poet was Ismâ'îl ibn Yasâr, a client of an Arab tribe, and a partisan of the Zubairids. He accompanied 'Urwa, the son of Zubair, on his journey to the court of the Caliph Walîd, and wrote an elegy on the death of his patron's son, who fell off a roof among a drove of horses, and was kicked to death by them. Later he paid a second visit to Walîd, when the Caliph was at the Syrian Ruṣâfa, built to the west of Raqqa by Hishâm. There, and during that prince's time, he

began chanting the praises of the Persians instead of extolling his host. The Caliph fell into a violent rage and had him thrown into a pond, out of which he was dragged half dead, and banished to the Ḥijâz. He had two brothers, Muḥammad and Ibrâhîm, both of them poets, and descended from slaves taken in the province of Fârs. Ismâ'îl is the earliest instance of these *Shu'ûbiyya*, fanatical adherents of their own race, who, notwithstanding their Arab education, openly declared themselves to be of a different origin from that of their barbarous conquerors.

Amongst other poets of foreign birth whom the ascendency of the conquering race and of the desert bards converted to the language of the Koran, we must not omit to mention Abû 'Aṭâ Aflaḥ ibn Yasâr. His father was an Indian from the banks of the Indus. The chances of life so fell out that the child was born at Kûfa, but he never spoke Arabic well, a remark we have already made as to the Persians who had adopted the dominant tongue. He was the chartered panegyrist of the Omeyyads, and was obliged to direct the shafts of his satire against the 'Abbâsids. He lived long enough to see these last—victors, thanks to the help of the Persian Shî'ites—found the city of Bagdâd on the banks of the Tigris, for his death only occurred when Manṣûr was Caliph in 774. So faulty was his pronunciation that he was obliged to have his stanzas recited by a Barbary slave who had a fine voice. The eulogies he offered to Manṣûr were not well received by that Caliph, who could not forget that he had written verses mourning the death of Naṣr ibn Sayyâr, the adversary of Abû Muslim. The poet, thus repulsed by the 'Abbâsid prince, took vengeance on him in his

satires, jeering at the decree whereby the populace was commanded to dress in black, the chosen colour of the ʿAbbâsids.

The Caliph Walîd was a poet, a musical composer, and a singer. A born artist, he early plunged into the greatest excesses, and drank wine during his pilgrimage to Mecca. He lost the affection of the people, and was killed by the Yemenites in 742, just a year after the death of his uncle Hishâm. He modelled his drinking songs on the works of ʿAdî ibn Zaid, and his successor in this line was the great poet, Abû Nuwâs. This Caliph, brilliant though he was, and full of showy qualities, necessarily displeased the Moslems by his shameless debauchery, and they accused him of having entered into a compact with Persian teachers, and of being a secret believer in their faith. He composed numerous airs, could play the lute, mark the rhythm on cymbals, and walk in cadenced step to the sound of the tambour—he denied this, it is true, and forbade his comrades to speak of it. At Mecca his chief care was to send for the best singer of the locality, Yaḥyâ, surnamed the Elephant (*Fîl*), and take lessons from him. Yaḥyâ, transported with admiration, besought the Caliph to receive him amongst his followers, so that he might profit by the teaching of a renowned artist, whom he acknowledged his superior.

AL-KUMAIT was acquainted with the different Arabic dialects, and knew the history of the various Arab wars. He was a fierce partisan of the Muḍar tribes, celebrated their exploits, and scoffed at the southern tribes. He had attached himself to the family of Hâshim, descended from the Prophet, and to it his finest panegyrics are addressed. His friendship with the poet Ṭirimmâḥ has

become a proverb, and was all the more phenomenal because the views of the two friends were diametrically opposed—Kumait was a Shîʿite, and championed the men of Kûfa, while Ṭirimmâḥ was a Khârijite, and supported the men of Damascus, his native city. "How can you agree," it was asked, "seeing you differ in every respect?" "We have one thing in common," replied Kumait, "our hatred of the vulgar." *Odi profanum vulgus et arceo:* every poet is an aristocrat. His attacks on the reigning dynasty earned him arrest and imprisonment at the hands of Hishâm, who would have cut out his tongue and cut off his hand; but he was saved by the devotion of his wife, who lent him her own garments to enable him to escape from durance. Maslama, the Caliph's son, afterwards obtained the poet's pardon as a reward for a funeral eulogy of his grandfather, Muʿâwiya—which is asserted to have been really improvised. He died a violent death in 743—killed during a riot by the soldiery.

At this period, also, flourished a very remarkable man, Ḥammâd ibn Sâbûr, surnamed Al-Râwiya, or the Quoter—because his extraordinary memory held thousands of ancient Arab stanzas and complete poems. To him the preservation of great part of the pre-Islamic poetry is due, and to him we owe the collection into one volume of the Muʿallaqât. He was an Iranian. His father, Sâbûr (Sapor), who was taken prisoner in war, belonged to that redoubtable race of the Dailamites, which braved the Arabs and maintained its independence in the inaccessible mountains of Gîlân, and which was later, under the name of Buwaihids, to seize Bagdâd, and reduce the Caliph's power to a purely spiritual sovereignty. This early commentator and

scholar, whose linguistic blunders bewrayed his foreign origin, was also born at Kûfa. The favour shown him by Yazîd had displeased Hishâm. When he succeeded, Ḥammâd was fain to hide himself a whole year in his own house, never leaving it, save to pay secret visits to trusted friends. But the new Caliph soon summoned him to Damascus. He is said to have died either in 771 or 774. His learning extended over the legendary history of the pre-Islamic Arabs, their poetry, their genealogies, and their dialects. He could distinguish the ancient from the modern style; he boasted that he could recite long odes, belonging to the heathen times, rhyming on every letter of the alphabet. He was a living encyclopædia. He had begun by being a thief and a rogue. Some verses which he found on the person of a man he had robbed in the middle of the night stirred his vocation in him. He wrote poetry himself. Al-Mufaḍḍal al-Ḍabbî accused him of interpolating his own lines amongst those of the ancient poets, so that it was impossible to detect the difference, and it is even said that, when pressed by Caliph Al-Mahdî, Ḥammâd confessed his fraud.

History first makes an appearance under the sway of the Omeyyads. We are told that Ziyâd, brother to Muʿâwiya, and his lieutenant, wrote a book on the pretensions of the Arab families, which was intended to serve as a weapon in the hands of his own descendants, in case their origin should be attacked (he was the son of Abû Sufyân, Muʿâwiya's father, by a slave); but this is by no means a certainty, though the assertion is supported by the authority of the *Fihrist*. ʿAbîd ibn Sharya was an Arab from the South; he was summoned to Damascus from Ṣanʿâ, by Muʿâwiya, to whom he

used to recite the stories of the kings of Yemen, and biblical legends, as also did Wahb ibn Munabbih (638–728), a Jew by origin, and either a Moslem convert, or, possibly, a Ṣâbian, or Christian follower of St. John Baptist. His surname, Abnâwî, indicated his descent from the Persian colony left in Southern Arabia by the troops sent by Chosroes I. Anûshîrwân against the Abyssinians. He played an important part in the elaboration of Moslem jurisprudence and theology, which are based, after the Koran, on the *ḥadîth*, or traditions of the Prophet. Wahb was one of the most ancient and popular of the traditionists. He was born at Dhimâr, near Ṣan'â. Abû Mikhnaf Lûṭ wrote three-and-thirty treatises on different persons and events. They deal more especially with the history of the conquest of 'Irâq, a subject on which he was, in the earliest days, the uncontested authority. He died in 774.

Muḥammad ibn Muslim al-Zuhrî, who was called Ibn-Shihâb, after one of his ancestors, was one of the learned men who devoted themselves to the study of the traditions of Mahomet. He belonged to Medina, but was not a member of the irreconcilable party which regarded the Omeyyads of Damascus as usurpers. He went to Syria, was chosen by the Caliph Hishâm to be his children's tutor, and became a magistrate under Yazîd II. His connection with the Omeyyad dynasty stirs some mistrust as to the tendency, unconscious no doubt, of his theological studies. Caliph 'Umar II. sent letters into the various provinces of the Empire, recommending that al-Zuhrî should be consulted in any legal difficulties, "for no man," he says, "is better acquainted with the customs of the past days." When at home, he was so absorbed in the study of his books that he forgot every-

thing else, and his wife one day exclaimed : " These books are more trying to me than the three other wives the law permits him, though he has but one!" He died, aged seventy-three, on his farm at Adama, in Arabia, between Syria and the Ḥijâz.

The conquest of Syria, and the selection of Damascus as the seat of the capital, had brought Moslems and Christians into close contact. St. John of Damascus, whose father was received at the court of ʿAbdal-Malik, wrote a defence of the Christian religion against the doctrine of Islam. In ʿIrâq, the great theologian Ḥasan Baṣrî, who died in 728, held uncontested sway as a doctrinal instructor. The elegance and purity of his Arabic are famous even now. He had been singularly handsome, but he fell when riding, broke his nose, and was disfigured for life. His father, who lived in Maisân, was made a prisoner and carried into slavery when Khâlid conquered that province in 633. His disciple, Wâṣil ibn ʿAṭâ, left him, and founded the Muʿtazilite school, who professed a kind of rationalism. He had a burr in his speech, and as he never could correct this defect, he obliged himself to avoid all words with the letter *r* in them. He had a long neck, and was somewhat gibed at on this account. He died in 748. But the theological works of those days have not come down to us. The collection of the Arab proverbs now began to attract some attention. Prince Khâlid, the son of Yazîd, practised alchemy, a science taught him by a monk of the name of Marianus. He wrote three treatises, the first of which deals with his teacher and the instruction he bestowed on him.

CHAPTER V

THE 'ABBÂSIDS

THE battle of the great Zâb was the Persians' revenge on the Arabs—a very incomplete revenge, for it did not come till a whole century had rolled by, and by that time Persia bore indelible marks of the Arab domination, both in religion and in language. The religious code of the Sâsânian dynasty, the Avesta, a revival of the old worship of Ahura-Mazda, had disappeared, and was only preserved round the very few fire-altars the victors' tolerance still permitted to exist. The Persian language was nothing but a spoken tongue; all the literary character had departed from it. All Persians now wrote in Arabic, and so strong was the impression made by the Semitic tongue that it has maintained itself to this day. But Persia possessed another and an intangible force, the Aryan genius, the powerful, imaginative, and creative mind of the great Indo-European family, the artistic, philosophic, and intellectual brain which, from this period onward, so mightily affects Arab literature, enabling it to develop in every quarter of the Caliphs' realms, and to produce that enormous aggregate of works, of which many, no doubt, were lost in the destruction attending the Mongol conquest. But the chief specimens have been preserved, and their effect on the Europe of the Middle Ages has been far greater than many have imagined.

When the ʿAbbâsids founded the city of Bagdâd, on the right bank of the Tigris, they seem to have sought for a site which would be a compromise between the Arab creators of the Caliphs' Empire and the Persian authors of the revolution which had placed the sons of ʿAbbâs on the throne. To the right of the Tigris lies Mesopotamia, a Semitic country from times immemorial, and overrun, since the fall of the ancient empires, by the nomad Arabs. To the left, Iranian territory begins at once. The very name of the city is Persian, and signifies *given by God.* The Bagdâd of the Caliphs now lies in ruins—only a very small number of the buildings remain; modern Bagdâd, which stands, as my readers are aware, on the left bank of the Tigris, being still inhabited by many Persians.

From the very outset of the eighth century, Persian influence was so strong in political matters that Manṣûr did not hesitate to rid himself, by the assassin's hand, of Abû Muslim, the leader who had overthrown the Omeyyad dynasty, just as Hârûn al-Rashîd, at a later date, rid himself of the Persian Barmakides, who had supplied him with two powerful ministers. In literature, this Persian influence is immense. It pervades everything—poetry, theology, jurisprudence: the Arabs had ceased to write; all posts, administrative, court, and legal, were held by men who were not Arabs, and the same applies to all the literature of the time. From this period onward, Arabic became the language, and the sole language, of the huge Empire of the Caliphs. But it was Arabic spoken and written by men who were Arabs by education, not by blood. All races, Persians, Syrians, Berbers from Maghrib, were melted and amalgamated in this mighty crucible. The most intel-

lectual parts of this medley were finally to recover their identity; the Persian tongue, which was never to drop the cloak cast upon it by the Semite domination, was once more to become a literary language, and to have the glory of giving birth to other literatures, such as the Ottoman-Turkish and the Hindu; but in the west, Arabic was only to be driven out of Spain together with the Moors, and the Maghrib was to keep the language of its conquerors, now become its native idiom, for ever.

Poetry now began to alter. The lengthy *qaṣîdas* of the desert, held up as models for students by the theorists, found no more original exponents. This form was doomed to servile imitation, and hence to platitude. But a new kind of poetry appeared on the banks of the Tigris, whither the imperial splendour was attracting the most brilliant talents.

A family from Palestine produced MUṬÎ' IBN AYÂS. His father had been with Al-Ḥajjâj when that general went into the province of Mecca to reduce the pretender 'Abdallah ibn Zubair to submission, and also when he defeated another pretender, Ibn al-Ash'ath, who came out of the distant land of Arachosia and very nearly succeeded in overthrowing the Caliphate. Muṭî' ibn Ayâs himself took service, first of all, with Caliph Walîd ibn Yazîd, but after the fall of the Omeyyads he appealed to Ja'far, son of Caliph Manṣûr, who took him into his service, and kept him till he died, thereby greatly displeasing the Caliph, his father. His poems are marked by elegant expression and deep feeling. His description of the two palm-trees at Ḥulwân would in itself suffice to make him famous. Under an apparent indifference in religious matters, he seems to have concealed heretical leanings. He was

accused of not being really a true Moslem. He denied the imputation of being a Zindîq (Manichean), but he was caught in the act of reciting suspicious verses. Men fought shy of his company, for he was a debauchee. His verses were very loose. One day he told a woman she was just as fit as the Caliph Al-Mahdî to mount the preacher's pulpit, which caused the sovereign to laugh most heartily.

As a maker of jokes and court jester, we must glance at Abû Dulâma Zand ibn al-Jaun, an Abyssinian negro, who had fought against the Omeyyads, and was permitted to entertain the Caliphs Manṣûr and Mahdî. He was the favourite of Manṣûr, to whom he certainly rendered good service by praising him, in a panegyric, for having put Abû Muslim to death. For the populace found it hard to understand why the 'Abbâsids rewarded the great general who had set them on the throne in such ungrateful fashion. He mocked at the Caliph's order that his subjects should wear black, the 'Abbâsids' colour, and a witty sally earned him leave, alone of all the population, to disregard the edict. When Mûsâ ibn Dâ'ûd made his pilgrimage to Mecca, he promised the jester 10,000 drachmas if he would travel with him. Abû Dulâma pocketed the cash and disappeared into the villages, whither he went to drink wine. Mûsâ, fearing to miss the pilgrimage season, started on his journey, came across the toper, had him bound and thrown into a palanquin. But so impudent were the fellow's repartees that he was fain to get rid of him, and leave him to spend the rest of the money he had given him. Abû Dulâma died in 778. He suggested to a physician to whom he owed money for curing his son, that, to secure payment of the debt, he should

bring a suit against a certain rich Jew, he himself offering to bear false witness to prove the claim. The judge well knew the real value of the demand, but such was his dread of the negro's wicked tongue that he preferred to pay the sum claimed out of his own pocket. Thus Abû Dulâma got his doctoring for nothing. One day, when he had alluded in verse to a supposed relationship between himself and the Caliph, Al-Mahdî, greatly enraged, inquired to whom he traced this kinship. "To Adam and Eve," replied the jester, and the Caliph laughed. It was said of him that he would make the very devil laugh. Al-Mahdî once ordered him, on pain of death, to satirise every member of the numerous company present. Abû Dulâma's presence of mind saved him in this hour of peril. He attacked himself, called himself "monkey-face, with a turban upon it," "forerunner of the Last Judgment," with other amenities, which vastly amused the gathering. On another occasion, out hunting, the Caliph killed a gazelle with an arrow, whilst his companion, 'Alî ibn Sulaimân, only hit one of the hounds, which died. Abû Dulâma summed up the incident in comical fashion. "The Caliph kills a gazelle and 'Alî kills a dog! Bravo! Each shall feed on the provisions he has provided for himself." Whereupon Al-Mahdî laughed till he nearly fell out of his saddle.

BASHSHÂR IBN BURD (693–783) was of Persian, and possibly even of royal race, as he himself asserted. He was born in the neighbourhood of Bassora, whither his father had been carried into slavery; his grandfather had been made a prisoner of war in Ṭukhâristân, far away in Khurâsân. He was a skilful worker in clay, although he was born blind. Later in life he obtained

his freedom from the Arab woman whose property he was, and lived partly at Bassora, his birthplace, and partly at Bagdâd. He made the acquaintance of the theologian Wâṣil ibn ʻAṭâ, the founder of the school of the Muʻtazilites, who ascribed the demoralisation of Bassora to his poems, and remained a free-thinker. He had broken through the rule of saying his prayers five times a day; he was really a Zindîq, that is to say a secret believer in the Avesta, while preserving the outward appearance of Islamism. He was always a suspected man. His panegyric of Caliph Mahdî saved him once. The Caliph contented himself with forbidding him to make any mention of women in future poems. But he imprudently wrote against the minister Yaʻqûb ibn Dâ'ûd, who revenged himself by the infliction of seventy lashes, and of these the poet died at the age of ninety.

He was ugly, for besides his congenital infirmity, which had left him with two pieces of red flesh instead of eyes, he was deeply pitted with smallpox. Bashshâr held the element of Fire to be superior to that of Earth, and justified Satan, who was created out of Fire, for having refused to bow down before Adam, who was made of clay, as the Koran relates. He even wrote a stanza which strongly betokens his Zoroastrian views. "The Earth is dark, and Fire is brilliant. Ever since it has existed men have worshipped it." He was a misanthrope, who thanked God for having made him blind, "so that I need not see that which I hate." When he was about to recite a poem he would clap his hands, cough, and spit right and left. But when once he opened his mouth he won the admiration of his hearers. He had begun to compose verses before he was ten years old, and boasted that he had known

Jarîr, and had even satirised him, but the great desert poet had thought him too young to deserve his notice. "If he had answered me," Bashshâr would say, "I should have been the greatest man of my time." What the grammarian Aṣma'î thought most admirable in his work was that his lines were the evident production of a natural genius, which would not submit to any lengthy process of polishing before publication; they were, so to speak, almost improvised. When the poet was questioned as to the source of his purity of expression he ascribed all the credit to the old men and the women of the Bedouin tribe of the 'Uqail, with which he was connected as a freed slave. Yet he was accused of carrying his use of expletives to the greatest excess and of introducing into his lines names of men and places which had never existed. He had dubbed several chambers in his house with poetic surnames, a source of gentle astonishment to the uninitiated persons to whom he would recount their beauties.

MARWÂN IBN ABÎ ḤAFṢA (721–797) was the son of a Khurâsân Jew who was taken by Marwân ibn al-Ḥakam, then Governor of Medina, to Yamâma in Arabia, as tax-collector, and there married an Arab woman of free blood. He was strangled in private vengeance for some political verses directed against the claim of the 'Alids. The criminal's confession—he himself was never discovered—is still in existence. Marwân was an imitator of the ancient desert poets. According to Ibn Khallikân, he was great-grandson to Abû Ḥafṣa, Marwân's freedman, whose liberty had been granted as a reward for service rendered during the siege of Caliph 'Uthmân's house at Medina—he had saved his life. Some say he was a

Jewish physician who turned Moslem. But at Medina he was believed to have been the freedman of Samaual, the famous Syrian nobleman and poet. We are also told that Abû Ḥafṣa was made prisoner when Persepolis was taken under ʿUthmân. As for Marwân, who was born in Yamâma, he made his way to Bagdâd, composed panegyrics in honour of Al-Mahdî and Hârûn al-Rashîd, and wrote satires directed against the descendants of ʿAlî. His most celebrated work is a *qaṣîda*, rhymed in *l*, in praise of Maʿn, son of Zâ'ida, Governor of Yemen, in which he lauds his inexhaustible generosity. "When a favour is asked of him, Maʿn will not speak the word *No*, for this seems a forbidden word to him." The poet was very stingy, and came to the Caliph's court dressed in a sheepskin and the coarsest cotton garments. So thrifty was he that he never bought any meat except sheep's heads, and on these he lived, winter and summer alike. It was of him that the line was written : "Marwân has no zeal for pleasure; the only jealousy he feels concerns the cooking-pots."

Beside the work, not unattended by risk, of the poets who dedicated their powers to politics, we find the far more kindly productions of the love poet, Abû'l-Faḍl al-ʿAbbâs IBN AL-AḤNAF, a descendant of Arab settlers in Khurâsân, allied with Iranian families. He was a comrade of Caliph Hârûn al-Rashîd, followed him in his campaigns, and died at Bagdâd (807 or 813). The grace and elegance of his diction made him the delight of men of taste. He was a man of fine manners, with nothing of the debauchee about him. Polished though he was, he never went beyond writing love poems. He was no artist either in satire or in

panegyric. His only known enemy was the great Mu'tazilite theologian, Hudhail al-'Allâf, who accused him of having written a stanza affirming the doctrine of predestination.

But the most famous of this group, beyond all contradiction, is ABÛ NUWÂS, the lyric and Bacchic poet *par excellence*, whose works have been studied by Nöldeke and Alfred von Kremer. He was born at Al-Ahwâz in the heart of Susiana (about 756), where his mother, of Persian origin, laboured as a washerwoman in a fuller's yard. But it was at Bassora that he received the teachings of his master, the poet Wâliba, who made him known to the Barmakides, and had cause, later, to regret his kindness, by reason of his pupil's ingratitude. He spent a year wandering about the desert, to study the pure Bedouin tongue. At Bagdâd, in spite of his loose life, he was valued by the Caliphs Hârûn and Amîn. When he grew old, he relinquished his bad habits, and gave himself up to religious observances. His jests about a member of the Beni-Naubakht clan earned him rough treatment, of which he died, about 810. Abû Nuwâs practised every form of Arabic poetry. Not only did he sing the praises of the grape, after the manner of 'Adî ibn Zaid and Walîd ibn Yazîd. Like his forerunners, he composed elegies, amatory poems, satires, panegyrics, humorous verses, and hunting scenes, in which last he reproduced the style of the ancient and intrepid hunters of the desert, and he also wrote the devout poems which mark the last stage of his career. His memory was extraordinary, and, what is no less remarkable, he possessed no library. Nothing was found after his death save a book cover, within which lay a manuscript containing notes on grammar. The

Caliph cast him into prison, and the poet wrote: "If you kill Abû Nuwâs, where will you find another?" The only woman he ever really loved was a slave, Janân. She was well taught and witty, learned both in history and poetry. She started on pilgrimage to Mecca, and the poet followed her. There it was that he spoke the lines: "Do you not see that I spend my life in pursuing her—a difficult enterprise? We made the pilgrimage together. This journey alone it was which could unite us." Janân did not care for him at first, but the lover's persistence broke down the severity of the cruel fair at last. He was the first poet who employed bold metaphor to describe the different parts of the beloved one's person. Amongst others, he has this line: "She taps the rose with jujubes"—that is, "her cheek with her finger-tips." Scenes in which deep drinkers, ever athirst, turn deaf ears to the muezzin's call to prayer, refusing to forsake their serious business, praise of good wine, purchased with gold from Jew or Christian merchant, and grown mellow in its cobwebbed jar, the heat of which cheers and warms the darkness of the night—such are the themes of Abû Nuwâs' most famous poems. Here and there we catch a note of sadness, a sudden memory of past days and comrades now no more, dark thoughts, swiftly washed away by a fresh draught of the divine juice.

MUSLIM ibn el-Walîd, known by the surname of *Ṣarîʿ al-Ghawânî*, "the victim of the fair," which had been bestowed on him by Hârûn al-Rashîd, was client of a family of Anṣârs or auxiliaries—otherwise those dwellers in Medina who had attained noble rank by their support of the Prophet against his enemies. He was born at Kûfa, somewhere between 747 and 757. His

father was a weaver, and Ibn Qanbar later cast cruel reproach on the poet concerning his parent's handiwork. "Where could I find a being more degraded than thy father? Nay, I was mistaken! One yet lower there is—thyself! For many a day he wove his cloaks as ill as thou now weavest thy verse!" No one knows who Muslim's teachers were. He may proceed directly from the great poets of the heroic period, whose works he studied. He was a careless wanderer, a spendthrift, who gave no thought to the morrow, and often, lacking any other shelter, slept under the starry sky, wrapped in his only cloak. His patrons, the valiant General Yazîd ibn Mazyad, Muḥammad, son of Caliph Manṣûr, and Faḍl ibn Sahl, the minister, lifted him out of this parlous state. The latter, indeed, went so far as to give him a post about the Court of Justice of the Province of Jurjân, and then promoted him to the delicate functions of director of the horse-post in the same place. But he appointed a steward to receive the income from the farms he had given the poet near Ispahan, to put aside the sum necessary for his daily expenses, and invest the rest in the purchase of more land. Muslim was a great admirer of the produce of the vines grown by the Zoroastrians at Ṭîzanâbâd, and has sung the praise of wine. "The daughter of the Magians turned Moslem by her union with the guests. We have asked her in marriage, and the negotiator who leads her to us walks with grave and solemn step." The whole of this poem is worth reading, in the charming translation given us by M. Barbier de Meynard. His enemies scoffed at his passion; ʿAbbâs Ibn al-Aḥnaf derisively called him "the victim of the sorceresses," and others "the victim of the brimming cup." But his intoxication was elegant, and his style was

classic, like that of the ancient authors whom he closely followed, even when he gave new metaphors to the world. His amorous poetry is less sincere, and he himself acknowledged that he sang of the object of his thoughts because fashion demanded it, but that his personal taste was for less exalted ladies. As a satirist, he seems to have been inferior to his opponents. His dispute with the poet Ibn Qanbar was violent, but the advantage, as Abû'l-Faraj al-Iṣfahânî and Al-Mubarrad have established, remained with his adversary. He died in 803, while still holding his appointment, a stranger in Jurjân, like the palm-tree he sang in the last stanza he composed. When at the point of death, he caused the rough copy of all his poems to be cast into the river, as a proof of penitence on account of his Bacchanalian compositions.

ABÛ'L-ʿATÂHIYA Ismâʿîl ibn Qâsim (748–828) belonged to the tribe of ʿAnaza. He was born in the Ḥijâz, lived at Kûfa, took his way to Bagdâd, when his poetry had already made him a name, and there fell in love with one of Mahdî's slaves, named ʿUtba. The prominent characteristic of his style is his use of simple expressions which every one can understand, because his poems are sermons in verse on the instability of the things of this world. On this account he is the ancestor of that long series of hortatory works which flourish more especially in Persian literature. He avoided all studied forms of expression, so that he might be understood by the populace.

He was surnamed Al-Jarrâr, "the jar-seller," because he had originally plied that trade. Men used to go and listen to his verses, and wrote them, at his dictation, on the fragments of broken pottery they picked up on the ground.

Abû'l-'Atâhiya boasted that he could put everything he said into verse, and when he was asked if he understood prosody, he would reply: "I am above all prosody." As a matter of fact he did use certain metres of his own invention, which do not follow the classic rules. 'Umar ibn al-'Alâ, Governor of Ṭabaristân, rewarded him richly for some verses written in his honour, and the jealousy of the other poets ran high. The governor called them together, and made them the following speech: "It is strange that you poets should be so jealous of each other. When one of you comes to us with a *qaṣîda* written in our honour, fifty lines are devoted to the celebration of his mistress' charms, and not till all his praise of her is exhausted does he enter on the real subject of his poem. Now Abû'l-'Atâhiya, on the contrary, devotes only a few lines to his beloved, and at once begins his panegyric. Why are you envious of him?" When he was at the point of death, he sent for Mukhâriq, the great singer, that he might hear him sing the lines he had himself written: "When my life closes, the sorrows of the women who weep me will be short. My mistress will cease to think of me. She will forget my love, and will soon find another lover." His last desire was that the following words should be inscribed on his tomb: "A life which ends in death is a life filled with bitterness." Abû Nuwâs found fault with his extreme facility, which permitted Abû'l-'Atâhiya to produce one or two hundred lines a day. He, too, gave up writing poetry, in his old age, probably from pious motives, but this step led to his being thrown into prison among malefactors, and then haled before Al-Mahdî, who gave him his choice between carrying on his art or suffering death. "I would rather write poetry," quoth the bard,

and forthwith regained his freedom. He was said to have adopted the views of the Greek philosophers, because in his lines he spoke of death, and made no mention of the Resurrection. He was also taxed with avarice, which was all the more incomprehensible because he had amassed great wealth. The surname by which he is known, which probably signifies "the Intriguer," was given him by Caliph Al-Mahdî. He made some enemies, such as 'Abdallah, the son of Ma'n, who caught him in a trap, and gave him a hundred lashes, but very light ones, seeing he dreaded the poet's vengeance. Nevertheless Abû'l-'Atâhiya took advantage of this forbearance to abuse his foe yet more roundly, and likened him to a woman with eunuchs all about her. "She struck me with her hand, the daughter of Ma'n. She hurt her hand, and I felt nothing at all!" He declared that most men spoke in verse without being conscious of it, and that all would be poets if they only knew how to compose their speech correctly. The grammarian Al-Aṣma'î said of Abû'l-'Atâhiya: "His lines are like the public square in front of the King's palace, whereon fall pearls, and gold, and dust, and potsherds, and fruit-kernels." Abû'l-'Atâhiya himself regarded the line in which he said, "Men lie in apathy, while the mill of Fate grinds on," as his masterpiece. Hârûn al-Rashîd also cast him into prison when he would have plunged into asceticism, so as to force him to compose erotic poems.

'Alî ibn Jabala, who was surnamed AL-'AKAWWAK (the crop-eared) (776–828), was born in the class of freed slaves. His family had originally belonged to Khurâsân. He was either born blind, or became blind when he was seven years old, from an attack of smallpox. His skin was blackish and stained with leprous patches. Caliph

Ma'mûn was very wroth with him because of a set of verses composed in honour of Ḥumaid al-Ṭûsî, in which the sovereign detected excessive eulogies such as should only be offered to Divinity, and also because he had asserted that all the Arabs on the earth borrowed their finest qualities from Abû Dulaf, without making any exception in favour of the Caliph himself. The poet, who was in the mountains of 'Irâq 'Ajamî, was forced to flee. He was taken in Syria and carried to Bagdâd, where his tongue was torn out, and he died of hemorrhage.

Abû Dulaf, whom Al-'Akawwak had extolled, was passing, one day, through a town in 'Irâq, when he heard one woman say to another: "That is Abû Dulaf, of whom the poet said: 'Abû Dulaf is the whole world, nomad or of the cities. If he turns out of his road, all the world follows him.'" And the great man wept, repenting that he had not rewarded Al-'Akawwak according to his deserts.

Two men of Persian origin, IBRÂHÎM AL-MAUṢILÎ and his son ISḤÂQ, won celebrity as poets, and were incomparably superior to all their competitors as singers and musical composers. The father was not born at Mosul, as his surname would seem to imply, but ran away to that place, to study music. He first saw the light at Kûfa, and was the son of a high-born Persian, Mâhân (whose Iranian name was corrupted to Maimûn), who had emigrated from the province of Fârs, in 742. Caliph Al-Mahdî was the first to appreciate his music, and he rose in favour under each of his successors. When Hârûn al-Rashîd fell out with his slave Mârida, and Ja'far the Barmakide, whose post of Grand Vizier has been made so famous by the *Thousand and One Nights*,

desired to bring about a reconciliation between the sovereign and his favourite, he caused the impassioned stanzas which brought the lovers together again to be written by the poet 'Abbâs Ibn al-Aḥnaf, and set to music by Ibrâhîm. Ibrâhîm was succeeded by his son Isḥâq, who was born in 767. Of him the Caliph Mu'taṣim used to say: "When Isḥâq sings, the borders of my Empire seem to me enlarged." He was as proficient in the traditions of the Prophet, in jurisprudence and scholastic theology, as in music. Al-Ma'mûn said of him: "If Isḥâq were not such a famous singer I should have made him a judge. He deserves it better than our present *qâḍîs*, and his conduct, his piety, and his uprightness surpass theirs. But his talent for music outshines all the rest." He was the second author to produce a *Book of Songs* (Kitâb al-Aghânî), in which the various pieces he sang were collected together.

Al-Mahdî had forbidden Ibrâhîm to go and see his sons, Mûsâ (al-Hâdî) and Hârûn (al-Rashîd); he disobeyed, was punished by the infliction of three hundred lashes and cast into prison. In later years Al-Hâdî was so lavish in his gifts to Ibrâhîm that Isḥâq was able to say that if the Caliph had lived they might have rebuilt the walls of their house with silver and gold.

Amongst the Bagdâd poets of Arab, or at all events of Semitic extraction, we must also mention DI'BIL ibn 'Alî AL-KHUZÂ'Î (765–860), who was born either at Kûfa or at Karkîsiya (Circesium). For some time he discharged administrative functions as governor of a small town in Ṭukhâristân, in North-Western Persia. He died in Babylonia. He was a satirist, who employed himself in collecting a volume of biographies of the poets. He had a spiteful tongue which spared no one,

not even the Caliphs. He was consequently in a constant condition of flight and concealment. So great was the terror he inspired that, when he came one day on an epileptic writhing in convulsions on the ground, he only had to shout his own name into the sufferer's ear to effect a cure. He had yet other sins upon his conscience. One night he fell upon a money-changer just going to his home, and whom he believed to be carrying his purse as usual. But all the poor man had in his sleeve that day was a rag wrapped round three pomegranates. The victim lay stone dead, and justice pursued the assassin, who, after long hiding, was fain to quit Kûfa altogether. He wrote his satires beforehand, and when he had a vengeance to wreak, would insert his enemy's name in a ready-made set of verses. Al-Buḥturî preferred Di‘bil to Muslim, because, according to Arab taste, his language and the character of his work were superior.

In his old age he would say: "For more than fifty years I have borne my cross on my shoulder, but nobody has been able to nail me to it yet."

He was a friend of Muslim, who had given him useful counsel. Yet, when Muslim was appointed governor of a Persian town, he refused to acknowledge him, an affront avenged by Di‘bil in a biting satire. He was an earnest Shî‘ite, and supported the claim of ‘Alî to the Caliphate.

He it was who wrote that verse, which stings like a whip, on Caliph Mu‘taṣim: "The ‘Abbâsids number seven, according to the books, which do not tell us of an eighth. Unless, indeed, like the Seven Sleepers in their cave, they are seven brave fellows, with an eighth who was a dog!" It is true he denied having written this, in later days.

The habitual guest and companion of Caliph Al-Mutawakkil, 'ALÎ IBN AL-JAHM, surnamed Al-Sâmî, because he was descended from a branch of the Quraishites which bore that name, was born in Khurâsân, whence Al-Ma'mûn summoned him to Bagdâd. He opposed the Shî'ites; he wrote many lines against the claim of the 'Alids; he also heaped insults on the Christians, amongst others on the famous physician Bôkhtyishû', and on the Mu'tazilites. For a satire which displeased his patron, already greatly irritated by his perpetual accusations against his comrades, he was imprisoned and exiled. He went back to his own country, then governed by Ṭâhir, and, by order of the Caliph, was fastened naked to a cross for a whole day, as he has himself related. "It was no unknown man, nor person of inferior merit, who was crucified at Shâdhiyâkh on Monday evening. By this execution they satisfied their vengeance. But, thanks be to God! their victim was a man of honour, and worthy of respect!"

He proceeded into Syria, and while travelling towards 'Irâq from Aleppo, fell in a fight with a Bedouin *Ghazw* (in 863). When help reached him, he was found to be dying, but still whispering verses. "Has the darkness of night been deepened? or has the torrent swept away the morn? I think of the folks in the street of Dujail in Bagdâd—but how far am I from there!" The Orientals admire the following delicate thought: "The enmity of a man without honour or religion is an affliction which has no equal, for he leaves you his own reputation, while he assails yours, which you have guarded with such care."

He has himself related that his poetic vocation first manifested itself when his father had him detained in the

school he was attending. He wrote to his mother, complaining of his father's inhumanity: "All the pupils have left school, and I stay here in prison, without having committed any fault." Whereupon his mother obtained his enlargement. But such was his reputation for lying that many people asserted the stanzas were written when he was sixty, and could not, consequently, have been composed while he was at school.

Under the rule of Mutawakkil, an artist prince, who loved games and buffoonery, and was the first to introduce them into the Palace of the Caliphs, music and the dance reached a development far beyond that of the old days. Among the court poets of this period we find FAḌL, a woman of Central Arabian blood, who led a somewhat loose life at Bagdâd. Her *liaison* with Sa'îd ibn Ḥumaid, a poet of Persian birth, and exceedingly orthodox opinions, who was head of the despatch office under Caliph Musta'în, whereas his mistress was a Shî'ite, fills up the whole story of her life. She used to be summoned to the Caliph's harem, to delight his fair favourites. She was a quick-witted woman, ready in repartee, and skilled in penmanship. Her lover, Sa'îd, perceived, at last, that he was dropping into unconscious imitation of her style. She went to see him when she chose. One day, as she entered, Sa'îd rose eagerly, greeted her, and begged her to remain with him. She replied; "A messenger from the Palace has just been at my house, so I cannot stay. But I came up, because I could not bear to pass thy door without coming in to see thee"; and Sa'îd replied: "Thou art like the sun that lights the world; its rays seem close to us, but who can reach it?" Sa'îd's devotion did not prevent the inconstant Faḍl from accepting the suit of Bûnân, a young singer. But at all

events she was swayed by a genuine and sincere feeling. How different from the female slave-musicians, who, as the poetess herself tells us (and other testimony proves her truth), "receive a poor man as if he were a dog, and never ask for less than a gold-mine!" When at the point of death, Faḍl desired to see her lover once more, and found strength to write to him. "My patience is worn out, and my sufferings increase. My house is near thee, it is true, but thou art still a long way off!" This happened under the Caliphate of Mu'tamid, in 873. In Mutawakkil's own harem, a singing-woman named MAḤBÛBA, born at Bassora, but of foreign blood, was greatly admired. She composed stanzas which she sang, accompanying herself on the lute. But her verses were thought better than her singing, which was mediocre. When Mutawakkil was murdered, Maḥbûba put on mourning and forswore all pleasure till she died. This persistent fidelity displeased the new owner into whose hands she passed when the Caliph's harem was dispersed: but an officer of Turkish birth asked for her as a gift, set her free, and bade her quit Sâmarrâ and settle wherever she chose. She died at Bagdâd, in the deepest seclusion.

IBN AL-RÛMÎ, "son of the Greek," a surname he owed to his grandfather, Juraij, or George, was born at Bagdâd in 836, and was poisoned by Abû'l-Ḥusain Qâsim ibn 'Ubaidallah, Caliph Mu'taḍid's vizier, who dreaded his satires. The minister suborned a servant, who served the poet with a poisoned biscuit. When Ibn al-Rûmî had eaten it, he perceived he had been poisoned, and rose to depart. "Where are you going?" said the minister. "Whither you have sent me." "Very good," replied the vizier. "Present my duty to my father." "I am not on my road to hell!" answered the poet, who

forthwith retired to his own house, sent for a physician, who is said to have used the wrong drugs, so that the patient died within a few days.

His lines are admirable, both for beauty of expression and originality of conception. The novelty of his ideas was especially praised. He derided the Eastern mania for dyeing the beard. "When a man's hair remains black, although his youth has gone by, it must of necessity be artificially dyed. How can any old man believe that jetty colour will be thought natural, and he himself considered young?"

A poet of the tribe of Ṭai, AL-BUḤTURÎ (Walîd ibn 'Ubaid), was born at or near Manbij in 820. He was first of all the comrade of his fellow-tribesman Abû Tammâm, and finally travelled to Bagdâd, where he long lived, as the panegyrist of Mutawakkil and his courtiers, and of the heads of his civil administration. He died in 897, either at his native town or at Aleppo. Like Abû Tammâm, whose chief claim to glory lies in his collection of the *Ḥamâsa*, Al-Buḥturî made a book of the same description. And his poetry, too, is written in imitation of the ancient style. He often mentions Aleppo and the surrounding plain, for that country had grown dear to him. It was Abû Tammâm who, hearing him recite a poem of his own composition, at Ḥimṣ, divined his poetic gift, and, as he knew him to be poor, wrote a letter recommending him to the inhabitants of Ma'arrat al-Nu'mân. As a result of this letter, he was given a pension of four thousand dirhems, the first money he ever earned. Abû'l-'Alâ al-Ma'arrî considered Abû Tammâm and Mutanabbî moralists, while he took Al-Buḥturî to be a genuine poet. Al-Buḥturî was very avaricious, wore dirty garments, and starved the brother and the servant

who lived with him. He left very few satires behind him. His son related that his father charged him on his deathbed to burn everything he had written in anger, or with a desire for revenge, so as to save his descendants from any inconvenience caused by other men's resentment. But Abû'l-Faraj al-Iṣfahânî has proved Al-Buḥturî's inferiority in this department, by means of fragments of satires admitted to be his.

Even the sons of kings dabbled in poetry. ʿAbdallah Ibn al-Muʿtazz, the son of Caliph Al-Muʿtazz (861–908), led the unfettered existence of a poet and man of learning under the reign of Al-Muʿtaḍid. After the death of that Caliph, he was mixed up in court intrigues. The party which was discontented with the policy of Muqtadir, who was ruled by women and eunuchs, chose ʿAbdallah to be Caliph, under the title of Al-Murtaḍî (December 17, 908). But the reigning Caliph's guard overcame ʿAbdallah's partisans. His sovereignty lasted one day only. He fled to the house of a jeweller, but was soon discovered and strangled (29th December) by the Caliph's chamberlain and treasurer, Mu'nis, a eunuch. His poetry, which resembled that of Abû Nuwâs, contained no imitation of the ancient styles. He wrote charming little occasional poems, full of aristocratic grace. Besides this, he took an interest in literature, and was the author of the first great Arabic work on rhetoric (*Kitâb al-badîʿ*), now preserved at the Escurial. His verses are marked by lucidity and ease of style.

He formulated the rule for healthy rhetoric in the following dictum : " Eloquence is the accurate expression of ideas, in few words." Some poets wept his tragic end, among them the refined and subtle ʿAlî ibn Muḥam-

mad Ibn Bassâm, and his friend Ibn al-'Allâf Ḥasan ibn 'Alî, the blind poet of Nahrawân, who, to avoid persecution, wrote a celebrated elegy on a cat, his pet, which was in the habit of climbing into his neighbours' pigeon roosts and devouring their denizens, whose owners ruthlessly destroyed it. "Thou hast left us, puss (*hirr*), and thou wilt return no more! Thou wast as my own child to me. How could we cease to love thee, thou who wast so sure a protection to us!" Ibn al-Mu'tazz was fond of drinking wine of a morning in the meadows of Maṭîra, near Sâmarrâ, not far from the Christian Convent of 'Abdûn. "How often have I been wakened at dawn by the voices of the monks at their prayers! Robed in black, they chanted matins, girt with their rope-girdles, and with a crown of hair about their shaven heads."

The 'Abbâsid administration may also claim the honour of numbering Ibn al-Ḥajjâj, a *Muḥtasib*, or commissioner in charge of the markets, weights and measures, and popular morals of Bagdâd, among its servants. He was ultimately deprived of his office, and died in the year 1000. His light poetry earned him considerable fame and applause. Its ease and gaiety were highly praised. He has been likened to Imru'ul-Qais, inasmuch as that, like him, he created a new style, in which he never was surpassed. He was a fervent Shî'ite, and ordered in his last will that his body should be laid at the feet of that of the Imâm Mûsâ, whose tomb is not far from Bagdâd. With him we must also mention Sharîf Muḥammad al-Riḍâ, a descendant of the Prophet. His father, Ṭâhir, had performed the functions of inspector of the descent of 'Alî, or judge of that final Court of Appeal known as al-Maẓâlim, and leader of the

Pilgrim Caravan. He began to write verses very early in life, and went on producing them in considerable numbers till he died. He also took an interest in Koranic exegesis, and wrote works dealing with the rhetoric of the Sacred Book. He died at Bagdâd in 1015.

One of his pupils, MIHYÂR IBN MARZÛYA, was converted to Islam by his means. He had been a Zoroastrian, born in Dailam, the mountainous region south of Gîlân, on the Caspian coast. He died at Bagdâd in 1037. He acted as Persian secretary, and studied poetry with Sharîf Al-Riḍâ. His Shî'ite opinions were abhorred by the Sunnites, one of whom said to him, at last: "Mihyâr, when you were converted, all you did was to shift from one corner of hell into another!" The delicacy of thought and remarkable sweetness of expression characterising his verses were greatly admired.

THE PROVINCES

All the poetic genius of the country was not attracted to the capital. From one end of the Empire to the other, we find poetical works produced. Their authors, for political or religious, or other more personal reasons, remained far from the central point, and were content with the patronage of the provincial governors. Ismâ'îl, the ḤIMYARITE SAYYID, born at Bassora about 729, was driven by his Shî'ite opinions to leave that town for Kûfa. He acknowledged Abû'l-'Abbâs Saffâḥ when that city fell, but he held apart from him and his successors on perceiving that they persecuted the 'Alids, and died at Wâsiṭ in 789. His poetry, like that of Abû'l-'Atâhiya and Bashshâr ibn Burd, is remarkable for its simplicity of diction.

This poet, who came of Khârijite parents, belonging to the ʻIbâdite sect, spent forty years in celebrating the glories of the house of ʻAlî in numberless poems, and with a talent which compelled the admiration even of his enemies. He himself has related that it was a dream which converted him to the tenets of the Kaisânites, the partisans of Muḥammad, son of the Ḥanafite woman. His bronzed complexion bore witness to the many crossings of races which had taken place in Southern Arabia. He was tall and well proportioned, with fine teeth and luxuriant hair. His fecundity of language and boldness of conception were remarkable. The Bedouins themselves highly esteemed his style. His drunken habits led to his being arrested one night, in a state of intoxication, in the streets of Al-Ahwâz, in Susiana. In his satires, which are full of the most violent hatred of the companions of the Prophet, he goes so far as to compare ʻÂ'isha to "the serpent which seeks to devour its young."

Abû'l-Shîṣ Muḥammad ibn ʻAbdallah attached himself as panegyrist to the service of the Amîr of Raqqa, ʻUqba ibn Jaʻfar ibn al-Ashʻath al Khuzâʻî, wrote Bacchic poetry and elegies on the loss of his own eyesight, which overtook him in old age, and died in 811. He was cousin to Diʻbil al Khuzâʻî, and his reputation was overshadowed by those of Muslim ibn al-Walîd, Ashjaʻ, and Abû Nuwâs. The Amîr of Raqqa was both rich and generous, and his largess kept the poet near him. He was a quick thinker, and composed with great rapidity.

No more poets are to be discovered in the Arabian Peninsula. It is scarcely worth while to mention Ibn Harma Ibrâhîm ibn ʻAlî (685–767), who dwelt at

Medîna, was a hot partisan of the ʿAlids, and a great lover of wine. Syria, however, continues to shine with brilliant splendour. Abû Tammâm Ḥabîb ibn Aus, who was born near the Lake of Tiberias in 807, the son of a Christian named Tadûs (Thaddeus) the druggist, was a great traveller. In his youth he was at Ḥimṣ, where, when the poet Al-Buḥturî met him, he already enjoyed considerable reputation as a poet. But some authorities aver that, as a child, he carried water in the mosques of Cairo. Certain it is that Egypt was the country in which his literary efforts first found favour. He went to Damascus, and failing to find a patron there, seized the opportunity offered by a journey into Syria, undertaken by Al-Ma'mûn, to wait on him, but could not obtain an audience. Having reached Mosul, he travelled into Armenia, where rich gifts from the governor, Khâlid ibn Yazîd, awaited him. The death of Caliph Al-Ma'mûn recalled him to Bagdâd, where he was received into favour by Al-Muʿtaṣim, and to this prince or to his courtiers many of his poems are dedicated. The increasing renown of ʿAbdallah ibn Ṭâhir, then well nigh independent in his government of Khurâsân, attracted the poet thither. On his return, being delayed at Hamadhân by a snowstorm which had choked the Zagros passes, he made the acquaintance of the learned Abû'l-Wafâ ibn Salama, who made him free of his library, inspired him with a taste for searching out and collecting the old Arab poets, and thus enabled him to compose, among other works, his *Ḥamâsa*—which has preserved the knowledge of a great number of poets and poetical works of the early Arab times to us. His own verses might, perhaps, have been swiftly forgotten; but his celebrity as the compiler of the

Ḥamâsa has endured, and his commentator, Tabrîzî, has been able to declare that "Abû Tammâm, when he collected this anthology, proved himself a better poet than in his own verse." Yet he is also said to have surpassed his contemporaries in purity of style, in the intrinsic merit of his work, and the excellence of the way in which he could handle a subject. Ibn Khallikân has ascertained that Abû Tammâm spent the close of his life at Mosul, whither Ḥasan ibn Wahb, secretary to the chief of the Chancery, had sent him as director of the horse post. This, under the Arab Empire, was a most confidential position, for, apart from his public functions, the director had to keep the central authority informed of all that was happening in the provinces. He died in this town, about the year 846.

In DÎK AL-JINN ("the Cock of the Genii," thus surnamed because he had green eyes and was very ugly) 'Abdal-Salâm ibn Raghbân, we have an instance of that interesting intellectual movement which stirred all the vanquished races just beginning to raise their heads, and find rhetoricians to defend their (purely imaginary) rights against the Arabian Arabs' pretensions to superiority and nobility of race. These rhetoricians were known as *shu'ûbiyya*. One thing they forgot—that they could only express their patriotism in the Arabic tongue, and that the use of that tongue was the indelible symbol of their vanquished state. The Cock of the Genii was a famous Shu'ûbî. He was born at Ḥimṣ in Syria, a country he never left, and he asserted the superiority of the Syrian race. He was also a Shî'ite, and wrote elegies on the sad death of Ḥusain, son of 'Alî, at the battle of Kerbelâ. He died in 849, when over seventy years of age. He had squandered his whole

patrimony in pleasure and dissipation. He had a slave of the name of Dunyâ, of whom he was passionately enamoured and to whom he wrote many poems. But in a fit of wicked passion and jealousy he put her to death, suspecting her of loose conduct with a slave called Waṣîf. He lived to repent his crime most bitterly. To his outpourings of sorrow we owe verses in which he vents his lamentation. "O cluster of dates, destruction has fallen upon thee! I have watered the earth with thy blood. . . ." Her form used to appear to him at night. "After she was buried she came to my couch, and I said to her: 'Joy of my eyes, art thou restored to me? But how? Can it be possible?' and she replied: 'My corpse lies yonder, but this, my soul, is come to visit thee.'" My readers will note the expression of regret. There is no expression of remorse. The poet's conscience was easy. In committing the murder, he had done no more than use the right conferred on him by law.

The rule of the Ḥamdânids at Aleppo engendered a most important literary movement in that city, and it soon spread to every Arabic-speaking country. Saif al-daula, who established himself at Aleppo when the sovereignty of Bagdâd was being disputed by military leaders of Turkish or Persian origin, was forced to defend the state he had set up against many external foes, and especially against the Roman troops of Byzantium. Notwithstanding this, he saw several poets flourish about him, the most famous being Mutanabbî and Abû Firâs al-Ḥamdânî.

The son of a water-carrier, MUTANABBÎ was born at Kûfa in 905; he spent his boyhood in Syria and amongst the desert Arabs. As a young man, he fancied

himself a prophet, founded a new religion in the plains round the little town of Samâwa on the Euphrates, received revelations after the manner of the Koran, and collected a few followers about him. But in a very short space of time he was overthrown by Lu'lu', the Ikhshîdite general in command at Ḥimṣ, and was cast into prison. Thence his surname of Mutanabbî, "he who counts himself a prophet." His prison, which did not open its doors till he had acknowledged the true Faith, revealed his poetic gift to him. In 948 he reached Saif al-daula's court, and composed such beautiful poems in his honour that the names of poet and patron are thereby indissolubly united.

This good understanding only lasted for nine years. After a dispute with the Persian philologist, Khâlawaih, of Susiana, who so far lost his self-control as to strike his adversary in the face with a key, the poet quitted Aleppo and offered his services to foes of the Ḥamdânid dynasty, Kâfûr, a negro eunuch, and Anûjûr, both of them ministers of the Ikhshîdite princes, who had made themselves independent in Egypt. But this attempt ended in disappointment, and Mutanabbî, in a rage, fled to Bagdâd, where the real ruler was the Vizier Al-Muhallabî, who would fain have been the object of the illustrious poet's praise. But this honour the poet would not grant him, and so departed to Shîrâz in Persia, to ʿAḍud al-daula, the Buwaihid, who heaped generous rewards upon him. On his way back from Persia, Mutanabbî fell amongst a marauding band of Bedouins, and was killed, not far from Bagdâd (965).

Mutanabbî's poems have been inordinately praised and criticised, both in the Arab and the European world.

Qâḍî Abû'l-Ḥasan boasted that he kept the golden mean between the poet's admirers, who preferred him to every other of his time, and set him above all his rivals, and his detractors, who declared his dissertations to be empty chatter and his expressions mere barbarisms. Tha'âlibî, the author of the *Yatîmat al-Dahr*, justly held this division of opinion to be an evident proof of the poet's merit and superiority. He also praised his skill. "Rhythm is subject to his will, and thoughts are his slaves." A close examination of Oriental criticism shows us that the qualities it most values in Mutanabbî's work are his refinement of expression, his neglect of the antique simplicity in favour of affected mannerisms, and his accumulation of fantastic imagery. Thus he was the first to compose lines in the style of the following: "He marched at the head of an army which raised a cloud of dust that darkened the sight. It was as though the soldiers saw with their ears." And this because the darkness was so great that nobody could see with his eyes! These regrettable inventions of the pseudo-prophet and his contemporaries won so much success that they reigned supreme over Oriental poetry, which we shall now see drop deeper and deeper into bombast and false imagery. In proof of Mutanabbî's popularity, Ibn Khallikân quotes the fact that more than forty commentaries have been written to explain his works. This is because the uncommon and far-fetched expressions he used so much too freely needed explanation before they could be understood. Avarice was the only vice with which he could be taxed. His moral conduct stood out in remarkable contrast to the looseness and debauchery of the life at Saif al-daula's court. One stern Moslem actually remarked that though he did not fast, nor

recite the canonical prayers five times a day, nor read the Koran, he never told a lie.

ABÛ FIRÂS al-Ḥamdânî, who was of the princely family, and cousin to Saif al-daula, who appointed him governor of the town of Manbij, and had him with him all through his wars with the *Domesticus*, general-in-chief of the Roman troops in Asia, was a man of a different temper. He was made prisoner in 959, when the fortress he commanded fell, was conveyed to Constantinople, and there remained till he was set at liberty in 965. During this captivity he wrote many elegies addressed to various members of his family. One, which is celebrated, to his mother, at Manbij, has been translated into German by Ahlwardt. When Saif al-daula died, in 967, Abû Firâs claimed the sovereignty of Ḥimṣ, but perished fighting with the troops sent against him by Saif al-daula's son. He was a valiant soldier, and his poems, quite devoid of any pedantic affectation, breathe brave and straightforward feeling, expressed in noble and elevated language. They form a diary of his eventful life.

With these two masters of the Arabic tongue, we may mention a member of Saif al-daula's circle known as Al-Sarî AL-RAFFÂ, because in his youth he had been a patcher or darner of stuffs at Mosul. After Saif al-daula's death, he went to Bagdâd, to the Vizier Al-Muhallabî; Thaʿâlibî accuses him of many plagiarisms. He had chosen Kushâjim, then famous in the East, to be his model, and to increase the volume of the copies he made from that author's works, he contracted the habit of inserting lines of his own composition. Al-Nâmî (Abû'l-ʿAbbâs Aḥmad), who succeeded Mutanabbî as court poet, died at Aleppo between 980 and 1008. He

was called Al-Miṣṣîṣî, because his family came from Mopsuesta in Cilicia. We possess witty lines from his pen, addressed to the solitary black hair remaining on his bald pate. "I say to my white hairs, which are terrified by this stranger's presence: 'Respect her, I entreat you. A black African spouse will not tarry long in a house where the second wife has a white skin!" Abû'l Faraj, surnamed Al-Babbaghâ (the parrot) because of a defect in his speech, belonged to Naṣîbîn. After his patron's death he betook himself to Mosul, and thence to Bagdâd, where he died in 1007. Al-Zâhî 'Alî ibn Isḥâq was only a temporary visitor at Aleppo. He usually lived at Bagdâd, where he was born, and where he kept a shop for cotton stuffs. In Bagdâd he wrote poems in honour of the 'Abbâsids and of Al-Muhallabî; he died in 963. He was famed for his descriptions. His lines on the violet: "azure blossom, whose stalk seems too weak to hold up the flower," on wine: "so transparent in the goblet that it seems luminous," and the fair: "whose eyes seem to brandish swords and unsheathe daggers, whose faces, veiled, recall the crescent, and unveiled, the moon at the full," are frequently quoted.

Egypt was slipping more and more out of the sphere of influence of the Bagdâd Caliphate. The Ṭûlûnids and the Ikhshîdites had established their independence, and the African Fâṭimids was soon to establish a Shî'ite Caliphate on the Nile. With a glance at the *kâtib* (secretary), Râshid ibn Isḥâq, who flourished about 850, and has left a *dîwân* filled with obscenities behind him (now in the Berlin Library), we may notice Sharîf Abû'l-Qâsim IBN ṬABÂṬABÂ, who performed the duties of inspector of the descendants of 'Alî. He died in 956

His poems are mostly of the ascetic and mystic type. Yet his description of a long night is often quoted: "To-night the Pleiades seem to have travelled all day long, and to have been weary when they reached their evening station. They have set up their tents, so that their caravan may rest. Not a planet moves in its orbit, not a star hurries over its nocturnal course (so dark is the night)."

Abû'l Qâsim Muḥammad ibn Hâni' al-Andalusî was born at Seville, but his father came from a village near Mahdiyya, in Tunis. He was driven out of his native town at the age of seven-and-twenty, because the dissipation into which he had plunged had earned him the reputation of being tainted with the opinions of the Greek philosophers. This roused popular hatred against him, and forced his patron, who dreaded being accused of sharing his views, to beg him to depart for a season; he attached himself to Jauhar, a general who served Al-Manṣûr, the Fâṭimid, and later to the general's son, Al-Mu'izz, who replaced his father in 953, and was with him when he went forth to conquer Egypt in 969. After some time he returned to the Maghrib to seek his family and conduct it into Egypt. In the course of his journey he was murdered at Barqa in the ancient Cyrenaïca, in 973. He was still a young man, not over forty-two.

Al-Mu'izz heard of his protégé's death when he reached Egypt, and was deeply affected by it. "We had hoped," he said, "to see this man compete with the Oriental poets, but this pleasure has been denied to us." Abû'l-'Alâ al-Ma'arrî, who did not like Ibn Hâni''s poetry, compared it to wheat grains crushed in the mill, because of its harsh phraseology.

TAMÎM, the second son of the Fâṭimid Caliph, Al-

Mu'izz (948–985), composed dithyrambs in praise of his brother, Caliph Al-'Azîz, and died in Egypt. Al-'Azîz, who succeeded Al-Mu'izz, having been designated heir-presumptive in his lifetime, was also a poet. Tamîm wrote amorous poetry, and imitated the desert poets in his descriptions of thirst-stricken gazelles. With him we may refer to Ibn Wakî', who was born at Tinnîs, near Damietta, and died in the same town, in 1003. His originality of thought was much admired. He was a remarkable compiler, and devoted a whole volume to the plagiarisms ascribed to Mutanabbî. A defect in his pronunciation had procured him the surname of Al-'Âṭis (he who sneezes). He has sung the delights of a love which has cooled down. "My heart, once so fond, is now rid of thy love, and feels neither inclination nor desire for thee. Thy cruelty has reconciled me to thine absence. A parent may cease to mourn the death of a froward child." His ambition was a modest one. "An obscure position fulfils my desires, which shrink from exalted rank. Not that they do not know how sweet greatness is, but they prefer health."

Abû'l-Raqa'maq was a man of Antioch. He settled in Egypt, sang the praises of the Fâṭimid rulers and the great men of that country, and died there in 1008. Al-Tihâmî (Abû'l-Ḥasan 'Alî ibn Muḥammad) only produced a small volume of poems, but the greater part are exquisite, after the Oriental pattern, that is to say, full of exaggerated and unexpected comparisons. In his eulogy of an open-handed vizier, he exclaims : "Compared with his magnificence, the heavy rain-cloud is but a vapour, and the seas mere brooks!" But he wrote a very beautiful elegy on the death of his own child, a youth,

and it was asserted that in reward for having written such fine verses his sins had been forgiven him. His political action proved his ruin. He came secretly to Egypt, bearing letters from Ḥassân ibn Mufarrij, chief of the tribe of Ṭai, to the Beni-Qurra, a tribe dwelling in the province of Barqa, the ancient Cyrenaïca, which had just risen against the Fâṭimids, in support of a descendant of the Omeyyad line. He was arrested, cast into prison at Cairo, and executed secretly, in 1025.

Abû Ismâʻîl al-Ḥasan ṬUGHRÂ'Î was of Persian origin, and was born at Ispahan. He was at once a poet, a man of learning, and a statesman. His surname signifies "he who traces the *ṭughrâ*," a kind of design formed of interlaced letters, which figures at the head of diplomas and official documents, and stamps them as authentic. The caligrapher who traces this sign is in reality the State Chancellor. Ṭughrâ'î composed, at Bagdâd, the *Lâmiyyat al-ʻAjam* (Ode in *l* of the Non-Arabs), in opposition to Shanfarâ's celebrated *Lâmiyyat al-ʻArab*. It is an elegy on the misfortunes of the times. At a later date, the Seljûqid Sultan Masʻûd appointed him his minister, in his capital, Mosul. When Masʻûd was defeated in the Battle of Hamadhân (1121) by his brother Maḥmûd, the poet was taken prisoner, and put to death, on the advice of the vizier, Sumairamî, who accused him of atheism. His *dîwân* contains numerous panegyrics of Sultan Saʻîd, the son of Malikshâh, and of the great minister, Niẓâm al-Mulk. The Oriental scholars Pococke and Golius have exercised their skill in a Latin translation of Ṭûghrâ'î's *Lâmiyya*.

A copyist and bookseller of Bagdâd, Abû'l-Maʻâlî Saʻd AL-ḤAẒÎRÎ (died 1172), surnamed Dallâl al-Kutub (the book-broker), collected his poems, in alphabetical

order, into a book called *Lumaḥ al-mulaḥ*, and also made a collection of enigmas, now preserved at Cairo. His *Zînat al-dahr*, an anthology of the poets of his own day and those before it, enriched with biographies, and his numerous compilations, have all disappeared. Graceful thoughts, very elegantly expressed, abound in his compositions.

Mu'în al-Dîn Aḥmad ibn 'Abd al-Razzâq AL-ṬANṬARÂNÎ wrote his Echo Ode (*tarjî'*)—which Silvestre de Sacy has made known, and translated for his *Chrestomathie Arabe*—in honour of the great vizier of the Seljûqid dynasty, Niẓâm al-Mulk.

At this period Syria saw the birth of a philosopher who was the last of the great poets of the Arabic tongue, and whose pessimism, finely expressed in verse, stirred the admiration of many generations. ABÛ'L-'ALÂ AL-MA'ARRÎ, who was born at Ma'arrat al-Nu'mân, in Northern Syria, in 973, came of a family descended from the Yemenite tribe of Tanûkh. When four years old, he had an attack of smallpox, and lost one of his eyes. At a later date his healthy eye, too, was destroyed, and he became stone blind. In spite of this he received a careful education, under the superintendence of his own father, whose memory he has immortalised in an elegy. After continuing his studies at Aleppo, he made a first journey to Bagdâd, but this visit did not prove a success, for he felt himself a stranger in the place, and longed for his native town. Nevertheless he returned the following year, to make the acquaintance of 'Abdal-salâm of Bassora, who was at the head of one of the great libraries of the city. Every Friday 'Abdal-salâm gathered about him a circle of freethinkers, of which Abû'l-'Alâ soon became a member. Some of these men were rationalists, like the

Muʿtazilites; others were downright materialists. Their society exercised a powerful influence on the poet's opinions. When, however, he was recalled to Maʿarra, at the end of a year and seven months, by the news of his mother's illness, and arrived too late to see her draw her last breath, he mourned her departure in verses full of the deepest feeling, and never left his native town again. His youthful poetry has been collected under the title of *Siqt al-zand* (Sparks from the Tinder), and his later poems under that of *Luzûm mâ lam yalzam* (Obligation which is not Indispensable), an allusion to his conquest of the difficulty of a double or triple rhyme, which is not indispensable in prosody. He left a collection of letters, and a treatise on asceticism and preaching, in rhymed prose and verse. He was said to have written a Koran, an imitation of the Prophet's, and possibly the mere banter of a freethinker. When somebody complained to him that, though his work was well written, it did not produce the same impression as the true Koran, he replied: "Let it be read from the pulpits of the mosques for the next four hundred years, and then you will be delighted with it!"

IBN KUSHÂJIM Maḥmûd also left a *dîwân* or collection of poems arranged in alphabetical order. He was grandson of an Indian from the banks of the Indus, and lived at Ramla. He died about 961.

Abû'l-Faraj Muḥammad AL-WAʿWAʿ, of Damascus, was a dainty and euphuistic poet, who over-indulged in description and metaphor. He wrote the famous stanza, "She made the narcissus rain down its pearls, watered the rose, and bit the jujubes with her hailstones," a description which might be taken for that of a cloud, but this would be quite wrong. It is applied to a woman

—the pearls her tears, the rose her cheek, the hailstones her teeth, and the jujubes no other than her rosy lips. These jests seemed charming, no doubt, when they were first invented, but in later days, repeated *ad nauseam* by thousands of poetasters, in Persian, Hindustani, and Turkish, they constitute the most wearisome repetition of empty formulas that can well be imagined. Al-Wa'wa' died at the end of the tenth century.

Abû 'Abdallah AL-ABLAH was born, and lived, and died, at Bagdâd. This last event took place towards 1183. His poems, some of which are preserved at the British Museum, unite tenderness of feeling with artificiality of style. There were not many of them, but they were widely read. Musicians took possession of them, and sang them to old airs. They pressed about him and begged him to write more. His lines were recited to the author of the *Kharîda*, Kâtib 'Imâd al-Dîn, in 1160. The surname Al-Ablah signifies "the fool," but it is questionable whether it was not bestowed on him in irony; as the Arabs will call a negro "Kâfûr" (Camphor), and we ourselves will dub him "Boule de Neige" (Snowball).

Ibn AL-TA'ÂWÎDHÎ (Abû'l Fatḥ Muḥammad) was the son of 'Ubaidallah, a freed Turkish slave, whose real name was Nûshtakîn. He was grandson, on the maternal side, of the celebrated ascetic Ibn al-Ta'âwîdhî, and hence his surname. He was born at Bagdâd in 1125, was brought up by his maternal grandfather, and became a secretary in the Office for the Administration of Fiefs. In 1183 he lost his eyesight; many of his poems lament this deprivation, and regret the days of his active youth. Before the calamity befell him, he had collected his verses into a *dîwân*, which he afterwards completed

by adding what he entitled *Ziyâdât*, or Additions. When he became blind he was still holding his administrative post. He obtained the favour of having his sons' names registered instead of his own on the list of officials. They seem, however, to have been ungrateful, and did not support their father, who addressed so touching a poem to Caliph Nâṣir-Lidînillah, pleading for a pension for himself, that the Caliph granted his request. "If that poem had been recited to a rock it would have touched it," says Ibn Khallikân. His easy and graceful style was much admired. Correctness and sweetness of expression are therein allied to subtlety of thought, and all were considered to possess extraordinary charm. Al-Taʿâwîdhî's death occurred in 1188.

IBN AL-MUʿALLIM (the Professor's Son) was the surname of Abû'l-Ghanâ'im Muḥammad al-Ḥurthî, who came from Ḥurth, near Wâsiṭ, was born in 1108, and died in 1196. Pathetic sentiment is the dominant quality of his verse, and with it we note a natural delicacy of thought. His poetry is of the amorous and panegyric orders, easy in style, and apt in fancy. It met with considerable success, spread far and wide, and earned its author the public esteem, an easy fortune, and an influential position. It was much learnt by heart, and preachers would quote it in their sermons. Every ode he wrote was immediately committed to memory by the Dervishes of the religious order of the Rifâʿiyya, who sang them at their gatherings, in order to work themselves into their mystic ecstasies. The songs of carnal love led them up to the divine. There was a mutual jealousy between Ibn al-Muʿallim and Ibn al-Taʿâwîdhî, who addressed satires to each other. One day, when the first-named poet was passing a spot

where Shaikh Abû'l-Faraj Ibn al-Jauzî was wont to deliver pious exhortations, he saw a crowd blocking the street, inquired the reason, and was told that Ibn al-Jauzî was about to preach a sermon. He contrived to push through the press, and come near enough to the preacher to hear him say: "Ibn al-Mu'allim has expressed a very fine thought in this stanza: 'The reputation of thy name renews, in my ear, the pleasure of hearing it, and he who repeats it seems to me delightful.'" To hear himself thus quoted made an exquisite impression upon the poet, but neither the preacher nor any of that assembly knew of his presence.

'Îsâ ibn Sinjâr AL-ḤÂJIRÎ served, like his father, as a soldier in the Turkish army. He was born at Irbil. He was the close friend of a brother of Ibn Khallikân, named Ḍiyâ al-dîn 'Îsâ; when the Arab biographer left Irbil in 1229, the poet was detained in the citadel of the town, "for reasons too lengthy to relate"; he lightened the dulness of his captivity by writing poems on it. At a later period he obtained his liberty, and entered the service of Muẓaffar al-dîn Kûkburî (the Blue Wolf), who had reigned at Irbil since 1190; he supported the Ṣûfîs, and wore their dress. When his patron died in 1232, he left the town, and did not return till Bâtikîn, an Armenian slave, had been appointed to rule it in the Caliph's name. He was stabbed, one day, as he was leaving his house, by an assassin who had been dogging his steps for some time. He expired before night, in June 1235, after writing, in spite of his terrible wound, a poetic appeal to Bâtikîn's vengeance. He was barely fifty years of age. The surname Al-Ḥâjirî refers to Al-Ḥâjir, a village in the Ḥijâz. It was not his birthplace; he was born

at Irbil; the name was bestowed on account of his constant references to the locality in his poems. Here we have a telling instance of the artificiality of the poetry of that period, the authors of which, from pride of learning, would refer to places they had never seen, in which they had never set foot, and their only knowledge of which was drawn from the ancient Arab poets. Greece played the same part in the work of the French seventeenth century poets. Al-Ḥâjirî's *dîwân* has been collected and set in order by ʿUmar ibn al-Ḥusainî of Damascus, who has arranged it in seven chapters—the *ghazals*, or love-poems; the verses written in prison; the *mukhammasât*, or five-lined stanzas; the isolated verses; the satires; the popular poetry, called *mawâlî;* and, last of all, the quatrains, or *dû-bait.* The volume was printed at Cairo in 1888.

Another poet of Turkish origin, Aidamîr al-Muḥyawî, surnamed FAKHR AL-TURK (the glory of the Turks), was a freed slave of Muḥyî al-dîn Muḥammad ibn Saʿîd. He flourished during the first half of the thirteenth century. He is the poet of the garden and of flowers. He also wrote popular poems, known as *muwashshaḥ.* Another writer of the same type is Ibn al-Ḥalâwî of Mosul (Aḥmad ibn Muḥammad), born in 1206, who was court poet to Badr al-dîn Lu'lu', *atâbek* of Mosul, and died in 1258. He was one of the dandies of the city, a pleasant and good-natured companion, but very frivolous-minded. His odes celebrate the Caliphs and Kings of that epoch, such as Malik-Nâṣir Dâ'ûd, the lord of Karak. When the Prince of Mosul went to Persia to meet Hulâgû, the grandson of Jengiz Khan, then marching to the conquest of Bagdâd, his favourite poet accompanied him. But he fell ill on the journey,

and died near Salmâs, aged nearly sixty. At the outset, Badr al-dîn Lu'lu', far from treating the poet as his close confidant, did not even admit him to his board or to his own society. He merely employed him on feast days, to recite the panegyrics he had composed; but, pleased with the poet's witty sally on the subject of his nag, which the prince had found ill in a garden, he adopted him as one of his daily circle at meals, and gave him a pension.

If we cite, in addition, the names of 'Izz al-dîn 'Abd al-Ḥamîd Ibn Abî'l-Ḥadîd, the Shî'ite poet (died 1258), author of seven poems called *al-sab' al-'Alawiyyât*, on the glories of the Prophet, the taking of Khaibar and of Mecca, the death of Ḥusain, son of 'Alî, and a panegyric of Caliph Nâṣir-Lidînillah—a manuscript copy of which exists at Leyden; of Jamâl al-dîn Yaḥyâ al-Ṣarṣarî, of Ṣarṣar near Bagdâd (died 1258), who performed the feat of composing a poem in honour of Mahomet, every line of which contains all the letters in the alphabet, and of summing up Ḥanbalite law in lines written in the *ṭawîl* metre; of Majd al-dîn al-Wâ'iẓ al-Witrî, a preacher at Witr (died 1264), the author of lines in praise of Mahomet and on the merits of pilgrimage; of Shams al-dîn al-Wâ'iẓ al-Kûfî (a preacher at Kûfa), who died, aged eighty, in 1276, and whose manuscript poems are at Gotha; and of Majd al-dîn Ibn Abî Shâkir of Irbil, who was alive in 1277, and one of whose poems, *Tadhkirat al-arîb*, is now in the Bibliothèque Nationale in Paris, we shall have reviewed the whole of the poetic movement of which Bagdâd was the scene.

PERSIA

The town of Bust in Sijistân, which enjoyed a period of brilliant prosperity and learning during the Middle Ages, and the unexplored ruins of which now lie in the desert stretching between Persia and Afghanistan, gave birth, in 971, to Abû'l-Fatḥ 'Alî AL-BUSTÎ, who, in his youth, acted as secretary to Bâtyûr, the chief of the town, and passed into the service of the Turkish chief, Sabuktakîn, father of the celebrated Maḥmûd the Ghaznevid, when he defeated the ruler of Bust. Al-Bustî died at Bukhârâ during Maḥmûd's reign, in 1010. His works, poetic and prose, were especially admired on account of his use, or, let us say, abuse, of alliteration. An extract from his *dîwân* is preserved at Leyden. His most famous *qaṣîda*, know as *Qaṣîdat al-Bustî*, on which several commentaries have been written, is pretty frequently found in European libraries.

Abû Manṣûr 'Alî ibn al-Ḥasan is known by the surname of SURR-DURR (Purse of Pearls), bestowed on him for his poetic talent, whereas his father was dubbed Surr-Ba'r (Purse of Dung) on account of his avarice. This we learn from Abû Ja'far Mas'ûd al-Bayâdî's satirical verses. But he had the bad taste to add: "What your father had garnered, you, ungrateful, have squandered. And you call it poetry!" This is not just, for Surr-Durr's verses are charming. We know scarcely anything about his life. He was born before 1009. He was at Wâsiṭ when Fakhr al-daula Muḥammad ibn Jahîr was made vizier, and congratulated him on his appointment. He was killed by an accident in 1072. A pit to catch lions had been dug close to a village on the road to Khurâsân, and he fell into it.

The study of Shâfi'ite law did not hinder the development of the poetic powers of Abû'l-Ḥasan 'Alî AL-BÂKHARZÎ. He practised the art of penmanship, and was occasionally employed in the offices of the State Secretary. He was born at Bâkharz, the chief town of a district between Nîshâpûr and Herât in Khurâsân. His life was spent in alternate wealth and poverty, and he went through extraordinary vicissitudes during his journeys to, and sojourns in, various towns. Besides his own *dîwân* he wrote a continuation, carried up to the 450th year of the Hegira, of Tha'âlibî's *Yatîmat al-Dahr*, under the title of *Dumyat al-qaṣr* (Statue of the Palace). This, like the work it carried on, was a poetical anthology. He was murdered in the midst of a pleasure party in his native town during the summer of 1075, and the crime remained unpunished.

A member of the sacred family of Hâshim, a descendant of Ibn 'Abbâs, Sharîf Abû Ya'lâ Muḥammad, better known as IBN AL-HABBÂRIYYA, was born at Bagdâd. His talent was great, and his tongue bitter. Nobody escaped his satire. He was one of the circle of poets which surrounded Niẓâm al-Mulk, the great Seljûqid vizier. His favourite forms of composition were satires and humorous and obscene poems. "When he condescends to respect decency, his poems are of a high order of beauty," writes Kâtib 'Imâd al-dîn in his *Kharîda*. Niẓâm al-Mulk treated him with the most excessive indulgence. A spirit of hatred and jealousy had grown up between the vizier and Tâj al-Mulk Ibn Dârest, secretary to Turkân-Khâtûn, Malik-Shâh's wife, who, indeed, succeeded him when he died. This secretary asked Ibn al-Habbâriyya to compose a satire on Niẓâm al-Mulk, promising him a rich reward and

all the weight of his favour and support. "How can I attack a man to whose kindness I owe everything I see in my house?" asked the poet. Nevertheless, being pressed by Ibn Dârest, he wrote the following lines: "What wonder is it that Niẓâm al-Mulk should rule, and that Fate should be on his side? Fortune is like the water-wheel which raises water from the well—none but oxen can turn it!" When the vizier was told of this spiteful attack he only remarked that the poet had simply intended to allude to his origin—he came from Ṭûs in Khurâsân, and, according to the popular saying, all the men of Ṭûs are oxen (we should say asses, nowadays); not only did he abstain from inflicting any punishment on the poet—he even rewarded him, and took him into higher favour than before. This noble behaviour and proof of extreme indulgence is, on account of its rarity, greatly admired by the Orientals, who, irascible and prone to vengeance as they are, are little accustomed to anything of the kind. As a specimen of the poet's humorous efforts, the following lines are quoted: "When Abû Sa'îd perceived that I had abstained from wine for a whole year, he said to me: 'Who is the Shaikh who has converted you to a more honourable way of life?' and I replied: 'That Shaikh is Poverty!'"

One of his most original productions is a collection of apologues, fables, and moral maxims, on the plan of *Kalîla wa-Dimna;* this work bears the title of *Al-ṣâdiḥ wa'l-bâghim* (He who Speaks Low and Whispers); it is in verse, in the *rajaz* metre, two thousand lines in all, and the author spent ten years in writing it. He dedicated it to Abû'l-Ḥasan Ṣadaqa al-Mazyadî, the lord of Ḥilla, a town on the site of the ancient Babylon, and

sent him the manuscript by his son's hand, with an apology for being unable to bring it himself. A liberal gift was his reward. This book is also known under the name of *Natâ'ij al-fitna* (Results of Discord). The poet relates that once, when on a journey, he woke up in the night, and heard a Hindoo and a Persian discussing the pre-eminence of their respective countries. Each quoted fables and apologues to support his arguments. Such is the general plan of the work, a considerable part of which has been translated by Hammer into German verse, and published in the *Wiener Jahrbücher*. It was printed at Cairo and at Beyrout. As for Ibn al-Habbâriyya, he died in 1110, at Kirmân, where he spent the closing years of his life, after having resided for a considerable time at Ispahan.

Although Abû'l-Muẓaffar Muḥammad AL-ABÎWARDÎ came into the world on Persian soil, at Kûfân, a small village in Khurâsân, some six leagues from Abîward, he was a man of pure Arab blood and of a noble family, that of the Omeyyad Caliphs, belonging to the tribe of Quraish. He won great celebrity as a poet, but he was also a student, learned in tradition and genealogy. His poetical works are classed under three headings: *'Irâqîyât* (poems touching 'Irâq), youthful effusions, and panegyrics of Caliphs and their ministers; *Najdîyât* (poems in praise of Najd, or Central Arabia, the Arcady of the Oriental poet); and *Wajdîyât* (erotic poems). His *History of the Cities of Abîward and Nasâ* is unfortunately lost. His illustrious origin had inspired him with excessive vanity, pride, and arrogance. He habitually prayed in these words: "Almighty God! make me king of the East and the West of the earth!" Now and

again the scion of the Omeyyads betrays himself in his poetry. "We reigned over the kingdoms of the earth," he says, "and their great men submitted themselves to us, whether they would or no." His life was virtuous, and his conduct exemplary. He died of poison, at Ispahan, on the afternoon of the 4th of September 1113.

IBN AL-KHAYYÂṬ (the Son of the Tailor) was of Syrian origin. He was born at Damascus in 1058. He had earned the honorary title of Shihâb al-dîn (Luminary of Religion), and was a Government servant until he began to travel. A wandering troubadour, he composed eulogies on the great dignitaries he met on his travels, and thus made his way into Persia, where he died in 1123. At Aleppo he met the poet Abû'l-Fityân Ibn Ḥayyûs, and presented him with his poems. This elicited from the elder poet the remark that the young man's arrival betokened his own approaching death, because it was a rare occurrence in any profession when the appearance of a first-rate master did not portend the speedy demise of the oldest of his peers. Al-Khayyâṭ's *dîwân*, which was collected within a year of his death, and was exceedingly widely read in the Middle Ages, is preserved at the Escurial and at Copenhagen.

At the same period, the town of Gaza, in Palestine, also produced its poet, in the person of Abû Isḥâq Ibrâhîm ibn Yaḥyâ al-Kalbî AL-GHAZZÎ, born 1049. He went to Damascus to study law, in 1088, thence proceeded to Bagdâd, and lived there some years, in the Niẓâmiyya College, composing elegies and panegyrics. At last he departed to Khurâsân, where he found matter for the praise of princes who rewarded his eulogies most generously. Here it was that his work first found admirers. He himself made a selection of his best

poems, and collected them into a volume containing about five thousand lines. Al-Ghazzî travelled a great deal, went as far as Kirmân, and sang the praise of the governor of that country, Naṣr al-dîn Mukram ibn al-ʿAlâ.

He died in 1130, on the road between Merv and Balkh, and was buried in the latter town. When he felt the approach of death he exclaimed: "I hope God will forgive me, for three reasons. I am the compatriot of al-Shâfiʿî, I am an old man, and I am far from my own kin."

Nâṣiḥ al-dîn AL-ARRAJÂNÎ (1068–1149) belonged to a family which traced its noble descent from the Anṣârs, or Medina auxiliaries, who championed the Prophet's cause against the Meccans. He was a magistrate, assistant *qâḍî* at Shustar and at ʿAskar-Mukram, was born at Arrajân near Al-Ahwâz in Susiana, and studied at the Niẓâmiyya College at Ispahan. He began to write some years subsequent to 1087, towards the period of the death of Niẓâm al-Mulk, and continued till his own. His position as assistant to the regular *qâḍîs* was a source of amusement to him. He mentions it in his lines: "That I should act as assistant in such a profession is one of fortune's tricks. It is a miracle that I have enough patience to endure such changes;" and again: "I am without contradiction the most poetic jurist of my time, and at least I am the most learned Doctor of Laws amongst its poets!" His *dîwân*, which is principally composed of rather lengthy apologues, was collected by his son.

ʿAmîd al-dîn Asʿad ibn Naṣr AL-ABARZÎ, born at Abarz in the province of Fârs, was vizier to the *atâbek* Muẓaffar al-dîn Saʿd ibn Zangî; in the time of Abû Bakr, the patron of the poet Saʿdî, he was dismissed, and im-

prisoned as a traitor in the state prison at Ushkunwân, one of the three fortresses which crown the site of Persepolis (this was at the close of 1226), and there died within a few months. During his incarceration, he composed an ode which was preserved by his son Tâj al-dîn Muḥammad, and is still famous throughout Persia. It is remarkable for its involved and diffuse style, and is full of conventional expressions learnt at school, traversed, here and there, by a breath of true and genuine poetry. It has been published and translated into French by the writer of these pages.

Among the Persian poets who wrote in Arabic, SAʻDÎ, the charming author of *Gulistân* and *Bûstân*, those twin blossoms of Iranian poetry, must not be forgotten. Saʻdî composed Arabic *qaṣîdas*, the first of which is an elegy on the taking of Bagdâd by the Mongols and the death of the last ʻAbbâsid Caliph. He wrote the language as if it were his own, with that wonderful simplicity and inimitable artlessness which distinguish him from all his Persian fellow-poets. At the same time his lines are full of touching and pathetic feeling. His odes are twenty in number. He was born at Shîrâz, the capital of Fârs, about 1184, lost his father, who was in the service of the *atâbek* Saʻd ibn Zangî, at an early age, went to Bagdâd to attend the Niẓâmiyya University course, made the Mecca pilgrimage several times over, acted, out of charity, as a water-carrier in the markets of Jerusalem and the Syrian towns, was taken prisoner by the Franks, and forced to work with Jews at cleaning out the moats of Tripoli in Syria ; he was ransomed by an Aleppan, who gave him his daughter in marriage. He himself mentions his visits to Kashgar in Turkestan, to Abyssinia, and Asia Minor. He travelled about India,

passing through Afghanistan on his way there. He closed his wandering career by settling down in a hermitage outside the town of Shîrâz, close to the source of the Rukn-Âbâd canal. There he died, over a hundred years old, in 1291, and there, too, he was buried.

Arabia

Arabia is no longer that which she was in the olden days, the cradle of poetry, yet the sacred torch is not wholly extinguished. In Yemen we discover, in 1058, a native poet, ʿAbd al-Raḥîm al-Burʿî, whose verses are full of mystic and religious feeling. A hundred years later, and in the same region, another Ṣûfî poet, Abû'l-Ḥasan Ibn Khumârṭâsh, the Ḥimyarite, composed, when twenty-two years of age, a mystic ode on which commentaries were afterwards written. In the province of Baḥrain we find a poet named ʿAlî ibn Muqarrab ibn Manṣûr al-Ibrâhîmî, who belonged to the family of the ʿUyûnids, which, after the expulsion of the Carmathians, founded a State held in fief from the Caliphs of Bagdâd. After living at the court of his great-uncle, Muḥammad, and his son, Masʿûd, he quarrelled with the last-named ruler, and fled to Mosul, where the geographer Yâqût met him in 1220, and thence to Bagdâd, where he died, probably in 1234. His panegyrics were successively addressed to his ʿUyûnid kinsmen, to the ʿAbbâsid Caliph Nâṣir-Lidînillah, and to Badr al-dîn Lu'lu', Prince of Mosul. To conclude, a poet of Syrian birth, Amîn al-daula Abû'l-Ghanâ'im Muslim, who came from Shaizar on the Orontes, dedicated his poetical anthology, entitled *Jamharat al-islâm*, to the last of the Ayyûbite princes of Yemen, Malik Masʿûd Ṣalâḥ al-dîn.

Egypt

Alexandria saw the birth, in 1137, of Ibn Qalâqis (Abû'l-Futûḥ Naṣr-allah), also called *Al-Qâḍî al-a'azz* (the most illustrious Judge), whose beard grew so thin that his face looked quite smooth, a peculiarity for which he was greatly ridiculed. Yet he was a talented poet. Leaving Egypt, in consequence of the disturbances following on Saladin's establishment there, he proceeded to Sicily, where he made the acquaintance of a Moslem chief named Abû'l-Qâsim ibn al-Ḥajar—a proof that under William II., the third Norman king of that island, the Moslem leaders continued to hold exalted positions. Being generously treated by him, he dedicated a work, now lost, called *Al-zahr al-bâsim* (the Flower that Smiles), to his benefactor. At that time there was an Egyptian Ambassador in Sicily. Ibn Qalâqis desired to take advantage of his return journey to get back to Alexandria, but, it being the winter season, contrary winds drove the vessel on which the travellers had embarked back to her starting-point. Later the poet went to Yemen, and lived for some time at Aden. Then he tried to go back to Egypt, but his ship was wrecked near the Isle of Dahlak, in the Red Sea, and he was fain to get him back to Aden, having lost his whole fortune, the fruit of the generosity shown him by Abû'l-Faraj Yâsir, minister to the ruler of that city. He returned to his patron almost naked, 11th August 1168.

He died at 'Aidhâb, a small port near Jedda, on 29th May 1172. He said of himself, referring to his many journeys: "There are many men in this world, but I am fated to have no companions save sailors and camel-drivers."

Yet another Egyptian magistrate whose serious avocations did not prevent his successful cultivation of polite literature was Hibat-Allah Ibn Sanâ al-Mulk, surnamed *Al-Qâḍî al-sa'-îd* (the lucky Judge). He was born in 1150, and in March 1176 he proceeded to Syria, whither his patron, Al-Qâḍî al-Fâḍil Mujîr al-dîn of Ascalon, minister to Saladin, had accompanied his master, and where his reputation had already preceded him. Here the Kâtib 'Imâd al-dîn, author of the *Kharîda*, met him, and thought his intelligence marvellous. His merits and talents alone carried him to the high position he held, and earned him fortune's favours. He died at Cairo in 1211.

The one *dîwân* of his which has come down to us, the *Dâr al-ṭirâz* (Storehouse of Embroideries), consists in large measure of popular poems, known as *muwashshaḥât;* the *Fuṣûṣ al-fuṣûl* is an anthology of scattered verse and prose extracted from his literary correspondence. At Cairo he was one of a circle of poets who had meetings in the course of which they held pleasant converse—gratuitous academies, which, if properly organised, would possibly have become quite as famous as many another.

Kamâl al-dîn Ibn al-Nabîh was the panegyrist of the Ayyûbite princes. At a later date he entered the service of Al-Malik al-Ashraf Mûsâ, Prince of Naṣîbîn, in Mesopotamia, as his secretary, and he died in that town in 1222. His *dîwân* was printed at Beyrout in 1882. One of his poems, translated into English, appears in Carlyle's *Specimens of Arabian Poetry*. His lighter work is full of affectation and play on words.

The greatest mystic poet of the Arabs, 'UMAR IBN AL-FÂRIḌ, was born at Cairo in 1181, and died in that city

in 1235, after a prolonged sojourn at Mecca. His *dîwân* was collected and arranged by his grandson 'Alî. His Arabic works are a perfect model of the style used by the Ṣûfîs to describe their ecstasies. These pantheistic philosophers, as my readers know, sang the praises of the love of the Divine, and the longing for absorption into the great All, borrowing the most burning imagery from human life, and even going so far as to seek, in the use and abuse of wine, a state of exaltation which, as they believed, carried them closer to the Supreme Being. Hence one of Ibn Fâriḍ's odes is devoted to the praise of wine.

A secretary in the Egyptian Government, and court poet to the Ayyûbites, BAHÂ AL-DÎN ZUHAIR al-Muhallabî, died in 1258, leaving a *dîwân* which was published and translated into English by E. H. Palmer. In his work we realise how supple the Arab tongue had grown, and how fitted to the apt expression of the innumerable refinements of feelings polished by the brilliant era of civilisation which followed on that of Saladin.

Sharaf al-dîn Muḥammad AL-BÛṢÎRÎ (1211 – 1294) has earned universal renown in the Moslem world by his ode to the Prophet's mantle (*Qaṣîdat al-Burda*), an imitation of Ka'b ibn Zuhair's panegyric. Many commentators have expounded the beauties of this work. Monsieur R. Basset has translated it into French, and there are also German translations, and one into English. Moreover, poets have entertained themselves by writing paraphrases of it, called *takhmîs* —three couplets of padding, which, with two more of the original Arabic, make up five. Other panegyrics of the Prophet are also due to Bûṣîrî's inspired pen; an ode called *Umm al-Qurâ* (the Mother of Cities,

a surname applied to Mecca), and four others of a similar nature.

Jamâl al-dîn Yaḥyâ Ibn Maṭrûḥ was born at Siout in Upper Egypt, on the 8th of June 1196. There he spent his early years, and pursued the studies which enabled him to enter the civil department of the Government. After filling various posts, he was taken into the service of the Ayyûbite Prince Al-Malik al-Ṣâliḥ Najm al-dîn, son of Malik-Kâmil, and his lieutenant in Egypt, and accompanied the prince when his father sent him to govern his newly acquired Eastern possessions in 'Irâq and Mesopotamia (1231); he was also in attendance on him when he returned to Egypt in 1240, and was appointed Steward of the Treasury. When his master was invested, for the second time, with the Principality of Damascus, Ibn Maṭrûḥ was appointed to govern the city and surrounding district, with the title of vizier. Then he received orders to march with an army and retake the town of Ḥimṣ, which had fallen into the hands of Malik-Naṣir. While the siege was proceeding, the Sultan learnt that the Crusaders were collecting at Cyprus, with a view to attacking Egypt. He hastily recalled his troops into that country, and Ibn Maṭrûḥ, for certain acts which had displeased the ruler, fell into disfavour. Yet in spite of his disgrace he continued to perform his duties about his master's person. Damietta had been captured by St. Louis on the 11th of June 1249. Al-Malik al-Ṣâliḥ encamped at Manṣûra, and died there on 23rd November of the same year. Then Ibn Maṭrûḥ went back to Old Cairo, and dwelt there in his own house till he died on 19th October 1251. He was the friend of Ibn Khallikân, who describes him as a man of great powers and

amiable temper, who, with these merits, possessed the most estimable qualities of the heart. They kept up a correspondence when they were apart, and when they met they spent their time in literary discussions and amusing talk. Ibn Maṭrûḥ recited his verses to his friend, who inserted some of them in his Biographical Dictionary. When, after his patron's death, he retired from public life, his want of occupation weighed heavily upon him. He suffered from a disease of the eyes which became incurable, and finally deprived him of his sight. When quite young, in Upper Egypt, he had known Bahâ al-dîn Zuhair; they were like two brothers. Later in life, they kept up a correspondence in verse. Ibn Maṭrûḥ's *dîwân* was published at Constantinople in 1881. It contains a poem on the Battle of Manṣûra, which was won by Malik-Mu'aẓẓam, and in which St. Louis was taken prisoner.

Syria

The filiation of Ibn al-Sâ'âtî leads us to assign him an Iranian origin, for his father's name was Rustam and his grandfather's Hardûz. He was born at Damascus in 1161. Owing to some unknown circumstances, he spent his life in Egypt, sang the praises of that country in his poems, and died there, at Cairo, in March 1208. He left two collections of verses behind him—a large one, still preserved in the Mosque of St. Sophia, and a smaller, bearing the title *Muqaṭṭa'ât al-Nîl* (Fragments touching the Nile), in which, amongst other descriptions, he gives us one, in elegant and much admired language, of the delights of a day and night spent at Siout, in Upper Egypt. His verses are full of ideas

which Orientals think exquisite, but which strike us as finical and affected.

The *dîwân*, in four volumes, of Shihâb al-dîn Yûsuf ibn Ismâ'îl, of Aleppo, surnamed AL-SHAWWÂ (the Cookshop-keeper), has disappeared. He was born in Aleppo in 1166, and acquired great technical skill in the art of versification. He was fond of introducing grammatical expressions into his verses; he composed little poems of two or three lines, containing original and carefully studied ideas. He was on terms of friendship with the biographer Ibn Khallikân, who liked to discuss the difficulties and subtleties of Arab grammar with him. They were inseparable from 1236, till Al-Shawwâ died, in the following year. He belonged to the most extreme section of the Shî'ite sect, and believed 'Alî and the imâms, his descendants, to be incarnations of Divinity.

'ABDAL-MUḤSIN ibn Ḥamûd al-Tanûkhî (1174–1245) had learnt much in many journeys, and entered the service of the Mameluke 'Izz al-dîn Aibek, Prince of Ṣarkhad. He was first of all his secretary, and then his minister, which last position he held till the prince was murdered in 1229. He left, amongst other works, the *Miftâḥ al-Afrâḥ fî'mtidâḥ al-râḥ* (Key of Delights, Praise of Wine), a collection of Bacchic poetry in the manner of Abû Nuwâs.

Nûr al-dîn Muḥammad al-Is'irdî (1222–1254), born at Seert, was one of the poets most favoured by Malik al-Nâṣir, the Ayyûbite Prince of Aleppo, to whom he had specially attached himself, and to whom, too, he dedicated his *Nâṣiriyyât*, panegyrics, now at the Escurial. He was bold and shameless. One of his odes is devoted to the defence of wine against hashish.

Ibn al-Ṣaffâr (the Son of the Coppersmith) (1179–

1260), of Mâridîn, otherwise called Jalâl al-dîn 'Alî ibn Yûsuf, was secretary in the service of the Urtuqid Prince al-Malik al-Manṣûr, and perished at the taking of the fortress by the Mongols. His poems, loose and erotic, are among the manuscripts preserved at Gotha.

Najm al-dîn Abû'l-Ma'âlî Ibn Isrâ'îl (Muḥammad ibn Sawwâr) (1206–1278) was born at Damascus, and died in the same city. He was a dervish, who retired from the world and travelled about. His *dîwân* is in the Escurial.

IBN MUNÎR AL-ṬARÂBULUSÎ (Abû'l-Ḥusain Aḥmad) (1080–1153) was the son of a wandering singer, who recited poems in the market-places of Tripoli in Syria, where he was born; as he grew up, he learnt the Koran by heart, studied grammar and philology, and began to write poetry on his own account. He went to Damascus and settled there. His religious views were Shî'ite. His satires were so many, and his language so caustic, that Bûrî, son of the *atâbek* Ṭughtakîn, and Prince of Damascus, cast him into prison for some time, and would have had his tongue cut out, but influential intervention saved the poet from this torture, and he was banished from the city instead. He went to Aleppo, where he died, and was buried on the hill of Jaushan, outside the town, where the biographer Ibn Khallikân saw his tomb. The *atâbek* 'Imâd al-din Zangî was laying siege to the Castle of Jabar when he heard his musician singing some lines by Ibn Munîr which took his fancy; he gave orders that their author should attend him with all haste; but on the very night of the poet's arrival in camp, the *atâbek* was murdered, and his army retired to Aleppo, carrying the discomfited

poet along with it. His enemy, Ibn al-Qaisarânî, at whom he had so often scoffed, declaring he had the evil eye, sent him ironical congratulations on his adventure. Ibn Munîr's poetry is eminently refined. His *qaṣîda al-Tatariyya*, an ode in ninety-one lines on his slave Tatar, whom he sent with presents to Sharîf Al-Mûsawî, and who was by him detained, is preserved in the Berlin Library. He gives it to be understood in this poem that he would be ready to renounce his profession of Shî'ite opinions if only he might regain possession of his servant.

The son of the chief of a tribe of desert Arabs, and therefore surnamed Al-Amîr, IBN ḤAYYÛS was born at Damascus on 27th December 1003. His real name was Abû'l-Fityân Mûḥammad ibn Sulṭân. Ḥayyûs was his grandfather. He was on terms of intercourse with many princes and great personages, who rewarded him richly for the praises he heaped upon them; but he attached himself more particularly to the Beni-Mirdâs, then the reigning family of Aleppo, to which town he went in 1072. Maḥmûd ibn Naṣr, one of the princes of this dynasty, had presented him with a thousand gold pieces. When Maḥmûd died in 1075, the poet sought the presence of his son and successor, Jalâl al-daula Naṣr, to offer him compliments and condolence in verse. In the course of his poem he said: "Maḥmûd gave me one thousand pieces of gold out of his treasury; I know for a certainty that his son Naṣr will do the same." This elegy so delighted Naṣr that he exclaimed: "If, instead of saying he would do the same, he had said Naṣr would double the sum several times over, I should certainly have done it!" The benefits conferred on him by the Mirdâs

family enabled the poet to build himself a house at Aleppo, over the door of which he set up odes of his own composition, praising "the goodness of those who had delivered him from adversity and the tyranny of fortune." In this house he died, in 1081.

Ja'far ibn Shams al-Khilâfa al-Afḍalî (1148–1225) was surnamed after Al-Afḍal Amîr al-juyûsh, the Egyptian minister, in whose service he had been. He was a clever copyist, and his transcriptions were much sought after, for the sake of the beauty of their penmanship and their correctness, qualities which, in the East, hardly ever coexist. Most of his works are compilations, in which we can only praise the good taste with which he has selected the poems they contain. He has, indeed, left some poetical compositions of his own. Ḥâjî Khalfa mentions his *dîwân*. The lines in which he says: "Suffering is followed by joy. Consider that the evil which has ceased is better than the joy that is passing from us," have been much admired.

Saif al-dîn al-Mushidd (1205–1258), of Cairo, was of Turkoman extraction. His name was 'Alî ibn 'Umar ibn Quzal ibn Jildak el-Yârûqî. He was called to Damascus as inspector (*mushidd*) of the Office of Public Administration by Al-Malik al-Nâṣir Yûsuf, and died there. He was an agreeable social companion, and a witty conversationalist. His *dîwân* may be seen both at the Escurial and in the British Museum.

The only other names of this period worthy of recollection are those of Ibn al-Zaqqâq al-Bulqînî, who died before he was forty, in 1134, and is well known for his *muwashshaḥât;* Ẓâfir al-Ḥaddâd of Alexandria, who died at Cairo in 1135, and whose *dîwân*, largely composed of elegies and panegyrics, is preserved at Berlin;

'Alî al-Hamadhânî] al-Sakhâwî, author of seven odes in praise of the Prophet, a commentary on which, written at a later date by 'Abd al-Raḥmân ibn Ismâ'îl ibn al-Maqdisî, is now in Paris; Zain al-dîn Katâkit, who belonged to Seville, was born in 1208, and died at Cairo in 1285—his poetry is now in the Gotha Library; Nâṣir al-dîn Ibn al-Naqîb al-Nafîsî, who died at Cairo in 1288—he wrote fragmentary verses, some of which will be found in Al-Kutubî's *Fawât al-Wafayât*, and an anthology entitled *Manâzil al-Aḥbâb*, a copy of which may be consulted in the Nûri-'Osmânieh Mosque at Constantinople; and of Sirâj al-dîn al-Warrâq, a copious and prolific poet, born 1218, died 1296, who was a caligrapher and copyist in the service of the Governor of Cairo, and whose exceedingly numerous poems, filling some thirty volumes, were reduced by himself into a *dîwân* of seven bulky tomes—none of these, save an extract made by Ṣafadî in 1346, are now in existence.

Shihâb al-dîn al-Talla'farî (Muḥammad ibn Yûsuf) (1197–1277) was born at Mosul. His panegyrics on the Prince Malik-al-Ashraf did not prevent his banishment from that city, on account of his addiction to games of chance, which the Moslem law forbids. The money bestowed on him by his patron was forthwith gambled away. He betook himself to Aleppo, and was at first well received by the prince, till he earned his displeasure by the same vice. It became necessary to make it known by the public crier, that any one seen gambling with him would have his hand cut off.

He was not more fortunate at Damascus, where, after gambling away the money he wormed out of various great people, he was obliged to sleep on the stoves used to heat the public baths. Then we come on him

again at the court of the Princes of Ḥamât, and in that town he died. His poems are in the Escurial and at Berlin; he occasionally abandoned the classic metres, and wrote popular songs called *muwashshaḥât.*

'Afîf al-dîn Sulaimân al-Tilimsânî (1213–1291) lived at Cairo and at Damascus, at one time as a Ṣûfî, at another as an author, and died in the latter town. His family belonged to Kûfa. He claimed to be a mystic, and was fond of using the expressions peculiar to the Ṣûfîs; he was even suspected of leanings towards the beliefs of the Nuṣairîs or Anṣârîs. When he was dying, he uttered these words: "He who knows God cannot dread Him. I, on the contrary, rejoice to go to be with Him." At Damascus he acted as bailiff to the Collector of the Public Revenues. His son, Muḥammad ibn Sulaimân, the gentle poet, of whom it was said that he reached men's hearts before he touched their ears, wrote elegant verse, which was the admiration of Damascus. He was surnamed *al-Shâbb al-Ẓarîf* (the Witty Young Man). Born in Cairo in 1263, he died at Damascus in 1289.

If to these names we add those of 'Abdallah al-Khafâjî (died 1074), who sang the praises of the great Amîr Sa'd al-daula 'Alî ibn Munqidh; of Ma'dân ibn Kathîr al-Bâlîsî, none of whose work is known to us, save some panegyrics and elegies preserved at Gotha; of Prince Bahrâm-Shâh ibn Far-rukh-Shâh, Saladin's great-nephew, who ruled Baalbek in 1182, and was murdered in 1230, leaving a *dîwân* consisting of love poems and poems of chivalry, now in the Bibliothèque Nationale; of Ṣadr al-dîn al-Baṣrî, who dedicated his *Ḥamâsat al-Baṣriyya* to Malik-Nâṣir Abû'l-Muẓaffar Yûsuf, Prince of Aleppo; of Tâj

al-dîn of Ṣarkhad, born in 1201, who taught Ḥanafite law at Damascus, where he died in 1275; and of Shams al-dîn al-Khaffâf, a panegyrist of the Prophet, we shall have reviewed all the lesser Syrian poets belonging to this period.

Sicily

Abû Isḥâq Ibrâhîm al-Ḥuṣrî, a poet belonging to Qairawân in Tunis, was born in that town, and died there in 1061. He wrote poems on his native place which are now in the Escurial, and has left us three anthologies of different sizes—the *Zahr al-Âdâb* (Flowers of Literature), printed at Bûlâq, on the margins of Ibn ʿAbd-Rabbihi's *ʿIqd al-Farîd;* the *Kitâb al-maṣûn* (Well-guarded Book), and the *Nûr al-ṭarf* (Light of the Glance).

A prince who likewise was the poet of a day was Al-Muʿizz Ibn Bâdîs, a member of the Zairid dynasty, who propagated the Mâlikite, to the exclusion of the Ḥanafite rite, which had hitherto held exclusive sway in Northern Africa. He felt himself strong enough to break the bonds of his vassalage to the Egyptian Fâṭimids, and publicly recognised the Caliph of Bagdâd as his purely nominal suzerain. He was born in 1007, and died in 1061, after having reigned for many years. To celebrate his declaration of independence as regards the Fâṭimids he composed an ode entitled *Nafaḥât Qudsiyya* (Sacred Odours), now preserved at the Escurial.

Ibn Sharaf al-Qairawâni al-Judhâmî had only one eye. He carried on a literary duel with Ibn Rashîq, who wrote several satires against him. He died in 1068. In the Escurial there is a literary *Lecture* of his, dealing

with the most famous poets. He wrote a graceful line on the wood of which a lute was made: "When it was green, birds sang in its branches; now it is dry, men sing to their own accompaniment upon it."

Abû 'Abdallah Muḥammad al-Shuqrâṭisî, who died in Jarîd (Tunis) in 1072, was the author of an ode in praise of the Prophet, frequently noticed by commentators; Abû'l-Faḍl al-Tûzarî (1041–1113) wrote another, called *al-Munfarija*, which has been the subject of many commentaries, and has been much amplified and imitated; Abû'l-Ḥasan Ḥâzim al-Qarṭâjinî (1211–1285) composed several odes in honour of the Ḥafṣid sovereign of Tunis, Al-Mustanṣir-Billah. These three close our list of Northern African poets from the eleventh to the thirteenth century.

'Abd al-jabbâr Ibn Ḥamdîs (1048–1132) was born in Sicily; while still young he made his name as a poet. He had reached his thirtieth year when the Normans took the island from the Arabs. He fled to the court of the Spanish Caliph Al-Mu'tamid, was kindly received by him, and accompanied him when he was carried into captivity by the African Prince Yûsuf ibn Tâshifîn in 1091. At the end of four years the Caliph died, and the poet remained at Mahdiyya in Tunis. Later on we find him at Bijâya, where he died, blind and over eighty years old. Some authorities assert he died in the Island of Majorca. His *dîwân* has been published at Palermo, by Monçada, and his songs at Rome, by Schiaparelli.

SPAIN

Even in the first century following on the Arab conquest of Spain the victors successfully cultivated the art of poetry, but not till the eleventh do we find any sufficient information as to the literary life of that country. We first come upon Yûsuf ibn Hârûn al-Ramâdi, a Cordovan poet, who died there in 1013, after gaining great glory. He was noted for his fecundity of production and the swiftness with which he expressed his thoughts; yet all we now possess of his works is a few scattered lines in various anthologies, and one ode, composed to pass the idle hours when he was shut up in prison. After him we have 'Abdallah ibn 'Abd al-Salâm, who wrote the *Durr al-manẓûm* (Pearls ranged in Order), a *dîwân* arranged in alphabetical order and composed of panegyrics and New Year congratulations; Abû'l Fatḥ Ibn al-Ḥaṣîna (*circa* 1048); 'Alî al-Mayurqî, who came from the Balearic Isles, and died at Bagdâd in 1048; the 'Abbâdid Caliph of Seville, Al-Mu'tamid, a friend and patron of men of letters, and himself a poet; Aḥmad al-Numairî (early in the twelfth century); and Abû'l-'Abbâs al-Ṭutîlî al-A'mâ, the blind poet of Tudela, who died young in 1126, sang the glories of 'Alî ibn Yûsuf ibn Tâshifîn the Moravid, and wrote several *muwashshaḥât*.

Ibn Zaidûn (Abû'l-Walîd Aḥmad) belonged to a prominent family in Cordova, where he was born in 1103. The prominent position he occupied when still quite young brought him to the notice of Wallâda, daughter of the Omeyyad Caliph Al-Mustakfî, who was murdered in 1025. Their loves were crossed by Abû'l-

Ḥazm ibn Jahwar, then master of Cordova, who cast the poet into prison; he escaped, but his longing to see Wallâda tempted him back to the city. When the tyrant died, his son, Abû'l-Walîd, ascended the throne, recalled Ibn Zaidûn, and made him his vizier. When Abû 'Âmir ibn 'Abdûs sought Wallâda's hand in marriage, Ibn Zaidûn, in her name, sent him a famous epistle refusing his request. His relations with Idrîs II., Prince of Malaga, a lover of the arts, stirred the suspicions of his patron, Abû'l-Walîd, who sent him into exile. He went to Seville, where Al-Mu'taḍid was then in power. This monarch gave him a brilliant reception, and shortly afterwards appointed him to the twofold position of Prime Minister and commander of his troops. So well did he perform these functions that Mu'taḍid's successor, Al-Mu'tamid, continued him in his post till he died, in 1070. His letter to Ibn 'Abdûs was translated and published by Reiske in 1755. In later years his work occupied the attention of the Dutch Orientalist, Weijers, and yet more recently his life has been studied, and his letter to Ibn Jahwar published, by M. Besthorn.

'Abd al-Majîd Ibn 'Abdûn, who was born at Evora, early attracted the notice of 'Umar ibn Afṭas, then governor of that town. When 'Umar succeeded his brother Yaḥyâ, he sent for the poet to Badajoz, and made him his secretary. When the prince lost his territory and his life, in the Moravid irruption (1092), Ibn 'Abdûn entered the service of Sîr ibn Abî Bakr, commander of the African troops, in the same capacity. Then he went on to Morocco, where the son of Yûsuf ibn Tâshifîn also employed him as his secretary. He died in his native town, whither he had returned to

visit his kinsfolk, in 1134. His ode on the disappearance of the Afṭas family has become celebrated. Commentaries on it have been written by Ibn Badrûn and Ismâ'îl Ibn Athîr.

Between Jativa and Valencia lies the village of Jucar, which the Arabs called an island, because it was surrounded by the waters of a river of the same name. Here was born, in 1058, Ibn Khafâja (Abû Isḥâq Ibrâhîm), and here he dwelt, without seeking to pay court to the kinglets who had divided up the country amongst them, and who, nevertheless, prided themselves on being patrons of letters. In spite of this, as we perceive on consulting his *dîwân*, published in Cairo in 1869, he did address numerous panegyrics to Abû Isḥâq Ibrâhîm ibn Yûsuf ibn Tâshifîn.

The Almerian Spaniard who entered the service of the Seljûqid Sultan Maḥmûd ibn Malikshâh in 1127, and provided him with a campaigning hospital, transported on forty camels, was both a physician and a poet. His name was 'Ubaidallah ibn Muẓaffar. Born in 1093, he made the Mecca pilgrimage in 1122, sojourned at Damascus and Alexandria, spent some time as a teacher at Bagdâd, and finally returned to Damascus, where he died in 1154. With the exception of such of his verses as are quoted in various anthologies, scarcely anything remains to us except a poem in the *rajaz* metre, called *Ma'arrat al-bait*, the manuscript of which is preserved at Berlin.

Abû Bakr Mûḥammad Ibn Quzmân, a wandering troubadour, travelled from town to town, singing the praises of the great, and living on the rewards he thus obtained. He wrote popular poetry in the form called *zajal*, till then left entirely to improvisators, but which

he raised to the dignity of a literary form. Indeed he has been regarded by some as the inventor of this particular style of poetry. He even adopted it to sing the praises of princes, whereas until his time the lordly *qaṣîda* had been solely devoted to this use. The unique manuscript belonging to the Asiatic Museum in St. Petersburg has been published by M. D. de Gunzbourg.

Abû Isḥâq Ibrâhîm Ibn Sahl, a Sevillian Jew, ultimately became a Moslem convert. He was drowned, with Ibn Khallas, Governor of Ceuta, in 1251 or 1260. He was a little over forty years of age. He lived much with Moslems before he was converted, and even wrote a poem in honour of Mahomet before he actually joined his followers. Yet some, noting that he continued to drink wine, were sceptical as to his conversion. He wrote verses in the popular metre known as *muwashshaḥ*, which have been collected by Ḥasan ibn Muḥammad al-'Aṭṭâr, and lithographed at Cairo.

The Spanish Government might also reasonably claim Abû Zaid 'Abdal-Raḥmân Ibn Yakhlaftan, who, after having acted as secretary to various Arab princes, was banished by the Almohad Al-Ma'mûn. He took refuge in Morocco, and made his peace with the Sultan in 1230, yet this served him but little, seeing he was dead within three months. One of his pupils collected his complete works, in prose and verse, into a volume, which is now at Leyden, and which treats of edification and asceticism. The poems included in a manuscript now at the Escurial are of the same type, and to these we must add a certain number of odes in praise of the Prophet. A Spaniard, Abû'l Ḥusain 'Alî al-Shushtarî, born at Shushtar, in the district of Wâdî-Âsh in Andalusia, who died at Damietta in 1269, wrote Ṣûfî poems in the popular form known

as *muwashshaḥ*. A native of Malaga, Abû'l Ḥakam Mâlik Ibn al-Muraḥḥal, wrote a panegyric of the Prophet in popular form.

Cultured Rhymed Prose

The same period witnessed the appearance of prose works worthy to rank with those of the poets. Rhymed prose, of which the Koran is the masterpiece, had fallen out of fashion before the days of Islam, and was utterly neglected when a recrudescence of this style occurred in the form of sermons (Khuṭba), epistolary art, and poetic compositions, which have grown famous under the name of *Lectures* (Maqâmât).

A preacher at the court of Saif al-daula at Aleppo was Ibn Nubâta (946–984), who was born at Mayyâfâriqîn in Mesopotamia, and died in his native town. He is called Al-Khaṭîb, the preacher, to distinguish him from Ibn Nubâta the poet, who also lived at Saif al-daula's court. A large number of Ibn Nubâta's sermons are devoted to the duty of prosecuting the Holy War. They were intended to stir the courage of the populace, and excite it to support the prince, to whose perpetual struggle with the Roman troops of Byzantium reference has been already made. The most famous of these sermons is one known as the Sermon of the Dream, or Vision. It was composed during a dream in which the preacher believed he had seen the Prophet in person. This has been translated and published by MacGuckin de Slane, in the *Journal Asiatique* for 1840. As for Ibn Nubâta the poet, he wandered from one country to another, reciting poems extolling their greatness to the various princes and great lords on whom he happened. He was born in 938, and died at Bagdâd

in 1015. A curious incident, related by Ibn Khallikân, befel him. He was taking a siesta one day in the vestibule of his house, when a man lately arrived from the East came to inquire whether he was author of the lines: "He who does not die by the sword will die in some other fashion. The manner may be different, but the misfortune never changes." And before the end of that same day, a native of Tâhart (Tiaret) in Algeria appeared and put the same query. What greatly surprised Ibn Nubâta was that the fame of this stanza should have simultaneously reached the eastern and western extremities of the Moslem world.

The mother of Abû Bakr AL-KHWÂRIZMÎ was own sister to the historian Ṭabarî. He was born in 935, and was the first author who left a collection of letters behind him. He was a letter-writer who had seen many adventures. He was of Persian origin. His father belonged to Khwârizm, now the Khânate of Khiva, and his mother to Ṭabaristân or Mâzandarân, in Northern Persia. In his youth he spent some time at Saif al-daula's court at Aleppo, then went to Bukhârâ, to that of Abû ʻAlî al-Balʻamî, but soon left it, and sojourned both at Nîshâpûr in Khurâsân, and in Sijistân, where he lay a long time in prison, because he had written a satire against the governor, Ṭâhir ibn Muḥammad. Returning from Nîshâpûr, he settled, after a certain amount of travelling, at Ispahan and at Shîrâz. His mania for satire earned him confiscation and imprisonment at the hands of Al-ʻUtbî, minister of Maḥmûd the Ghaznevid. Then he departed into Jurjân, whence he was recalled, after ʻUtbî's assassination, by his successor, Abû'l-Ḥusain al-Muzanî. Towards the end of his life his reputation was somewhat overshadowed by that of

Hamadhânî. He died either in 993 or in 1002. Tha'âlibî has preserved extracts from his poems, in his *Yatîmat al-dahr;* but his *Rasâ'il*, or letters in rhymed prose on every possible literary topic, have made his name famous. When he went to wait on the Vizier Ibn 'Abbâd, he was told by the chamberlain that no man of letters was admitted to his master's presence unless he knew by heart twenty thousand lines written by desert Arabs. "Twenty thousand lines written by men or by women?" inquired the poet. He was recognised at once. "It can be no one but him," said the vizier. "Let him come in!" The welcome this personage bestowed on Al-Khwârizmî did not save him from the poet's jeers at a later date. "Praise not Ibn 'Abbâd, even if he showers so many benefits that the very rain-cloud is ashamed. For with him such actions are the suggestions of his fancy. When he gives, it is not out of liberality, nor is it from avarice that he denies." "God's curse on the ungrateful fellow!" cried the vizier. One of his fellow-countrymen has left us this unflattering sketch of the poet's character: "Abû Bakr has learning and talent, but he is not faithful to his engagements. His friendship lasts from morning till the darkness, but no later."

Badî' al-zamân AL-HAMADHÂNÎ (the Wonder of his Time) was still a young man when he left his native town of Hamadhân in 990. He travelled through the same countries as Al-Khwârizmî, made a stay at Nîshâpûr, held an oratorical duel in that town with the said Al-Khwârizmî, an older and better known man than himself, and seems to have finally settled at Ghazna, in Afghanistan, and to have died at Herât, aged forty, in the year 1008. He was actually buried prematurely, while he lay in a state of

lethargy. His screams were heard in the night, and the tomb was opened, but he was found to have died of terror, with his hand clutching his beard. His memory was so prodigious that he could recite four or five pages of a book correctly after having read them over once, and he could repeat any poem without hesitation after having once heard it declaimed. He composed with the same ease, either in prose or verse, and improvised at will upon any subject he was given. Any poem put into his hand he could at once read in prose, and *vice versâ;* and, yet more astonishing, he would sometimes answer a question addressed to him, writing his answer backwards, from what should have been its last line. He translated Persian verse into Arabic poetry in the same rapid fashion. While at Nîshâpûr he wrote his *Lectures*, in which he introduces us to a fictitious character called Abû'l-Fatḥ Iskandarî, and which contain anecdotes about mendicants and other topics. These lectures are, in fact, tales, the Aryan origin of which is at once evident. They are rather short, but written in a brilliant and difficult style, the words of which are, for the most part, the rarest in the Arabic dictionary. The fictitious hero is a *chevalier d'industrie*, who passes himself off now as a Nabatean, now as an Arab, then as a Christian, and again as a Moslem: "I am the chameleon," says he, "and am perpetually changing my hue. Be not deceived by reason! Madness is the only real reason!"

The word *maqâma* (lecture or séance) had long been used to describe the gatherings of the learned men and poets clustered about the Caliphs and Governors, at which they exchanged ideas on grammatical points, and vied with one another in wit and erudition. Ibn Qutaiba mentions them in his *'Uyûn al-Akhbâr.* But to

Hamadhânî belongs the credit of having been the first to create a new form of literature, by making a volume of short stories of the comic adventures of beggars and rogues, painted in the most brilliant colours by a learned author, thoroughly acquainted with the homonymy of the Arab tongue. The masterpiece in this particular style was to be the celebrated *Lectures* of Ḥarîrî, which appeared at a later date. The Berlin Museum has preserved a lecture in the same style, and written at the same period, by ʿAbdal-ʿAzîz ibn ʿUmar al-Saʿdî (939–1015), who was born at Bagdâd, was a court poet at Aleppo in the days of Saif al-daula, and afterwards at Rai, under the governor, Muḥammad ibn al-ʿAmîd, and died in his native town.

At the same period we may cite, as authors of literary correspondence, Abû'l-Husain al-Ahwâzî, and that Hellenising pagan belonging to Ḥarrân, a member of the sect which preserved the ancient Syrian religions, with their strong tincture of Greco-Roman syncretism, long after Islam was in full power, and which were believed to be derived from the Ṣâbians, or disciples of St. John Baptist, formerly included by the Koran among the *Men of the Book*—I refer to Abû Isḥâq Ibrâhîm ibn Hilâl, surnamed al-Ṣâbî, who was head of the Official Correspondence Office under ʿIzz al-daula, the Buwaihid, and whom, in his hatred, ʿAḍud al-daula would have caused to be trampled by elephants, when Bagdâd was taken in 977. He was fortunate enough to be imprisoned instead, and was pardoned, on condition of his writing a history of the Buwaihids. He died in want, in 994.

The honour of writing the most brilliant literary work in rhymed prose was reserved for Abû Muḥammad al-Qâsim al-Ḥarîrî (1054–1122), author of the famous

Lectures. He was born at Bassora. His family belonged to Mashân, a small unhealthy village hidden in the palm groves near the great commercial city. His country property ensured him an income which allowed him to lead an independent life, and devote himself with a quiet mind to his studies, linguistic and literary. His collection of *Lectures,* coming as they did after Hamadhânî's, was modelled on it, but he excelled his predecessor in wealth of fancy, and in his vocabulary, which is even more full and studied. Like his predecessor, he brings a fictitious hero on the scene, a vagabond, nursed on literature, called Abû Zaid of Sarûj, whom he meets in the most extraordinary situations. The name is not altogether imaginary. Ḥarîrî's son has told us of the circumstances under which it was adopted. A stranger of poverty-stricken appearance, but who expressed himself in elegant language, had come into the mosque. To every question addressed to him he replied: "I am Abû Zaid of Sarûj." This town in Mesopotamia had been seized by the Christians during the First Crusade, and sacked by the captors. Abû Zaid's daughter had been carried into captivity, and he himself, stripped of everything he possessed, was fain to live on public charity. But the richness of the style is even more wonderful than the delicate web which connects the fifty stories of which this collection consists.

The great Oriental scholar, Silvestre de Saçy, the chief master of Oriental study at the beginning of the nineteenth century, has published the Arabic text of al-Ḥarîrî's work, with a preface and commentary of his own, also written in Arabic. This is not the least feat performed by this master mind.

In addition to this famous book, Ḥarîrî has also left other works, such as the two letters in which every word begins either with an *s* or a *sh*, a puerile trick, of considerable difficulty, in which Western writers of the Middle Ages also took delight; a grammatical work dealing with the mistakes in language generally made by educated persons, which he entitled *The Pearl of the Diver into the False Notions of Men of the World* (Durrat al-Ghawwâṣ fî auhâm al-Khawâṣṣ); and *Grammatical Recreations* (Mulḥat al-Iʿrâb), a didactic poem, which has been translated into French by M. L. Pinto.

CHAPTER VI

THE 'ABBÂSIDS—*Continued*

GRAMMAR—THE SCHOOLS OF KÛFA AND BASSORA

MEANWHILE, the study of the Arabic language and grammar, arising out of the exegesis of the Koran, and destined to supply the needs of the constantly increasing number of nations and individuals to whom a knowledge of the conqueror's tongue was an absolute necessity, was steadily proceeding. It is to the Aristotelian logic taught in the Syro-Persian school of Gundêshâpûr that, as Ernest Renan has demonstrated, we must trace back Arab research into the construction of the national language. The interpretation of the Koran, and the necessity for explaining the difficulties of its text, gave rise to inquiries ultimately continued for the sake of their intrinsic interest, and which resulted in the final organisation of the lexicography of the language, and the restoration of its ancient literary monuments. Thus the criticism of the ancient texts sprang from these texts themselves, within the limits permitted by Oriental erudition, always incomplete, because Easterns can very seldom go beyond the range of their native tongue. Two schools of grammarians simultaneously appear, on the banks of the Euphrates and the Tigris. At Bassora, founded in 636 by one of Caliph 'Umar's generals, and

the centre of a mixed Arab and Persian population, speaking two different languages—not only on account of the striking difference between the two idioms, but of the real though less striking variation of the Arabic literature, derived from the Quraishite dialect of the Koran, and from the others spoken in the Arabian Peninsula—a school, the origin of which is wrapped in obscurity, had arisen. Some go back to Abû'l-Aswad as its founder, but to be more certain we must come down to 'ÎSÂ IBN 'UMAR al-Thaqafî, died 766, the master of the famous grammarians Khalîl and Sîbawaih; he had a reputation as a reader of the Koran. Near him his friend Abû 'Amr ibn al-'Alâ, born at Mecca in 689, died at Kûfa in 766, just as he had come back from a journey to Damascus, collected the ancient Arab poets. It is said that in a fit of religious fervour he put his whole collection into the fire, so that he might devote himself exclusively to the study of the Koran. He is recognised, indeed, as one of the seven authoritative readers of the sacred book. He had a pupil, Yûnus ibn Ḥabîb, the freed slave of an Arab tribe, possibly of Persian, more probably of Aramean origin, and born at Jabbul, a small town on the Tigris, between Wâsiṭ and Bagdâd. He busied himself in collecting the rare peculiarities occurring in the language, dialect words, and proverbs, and studied syntax. The great master of this school was an Arab from 'Umân, KHALÎL ibn Aḥmad, to whom is ascribed the invention of the rules of prosody (he is said to have discovered them by hearing a smith's hammer ringing on the anvil), and who was the author of the first known work on lexicography, the *Kitâb al-'Ain* (Book of the Letter *'Ain*), in which the letters are not arranged in the order of the Arab alphabet, nor in

that which may be called the historic order (because it passed from its Phœnician inventors into the Greek and Latin languages), but in an order suggested by linguistic and phonetic laws. The alphabet thus conceived began with the letter *'ain,* so characteristic of the Semitic tongues, and especially of the Arab (my readers are aware that the *'ain* is the guttural cry of the camel on whose back the pack is being placed), and ended with the letter *y.* Lepsius has adopted a rational and experimental order of this nature in his *Standard Alphabet,* which is the delight of linguists, and obliges men of learning to acquire yet another alphabet. It is interesting to note the order adopted by a learned Arab of the eighth century. First come the gutturals (*'ain, ḥ, h, kh, gh,* and *q*), next the palatals (*k, j*), then the whistling and sibilant letters (*sh, ṣ, ḍ, s, z*), the lingual (*ṭ, d, t, ẓ, dh, th, r, l, n*), the labials (*f, b, m*), and the semi-vowels (*w, hamza,* and *y*). This work, begun during a visit paid by its author to Khurâsân, and finished after his death by Laith ibn Muẓaffar, was in the library of the Ṭâhirid family, and was removed, in 862, to Bagdâd, where it became the subject of constant study and alteration.

It is more especially by means of the famous book written by Khalîl's pupil, SÎBAWAIH, the *Kitâb,* or Book above all others, that we are enabled to gauge Khalîl's influence over the Bassora School. Sîbawaih is the Arab pronunciation of the Persian name Sîbûya, the meaning of which was given as "perfume of apple," and which may possibly be the ancient historical name of Sêbukht. He came to Bassora when he was thirty-two years of age, completed his studies there, and then moved on to Bagdâd, where he found

life intolerable on account of his altercations with Al-Kisâ'î, tutor of Hârûn al-Rashîd's son, as to the accusative or nominative of a word. Infuriated at the venal testimony borne against him by desert Arabs on whose honour he had fully depended, he returned to his native country, and died young, before he was fifty, in the neighbourhood of Shîrâz (793 or 796). His *Kitâb* was famous all over the East, and has remained the great and favourite authority ; no other work has ever been acknowledged its equal. The text has been published by H. Derenbourg, and translated into German by G. Jahn.

Besides Sîbawaih, Khalîl had other pupils. MU'ARRIJ ibn 'Amr al-Sadûsî, who was born in the desert, and accompanied Caliph Ma'mûn into Khurâsân, lived some time at Merv and at Nîshâpûr, and came back to die at Bassora in 810. Naḍr ibn Shumail was born at Merv, and lived there after he had studied grammar and law at Bassora. He was appointed a judge in his native town, and died there in 818, leaving exegetical works on the Koran and on the traditions, and also an encyclopædia of the Bedouin tongue, which attained great celebrity (*Kitâb al-ṣifât*).

To the same school belongs one of Sîbawaih's pupils, Muḥammad ibn Aḥmad al-Mustanîr, whom his master surnamed QUṬRUB (Were-Wolf), *quṭrub* being a mere corruption of the Greek term *lykanthrôpos :* the surname was bestowed because, in his eagerness to learn, he always came to his lessons before any of the other pupils. He was a freedman, born at Bassora, acted as tutor to the children of Abû Dulaf, a general in the service of Ma'mûn and Mu'taṣim, and left a collection of lexicographical works, numbering twenty-eight, four of which

have survived to the present day, and have been the subjects of copious commentary, more especially his book on triliteral roots, the signification of which alters according to their vocalisation (*Kitâb al-Muthallath*), a subject on which he was the first to write, and on which he has found many imitators. He died in 821.

Amongst Quṭrub's pupils we must place Muḥammad ibn Ḥabîb, to whom we owe our collection of the verses of Ferazdaq. He also studied the ancient history of the Arab tribes, and wrote a book on the subject, which is now lost. He died at Sâmarrâ in 859. His mother's name was Ḥabîb.

Abû 'Ubaida Ma'mar ibn al-Muthannâ was born at Bassora in 728, of Jewish parents, settled in Persia. He attended the lectures of Abû 'Amr ibn al-'Alâ. He was attached to the religious and political views of the Khârijites, and his leanings were also *Shu'ûbite*—that is to say, he asserted the superiority of the conquered races over the Arab victors, as we have previously explained. Hârûn al-Rashîd summoned him to Bagdâd in 803. He had made himself so many enemies by his book called *al-Mathâlib* (Book of the Arabs' Faults) that when he died at Bassora in 825, poisoned by a banana, not a soul followed his coffin to the grave—a most unusual occurrence in the East. He wore dirty garments, and had a burr in his speech. He wrote two hundred grammatical and philological treatises, composed of extracts from the poems and proverbs of the Arabian Peninsula. The poet Abû Nuwâs took lessons from Abû 'Ubaida. He thought very highly of him, and despised Al-Aṣma'î, of whom he used to say that he was a caged nightingale—in other words, that he made fine speeches without understanding a word of them. Of

his own master he said : "He is a bundle of knowledge done up in a skin." When he recited verses, he would not mark the rhythm, and when he repeated passages from the Koran or from the traditions, he made deliberate blunders ; on being asked the reason, he would say : "Because grammar is an evil portent." His *Book of the Arab Days* was the foundation on which the *Aghânî* of Abû'l-Faraj al-Iṣfahânî and the *Kâmil* of Ibn al-Athîr were written.

Abû Zaid SA'ÎD IBN 'AMR al-Anṣârî was another of Abû 'Amr ibn al-'Alâ's pupils. His family belonged to Medina, but he was born at Bagdâd, just when Caliph Mahdî came to the throne, and died there in 830, aged nearly a hundred years. He was a *qadarî*, which means that he acknowledged man's free will, a theological opinion then considered heretical. Yet he is regarded as a trustworthy authority on the Prophet's traditions.

But the most famous of all Abû 'Amr's disciples was AL-AṢMA'Î 'Abdal-Malik ibn Quraib, a man of true Arab descent, who was born at Bassora in 739. His astonishing erudition earned him the highest consideration at the court of Hârûn al-Rashîd, while, both as an instructor and as a writer, he wielded great influence in literary circles. He is distinguished from his predecessors by his excessive piety, the expression of which is evident even in his philological works. He died towards 831. He wrote books on a great many subjects, amongst others the *Kitâb al-Khail* (Book of the Horse), in which he enumerates the names given by the Bedouins to every part of the noble creature's body, and quotes an appropriate Arabic verse to accompany each. This book gave rise to an incident which Al-Aṣma'î himself relates to us. He went one day, with Abû 'Ubaida, to

the Vizier Faḍl ibn Rabî', who asked him the number of volumes in which his treatise on the horse was contained. "One only," replied the grammarian. To a similar question Abû 'Ubaida, who had also written a book on the horse, replied that his work was in fifty volumes. "Go up to that horse," said the vizier, pointing to one which had just been led out of his stables, "and lay your hand on every part of his body, one after the other, giving me their names." "I am not a horse-doctor," replied Abû 'Ubaida; "I got everything I have written on the subject from the Bedouins." But Al-Aṣma'î undertook to do what the vizier desired, and taking hold of the horse by the mane, he named every part of its body, and quoted a verse of Bedouin poetry in which each was mentioned. Of course the horse was bestowed on him as the reward of his knowledge. Afterwards, whenever he desired to nettle Abû 'Ubaida's feelings, he would call on him, riding the horse which had been the cause of his confusion. So profound was Al-Aṣma'î's respect for the Koran and the traditions of the Prophet, that he would never apply his learning to the elucidation of their difficulties and obscurities. He always answered: "The Arabs of the desert say that such an expression means such and such a thing, but I do not know what it may mean in the Koran." This timidity in exegetical matters arose out of his religious feelings, and prevented him from using the gifts which had brought him fame in profane subjects, for the study of the sacred texts.

AL-AKHFASH (surnamed *Al-Ausaṭ*, "the Middle," to distinguish him from an older grammarian of the same name) Sa'îd ibn Mas'ada was born at Balkh, and was probably of Persian descent. He was a freedman,

belonging to an Arab tribe. Though older than Sîbawaih, he had been his favourite disciple, and was in the habit of saying: "My master never put a single passage into his *Kitâb* without having first submitted it to me." To him, in fact, we owe the preservation of that famous grammar, certain tendencies of which, however, he opposed. His surname Akhfash signifies "he who has little eyes," or can only see plainly in the dark. Besides this peculiarity, his mouth was always open, and he could not bring his lips over his teeth. He died towards 835.

Al-Aṣma'î had several pupils. The first is Abû 'Ubaid AL-QÂSIM IBN SALLÂM (773–837), the son of a Greek slave, born at Herât. He not only studied at Bassora with Al-Aṣma'î, Abû 'Ubaida, and Abû Zaid, but also at Kûfa with Ibn al-A'râbî and Al-Kisâ'î. He was first of all appointed tutor to the children of Harthama, Governor of Khurâsân under Hârûn al-Rashîd, and to those of Thâbit ibn Naṣr, Governor of Tarsus in Cilicia. This latter functionary gave him a post as *qâḍî*, which he held for eighteen years. Then he travelled to the court of 'Abdallah ibn Ṭâhir, Governor of Khurâsân, who gave him a generous welcome. There was a wonderful prudence about his literary efforts. To avoid the disagreeable consequences of the satirical lines he introduced into them, he replaced the proper names by substantives fabricated by himself to suit the rhythm. In his later years we find him back at Bagdâd. He died at Mecca, or at Medina, in the course of a pilgrimage. He was said to have divided the night into three parts—one for prayer, one for sleep, and one for the composition of his literary works. Of these latter, the *Gharîb al-Muṣannaf*, on which he laboured for forty years, is preserved in the

Khedivial Library at Cairo, the *Gharîb al-Ḥadîth* is at Leyden, and the *Book of Proverbs* in Paris.

The second of Al-Aṣma'î's pupils is ABÛ ḤÂTIM Sahl ibn Muḥammad, who belonged to Sijistân, and died towards 864. He lived for some time at Bagdâd, and towards the close of his life forswore study, becoming a bookseller instead. He is well known as the author of the *Kitâb al-Mu'ammarîn*, which is preserved in the Cambridge University Library and deals with men of remarkably long life. His book of the palm-trees (*Kitâb al-Nakhl*) has been studied by Cusa and Lagumina. He was the teacher of Ibn Duraid and of Al-Mubarrad. He was a man of piety, who spent a gold coin in alms every day, and read the whole Koran through every week. We are told he was a better poet than grammarian. One anecdote related of him shows he was acquainted with the use of sympathetic inks to conceal writings. He used to say to his pupils: "If you desire to consign a secret to paper, write it in fresh milk; the words will come out when you throw hot ashes from burnt paper upon them: or else write with a solution of sulphate of iron; the writing will become legible if you pour an infusion of gall-nuts upon it. You can also write with the gall-nut infusion, and pour sulphate of iron on it."

The third pupil of this great master, Abu 'Umar ṢÂLIḤ IBN ISḤÂQ al-Jarmî, was a jurisconsult and grammarian, born at Bassora. He went to Bagdâd, where he held great discussions with Al-Farrâ. He died in 840. The fourth, Abû'l-Faḍl al-'Abbâs ibn Faraj al-Riyâshî, perished at Bassora during the insurrection of the Bassoran 'Alid, the sham 'Alî ibn Muḥammad, Chief of the Zanj, in 874. When the town was taken by

these savage negroes, the grammarian fell in the general massacre of the inhabitants which ensued. A fifth was Al-Sukkarî Abû Sa'îd al-Ḥasan ibn al-Ḥusain (827–888), who made a collection and a critical edition of the ancient Arab poets, the Hudhailite *dîwân*, and that of Imru'ul-Qais. A sixth was Abû 'Uthmân Bakr ibn Muḥammad al-Mâzinî, died 863; he refused, one day, to give lessons in grammar out of Sîbawaih's book to a man who was not a Moslem, because that book is full of quotations from the Koran, which he would not explain to the learner for fear of profanation—and this in spite of the large sum offered him by the student, and of his own poverty. He was summoned to Bagdâd, and explained a grammatical difficulty occurring in a verse written by the erotic poet Al-'Arjî, of Mecca, grandson of Caliph 'Uthmân, to Caliph Wâthiq.

One of the chief props of the Bassora School was AL-MUBARRAD Muḥammad ibn Yazîd al-Azdî, author of the *Kâmil*, or complete treatise on grammar. Born at Bassora towards 826, and trained by Al-Mâzinî and Abû Ḥâtim, he opposed several of the theories of Sîbawaih. Towards the close of his life he settled at Bagdâd, and died there in 898. He himself has related the origin of his surname Al-Mubarrad (the Cooled). One day, when the Chief of the Police wished to have him with him, and enjoy his conversation, Al-Mubarrad, to avoid a society which he found very wearisome, went to a friend's house. When the messenger came there to fetch him, he hid himself in the great osier basket used to cover drinking jars, and was not discovered. When the messenger had departed, his host called him, shouting out *Al-Mubarrad* (the Cooled One), and the nickname stuck. A whole dynasty of philologers and teachers of

grammar is formed by the Al-Yazîdî family, from Abû Muḥammad Yaḥyâ, a freedman of the 'Adî tribe, who died at Merv in 817, and his five sons—Muḥammad, who was a poet too; Ibrâhîm, who went with Ma'mûn into Asia Minor, and died in 839; Ismâ'îl, 'Ubaid-Allah, and Isḥâq—down to his descendant Abu 'Abdallah Muḥammad ibn al-'Abbâs, tutor to the children of Caliph Muqtadir, who died in 922. He wrote a history of the family. Yazîdî was present one day at a musical gathering in the palace of Ma'mûn. "Tell me," said the Caliph, "if there is any better thing in life than this gathering of ours." "Yes," responded Yazîdî, "there are the thanksgivings due to the Most High for the signal favour He has granted you in permitting you to have it!" A pious answer which greatly pleased the monarch.

Among Al-Mubarrad's pupils was numbered Al-Zajjâj Abû Isḥâq Ibrâhîm ibn Sahl, originally a glass-worker, who became a philologist, and died, aged over eighty, in 922, having acted as tutor to Al-Mu'taḍid's vizier, and later entered the Caliph's own service. He transmitted his name as surname to his pupil, 'Abd al-Raḥmân ibn Isḥâq al-Zajjâj, who was born at Nahâvand, taught at Damascus and at Tiberias, and died at the latter place in 949. His *Kitâb al-Jumal* (Book of Sentences) is an instructive work on Arabic grammar, but lengthened and overloaded by a plethora of instances. He is said to have written it at Mecca, and at the end of each chapter to have circumambulated the Ka'ba seven times according to the pilgrimage rites, praying God to forgive him his sins, and make his book useful to its readers. Amongst Al-Zajjâj's pupils we must not overlook Al-Ḥasan ibn Bishr al-

Âmidî, born at Diyârbakr (the ancient Amida), who died in 987, and wrote a critical book on poetry, devoted to a comparison of the two poets, Abû Tammâm and Buḥturî.

IBN DURAID (Abû Bakr Muḥammad ibn al-Ḥasan) (837–934) was at once a poet and a man of learning. Born at Bassora, of a family belonging to 'Umân, he contrived to escape the massacre that followed the capture of his native city by the negro rebels known under the name of Zanj. He returned to the land of his fathers in 871, and remained there for twelve years. Then he went on into Persia, and by his panegyrics—and notably by his ode called *al-Maqṣûra*, which has been translated into Latin by Haitsma, Scheidius, and Nannestadt Boysen—he acquired the favour of the Governor of Susiana and Fârs, 'Abdallah ibn Muḥammad ibn Mîkâl, commonly called al-Shâh, "the king." In honour of this dignitary and his son he wrote a great dictionary, entitled *Jamhara*. After the dismissal of his patrons he went to Bagdâd in 920, and the Caliph Al-Muqtadir granted him a pension which enabled him to continue his studies there until his death. Under the title of *Kitâb al-Ishtiqâq* (Book of Etymology), he wrote a genealogical dictionary of the Arab tribes, which has been published by Wüstenfeld. He had earned large sums in the service of the Governors of Fârs; but, owing to his generous and even prodigal disposition, he never had any money in his pocket; he had also, while in Persia, contracted a taste for wine, and was fond of getting drunk. Once, when a beggar asked alms of him, he gave him a keg of wine, having nothing else in his possession. When some one expressed disapproval, on the score of the Koranic injunction not to drink wine, he replied: "It was all I had."

He became paralytic in his old age, but lived two years after his last attack.

Al-Mubarrad's favourite pupil, IBN AL-SARRÂJ (Muḥammad ibn al-Sarî), had a defect in his pronunciation which was a serious one for a grammarian—he burred his *r*'s, which the Arabs pronounce with a roll on the tip of the tongue. He died in February 929. Another of the master's pupils was a Persian from the town of Fasâ in Fârs, Ibn Durustawaih (ʿAbdallah ibn Jaʿfar), born in 871, died at Bagdâd in May 958.

Behzâd, a Persian, who professed belief in the Avesta, and lived in the town of Sîrâf on the Persian Gulf, had a son who became a grammarian under the name of Al-Ḥasan ibn ʿAbdallah AL-SÎRÂFÎ. He travelled much, left his native town when he was twenty, studied law in ʿUmân, metaphysics at ʿAskar-Mukram in Susiana, and ended his studies at Bagdâd, under Ibn Duraid, who taught him philology. For forty years he acted as coadjutor to the Grand Cadi of the Ḥanafites in the Mosque of Ruṣafa, and also gave lessons in grammar. He died in 979. He lived a retired and very serious life. He had imbibed Muʿtazilite views, which he concealed, from the teachings of Abû Muḥammad ibn ʿUmar. He lived by the work of his hands, gaining his bread by copying manuscripts.

Al-Sarrâj and Ibn Duraid had a pupil named Abû'l-Ḥasan ʿAlî ibn ʿÎsâ al-Rummânî, the Ikhshîdite (the Bookseller) (908–994), whose family originally belonged to Sâmarrâ. He was born and died at Bagdâd. If we may judge by the work he has left, and which is now in the Bibliothèque Nationale—the sole survivor of the eighteen books he wrote—he chiefly applied himself to the solution of grammatical difficulties.

Yet another Persian we find in the person of Abû 'Alî al-Ḥasan ibn Aḥmad al-Fârisî, of Fasâ (902–987). He came to Bagdâd for purposes of study at the age of eighteen, went to the court of Saif al-daula at Aleppo in 952, and thence to Shîrâz, to that of the Buwaihid ruler, 'Aḍud al-daula, to whom he dedicated his *Kitâb al-Îḍâḥ* (Book of Grammatical Explanation) and his *Takmila* (Supplement). He came back to Bagdâd, and died there.

Very soon after the Bassora School, arose that of Kûfa, of which it may be predicated that it aimed much less than did its elder at confining the Arab tongue to narrow paradigms. It consequently relied more on the customs of the living language than on the artificial constructions of the grammarians. Its foundation was attributed to a contemporary of Khalîl, Abû Ja'far Muḥammad ibn Abi Sâra al-Ru'âsî. His pupil, AL-KISÂ'Î ('Alî ibn Ḥamza), was of Persian descent. He, too, studied under Khalîl at Bassora, and, advised by him, undertook a long journey amongst the desert tribes, considered the depositaries of the purest form of the language. He was the author of a particular manner of reading the Koran, and ranks as one of the seven canonical readers. Hârûn al-Rashîd entrusted him with the education of his two sons, Amîn and Ma'mûn. He was an adversary of Sîbawaih. He died at Ranbûya, near Rai (Rhages, not far from the present Teheran), towards 805.

The only work of his remaining to us, with the exception of the frequent quotations to be met with in other authors, is a treatise on the mistakes in the language of the vulgar (*Risâla fî laḥn al-'âmma*), preserved in the Berlin Library, and probably the most ancient work on the subject.

His chief disciple was AL-FARRÂ (Abû Zakarîyâ ibn Ziyâd), like him, of Persian origin, his family being of the rough mountain race of Dailam. Caliph Ma'mûn chose him to be his sons' tutor: he taught grammar at Bagdâd. He died on his road to Mecca, in 822, at the age of sixty.

AL-MUFAḌḌAL AL-ḌABBÎ employed himself in collecting the lines of the ancient poets, and the Arab proverbs. Both these works have been preserved. The first is the *Mufaḍḍaliyyât*, which he put together for his pupil Prince Al-Mahdî; the second, the *Kitâb al-Amthâl.* At one moment Al-Mufaḍḍal played a part in politics which very nearly cost him dear. He took part in the rebellion of the 'Alid, Ibrâhîm, called by his own partisans the *Pure Soul*, against the Caliph Manṣûr. The grammarian was thrown into prison, but ultimately pardoned, and appointed tutor to the ruler's son. He died in 786, leaving as his disciple Abû 'Amr Isḥâq ibn Mirâr al-Shaibânî, who also collected the ancient poetry, and who died in 821. He made a special study of the anecdotes, rare forms of expression, and improvised poetry of the nomad tribes. His son tells us that he collected and classified the poems of more than eighty tribes: when he had gathered all he could find in one encampment, he published the result of his labour there, and deposited a copy in the mosque at Kûfa. He also wrote more than eighty volumes with his own hand. Another of Mufaḍḍal's pupils was IBN AL-A'RÂBÎ (Muḥammad ibn Ziyâd); Mufaḍḍal had married his mother, whose first husband, the father of Ibn al-A'râbî, had been a slave from the Indus. He died at Sâmarrâ in April 846. His knowledge of the rare forms of expression placed him in the foremost rank, and he criticised the philological works of

others, pointing out the faults they contained. He had a prodigious memory. One of his pupils, Abû'l-'Abbâs Tha'lab, attended his lectures for ten years, and never once saw a book in his hand: yet he dictated several camel-loads of philological texts to his pupils.

IBN AL-SIKKÎT (Abû Yûsuf Ya'qûb ibn Isḥâq) was the son of a Susian, and probably of Aramean descent. He, too, spent much time amongst the Bedouins, to complete his knowledge of the Arab tongue. The celebrity of his works induced Caliph Al-Mutawakkil to entrust him with the education of his son Al-Mu'tazz. His avowed support of the pretensions of the 'Alids, which he never concealed even from the Caliph himself, brought him rough treatment at the hands of the ruler's Turkish body-guard, by whom he was so chastised and trampled upon that he died two days afterwards, in 857. He is said, as a grammarian, to have lacked acumen. His best work is his *Iṣlâḥ al-Manṭiq* (Correction of Language); he also wrote commentaries on the *dîwâns* of Al-Khansâ and Ṭarafa. One of his pupils was Abû Ṭâlib al-Mufaḍḍal ibn Salama, who was the comrade of Fatḥ ibn Khâqân and of Ismâ'îl ibn Bulbul, both of them ministers in the service of Mutawakkil, wrote a collection of proverbs, under the title of *Ghâyat al-Adab* (The Height of Morality), and died in 920.

But the man who really carried on the teaching of Ibn al-A'râbî was Abû'l-Abbâs Aḥmad ibn Yaḥyâ THA'LAB (815–904). Complete confidence was placed in his competence as to all matters of tradition: even as a young man, his reputation as a good relater of Arabic poems was widespread. His master, Ibn al-A'râbî, did not hesitate to appeal to his pupil's knowledge in the case of doubtful questions. He wrote the *Kitâb al-Faṣîḥ*, on the form

and meaning of doubtful words, and the *Qawâ'id al-Shi'r*, rules for poetical composition, and also collected and published the *dîwâns* of Zuhair and Al-A'shâ. He died at Bagdâd, from an accident.

His pupils were: First, IBN AL-ANBÂRÎ (Abû Bakr Muḥammad ibn al-Qâsim) (885–939), the son of a learned traditionist and grammarian, who communicated his knowledge to his son. He was a pious man, who made it his rule of life to follow the *Sunna*, or tradition of the Prophet. He wrote the *Kitâb gharîb al-Ḥadîth* (Book of Rare and Curious Expressions found in the Traditions), which is quoted by Ibn al-Athîr in the preface to his *Nihâya;* the *Kitâb al-Aḍdâd* (Book of Words possessing opposite Meanings), published by Houtsma; the *Kitâb al-îḍâḥ* (Book of the Explanation), dealing with the pauses and openings of the verses in reading the Koran. He had a pupil named Ibn al-'Uzair (or Ibn al-'Uzairî) Abû Bakr Muḥammad ibn 'Umar, whose family belonged to Sijistân. He died in 941, having written, under the title of *Nuzhat al-qulûb* (Pleasure of the Hearts), a dictionary of the rare expressions in the Koran.

Secondly, AL-MUṬARRIZ (Abû 'Umar Muḥammad ibn 'Abdal-wâḥid al-Zâhid) (874–956), whose fidelity to his master won him the surname of Ghulâm Tha'lab (Faithful Servant of Tha'lab). His pupil, Ibn Khâlawaih (died in 980), arranged and edited his *Kitâb al-'Asharât* (Book of the Tens), explaining words which ten by ten have the same beginning. His astounding memory and infallible erudition attracted the hatred of his rivals, who vainly strove to find weak spots in his truth and correctness.

The two rival schools of Bassora and Kûfa disappeared

in the fourth century of the Hegira, and were fused into what may be called the Bagdâd School, which endeavoured to amalgamate, naturally, the opposing tendencies of the two provincial towns, whose glory faded day by day before the splendour and power of the city founded by Al-Manṣûr. To Bagdâd, as the capital of the States, gathered all the chief intellects of the Empire.

Ibn Qutaiba (Abû Muḥammad Abdallah ibn Muslim) (828–889?) was born either at Bagdâd or at Kûfa. His father came from Merv, and he was consequently of an Iranian stock. For some time he acted as *qâḍî* at Dînawar in ʿIrâqʿAjamî, and afterwards taught at Bagdâd, where he died. He proved himself not only a grammarian, but an historian: he bore his share in the theological discussions which occupied men's minds at that period, and championed Moslem tradition against the scepticism arising from the perusal of Syrian, and later, Arabic, translations of the Greek philosophers. He wrote the *ʿUyûn al-Akhbâr* (Sources of the Traditions), published by Brockelmann, a kind of "select extracts" from the works of the pre-Islamic poems, with selected specimens from the traditions and from history; the *Kitâb al-Maʿârif* (Book of Knowledge), a manual of history, published by Wüstenfeld; the *Adab al-Kâtib*, or Secretary's Guide; and the *Ṭabaqât al-Shuʿarâ*, on the different classes of poets.

Abû Ḥanîfa al-Dînawarî (Aḥmad ibn Dâ'ûd) was of Persian extraction, as his grandfather's name, Wanand, denotes. He was a man of really encyclopædic intellect, who, after studying literature under Ibn al-Sikkît, learnt mathematics, geography, astronomy, and history. He died in 895. His *Kitâb al-Nabât* (Book of Plants) was not, properly speaking, a treatise on natural history, but

a literary work. It dealt with the plants mentioned in the ancient Arab poems. This book is known to us through the extracts from it preserved in the *Khizânat al-Adab*. On the other hand, his historical work, *Kitâb al-Akhbâr al-Ṭiwâl* (Book of Long Stories), now in the St. Petersburg Library, has been published by W. Guirgass. It is written from the Persian point of view, Alexander and the legendary history of the ancient Persians, the conquest of 'Irâq by the Arabs, and the long struggles of the Caliph with his competitors, occupying an important place in its pages.

AL-NÂSHÎ AL-AKBAR (that is to say, *senior*) Abû'l-'Abbâs Ibn Shirshîr was born at Anbâr, a village on the Lower Euphrates, the name of which reveals its Persian origin; it signifies "shop" in that tongue—not, as has been thought, the Greco-Latin term *ἐμπόριον, emporium*. He lived at Bagdâd, and died in Egypt in 906. He was a poet, and wrote hunting scenes and didactic poems relating to sport. He has written fine verses descriptive of falcons. He also turned his attention to grammar, prosody, and scholastic theology. Great praise has been showered on his logical skill and subtle dialectics, which enabled him to controvert all the proofs brought forward by the grammarians in support of their doctrines. He attacked the principles of versification established by Khalîl, and invented an entirely different system.

The same school may also claim the Shaikh al-Islâm Ibrâhîm ibn Isḥâq AL-ḤARBÎ, of Merv (814–898), who wrote on legal and theological subjects; he was the pupil of Aḥmad ibn Ḥanbal, founder of the orthodox rite of the Ḥanbalites: Al-Washshâ (Abû'l-Ṭayyib Muḥammad ibn Aḥmad), the follower of Al-Mubarrad and

of Tha'lab, who died at Bagdâd in 936, a humble schoolmaster, but an elegant writer, who, in his *Kitâb-al-Muwashshâ*, published by M. Brünnow, has left us a lively and most interesting picture of the civilisation of his day, and a collection of model letters as well; these are now at Berlin: Abû'l-Faḍl al-Harawî, a Persian, born at Herât, and disciple of the same masters; he died in 940, after writing a *Kitâb Mafâkhir al-maqâla* (Book of Glorious Discourses), the manuscript of which is preserved at Constantinople: and Al-Akhfash the Little, editor of the *Kâmil* of Al-Mubarrad, and commentator of Sîbawaih's Book, who travelled to Egypt in 900, returned in 918, and died at Bagdâd in 920.

IBN AL-MARZUBÂN (Abû Bakr Muḥammad ibn Khalaf), died 921, wrote a book to demonstrate the superiority of the dog over most men (the manuscript is now in Berlin), but nothing further is known about him. Ibn Khâlawaih (Abû 'Abdallah al-Ḥusain), the pupil of Ibn Duraid and Al-Anbârî, studied the traditions of the Prophet, and was even professor of that subject for a time, in the great Mosque at Medina. In later years he went to Aleppo, entered the service of the Ḥamdânids, and was much in the company of the poet Mutanabbî. He died at Aleppo in 980. He was the author of a book called *Laisa*, on the exceptions occurring in the Arabic tongue, the text of which, from the unique manuscript now in the British Museum, has been published by H. Derenbourg. Ibn Jinnî (Abûl-Fatḥ 'Uthmân), of Mosul, was the son of a Greek slave. He taught in his native town, after having studied at Bagdâd under the grammarian Abû 'Alî al-Fârisî, of the Bassora School. He ultimately returned to the capital, actually took his former master's place, and died there in 1002. His

many works, of which only a few are now in existence, are remarkable for the way in which he has applied philosophy to the study of grammar. His treatise on the principles of inflection has been translated into Latin, and published by G. Hoberg. Abû Hilâl al-'Askarî (al-Ḥasan ibn 'Abdallah) was the author of a collection of proverbs, of works on the rules of composition in prose and verse, and on various literary subjects, and of a commentary on the *dîwân* of Abû Miḥjan. Ibn Asad al-Bazzâz, the cloth merchant (Abû 'Abdallah Muḥammad), author of a book to explain difficult lines of poetry, was celebrated for his penmanship—hence his surname, al-Kâtib, the secretary; he was the master of the famous caligrapher Ibn al-Bawwâb. Al-Zujâjî (Abû'l-Qâsim Yûsuf ibn 'Abdallah), who died in 1024, wrote a book containing the names of the different parts of the human body, in alphabetical order.

In Persia, about the same period, 'Abdal-Raḥmân ibn 'Îsâ al-Hamadhânî, a secretary and caligrapher, who died in 932, was writing his *Kitâb al-Alfâẓ al-Kitâbiyya*, a book on synonymy, edited by the Rev. Father Cheikho, at Beyrout. Abû Ibrâhîm Isḥâq ibn Ibrâhîm, of the town of Fârâb (or Otrar), in Turkestan, lived for some time at Zabîd, where he wrote his *Dîwân al-Adab*, for Atsiz, King of Khwârizm (Khiva). He then returned to his native town, and taught there till he died, in 961. He was the master and instructor of his nephew, the famous lexicographer AL-JAUHARÎ (Abû Naṣr Ismâ'îl ibn Ḥammâd), who, after having studied under his uncle at Fârâb, proceeded to Bagdâd, where he took advantage of the lessons given by Al-Fârisî and Al-Sîrâfî. To perfect his knowledge of the Arabic tongue, he travelled about 'Irâq 'Arabî and the Syrian Desert, then returned east-

ward, and settled, in the first place, at Damghân, and then at Nîshâpûr, in Khurâsân, where he died, towards 1002, from the effects of a fall either from the roof of his own house, or from that of the great Mosque. On this point versions differ. His great dictionary, *al-Ṣaḥâḥ fî'l-Lugha*, is alphabetically arranged, according to the order of the last radical letter, a curious arrangement, to which his successors have adhered, and which, useful as it is to poets, is perhaps more useful still to their critics, for my readers are aware that several Arabic letters are only differentiated by their distinguishing dots. When one of these dots is forgotten by the copyist, which frequently occurs, the word becomes unintelligible. The order adopted by Al-Jauharî perhaps allows of an easier rectification of these errors than would be the case if our plan of arranging the Arabic roots according to the order of the first radical were adhered to. He himself drew up about one half of the work; the rest was completed by one of his pupils, Abû Isḥâq Ibrâhîm ibn Ṣâliḥ al-Warrâq (the Paper-seller or Bookseller), who allowed a few errors to creep in.

Other lexicographers were working at the same time and on the same subject. Ál-Azharî (Abû Manṣûr Muḥammad ibn Aḥmad), born at Herât in 895, was coming back from his pilgrimage to Mecca when the caravan was pillaged (26th April 924), and he fell into the hands of a Bedouin tribe which shifted its camp, according to the seasons, from one part of the peninsula to another. This fact enabled the Persian prisoner, much against the grain, to learn his Arabic at the fountain head. Once delivered out of his captivity, he returned to his native town, taught there for many years, and died there in 981. His dictionary, the *Tahdhîb al-*

Lugha, adopts the arrangement followed by Khalîl in his *Kitâb-al-ʿAin.*

The *Ṣâḥib* Ibn ʿAbbâd (Abûl-Qâsim Ismâʿîl) al-Ṭâlaqânî, born at Ṭâlaqân, near Qazvîn, in 938, was the son of the vizier of the Buwaihid princes Rukn al-daula and ʿAḍud al-daula; he was the first to receive the title of *ṣâḥib*, or comrade. He attended the lessons of Ibn Fâris at Rai, and completed his studies at Bagdâd. When he returned from this city, the Buwaihid prince Mu'ayyid al-daula, whose companion he had been in boyhood, chose him to be his minister, and he continued to hold the post under the prince's successor, Fakhr al-daula. He was a patron of art and science, and himself wrote poems and letters which have been collected under the title of *Kâfî'l-Kufât.* The third volume of his *Muḥîṭ*, a dictionary in alphabetical order, in seven volumes, now preserved in the Khedivial Library at Cairo, contains a very large number of words, insufficiently supported by a very few instances. He died in 995. He was popular at Rai, and his funeral, over which the prince presided in person, called forth a great demonstration of sorrow.

Ibn Fâris al-Râzî (Abûl-Ḥusain Aḥmad) was a teacher at Hamadhân, where one of his pupils was Badiʿ al-Zamân Hamadhânî, author of the *Lectures.* He was presently summoned to Rai by Fakhr al-daula, to be tutor to his son Abû Ṭâlib. He is the first instance we have of a writer of Iranian descent who takes the Arab side in the conflicts of the *Shuʿûbiyya.* He also wrote polished verses, amongst others those in which he satirised the natives of Hamadhân, whose ignorance was proverbial: "Why should I not offer up a silent prayer for the town in which I have had the advantage of for-

getting everything I ever learnt?" He died at Rai in 1005. His *Mujmal fî'l-Lugha* is a dictionary arranged in the order of the first radical letter. His *Fiqh al-Lugha* (Jurisprudence of the Language) is an introduction to Arabic lexicography, full of philosophical reflections.

Aḥmad ibn Muḥammad al-Harawî came from Herât. He was the pupil of Al-Azharî, and died in 1010. He wrote the *Kitâb al-Gharîbain* (Book of the Two Wonders), a treatise on the obscure expressions found in the Koran and the traditions. This work, which was considered exceedingly practical, was copied over and over again, and several of these manuscripts are now in Europe. The author of this serious book was fond of conversing on loose subjects, did not deny himself the luxury of drinking wine in private, and surrounded himself with witty companions, whose pleasure parties he shared. His contemporary, Niẓâm al-dîn Ḥasan ibn Muḥammad of Nîshâpûr, wrote a book of the same nature on the Koran, and simultaneously composed a commentary on the *Almagest* of Ptolemy.

Egypt, too, shared in the movement, as is proved by the labours of Ibn Wallâd (Aḥmad ibn Muḥammad), a pupil of Al-Zajjâj, who died at Cairo in 943, and wrote a dictionary of the words ending with the vowel *a*, long or short (*Kitâb al-maqṣûr wa'l-mamdûd*); of Al-Naḥḥâs (Abû Ja'far), a pupil of the same master, a teacher at Cairo, who was thrown into the Nile in May 950 by a man of the lower orders, who took the verses he was reciting as he sat on the steps of the *Miqyâs* or Nilometer on the Island of Rauḍa for an incantation intended to prevent the rise of the river, and thus to bring about famine and dearness of food. He

was a man of sordid habits. So mean was he that if anybody gave him a piece of muslin to roll round his turban, he would cut it into three strips.

Spain had enjoyed the benefit of the teaching of ABÛ ʿALÎ (Ismâʿîl ibn al-Qâsim) AL-QÂLÎ (901–967), of the town of Qâlîqalâ, in Armenia. He was a student at Bagdâd in 915, left that city in 939, travelled into the distant regions of the Maghrib, and wandered at last to Cordova, where he settled as a teacher of grammar. The work dictated by him to his Spanish pupils is known under the title of *Kitâb al-Amâlî* (Book of Dictations); it is an anthology, filled with traditions relating to the Prophet, an immense number of notes on the proverbs, language, and poetry of the ancient Arabs, anecdotes concerning the poets at the Caliphs' courts, prose pieces, and verses preserved by oral tradition. Another book of his, the *Kitâb el-Bâriʿ*, was devoted to the traditions of the Prophet. His chief disciple was ABÛ BAKR Muḥammad ibn al-Ḥasan AL-ZUBAIDÎ, who completed, under his guidance, the studies he had begun under Spanish teachers. His family belonged to Emesa, in Syria, but he was born at Seville in 918. When his studies at Cordova were completed, he was appointed by the Caliph Mustanṣir al-Ḥakam to superintend the education of his son Hishâm, who, when he succeeded his father, made his old tutor *qâḍî* and chief watchman over the city of Seville. Here he died in 989. His appointment brought him wealth, which his descendants enjoyed for many a year. He composed a considerable amount of poetry; the *Wâḍiḥ* (Clear Treatise) on grammar, now in the Escurial Library; the *Istidrâk*, published by Guidi; and a classified list of the grammarians and philologists

who had flourished before his own time, both in Spain and in the East, of which use has been made by Suyûṭî in his *Mizhar*.

The Niẓâmiyya University at Bagdâd

The foundation of the Niẓâmiyya University at Bagdâd provided a natural rallying-point for the study of classical literature. Here numerous works on poetry, rhetoric, and lexicography were elaborated, for the most part by professors of Persian origin.

Yaḥyâ ibn ʿAlî, surnamed Al-Khaṭîb, and known under the name of Al-Tabrîzî (1030–1109), was born at Tabrîz, in Persia. He studied the traditions at Ṣûr, the Tyre of the ancients; he had learnt philology under the poet Abû'l-ʿAlâ al-Maʿarrî; he taught for some time in Egypt, and then went to Bagdâd, where he was a professor at the Niẓâmiyya till he died.

We are told that, when he would have gone to ask Abû'l-ʿAlâ al-Maʿarrî to direct his study of Abû Manṣûr al-Azharî's *Kitâb al-Tahdhîb*, he had no money wherewith to hire a horse, so he put the book into a sack and started to walk the long journey from Persia to Syria. The sweat on his back oozed through the material of his sack and stained the precious manuscript, which was long preserved and shown to visitors in one of the libraries of Bagdâd. He wrote a treatise on prosody and metre, an abridgment of the grammar of the Koran, and commentaries on the *Muʿallaqât*, the *Ḥamâsa*, the *dîwân* of Abû Tammâm, and that of his own master, Abû'l-ʿAlâ al-Maʿarrî.

His pupil was Abû Manṣûr Mauhûb Ibn al-Jawâlîqî (1073–1145), of Bagdâd, who is known by

his book on foreign words introduced into the Arabic, which has been published by Monsieur Sachau, and by his *Takmila*, a supplement to Ḥarîrî's *Pearl of the Diver*, which has been edited by H. Derenbourg under the title of *Book of Faulty Locutions*. Another work of his, on the names of Arab horses and of their riders, may be seen in manuscript in the Escurial and at Munich. He was famous for his penmanship, and manuscripts in his hand were eagerly sought after. He acted as Imâm to the Caliph Al-Muktafî, and led the five daily prayers at which the monarch was habitually present. A pupil asked him, one day, to explain two lines of poetry which contained some technical terms of astronomy, and he, perceiving he knew nothing of that science, made a vow never to teach again until he had mastered the movements of the sun and moon.

Abû'l-Ma'âlî Muḥammad ibn al-Ḥasan IBN ḤAMDÛN (1101–1167), surnamed *Kâfî'l-Kufât*, or "the Most Perfect of Men," was born at Bagdâd, of a well-to-do family, members of which had served the government as statesmen. He began his career in the army; under Caliph Al-Mustanjid, he was first Inspector of the Palace and afterwards Secretary of State. While holding this latter post, he was so imprudent as to blame openly, and in an official document, the evils he saw around him. He was dismissed and cast into prison, where he shortly died. He left, under the title of *al-Tadhkira*, an historical and philological anthology in twelve volumes, on which Alfred von Kremer has founded his researches into pre-Islamic Arab history and customs.

Sa'îd ibn al-Mubârak IBN AL-DAHHÂN, who was born at Bagdâd in 1101, made his reputation there as a first-

rate grammarian. He ultimately left that city to pay a visit to the Vizier Jamâl al-dîn al-Iṣbahânî at Mosul. During his absence the Tigris overflowed its banks and flooded his library. Such of his books as had been saved were conveyed to him at Mosul. As they had been damaged by the river water, he tried to repair them by plunging them into the vapour of *ladanum*, the resin of the Cretan *gum cistus*, which destroyed his sight. He died shortly afterwards, in the year 1173, in this same town of Mosul. All that remains to us of his work is his *Fuṣûl*, on the art of prosody, and one *qaṣîda*, both at Gotha.

Another member of the Niẓâmiyya University was Kamâl al-dîn ʻAbdal-Raḥmân IBN AL-ANBÂRÎ (1119–1181), who studied and afterwards taught philology there. In the last years of his life he renounced all society, shut himself up in his chamber, and gave himself up to study and to pious exercises. His *Mysteries of the Arab Tongue* (Asrâr al-ʻArabiyya), a grammar, has been published at Leyden by Herr Seybold. His book "of the Just Decision between the grammarians of Bassora and those of Kûfa," written at the request of his pupils at the Niẓâmiyya, has been the subject of a grammatical treatise by Koschut. His *Nuzhat al-alibbâ* (The Delight of Men of Feeling, on the Classes of Literary Men) is a history of Arabic literature from its earliest origin down to the author's own times. It has been lithographed at Cairo. Other works on grammar by the same hand are at Leyden and Paris.

Muḥibb al-dîn Abû'l-Baqâ ʻAbdallah AL-ʻUKBARÎ, born in 1130, died 1219, was regarded, towards the end of his life, as a distinguished philologist. He had also made a study of the jurisprudence of the Ḥanafite rite.

His skill in arithmetic had facilitated his study of the division of inheritances. His family belonged to ʿUkbara, a village on the Tigris, above Bagdâd, which has been the cradle of several remarkable men. He was completely blind. He was the author of commentaries on Mutanabbî's poetry, and on Ḥarîrî's *Lectures*, on the unusual syntactic expressions occurring in the ancient poets (*Kitâb al-Mûjiz*), and on the causes of inflection, and the absence of it, in certain words (*al-Lubâb*).

The Arabic tongue was still lovingly studied in Persia. It was the language of science *par excellence*. There were many ideas which seemed incapable of clear and precise expression in any other. The Persian language was at this period just coming back to life, and the dawn of that brilliant constellation of poets who have ensured its eternal glory was beginning. But the vulgar tongue, which the men of letters were yet forging afresh upon their anvil, lacked many words which had been lost, and must perforce be replaced by others, borrowed from the Arabic. Thus Arabic played the part of Latin in the Middle Ages; save in University discussions, it was no longer spoken, but everybody wrote it.

Abû Manṣûr ʿAbdal-Malik AL-THAʿÂLIBÎ, born at Nîshâpûr in 961, who died in 1038, was a busy compiler, in whose work we note the bad habit, growing daily more general, of not quoting the source from which he borrows, a duty which had been sedulously performed during the best period of Arabic literature. His great work, *Yatîmat al-dahr fî maḥâsin ahl al-ʿaṣr* (The Unique Pearl of the Time, on the fine qualities of contemporary authors), is an anthology of the poets of his time, arranged according to the countries of their birth; to each poetical extract is prefixed a biography, which

is, unfortunately, very brief. His *Laṭâ'if al-Ma'ârif* (Jests of Science) has been published by De Jong at Leyden. His *Fiqh al-lugha* (Jurisprudence of the Language) is a dictionary of synonyms. His *Laṭâ'if al-ṣaḥâba wa'l-tâbi 'în* (Jests of the Companions of the Prophet and their Successors) is a collection of *bons mots* dropped by authorities on Moslem law. Extracts from this have been published by Cool in the *Chrestomathy to Roorda's Grammar;* another collection of *ana* (*aḥâsin Kalim al-nabî*, &c.) has been studied by Valeton. We owe him many other grammatical works, too numerous to mention here. To conclude, he may possibly be the author of the *Kitâb al-Ghurar*, part of which, dealing with an ancient history of the Persians, has been translated and published by Zotenberg.

Abû'l-Ḥasan Ṭâhir IBN BÂBASHÂD, although he spent his whole life in Egypt, was of Persian descent, and belonged to the southern shores of the Caspian. He was attached to the Official Correspondence Office at Cairo, his duty, for the discharge of which he received a monthly salary, being to attend to the grammatical correctness of the documents submitted to him. At a later period, having seen a cat come and beg food for one of its fellows, which had gone blind, he gave up his employment, and trusted Providence to supply his needs. He died in January 1077, having fallen, one night, from the roof of the old Mosque at Cairo into the interior of that building. He left a manual of grammar, in ten chapters, behind him. It is called *al-Muqaddima* (The Preface), and has been the subject of commentaries both by himself and by other authors.

Abû Bakr 'Abdal-Qâhir al-Jurjânî, who died in 1078, wrote a grammatical treatise on the hundred governing

particles, of which numerous copies have been made, now to be found in every library. Both Erpenius (at Leyden in 1617) and Baillie and Lockett (at Calcutta) have given it their attention. Others of his works on syntax have been honoured by frequent commentaries.

Yet another Persian compiler, Abû'l-Qâsim al-Ḥusain AL-RÂGHIB AL-IṢBAHÂNÎ, of Ispahan, who died in 1108, collected a very copious literary anthology under the title of *Muḥâḍarât al-udabâ* (Conversations of Literary Men); he wrote a dictionary of the words of the Koran arranged in alphabetical order (*Mufradât alfâẓ al-Qur'ân*), with quotations from the traditions and from the poets; he also wrote a treatise on morals, which Ghazâlî always carried about with him (*Kitâb al-dharî'a*), and a commentary on the Koran.

The ancient Arab proverbs were put together at this period by Abû'l-Faḍl Aḥmad AL-MAIDÂNÎ, who died at Nîshâpûr, his native town, in 1124. His great work formed the basis of Freytag's *Arabum Proverbia.* His dictionary (*al-sâmî fî'l asâmî*) and his work on syntax (*al-hâdî li'l-Shâdî*) have been somewhat overshadowed by the success of the *Proverbs.*

Abû'l-Qâsim Maḥmûd AL-ZAMAKHSHARÎ, surnamed *Jâr-Allah* (the Neighbour of God), on account of his lengthy sojourn at Mecca, was born at Zamakhshar in Khwârizm (the present Khanate of Khiva), in 1074. His youth was spent in travelling for the sake of study. He made the holy pilgrimage to Mecca, and died in his native land, in the town of Jurjâniyya (Ourghendj, the ancient capital of the country), in 1143. One of his feet had been frost-bitten during a winter storm, necessitating its amputation, and he wore a wooden leg. He always

carried about the written testimony of ocular witnesses to prove he had been maimed by an accident, and not in consequence of a sentence in punishment of some crime.

He was a declared Muʿtazilite, and when he wrote his commentary on the Koran he began it with the words: "Praise be to God, who *created* the Koran!" Orthodoxy at a later date replaced the word "*created*" by "*revealed*." Although, as being more accessible to his readers, he used interpretations couched in Persian in his lexicographical works, he was so convinced of the superiority of the Arabic that he opposed all the *Shuʿûbiyya* tendencies to which we have already referred. His great commentary on the Koran is called the *Kashshâf* (That which Discovers the Truths of Revelation); it has been printed at Calcutta and at Cairo, and many commentaries on it have appeared. The *Kitâb al-Mufaṣṣal* (The Detailed) is a complete manual of Arabic grammar; it has been published by Broch at Christiania. The *Muqaddimat al-adab* (Preface to Literature) is an Arabic-Persian dictionary, which has been published by Wetzstein. The *Kitâb al-Amkina* (Book of Localities, of Mountains and Waters), a geographical lexicon, has appeared in print, thanks to the care of Salverda de Grave. The *Nawâbigh al-Kalim* (The Gushing Words), a collection of proverbs, had already attracted the notice of H. A. Schultens in the eighteenth century, and was by him translated into Latin; Barbier de Meynard has made a more recent study of the text. The *Aṭwâq al-dhahab* (The Golden Necklaces), moral allocutions, has been translated into German by Joseph von Hammer, by Fleischer and Weil, and into French by Barbier de Meynard.

The very year in which Zamakhsharî died witnessed

the birth, in the same country, of Abû'l-Fatḥ Nâṣir AL-MUṬARRIZÎ (died in 1213), who was commonly called his successor. While carrying on his literary studies, he taught Ḥanafite jurisprudence and the dogmatics of the Mu'tazilite School. He has left us a manual of syntax, the *Miṣbâḥ* (The Lamp); a dictionary of the rare terms employed in the style written by jurisconsults, *al-Mughrib fî tartîb al-Mu'rib;* a lexicon of synonyms, *el-Iqnâ';* and a commentary on Ḥarîrî's *Lectures.* In 1204, in the course of a pilgrimage to Mecca, he went to Bagdâd, held frequent controversy on the subject of the Mu'tazilite doctrines, and at the same time gave lessons in philology.

Khwârizm was also the birthplace of Sirâj al-dîn Yûsuf AL-SAKKÂKÎ (1160–1229). He was the author of the *Miftâḥ al-'Ulûm* (Key of the Sciences), a work on grammar and rhetoric which has had many commentators.

Kurdistan produced three Ibn el-Athîrs: Majd al-dîn, the theologian; 'Izz al-dîn, the historian; and Ḍiyâ al-dîn Fakhr al-dîn Naṣrallah (1163–1239), the man of letters. This last was born in the little town of Jazîrat Ibn 'Umar, on the banks of the Tigris, and at the foot of the Kurdistan mountains. He studied at Mosul, and entered the service of Saladin in 1191. In the following year we find him acting as minister to the great warrior's son, Al-Malik al-Afḍal. When his master evacuated Damascus, Ḍiyâ al-dîn, whose life was threatened, was fain to flee into Egypt, where he hid himself when Al-Malik al-Afḍal conquered that country, and he then rejoined his master at Samosate. In 1210 he entered the service of Al-Malik al-Ẓâhir at Aleppo, and in 1221 passed into that of Nâṣir al-dîn, Prince of

Mosul, as his secretary. He died at Bagdâd. It is difficult to understand how, in the midst of so busy a life, with such constant comings and goings, he contrived, in addition to his masterly correspondence, which is collected under the title of *Al-Washy âl-Marqûm*, has been printed at Beyrout, and studied by Margoliouth, to indulge in the æsthetic and critical literary studies which resulted in his book *Al-Mathal al-Sâ'ir*, to which Goldziher has given his attention, his *Poetics* (al-Burhân), and his *Language of Flowers* (al-Azhâr), all preserved in manuscript at Berlin and in Paris.

In Syria we find Abû'l-Baqâ Ya'îsh IBN YA'ÎSH, surnamed IBN AL-ṢÂ'IGH (the Goldsmith's Son), born at Aleppo in 1158. He was on his way to Bagdâd, to sit at the feet of Ibn al-Anbârî, when the news of the death of that master reached him at Mosul. He made some stay in that town, and then returned to Aleppo, where he acted as a teacher of literature till his death in 1245. He wrote a commentary on Zamakhsharî's *Mufaṣṣal*. Ibn Khallikân, the author of the Biographical Dictionary, took advantage of his teaching in 1229: he has recorded his lively admiration for his master, who had a rare gift for smoothing and explaining difficulties. He spoke in a soft voice, and his patience with such of his pupils as were beginners was exemplary. Beneath his grave and serious nature he hid a fund of humour. One day, after he had been explaining an Arabic verse, in which the poet, according to a well-known form of imagery, had compared his mistress to a gazelle, a lawyer of the company, who had listened attentively, and had apparently understood his meaning, suddenly interrupted him with the inquiry: "Master, will you tell me what point of comparison exists between a beautiful woman and a gazelle?"

"The tail and the horns," replied the angry sage, to the delight of all the company.

Jamâl al-dîn Muḥammad IBN MÂLIK al-Jayyânî (1203–1273) was of a family belonging to Jaen, in Spain, but he himself was born in Damascus. He finished his studies at Aleppo, became a teacher of literature at Damascus, and died there, having won the reputation of being the greatest philologist of his time. He wrote a great book, now lost, called *al-Fawâ'id* (Useful Teachings), on the subject of syntax, an extract from which appears in the *Tashîl al-fawâ'id;* the *Alfiyya*, a didactic poem on grammar, numbering about a thousand lines, which has been frequently printed, and on which many commentaries have been written—it has occupied the attention of Silvestre de Sacy, Dieterici, L. Pinto, and Goguyer; and the *Lâmiyyat al-Af'âl*, another didactic poem on the conjugations of the Arabic verbs, which has been autographed by Wallin, at Helsingfors, and published by Kellgren, Volck, and Goguyer. The manuscripts of other and less celebrated grammatical works, on syntax, prosody, and synonymy, are to be found in various libraries.

In Southern Arabia, NASHWÂN IBN SA'ÎD al-Ḥimyarî, a poet and man of learning, turned his attention to the traditions of his native country, and composed an Ḥimyarite ode, which has been edited by Alfred von Kremer and published by Prideaux, but on the historical accuracy of which no reliance should be placed. A dictionary, *Shams al-'ulûm* (Sun of Learning), and a treatise in rhymed prose on the true faith, as opposed to the tenets of the various sects, and the dreams of the philosophers, entitled *Kitâb al-ḥûr al-'în* (Book of the Houris with Great Eyes), make up the sum of his literary output.

Jamâl al-dîn 'Uthmân IBN AL-ḤÂJIB, the son of a Kurdish chamberlain to the Amîr 'Izz al-dîn Mûsak al-Ṣalâḥî, who was born at Esneh, in Upper Egypt, in 1175, first studied Mâlikite law and the reading of the Koran at Cairo, then devoted himself to literature, went to Damascus, and taught there in the great Mosque of the Omeyyads. Later, he returned to Cairo, and died at Alexandria, where he had just settled, in 1249. He wrote books which have been the subject of many commentaries, and are to be found in almost every library: the *Kâfiya*, a short manual of grammar; the *Shâfiya*, a work of the same kind; the *Maqṣad al-jalîl*, on prosody; the *Amâlî*, or dictated lessons on the Koran, on Mutanabbî, and on other poets; and the *Muntahâ al-su'âl wa'l-amal* (The End of Asking and of Hope), a manual of Mâlikite law.

In Northern Africa, Abû 'Alî al-Ḥasan Ibn Rashîq was born in 980, or, according to some authorities, in 1000. He was the son of a Greek slave, or, as others tell us, of a goldsmith. In 1015 he journeyed to Qairawân, and there addressed praises to Al-Mu'izz ibn Bâdîs, which gained him that prince's favour. When Qairawân was destroyed by the Arab tribes of Egypt, sent for that purpose in 1051 by the Fâṭimid Caliph, the poet fled to Sicily, and settled at Mâzar, where he died in 1064 or 1070. His *Kitâb al-'Umda* (The Stay), dealing with the beauties and the rules of poetry, and preceded by an exceedingly detailed introduction to the poetic art in general, earned the praise of Ibn Khaldûn, author of the *Prolegomena*, who regards him as the best of all the critics of modern Arabic poetry. His *Unmûdhaj* (Specimen) deals with the poets of the town of Qairawân.

In Spain, Abû'l-Khaṭṭâb 'Umar Ibn Diḥya al-Kalbî, born at Valencia in 1149, was surnamed *Dhû'l-nasabain* (With two Genealogies), because he was descended, on his father's side, from Diḥya al-Kalbî—that curious individual of Mahomet's time, who was said by the Prophet to be like the Archangel Gabriel, and whom he sent as his ambassador to Heraclius—and, on his mother's, from Ḥusain, the son of 'Alî. He travelled all over Spain in pursuit of his studies, was twice appointed *qâḍî* of Denia, and dismissed on account of his scandalous behaviour. He took up his traveller's staff again, wandered to Morocco, and to Bijâya, where he taught the knowledge of the traditions (1198). He sojourned some time in Egypt before starting on pilgrimage to Mecca, and, on his return from the Holy City, made a long detour, lasting over several years, by Syria, Chaldea, and Persia. On his return, Al-Malik al-'Azîz chose him to be tutor to his son Al-Malik al-Kâmil, and when that prince succeeded to power he built his old master the Madrasa Kâmiliyya, where he taught the traditions. He eventually fell into disgrace, was dismissed, and died on 30th October 1235.

About the same period we find Ḍiyâ al-dîn Muḥammad al-Khazrajî, who died in 1228. He was the author of a didactic poem on versification, called *al-Râmiza al-Shâfiya*, which was edited at Rome, by Guadagnoli, in 1642, and has been the subject of many commentaries.

CHAPTER VII

THE 'ABBÂSIDS—*Continued*

HISTORY — FABLES — ANECDOTES

WE have already seen how history began with the *Maghâzî*—works devoted to the story of Mahomet's wars. The constantly increasing development of the study of the tradition (*ḥadîth*), one of the fundamental bases of Moslem law, made it necessary to collect every possible information as to the life of the law-giver. Further, students of ancient Arab poetry were led to inquire into the old historic deeds, and the "days" or battles to which the poets referred, and chroniclers registered the events which took place after the establishment of Islam, adding legendary information, obtained at second-hand, as to what they believed to be the ancient history of Persia and of the Jewish nation. The translations into Arabic of the Sâsânian *Books of the Kings*, produced at an early date by Persians who wrote and spoke Arabic, certainly gave an impetus to historical study. We may be sure that the 'Abbâsid Caliphs, whose capital was close to the ruins of Seleucia and of Ctesiphon (not to mention the more ancient Babylonian towns, the memory of which was totally lost), were resolved, when they left the world the story of the events that took place under their rule, not to allow themselves

to be eclipsed by the monarchs whom the Arabs had overthrown.

Even at the close of the Omeyyad dynasty we find a writer of *maghâzî*, Mûsâ ibn ʿUqba ibn Abî'l-ʿAyyâsh, whose works earned him the singularly honourable title of *imâm al-maghâzî*, "chief, or director, of historical studies as to the wars of the Prophet." His work was put together in 1387 by Ibn Qâḍî Shuhba. The author himself, a freedman belonging to the Zubair family, at Medina, died in 758. But the great authority of those days, constantly quoted in later works, is Abû ʿAbdallah Muḥammad IBN ISḤÂQ, the original of whose work is now lost; but a great part of it has been preserved to us in a compilation by Ibn Hishâm (ʿAbdalmalik al-Ḥimyarî al-Baṣrî, died at Old Cairo in 834), known under the name of *Sîrat al-Rasûl* (Biography of the Prophet), published by Wüstenfeld, and translated into German by G. Weil. The ill-will Ibn Isḥâq brought on himself at Medina obliged him to leave that town for Alexandria, and thence he went to Kûfa and Rai. At Ḥîra he met the Caliph Al-Manṣûr, who invited him to settle at Bagdâd, a city he had then just founded, and there to make all the traditions of the Prophet he had collected into one volume. He died at Bagdâd in 768.

Another and most famous historian was AL-WÂQIDÎ, but he chiefly owes his renown to impostors, who—very probably at the time of the Crusades, and to stir the warlike spirit of the Moslems by reminding them of the brilliant period of their conquests—sent forth historical romances on the wars in Syria, Mesopotamia, Egypt, and Africa, under his venerated name. Nevertheless, his great historical work (*Kitâb al-Maghâzî*) has come down to us, and has been published at Calcutta by Alfred von

Kremer. Abû 'Abdallah Muḥammad ibn 'Umar al-Wâqidî, who was born at Medina in 747, began life as a corn merchant. Having ruined himself by extravagance, he was obliged to leave the city. At Bagdâd, the vizier, Yaḥyâ ibn Khâlid the Barmakide, furnished him with the wherewithal to arrange his affairs, and appointed him *qâḍî* over the western side of the city; Caliph Ma'mûn later sent him in the same capacity to Ruṣâfa, and there he died on 28th April 823.

A story reported by Mas'ûdî in the *Golden Meadows*, translated by Barbier de Meynard, casts a vivid light on the amicable relations between the historian and his friends. The incident is related by Wâqidî himself. "I had two friends, one of whom belonged to the Hâshim family, and we were, so to speak, but one soul. The festival at the end of the great Fast drew near, and I was in a state of great poverty, when my wife said to me: 'If it only affected ourselves, we could very well bear poverty and privation. But the poor children! I pity them, and it makes my heart bleed! They will see the neighbours' children dressed and adorned for the festival, and they will still have to wear their wretched rags. Couldst thou not, by some means or other, find enough money to get them clothes?' I wrote to my friend the Hâshimite, and begged him to help me in this circumstance. He at once sent me a sealed purse, telling me it contained a thousand dirhems. I had hardly time to get my breath before I received a letter from my other friend telling me of the same trouble as that I had just revealed to my Hâshimite comrade. I sent him the purse just as it had come to me, and went to the Mosque, where I spent the night, for I did not dare to go back to my wife. Nevertheless,

when I did go home, she approved what I had done, and did not utter one word of reproach to me. Thus the matter stood when my Hâshimite friend came to me carrying the purse, still just as he had sent it to me, and he said : 'Tell me honestly what you did with that which I sent you?' I told him everything, just as it had happened, and he continued as follows : 'At the moment when your message reached me, I had nothing in the world except the sum I sent you ; I therefore wrote to our mutual friend to beg him to come to my aid, and he sent me my own purse, still sealed with my own seal.' We then divided the money into three parts, and each took one, having previously set apart a hundred dirhems for my wife."

His secretary, IBN SA'D (Abû 'Abdallah Muḥammad, died 845), collected his works, of which he possessed one of the four copies existing when their author died, and himself produced a collection of biographies (*ṭabaqât*) of the Prophet, his companions, and his successors. His life of Mahomet is occasionally reckoned as a separate volume.

While these authors were writing history in general, Al-Azraqî was compiling a history of Mecca, founded on the fabulous traditions of the pre-Islamic period, and on the notes collected by his own grandfather, Abû'l-Walîd al-Azraq, a descendant of the Ghassânid dynasty, who died in 834. Al-Azraqî himself died soon after 858. A successor of his, Al-Fâkihî (Abû 'Abdallah), also wrote a history of Mecca, in 885; the two have been published by Wüstenfeld. Ibn Zabâla's history of Medina, 'Umar ibn Shabba's histories of Bassora and Kûfa, Aslam ibn Sahl's history of Wâsiṭ; that of Mosul, by Abû Zakarîyâ al-Azdî, *qâḍî* of that town;

of Raqqa, by Al-Qushairî; and of Ḥarrân, by Abû 'Arûba al-Ḥarrânî, who had travelled in Egypt, and taught the traditions at Bagdâd, have all disappeared. Gone, too, are those of various Persian towns, such as the history of Merv, by Aḥmad ibn Sayyâr; of Ispahan, by Ibn Mandah; of Bukhârâ, by Muḥammad al-Bukhârî; of Astarâbâd and Samarqand, by 'Abdal-Raḥmân al-Idrîsî. But we still possess, in the Bibliothèque Nationale, the *Riyâḍ al-Nufûs* (Gardens of Souls), a history of the learned lawyers and pious men of Tunis, by Abû Bakr al-Mâlikî. In the British Museum there is the sixth volume of the great history of Bagdâd, written by Abû'l-Faḍl Aḥmad ibn Abî Ṭâhir Ṭaifûr, who was of Iranian blood, and belonged to a family formerly holding princely rank in Khurâsân. He was born at Bagdâd in 819 and died there in 893.

IBN AL-KALBI (Abû'l Mundhir Hishâm) was the son of a warrior, who, after having fought at the battle of Dair al-Jamâjim, in the ranks of the troops brought back from Arachosia by the rebel chief Ibn al-Ash'ath, turned his mind to Koranic exegesis, and collected most careful notes on the history and genealogies of the ancient Arabs. He died in 763. His son carried on his researches, and wrote a great book on genealogy (fragments of which, in manuscript, are now preserved in the libraries of Paris and the Escurial), and also a curious and valuable treatise on the idols of the ancient Arabs, numerous extracts from which are to be found in Yâqût's *Geographical Dictionary*. This latter work, the subject of which was not calculated to please the Moslems, who hated all memories of the antique pagan period of the peninsula, as recalling an age of ignorance, elicited hot criticism on the part of contradictors, who

accused its author of falsification. Yâqût, who owed him a great deal of his information, defended him against this accusation, and modern critics have confirmed this view. Ibn al-Kalbî, who was born at Kûfa, lived for some time at Bagdâd, and died in 819. He also wrote a book on the genealogies of Arab horses in pagan times, and in those of Islam. His memory was very unequal. He himself relates that on one occasion, having been reproached by his uncle, he learnt the whole Koran by heart in three days; while, on the other hand, looking at himself in the glass one day, he took hold of his beard, meaning to clip all the hairs below his hand, but, instantly forgetting this intention, he cut his beard off above his hand, and consequently made it much too short.

A historian of great merit, whose work, unfortunately, has disappeared, after having been utilised by Balâdhurî and Ṭabarî, was AL-MADÂ'INÎ (Abû'l-Ḥasan 'Alî), who was born in 753, and died at some unascertained date between 830 and 845. The *Fihrist* enumerates one hundred and eleven titles of books written by him on the history of the Prophet, of the tribe of Quraish and of the Caliphs. His *Kitâb al-Maghâzî* and his *Ta'rîkh al-Khulafâ* are frequently quoted. He wrote several works on famous women, and made collections of anecdotes. His name indicates that his origin was connected with Ctesiphon (Madâ'in).

Beside this ancestor of the Arab historians we must place Al-Zubair Ibn Bakkâr (Abû' Abdallah), of the family of 'Abdallah ibn Zubair, who lived at Medina. Even in his youth his knowledge of the traditions, of history, and genealogy, had made him a name. Having quarrelled with the descendants of 'Alî, he went to

Bagdâd, but not meeting with the encouragement he had looked for at the court of the 'Abbâsids, where, indeed, he was suspected of serving the 'Alid party, he returned to his own country, and was appointed *qâḍî* of Mecca, a position which gave him several opportunities of revisiting Bagdâd. He was at Mecca, when, at the age of eighty-four, he fell off the roof of his own house, breaking his collar bone and one of his ribs. Of this accident he died, within two days, on 20th October 870. He was the author of a genealogy of the tribe of Quraish, the manuscript of which is now in the Bodleian Library, and of a collection of historical tales to which he gave the name of *Muwaffaqiyyât*, because they were intended for the instruction and entertainment of Al-Muwaffaq, son of Caliph Mutawakkil. The three last of the eighteen parts into which this work was divided are preserved at Göttingen.

AL-BALÂDHURÎ (Aḥmad ibn Yaḥyâ) was of Persian birth: he frequented the courts of the Caliphs Mutawakkil and Musta'în: Al-Mu'tazz entrusted him with the education of his son 'Abdallah, the poet who was Caliph for one day. He died in 892, after having lost his reason in consequence of taking too strong a dose of cashew nut or marsh nut (*balâdhur*), that curious Indian fruit which is supposed to develop the memory—hence his surname. It became necessary to shut him up in a madhouse, and there he ended his days. His *Kitâb Futûḥ al-Buldân* (History of the Moslem Conquest), published by De Goeje, is an exceedingly remarkable contribution to the history of the victorious expeditions of the Moslems in the first years of the Hegira. The care with which he indicates the sources whence he has procured his verbal information makes it a most

valuable historical document. It is, unfortunately, only a summary of a much larger work, which he never completed. Under the title of *Ansâb al-Ashrâf* (Genealogy of the Noble), he wrote another historical work, two volumes of which have been preserved. The first forms part of the Schefer Collection, which has lately become the property of the Bibliothèque Nationale; the second has been autographed by Ahlwardt at Greifswald. Finally, he translated other books from the Persian into Arabic, the only one of which now known to us is the translation into Arabic verse of the *'Ahd Ardashîr* (Epoch of Artaxerxes), probably devoted to the legends which surround the foundation of the empire of the Sâsânians by Ardashîr Bâbakân—but even this has entirely disappeared; all we know of it is that it is mentioned in the *Fihrist*.

The great historian of this epoch, ṬABARÎ (Muḥammad ibn Jarîr) (838-923), the publication of whose masterpiece has just been completed at Leyden, was also of Persian blood. He was born at Âmul in Ṭabaristân (Mâzandarân), to the south of the Caspian Sea. He travelled in Egypt, Syria, and 'Irâq, and then established himself as a teacher of the traditions and of jurisprudence at Bagdâd. In this latter department he originally followed the rules of the Shâfi'ite rite, which he had learnt during his stay in Egypt. He afterwards endeavoured to create a school of his own, but he failed: indeed, he attracted the enmity of the fierce Ḥanbalites of Bagdâd. To his inquiries into these two subjects we owe his *Tahdhîb al-Âthâr*, now at Constantinople (in the library belonging to Kyüprulu Muḥammad-Pacha), and his great *Tafsír*, or Commentary on the Koran, which was later translated into Persian and Turkish. But his most

interesting work, as far as we are concerned—because it is the most ancient written record of Arab history we possess—is his universal history (*Akhbâr al-rusul wa'l-mulûk*, History of the Prophets and Kings), the first complete history in the Arabic tongue. Great difficulties are connected with the verification of the full text of this work, which is scattered about, a volume here and another there, amongst many libraries, both European and Oriental. Ṭabarî died at Bagdâd, on 16th February 923. He possessed remarkable powers of work, and for forty years he wrote forty sheets a day.

AL-ṢÛLÎ (Abû Bakr Muḥammad ibn Yaḥyâ) was descended from a Turkish prince of Jurjân, named Ṣul-Takîn, who was a convert from Zoroastrianism to Islam. He was much valued at the courts of the Caliphs Muktafî and Muqtadir, on account of his skill in playing chess, which passed into a proverb: a man was said to play chess like Al-Ṣûlî. But his views as to the posterity of 'Alî rendered his position so critical that he was obliged to flee from Bagdâd and hide himself at Bassora, where he died, in 946. He had studied the Arab poets, and wrote a history of them, and special treatises on several of their number, such as Abû Tammâm, Abû Nuwâs, and Al-Buḥturî. He also wrote an historical work on the 'Abbâsids, and on those members of the dynasty who cultivated the poetic art. This is now preserved at Cairo.

In the person of the witty and attractive story-teller MAS'ÛDÎ (Abû'l-Ḥasan 'Alî) we hail the opening of a new branch of Arab literature, that of the historical anecdote. This writer, the scion of an Arab family tracing its descent from Mas'ûd, one of the comrades of the Prophet, was born at Bagdâd, took journeys

which brought him to Persia, where he visited Iṣṭakhr (Persepolis) in 915, and to India. He traversed Multan and Manṣûra, and then travelled by the Deccan peninsula to Ceylon : here he took ship, sailed over the China Sea and the Red Sea, touched at Madagascar, and returned to Arabia by ʿUmân. The Caspian Sea, Syria, and Palestine in turn attracted his curious attention. In 926 he was at Tiberias, in 943 we find him at Antioch and in Cilicia, and two years later he was at Damascus. During the latter years of his life he lived partly in Egypt and partly in Syria. In 947 and in 955 he was at Fusṭâṭ (Old Cairo), where he probably died, in 956 or 957. A man of curious and inquiring mind, Masʿûdî neglected no accessible source of information. He extended his researches beyond purely Moslem studies, examined the history of the Persians, Hindus, and Romans, and the traditions of Jews, Christians, and pagans. Touching the period of the Caliphs, the numberless anecdotes in his *Golden Meadows* (Murûj al-Dhahab) furnish us with the fullest and most entertaining fund of information as to the Eastern civilisation of that period. His great historical work, the *Akhbâr al-zamân*, of which the *Golden Meadows* is but an extract, was in thirty volumes. Of these the first only now exists, at Vienna. The *Kitâb al-Ausaṭ* (Middle-sized Book) was an abridgment of the greater work. The *Tanbîh wa'l-ishrâf* (Notice and Review) is a sort of philosophical epitome of Mas'ûdî's whole work. The text of this has been published by De Goeje, and translated into French by Baron Carra de Vaux.

ḤAMZA ibn Ḥasan AL-IṢFAHÂNÎ was of Persian blood, and in his historical works he has dealt with the legen-

dary history of his country according to verbal information given him by the fire priests, and that obtained from Iranian sources. He belonged to the sect of the Shu'ûbiyya, of which he was a fervent partisan, and endeavoured, in his writings, to re-establish the correct spelling of the Iranian names which had been corrupted in the Arabic. He probably lived at Bagdâd in the early part of the tenth century of our era. His *Annals*, with a Latin translation, have been published by Gottwaldt at St. Petersburg. The Munich Library contains a *Book of Proverbs* written by him, and in that of Cairo there is a Parallel between the Arab and the Persian.

The Book of Songs

Abû'l-Faraj al-Iṣfahânî ('Alî ibn al-Ḥusain) (897–967) was also born at Ispahan, but this was a mere chance, for by blood he was of pure Arab race and descended from the Omeyyads. He studied at Bagdâd, and led the life of many literary men of that period, travelling from Aleppo, where Saif al-daula was then in power, to Persia, to wait on the ministers in the service of the Buwaihid princes, Ismâ'îl Ibn 'Abbâd and Al-Muhallabî. He gradually lost his mental faculties, and died on 21st November 967. His connection with the Omeyyads by a common ancestry led to his being in constant relations with their descendants settled in Spain, from whom he received gifts in acknowledgment of the books he dedicated to them. His *Kitâb al-Aghânî* (Book of Songs) has been published at Bûlâq, and supplemented by a twenty-first volume published at Leyden by Brünnow. These songs are simply the history of all the Arab poetry that has been set to music. And as this has been done to an

enormous number of lines written both by pre-Islamic poets and during the first four centuries after the Hegira, the author has had the opportunity of collecting a mass of biographical details as to their writers. Under the pretext of giving us the songs, this admirable book supplies us with anecdotes and information touching desert and city life, and that led in private by sovereigns and Caliphs, such as are nowhere else to be discovered. It offers a rich mine to the student of Arab society at its most brilliant period. The Berlin Library possesses another work by the same author, the *Kitâb al-diyârât* (Book of the Monasteries), giving the history of many convents and places of pilgrimage on the banks of the Tigris and Euphrates, or in Egypt. It really is an anthology of the poetry in which these convents have been celebrated. We must not forget that, when Moslems went to Christian cloisters, it was not to seek devotional impulses, but simply for the sake of an opportunity of drinking wine, the use of which was forbidden in the Mahometan towns. The poets, out of gratitude, sang the praises of the blessed spots where they had enjoyed the delights of intoxication.

The court of Saif al-daula was also graced by the presence of two brothers, who had been surnamed the two Khâlidîs, Abû 'Uthmân Sa'îd and Abû Bakr Muḥammad, both of them good poets. The ruler of Aleppo rewarded them generously for their praises. They wrote a history of Mosul, biographies of Abou Tammâm and Ibn al-Rûmî, and an anthology of modern poets, entitled *Ḥamâsa*—this last work is now in the Cairo Library.

The Fihrist

A work of this period, which, in its way, is unique, is the bibliographical treatise known as the *Fihrist* (Index). Little, unfortunately, is known of its author, Abû'l-Faraj Muḥammad ibn Isḥâq ibn Abî Yâ'qûb al-Nadîm, surnamed the Bookseller (al-Warrâq) of Bagdâd. It is a catalogue of books, most of which have now disappeared, either because they did not survive the great catastrophes which overtook the Bagdâd Libraries (destroyed by the Mongols in the thirteenth and by Tamerlane in the fifteenth century)—disasters which may compare, as regards the Arab Middle Ages, with the various destructions of the Alexandrian Library in ancient times—or because, owing to their being epitomised in more recent and fashionable works, they were no longer copied, and so died out by a process of decay. The *Fihrist* was written in 988, and its author probably died eight years later, in 996. The opinion expressed by Sprenger, that this book was the catalogue of some library, has been quite put aside, for the historical reflections it contains are evidently a part of the fundamental plan of the work.

Provincial Histories

The *History of the Conquest of Egypt, Northern Africa, and Spain* was written by Ibn 'Abdal-Ḥakam (Abû'l-Qâsim 'Abdal-Raḥmân), the son of the Mâlikite *qâḍî* in Egypt, who died at Old Cairo in 871. This book, which is in the Bibliothèque Nationale, has been partially utilised by MacGuckin de Slane in the appendix to his translation of Ibn Khaldûn's *History of the Berbers:*

fragments of it have been published by J. Karle and John Harris Jones.

SA'ÎD IBN AL-BAṬRÎQ was the Arabic name of Eutychius (876–939), a Christian physician, born at Old Cairo, who was a remarkable historical student, appointed Melkite patriarch at Alexandria in 933. At a time when men were inquiring which was the oldest language, the Syrian or the Hebrew, he declared that the Greek must be the most ancient of all, because of its richness and volume. His universal history, called *Naẓm al-Jauhar* (Pearls Ranged in Order), has been translated into Latin by E. Pococke.

While Aḥmad ibn Yûsuf IBN AL-DÂYA (died 945) was writing the anecdotic history of the founder of the Ṭûlûnid dynasty, Aḥmad ibn Ṭûlûn, and of his son Khumârawaih, Ibn Yûsuf (Abû 'Umar Muḥammad) was composing, for Prince Kâfûr, and under the title of *Faḍâ'il Miṣr* (The Excellent Qualities of Egypt), an epitome of the history and geography of that country down to his own period, which has been translated into Danish by J. Oestrup, a history of the Egyptian *qâḍîs*, and another of the governors of the same country : these are now at the British Museum. At the same time Abû'l-Ḥasan Muḥammad of Alexandria was writing a journal of the government of Muizz Lidînillah, which may be seen in the Escurial Library, and Ibn Zûlâq al-Laithî (al-Ḥasan ibn Ibrâhîm), who was born in 919 and died on 30th November 998, was drawing up various works on Egyptian history and geography, which are now in the libraries of Paris and Gotha.

A beginning of written Spanish history was made by 'Abdal-Malik ibn Ḥabîb al-Sulamî al-Mirdâsî, who was born at Hiṣn Wâṭ, near Grenada, in 796, and died at

Cordova on 17th February 853. In the course of his pilgrimage to the Ḥijâz, he became imbued with the judicial theories of Mâlik ibn Anas, and spread them in his own country. But none of his many works remain to us, with the exception of the beginning of a book on the division of inheritances, which is at Berlin. As to the history now in the Bodleian Library, it has been ascribed to him, as Dozy has acknowledged, without due warrant. After him came Aḥmad ibn Muḥammad al-Râzî of Cordova, whose family came from Rai, in Persia. He died in 937. On his history of Spain and description of that country was based the Spanish work known under the name of *Cronica del Moro Rasis.* The most interesting figure of this epoch and country is that of the historian and philologist Ibn al-Qûṭiyya (Abû Bakr Muḥammad ibn 'Umar ibn 'Abdal-Azîz), that is to say, the *Son of the Goth woman;* his ancestor, 'Îsâ, had married a Spanish princess, Sara, the daughter of King Oppas the Goth, when she went to Damascus to lay her complaint concerning his uncle Ardabast before Caliph Hishâm ibn 'Abdal-Malik. 'Îsâ, with his wife, was sent to Spain, and his posterity continued to inhabit Seville. Abû Bakr, who was born at Cordova, was recommended to the Caliph Al-Ḥakam II. by Al-Qâlî, as being the most learned man in the country. He died at Cordova in 977, leaving behind him a *Ta'rîkh al-Andalus*—a history of Spain from the time of the Moslem conquest till the year 893—the manuscript of which is now in Paris. Cherbonneau and Houdas have translated and published extracts from it, and Cardonne has made use of it for his history of Africa and Spain. Abû Bakr also left a book on the conjugations of Arabic verbs, which has been published by J. Guidi.

Persia is remarkable for the production of biographies in rhymed prose, of a laudatory character, intended to cast lustre on the princes of the various dynasties which successively flourished on Iranian soil, as the power of the 'Abbâsid Caliphs faded. Abû Naṣr Muḥammad AL-'UTBÎ, who was born in Persia, came of a family of Arab extraction. He held important posts under the government of the empire founded by the Turkish chief Sabuk-Tekîn and his son Maḥmûd the Ghaznevid. He ended by being director of the horse post at Ganj-Rustâq. He died in 1036. His masterpiece, the *Kitâb al-Yamînî*, so called after the surname of the Sultan Maḥmûd, Yamîn al-daula (Right Arm of the Empire), is a history of that ruler's glorious reign down to the year 1018. The author took advantage of his presentation of this work to point out that he was being intrigued against by Abû'l-Ḥasan al-Baghawî, who had succeeded in ousting him from his post. The book, which is famous for its brilliancy of style, has been the subject of commentaries by various authors, and has been translated both into Persian and into English.

THE BIOGRAPHERS OF SALADIN

'IMÂD AL-DÎN (1125–1201), surnamed Al-Kâtib al-Iṣfahânî (the Secretary of Ispahan), devoted his pen to the history of his master, Saladin. He was called Alûh, a Persian word signifying *eagle*. Born at Ispahan, he went to Bagdâd to study at the Niẓâmiyya University. His protector, the minister 'Aun al-dîn Ibn Hubaira, procured him the lucrative post of Inspector of the Administrative Departments, first at Bassora and then at Wâsiṭ. But when his patron died, in 1165, he was dis-

missed and cast into prison, and for two years led a wretched life, till he made up his mind to go to Damascus, where he became known to Najm al-dîn Ayyûb and his son Saladin. Sultan Nûr al-dîn, son of the *atâbek* Zangî, gave him a post as copyist, and sent him on an embassy to Caliph Mustanjid. This mission earned him, when he returned to Bagdâd, the professorship of the newly built school, which was called by his name, Al-ʿImâdiyya, and, in the following year, his appointment to the presidency of the council. Nûr al-dîn's death brought about his downfall. The Caliph's son, who succeeded him in 1173, was a child, and ʿImâd al-dîn's enemies circumvented him, and forced him to relinquish his office and leave the court. He was on his way to Bagdâd, but, falling ill at Mosul, there heard that Saladin had seized Egypt and was marching on Syria. He succeeded in joining him at Aleppo; the great Moslem leader received him into his service, and took him with him on his campaigns. When his patron died, perceiving that his influence had departed, he retired into private life and devoted himself to literary work until his own death, on 20th June 1201. He thus wrote, under the title of *Fatḥ al-Qussî*, his history of Saladin's conquest of Syria and Palestine, which has been published by C. von Landberg; and, under that of *al-Barq al-shâmî*, the history of his own times, including his autobiography, in seven volumes. The fifth of these volumes is now in the Bodleian Library. His *Nuṣrat al-fatra* contains the history of the Seljûqid monarchs and their ministers; it really is an abridged translation, very pompous and exaggerated in style, of a Persian work by Sharaf al-dîn Anôsharwân. His *Kharîdat al-Qaṣr* is an anthology of the poets of the sixth century

of the Hegira, with comments written in a very pretentious style, and unfortunately containing scarcely any historical information ; it is a continuation of Tha'âlibî's *Yatîmat al-dahr*.

One of 'Imâd al-dîn's friends, known to us by his correspondence either with him or with other persons, was 'Abdal-Raḥîm ibn 'Alî of Ascalon, surnamed AL-QÂḌÎ AL-FÂḌIL (the excellent judge) (1135–1200). He was the son of the *qâḍî* of that small town in Palestine. He held posts in Egypt, was attached to the Secretarial Office in Cairo, then secretary to the Judge of Alexandria, and afterwards Secretary of State under the Fâṭimid Caliph Al-Ẓâfir and his successors. He continued in this office under Saladin, who appointed him Governor of Egypt during his own campaign in Syria. During a visit to Damascus he made the acquaintance of 'Imâd al-dîn, and they always remained friends. He died on the 26th of January 1200. Saladin's son and grandson, 'Azîz and Manṣûr, continued the favour extended to him by their predecessor.

Let us now continue the series of Saladin's biographers. Yûsuf ibn Râfi' Bahâ al-dîn of Aleppo was born at Mosul on the 6th of March 1145. Attracted by the renown of the Niẓâmiyya University, he went to Bagdâd, and was there employed as an assistant professor. Later he returned to Mosul, made the pilgrimage to Mecca, and then proceeded to Damascus, where he was honourably treated by Saladin, who appointed him military judge and *qâḍî* of Jerusalem in 1188. After his patron's death he retired to Aleppo, of which city he was *qâḍî* under Saladin's successors, and where he founded two *madrasas*, out of his own private fortune. His influence waned when 'Azîz resigned the sovereignty in

1231, and he lived another three years as a private citizen. The life of Saladin of which he is the author bears the title of *Al-Nawâdir al-Sulṭâniyya.* It has been published by Albert Schultens. Bahâ al-dîn also wrote a history of Aleppo, now preserved in manuscript in the Asiatic Museum at St. Petersburg, and some works on jurisprudence, which are at Paris, in the Bodleian, and at Cairo.

Shihâb al-dîn 'Abdal-Raḥmân ibn Ismâ'îl, surnamed ABÛ SHÂMA, because he had a blackish mole on his eyebrow, was born at Damascus on 10th January 1203. He studied in his native town, and also at Alexandria, and then returned to Damascus, where he taught in several *madrasas.* His house was attacked by a mob, which suspected him of having committed a crime, and he was so roughly handled that he was left for dead. Some time afterwards his enemies renewed their assaults, and he was assassinated on 13th June 1268. He wrote a history of the two Sultans Nûr al-dîn and Saladin, entitled *Kitâb al-Rauḍaṯain ;* it has been published and partially translated by Gœrgens and Röhricht, and has also appeared in the *Historiens des Croisades,* published by the Institut de France. He also left poems and commentaries on the panegyrics of the Prophet written by his master, Sakhâwi, and by Bûṣîrî.

Abû'l-Maḥâsin Muḥammad IBN 'UNAIN was born in the same city of Damascus on 20th October 1154. He was a precocious poet, and, having stirred Saladin's enmity by his biting attacks on all highly placed personages, he was banished. He wandered through Persia, Bukhârâ, India, and Yemen, where he remained for some time, then passed on into the Ḥijâz and to Egypt, and returned to Damascus after Saladin's death.

Saladin's successor gave him the title of vizier, and trusted him with diplomatic missions; he died on the 7th January 1233. He was a cheery, good-humoured man, with a facile talent for improvisation, and would answer rhymed riddles with others, yet more ingenious, containing the solution of the first question. He never took the precaution, during his lifetime, of collecting his poems into a volume, and they are now scattered and lost. The Berlin Library does possess an elegy written by him on the death of Al-Malik al-Mu'aẓẓam. The Turkish biographer Ḥâjî Khalfa saw and mentions his biography of Al-Malik al-'Azîz, the son of Saladin.

In Egypt, while Muḥyî al-dîn Abû'l-Faḍl al-Sa'dî (died 1293) was writing biographies of the Sultans Baibars and Ashraf, a Persian author was preparing a life in Arabic of Jalâl al-dîn Mankobirtî, Sultan of Khwârizm, the ill-fated adversary of Jengiz Khan. Muḥammad ibn Aḥmad AL-NASAWÎ was born at Khorendiz, near Nasâ: he became secretary to the Sultan when he returned from his expedition to India in 1221, and remained with him till his death in 1231. Ten years later he wrote the history of his patron, which has been translated into French and published by O. Houdas. As a historian he is cool and impartial, as a writer he is heavy. The reader generally feels that most of his Arabic phrases have been thought out in the Persian tongue.

THE AUTOBIOGRAPHY OF IBN MUNQIDH

Abû'l-Muẓaffar Usâma IBN MUNQIDH did something better than relate other folk's histories; he wrote his own, and was the first to introduce the novelty of an

autobiography. He was born on 25th June 1095, at Shaizar in Syria, a small fortress in the valley of the Orontes, the principal town of the hereditary principality of his family. He was exiled in 1138 by his uncle ʿIzz al-dîn, who feared his courage and ambition, and went to Damascus. His patron there, Shihâb al-dîn Maḥmûd, became prejudiced against him, and he departed to Egypt, where he gave his whole time to sport. In 1150 and 1153 he was fighting the Crusaders at Ascalon ; in the following year he returned to Damascus, made the Mecca pilgrimage, went with Nûr al-dîn on his campaign against the Franks in 1162, and afterwards took refuge at Ḥiṣn Kaifâ in Mesopotamia, where he devoted himself to literary pursuits. He was recalled to Damascus by Saladin, but he did not remain long in favour, nor follow the Conqueror of the Crusaders into Egypt. He died at the Syrian capital on 6th November 1188, leaving behind him his autobiography, which has been translated into French and published by H. Derenbourg, the *Kitâb al-badîʿ*, on the beauties and defects of poetic rhetoric, and the *Book of the Stick*, a monograph on celebrated sticks. Extracts from this work, and the few fragments of the author's poetry he has been able to bring together, have been published by Monsieur Derenbourg. Usâma was a man of original and observing mind, whose love of the chase led him to study the habits of wild animals. His natural bravery is reflected in the strong and simple style in which he tells his adventures : his poetical compositions are marked by literary skill.

Jamâl al-dîn ʿAlî ibn Ẓâfir, born in 1171, succeeded his father as a teacher in the Kâmiliyya Madrasa at Cairo, and subsequently acted as minister to Prince

Malik al-Ashraf. We owe him a history of past dynasties (*al-duwal al-munqaṭi'a*), down to 1225, and a collection of *bons mots* and witty replies entitled *Badâ'i' al-bidâya.* In 1226 Abû'l-Fatḥ al-Bundârî of Ispahan made an abridgment of 'Imâd al-din's history of the Seljûqids, under the title of *Zubdat al-nuṣra,* and translated the Persian poet Firdausî's *Book of Kings* into Arabic.

In the West the history of the Almohads engaged the attention of ABDAL-WÂḤID ibn 'Alî al-Marrâkushî, who was born at Morocco on 10th July 1185. Having finished his studies at Fez, he settled in Spain, and remained there till 1216. He then proceeded to Egypt, and continued in that country till his death, except when he made a short pilgrimage to Mecca. His *Kitâb al-Mu'jib,* written in 1224, has been translated by E. Fagnan and published by R. Dozy.

Jamâl al-dîn Muḥammad ibn Sâlim ibn Wâṣil, who was born in 1207, lived at Ḥamât in Syria, where he taught Shâfi'ite law, philosophy, mathematics, and astronomy. In 1261 the Egyptian Sultan Baibars summoned him to Cairo, and despatched him on a mission to Manfred, King of Sicily, son of Frederick II., for whom he wrote a short treatise on logic. On his return he was appointed *qâḍî* of his native town and professor at the *madrasa.* Under the title of *Mufarrij al-Kurûb,* he wrote a history of the Ayyûbites, which was continued up to 1296 by 'Alî ibn 'Abdal-Raḥmân, the secretary of Malik al-Muẓaffar, Prince of Ḥamât, and predecessor of the royal geographer Abû'l-Fidâ.

Abû'l-Ḥasan 'Alî ibn Yûsuf IBN AL-QIFṬÎ was thus surnamed after the little town of Qifṭ, the ancient Coptos, in Upper Egypt, where he was born in 1172.

He spent his whole life in Palestine and Syria. After a few years at Jerusalem, he settled, in 1202, at Aleppo. Malik al-Ẓâhîr, much against the historian's will, appointed him to govern that town in 1214, and as soon as that prince died he speedily rid himself of the responsibility. Yet he seems to have made himself indispensable, for twice over we see him again accept its duties, and he was discharging them at the time of his death, on 24th December 1248. He was a great lover of books, and had turned his back on all other earthly delights, so as to indulge his favourite passion. His principal work, *Ikhbâr al-'Ulamâ* (Information given to the Learned on the Subject of the History of the Wise), is known to us through an extract made from it in 1249, by Muḥammad ibn 'Alî al-Zauzanî, under the title of *Ta'rîkh al-ḥukamâ* (History of the Wise). These works have both been studied by A. Müller and J. Lippert. He also left a history of the grammarians, an extract from which, by Al-Dhahabî, is preserved at Leyden, and a posthumous work treating of the poets bearing the name of Muḥammad, which is now in the Paris Library.

Muwaffaq al-dîn Abû'l-'Abbâs IBN ABÎ UṢAIBI'A, the medical historian, was the son of an oculist settled at Damascus, and was born there in 1203. To complete his medical studies, which he had begun in Syria, he travelled to Cairo, where he met the botanist and physician Ibn Baiṭâr, who encouraged him. He kept up a correspondence with 'Abdallaṭîf, author of the *Account of Egypt*. Saladin appointed him to manage the hospital he founded at Cairo in 1236, but notwithstanding this, he responded in the following year to the summons of the Amîr 'Izz al-dîn Aidamir, and departed to Sarkhad in the Ḥaurân, near Damascus, where he

died in January 1270. His history of the physicians is called '*Uyûn al-anbâ*; it was published at Königsberg, by A. Müller, in 1884.

Shams al-dîn Abû'l-'Abbâs Aḥmad IBN KHALLIKÂN, whose family belonged to Irbil (Arbela) and was connected with the Barmakides, was born on 23rd September 1211. He was the son of a teacher in the Muẓaffariyya Madrasa at Irbil, and received his first lessons from his father. He then departed to Syria, was at Aleppo in 1229, at Damascus in 1234, and four years later at Alexandria and Cairo; for a time he filled the place of the Grand Qâḍî Yûsuf ibn al-Ḥasan of Sinjâr, and was appointed in 1264 to the important post of Grand Qâḍî of Syria, to reside at Damascus. This position was all the more influential because, though he himself was an adherent of the Shâfi'ite rite, the three other orthodox rites were all under his jurisdiction. In 1266, Sultan Baibars appointed separate *qâḍîs* for each of these, the Ḥanafite, Ḥanbalite, and Mâlikite, which considerably reduced Ibn Khallikân's importance, and five years later, he lost his post altogether. He then went to Cairo, to fill the post of professor in the Fakhriyya Madrasa, and took this opportunity of finishing, in the space of seven years, his great Biographical Dictionary. In 1280 he was reappointed *qâḍî*, but two years later he was so unlucky as to spend some weeks in prison, on suspicion of having abetted the governor of the town, who had revolted. Still he must have contrived to exculpate himself, for he was left in possession of his office till May 1281, when he was finally dismissed. He supported himself by teaching at the Amîniyya Madrasa till he died, on 30th October 1282. His *Wafayât al-A'yân* (The Deaths of Great Personages) is a diction-

ary of the famous men of Islam, with the exception of the companions of the Prophet, the four first Caliphs, and, broadly speaking, the personages of the first century of the Hegira. It was begun at Cairo in 1256, and finished in the same city in 1274, after an interruption caused by the author's mission to Damascus. The autograph manuscript is in the British Museum. The text has been published by Wüstenfeld. Its publication was also begun by MacGuckin de Slane, but was interrupted about half way. On the other hand, this Oriental scholar has given us a complete English translation of the work. Ibn Shâkir al-Kutubî, in his *Fawât al-Wafayât* (Omissions from the Book of Deaths), has written the biographies of illustrious persons not included in Ibn Khallikân's great work.

Abû Bakr Aḥmad AL-KHAṬÎB AL-BAGHDÂDÎ (the Preacher of Bagdâd) (1002–1071) was born in a large village on the Tigris, below that city, called Darzîjân. He was one of those learned men who wandered up and down the world, collecting traditions concerning the Prophet. His long journeys found their reward in the renown he gained as one of the chief masters of this branch of knowledge. He returned to Bagdâd, was appointed a preacher, and died there, leaving a history of the learned men of Bagdâd, in fourteen volumes, a treatise on the art of seeking out the authenticity of the traditions, entitled *al-Kifâya* (The Adequate Book), another (*Taqyîd al-'ilm*) to prove that traditions may be written down, and a third (*al-Mu'tanif*) on the correct manner of writing proper names.

Far away at Merv, in Khurâsân, Abû Sa'd 'Abdal-Karîm AL-SAM'ÂNÎ, surnamed *Tâj al-Islâm* (the Mitre of Islamism), who was born on 11th February 1113, had

left his own country to search out traditions, but he returned, and died there in January 1167. He wrote a supplement to Al-Khaṭîb's history of Bagdâd, in fifteen volumes, and the *Kitâb al-ansâb* (Book of Patronymics), in eight volumes, which is in the library of Muḥammad Kyüprulu at Constantinople, and which, according to a remark made by Sachau, is important as regards the history and proper names of Central Asia, on account of the biographical information it supplies. This great work has been abridged into three volumes by 'Izz al-dîn Ibn al-Athîr, in his *Lubâb*, and this again has been abridged by the polygraph Suyûṭî, in his *Lubb al-Lubâb*, published by Veth.

Damascus, the great Syrian city, also had her own historian, in the person of Ibn 'Asâkir ; and already possessed an historical topography, written in 1043, by Abû'l-Ḥasan 'Alî al-Raba'î, and entitled *I'lâm fî faḍâ'il al-Shâm*. Abû'l-Qâsim 'Alî Ibn 'Asâkir was born in September 1105. In 1126 he went to Bagdâd, and thence to Persia, to study the traditions of the Prophet. On his return he performed professional duties at the Nûriyya School, and died in his native town on 26th January 1176. Saladin himself attended his funeral. His *Ta'rîkh*, or history of the city of Damascus, is written on the same plan as the history of Bagdâd, that is to say, it is a collection of biographies of celebrated men of learning, who were either born at Damascus or spent some time there. The work is a large one, in eighty volumes, abridged in later days by various authors.

KAMÂL AL-DÎN Abû'l-Qâsim 'Umar Ibn al-'Adîm wrote the history of Aleppo, where he was born in 1191 or 1193. He belonged to a family of *qâḍîs*. Having travelled, for the sake of his studies, in Syria, the Ḥijâz and Mesopo-

tamia, he returned to his native town and discharged the duties of Departmental Secretary, of *qâḍî*, and even of minister to several princes, by whom he was also employed on diplomatic missions. He attended Malik al-Nâṣir to Egypt when that sovereign was obliged to abandon Aleppo to the devastations of the Mongols, who had taken possession of the town on 26th January 1260. Nevertheless, Hulâgû, grandson of Jengiz Khan, chose him to be Grand Qâḍî of Syria. Thus he returned to Aleppo, to find his birthplace in ruins, and mourned it in an elegy, of which a fragment has been preserved. But he died, not long after (21st April 1262), at Cairo. His great history is called *Bughyat al-Ṭâlib*: it is a history of the learned men of the city, in ten volumes. The author himself abridged it, and arranged it in chronological order, under the title of *Zubdat al-ḥalab* (The Cream of the Milk). Extracts from it have been published by Freytag, and it has been translated into French by Blochet. Kamâl al-dîn was a skilful caligrapher, and the St. Petersburg Library possesses some models of penmanship written by his hand.

Abû Muḥammad 'Umâra ibn 'Alî, who was born in Yemen in 1121, studied at Zabîd, went on pilgrimage to Mecca in 1154, and was sent by the Amîr of the sacred city, on a mission to Egypt, then ruled by the Fâṭimid Caliph Al-Fâ'iz. So successful was this embassy that, two years later, he was entrusted with another, and never returned to Yemen. He settled in Egypt in 1157, and hailed Saladin's conquest with a panegyric. At a later date he was mixed up in a plot to replace the son of the last of the Fâṭimid Caliphs on the throne, with the help of the Frank King of Jerusalem: the plot was betrayed, and 'Umâra was executed on 6th April

1175. H. Derenbourg has published his *Nukat al-'Aṣriyya* (Contemporary Subtleties), an autobiography, and accounts of the Egyptian viziers, together with a selection of poetry. Mr. H. Cassels Kay has translated and published his history of Yemen. His ode to Saladin appears in Maqrîzî's *Khiṭaṭ* and in Wüstenfeld's translation of Qalqashandî's geography of Egypt. Three stanzas written by him in praise of the pyramids have been translated into German by J. von Hammer in the *Mines of the East.*

In Egypt, likewise, flourished the Amîr AL-MUKHTÂR AL-MUSABBIḤÎ ('Izz al-Mulk Muḥammad), who came of a family belonging to Ḥarrân, and was born at Old Cairo in 976. He entered the Government service, and in 1007 was acting as secretary to the Fâṭimid Caliph Ḥâkim. He was appointed to administer certain districts in Upper Egypt, and was afterwards made head of the financial department of the Paymaster's Office. He died in April, 1029. One volume of his great history of Egypt is all we now possess out of the many books he wrote. This is in the Escurial Library.

Saladin's conquest of Egypt brought about the conversion to Islam of Abû'l-Makârim As'ad IBN AL-MAMMÂTÎ, who, with his family, was employed under the Government. His change of religion earned him the post of Minister of War. The enmity of the Vizier Ṣafî al-dîn 'Abdallah ibn Shukr obliged him to flee to Aleppo, where he took refuge with the prince who then ruled that town, Malik-Ẓâhir : and there he died, aged sixty-two, on 30th November 1200. In his *Qawânîn al-dawâwîn* he gives an account of Egyptian government under Saladin, and in his *Kitâb al-Fâshûsh*, which has been studied by J. Casanova, he satirises the

faulty administration of the Vizier Qarâqûsh. On this account it is, perhaps, that Qarâqûsh has become the Calino of magistrates in the East (*ḥukm qarâqûshî* is a sentence for which no ground exists, in which the specified "whereas" leads up to a perfectly illogical conclusion), and that legend has developed him into the type of the Oriental Punch, *Qaragyüz*. Ibn al-Mammâtî was a poet of some merit : his panegyric on the Conqueror of the Crusaders and his poem called *Kalîla and Dimna* are both lost.

ABÛ ZAKARÎYÂ Yaḥyâ ibn Abî Bakr was born at Wargla in Algeria ; he studied in Wad Rir', under the 'Ibâdite Sheikh, Sulaimân ibn Iḥlaf al-Mazatî, and died in 1078, having written a history of the 'Ibâdite imâms of Mzâb, which has been published by Masqueray.

Abû'l-Ḥasan 'Alî IBN SA'ÎD AL-MAGHRIBÎ, who was born in 1208 or 1214, at the castle of Yaḥṣub (Alcala Real), near Grenada, studied at Seville, and went with his father to Mecca in 1240. His father died at Alexandria in 1243, and Ibn Sa'îd, after some stay at Cairo, proceeded to Bagdâd, where he saw thirty-six libraries, and copied extracts from books contained in them, and thence to Aleppo and Damascus. On his return, he paid another visit to Mecca, came back to the West, and entered the service of the Amîr Abû 'Abdallah al-Mustanṣir, ruler of Tunis (1254). He was an inveterate traveller, and started again for the East in 1267. Desiring to know Hulâgû, whose victories had spread his fame far and wide, he went to that prince's court in Armenia, remained there some time, and returned to die, either at Tunis in 1286, as Suyûṭî and Maqqarî have it, or at Damascus in 1274, as Ibn Taghribirdî avers. Fragments of his *Mughrib* have been published by Vollers. In his *Basṭ al-arḍ*,

habitually used by Abû'l-Fidâ, he completed Ptolemy's Geography. The Bibliothèque Nationale now possesses the copy used by the Prince of Ḥamât. His '*Unwân al-Murqiṣât wa'l-Muṭribât* has been printed at Cairo. It contains samples of ancient and modern literature, arranged according to the author's own peculiar theory of taste. An extract from his *Qidḥ al-Mu'allâ*, which treats of the Spanish poets of the early part of the seventh century of the Hegira, is now in Paris.

Towards the end of this same century, Ibn al-Idhârî of Morocco wrote, under the title of *al-Bayân al-Mughrib*, a history of Africa and Spain, published at Leyden by R. Dozy.

In Spain, Abû'l-Walîd 'Abdallah Ibn al-Faraḍî wrote a history of the learned Moslems of that country, which has been published by F. Codera. He was born at Cordova in 962. On his way back from the Mecca pilgrimage, he passed through Egypt and Qairawân, where he finished his studies, and on his return to his own country, was appointed *qâḍî* at Valencia (1009). He was at Cordova when that city was taken and sacked by the Berbers in 1012, and lost his life in the carnage.

Abû Naṣr AL-FATḤ IBN KHÂQÂN came from Ṣakhrat al-Walad, a village near Alcala Real, not far from Grenada: as a youth he was a vagabond and a hard drinker: having succeeded in attracting the attention of Tâshifîn ibn 'Alî, Prince of Grenada, he obtained a post as secretary. He went to Morocco, and was strangled (1134 or 1140) in one of the caravanserais of the capital, possibly by order of 'Alî ibn Yûsuf ibn Tâshifîn, whose ire he had provoked by addressing verses to his brother Ibrâhîm, to whom he had also dedicated his *Necklaces of Native Gold and Beauties*

of the Great (Qalâ'id al-'Iqyân wa-maḥâsin al-A'yân), a work in rhymed prose, much admired for the splendour of its style; it contains anecdotes concerning princes, ministers of state, judges, and poets, with a selection from their poetical productions. The text of this book has been published in Paris by Sulaiman al-Ḥarâ'irî, and it has been translated by E. Bourgade. The *Maṭmaḥ al-anfus*, by the same author, published at Constantinople, seems to be no more than an earlier and less extended form of the same book.

Abû Marwân 'Abdal-Malik Ibn Badrûn, of Silves in Southern Portugal, who came of an old Ḥimyarite family which had emigrated, lived at Seville in the second half of the twelfth century, and wrote an historical commentary on Ibn 'Abdûn's poem, which has been published by R. Dozy.

Ibn al-Faraḍî's history of learned Spaniards was carried on by Abû'l-Qâsim Khalaf Ibn Bashkuwâl (Aben Pascualis), of Cordova, under the title of *Kitâb al-Ṣila* (The Gift): this work has been published by Codera. The author, who was born on 30th September 1101, was for some time an assistant judge at Seville. He died in his native town on 5th January 1183. Another biography of famous Spaniards of both sexes is the *Bughyat al-Mutalammis* (Desire of the Seeker), by Abû Ja'far Aḥmad ibn Yaḥyâ AL-ḌABBÎ, of Cordova. This work also contains a history of the conquest of Spain and of the Omeyyad Caliphs down to the year 1196. Ibn Bashkuwâl's *Ṣila* was continued by Abû 'Abdallah IBN AL-'ABBÂR, who was born at Valencia, and acted as secretary to the governor of that town, Muḥammad ibn Abî Ḥafṣ. When the governor's son, Abû Zaid, became a convert to Chris-

tianity, and betook himself to the court of the King of Aragon, Ibn al-ʿAbbâr was despatched on a mission to Africa to beg for help against the Christians, who were then laying siege to Valencia, and captured it, in 1235, in spite of the fleet brought back by the ambassador. He thereupon resolved to leave Europe, went to Tunis, and obtained a post as secretary in the *Dîvân*. He even rose to be vizier under Al-Mustanṣir. He was suspected of being involved in a conspiracy, and was murdered in his own house, by the prince's orders, 2nd January 1260. Besides the continuation already mentioned, he wrote the *Ḥullat al-siyarâ*, biographies of such princes and great men in Spain and Northern Africa as had been poets. His treatise on disgraced secretaries who recover favour, which earned him the renewed patronage of the Prince of Tunis, is now in the Escurial Library.

To return to the East. Abû ʿAlî Aḥmad ibn Muḥammad Ibn Maskawaih, treasurer and confidential adviser of the Buwaihid Prince ʿAḍud al-daula, died in 1030, after writing a universal history under the title of *Tajârib al-Umam*, the sixth book of which has been published at Leyden by De Goeje; a book of practical wisdom, called *Âdâb al-ʿArab wa'l-Furs* (Customs of the Arabs and Persians), which also deals with the Hindoos and Greeks; and a treatise on morality (*Tahdhîb al-Akhlâq*), which has been printed at Cairo.

An Egyptian magistrate, Abû ʿAbdallah Muḥammad ibn Salâma AL-QUḌÂʿÎ, who had studied the traditions, and Shâfiʿite law, at Bagdâd, and had been appointed *qâḍî*, was sent on an embassy to the Roman Emperor at Constantinople. When Abû'l-Qâsim ʿAlî al-Jarjarâ'î, whose two forearms had been cut off by order of the Caliph Al-Ḥâkim, was appointed vizier by the

Fâṭimid Caliph Al-Ẓâhir, in 1027, Al-Quḍâ'î was called on to perform the delicate and confidential duty of appending the seal which rendered the minister's decrees valid, to each document. He died at Old Cairo in 1062. He compiled, under the title of *Kitâb al-inbâ*, a universal history, from the creation of the world down to the eleventh century; under that of *'Uyûn al-Ma'ârif* (Sources of Knowledge), he wrote a history of the patriarchs, prophets, and Caliphs—Omeyyad, 'Abbâsid, and Fâṭimid; and under the name of *Shihâb* (The Flame), a treatise on such traditions of the Prophet as might serve as a basis of morality.

Abû'l-Ḥasan 'Alî 'Izz al-din IBN AL-ATHÎR, who was born at Jazîrat ibn 'Umar on the Tigris, at the base of the mountains of Kurdistan, on 13th May 1160, went to Mosul, when he was twenty years of age, with his father, who had just been dismissed from his post as governor. At Mosul he finished his education, and took advantage of his subsequent journeys to extend his knowledge of the traditions of the Prophet and of history, both at Bagdâd, whither he went several times, when on pilgrimage to Mecca or on missions from the Prince of Mosul, in Syria, and at Jerusalem. When he returned to Mosul, he lived as a private citizen, and devoted his leisure to work and study. His house became a rallying-point for learned men and foreigners. Ibn Khallikân met him at Aleppo in 1229 (he praises his excessive modesty); thence he went on, the next year, to Damascus. He returned to Aleppo, and then went back to Mosul, where he died in May 1234. His universal history, *al-Kâmil fî'l-ta'rîkh* (Complete Chronology), is carried down to the year 1231 : the portion covering the period from the Creation till the year of the Hegira 310

is an abridgment of Ṭabarî's work, to which, as lately demonstrated by Herr Brockelmann in a special dissertation, he has added certain information drawn from other sources. The text of this book has been published by Tornberg. The *Usd al-ghâba* (Lions of the Forest) is an historical treatise dealing with seven thousand five hundred companions of the Prophet : it has been printed at Cairo. This work is important because of its bearing on the history of the *ḥadîth*. In his *Lubâb* he has abridged Samʿânî's great work on patronymics.

Abû Isḥâq Ibrâhîm IBN ABÎ'L-DAM, who was born at Ḥamât in 1187, acted as Shâfiʿite *qâḍî* in that town. He was sent on an embassy to the Caliph Mustaʿṣim, with the object of inducing him to invest Malik-Manṣûr, Prince of Ḥamât, with the government of the district of Mayyâfâriqîn, which had fallen vacant owing to the death of Malik al-Muẓaffar Ghâzî (1244). The envoy fell sick on his way, was forced to turn back from Maʿarra to his native town, and there died shortly afterwards. To this same Malik al-Muẓaffar he had dedicated his *Ta'rîkh al-Muẓaffarî*, a general history of the Moslem peoples, in six volumes, which forms one of the sources whence Abû'l-Fidâ drew his information. That portion of the work which treats of Sicily has long been studied in Europe. As early as 1650 Inoegeo translated it into Italian, later (1723) Carusius translated it into Latin, and Gregorio (1790) gave it a place amongst his collection of Arabic works bearing on the history of the great Italian island.

Shams al-dîn Abû'l-Muẓaffar Yûsuf SIBṬ IBN AL-JAUZÎ, the son of a Turkish slave belonging to the minister Ibn Hubaira, set free and educated by him, was born at Bagdâd in 1186, and owed his surname to the

fact that his father had married the daughter of the famous preacher and polygraphist Ibn al-Jauzî, who brought up his grandson Yûsuf, for the boy's father died very soon after his birth. After prosecuting his studies at Bagdâd and travelling about, he settled at Damascus as a preacher and teacher of Ḥanafite law, and died in that city on 10th January 1257. His *Mir'ât al-Zamân* is a universal history, carried down to the year 1256; his *tadhkirat Khawâṣṣ al-umma* is a history of Caliph 'Alî and his family, and of the twelve imâms; a manuscript copy of this work is now at Leyden. Under the title of *al-Jalîs al-ṣâliḥ* (The Honest Comrade) he wrote a treatise on policy and on the education of princes, in honour of Mûsâ ibn Abî Bakr the Ayyûbite, which is now in the Gotha Library: the Paris Library possesses a collection of anecdotes called *Kanz al-Mulûk* (The Kings' Treasury).

But if there is one Arab historian whose name has long been known to the reader, he must be George AL-MAKÎN Ibn al-'Amîd (1205–1273), son of an unfrocked monk, a Christian employé at the Ministry of War, who was born at Cairo. He, like his father, entered the Government service, and was given a similar post at a very early age. When 'Alâ al-dîn Ṭîbars, Governor of Syria, fell into disgrace, all the persons employed in his office were conveyed to Egypt and imprisoned there. Amongst them went Al-Makîn and his father. The latter died in 1238; the son was soon set at liberty, and given back his post. He presently fell under suspicion once more, and spent some time in prison. These mishaps disgusted him with the public service; he retired to Damascus and died there. His universal history bears the title of *al-Majmû' al-Mubârak* (The

Blessed Collection); the second part, which covers the period between Mahomet's time and the year 1260, has been published and translated into Latin by Erpenius, into English by Purchas, and into French by Vattier.

Another Christian, a deacon of the Monophysite creed at the Church of the Virgin in Old Cairo, called *Mu'allaqa* (The Suspended), Abû Shukr Buṭrus (Petrus) Ibn al-Râhib, who was still alive in 1282, wrote a universal history carried down to 1259, which was translated into Latin by the learned Maronites, Abraham Ecchelensis, in 1651, and J. S. Assemani, in 1729.

Yûḥannâ ABÛ'L-FARAJ, also known under his Latinised Syrian name of BAR-HEBRÆUS (the son of the Hebrew), was the son of a baptized Jewish physician of Malatia, named Ahrôn. He was born in 1226, accompanied his father to Antioch in his flight before the Mongol invasion (1243), there became a monk, and lived the life of an anchorite in a cave; later he went as far as Tripoli, in Syria, to study dialectics and medicine. On 12th September 1246 he was appointed Bishop of Gubos, near Malatia, and in that quality assumed the name of Gregory. The Bishopric of Aleppo rewarded him, in 1252, for the zeal displayed in securing the election of the new Jacobite Patriarch, Dionysius. In 1264 he was appointed *maphrian* (Archbishop of the Eastern Jacobites). Mosul was the nominal seat of his see, but he usually lived in the Persian towns of Tabrîz and Marâgha, the habitual residence of the Mongol emperors of Persia. In the last-named town he died, on 30th July 1289. He displayed considerable activity in Syriac literature, but in this place we can only refer to his Arabic works. The *Mukhtaṣar al-duwal* (Epitome of Dynasties) is, in fact, an epitomised history, to which

its author has added information as to the medical and mathematical literature of the Arabs. It is an amplified translation of his Syrian chronicle, made, a short time before his death, at the request of a Moslem ; it has been published at Oxford, by E. Pococke, and at Beyrout, by the Rev. Father Salhani, and has been translated into German by Bauer.

The legendary history of the Hebrew prophets, as it reached the Arabs through the oral traditions preserved by the Jews of the Arabian Peninsula, has been treated by Abû Isḥâq Aḥmad al-Tha'labî of Nîshâpûr, a Shâfi'ite jurisconsult, who died in 1036. His *'Arâ'is al-majâlis* (The Brides of the Lectures) has been printed at Cairo. A more serious production is his *Al-Kashf wa'l-bayân* (Inquiry and Exposition), a commentary on the Koran : a curious little work on the victims of the Koran, entitled *Kitâb mubârak* (Blessed Book), is devoted to the story of those who died of listening to the reading of the sacred book.

The *Maṣâri' al-'ushshâq* is a collection of tales, anecdotes, and poetry, touching love and lovers, written by Abû Bakr Muḥammad ibn Ja'far Ibn al-Sarrâj of Bagdâd, who was born about 1027 and died in 1106. The success of this work accounts for its having been given an abridged form in the *Aswâq al-ashwâq* (Markets of Love) by Ibrâhîm ibn 'Umar al-Biqâ'î (died 1106), and for this latter book having furnished matter for a process of selection of which we have the fruit in the *Tazyîn al-aswâq* (Ornament of the Markets), arranged by Dâ'ûd al-Anṭâkî (died 1599).

Ḥujjat al-dîn Muḥammad IBN ẒAFAR, who was born in Sicily and brought up at Mecca, lived in his native country, and died at Ḥamât in 1169, leaving behind

him the *Sulwân al-Muṭâʿ* (Consolation of the Prince), a political treatise; the *Inbâ nujabâ al-abnâ*, characteristic traits and anecdotes of famous children—the manuscript of this work is in the Bibliothèque Nationale—and the *Khair al-bushar*, a collection of prophecies concerning the prophets.

The celebrated caligrapher Yâqût al-Mustaʿṣimî (Jamâl al-dîn Abû'l-Durr), who died at Bagdâd in 1298, compiled an anthology of anecdotes and poetry under the title of *Akhbâr wa-ashʿâr* (Tales and Poems), and a collection of sentences and apophthegms, called *Asrâr al-ḥukamâ* (Secrets of the Wise).

The Fables of Kalîla and Dimna

Some literary men had begun to translate works of a class not existing in Arabic literature, out of the Pehlevi tongue. It need scarcely be said that this labour was undertaken by Persians, who were equally skilful in the use of both languages. ʿAbdallah Ibn al-Muqaffaʿ was a Persian, who, before he became a convert to Islam, bore the name of Rûzbih. He lived at Bassora, where he became the close friend of Khalîl, the grammarian. He was put to death in 757 by order of Caliph al-Manṣûr, whose anger he had stirred by the fashion in which he had drawn up the deed of amnesty touching his uncle ʿAbdallah ibn ʿAlî. The Governor of Bassora eagerly seized this opportunity for avenging the sarcasms of which he had been made a victim by the Persians; he had his enemy's limbs cut off and thrown into an oven. Ibn al-Muqaffaʿ translated the fables of Kalîla and Dimna out of the Pehlevi into Arabic. These fables are simply an adaptation of the Indian tales of

the Panchatantra, originally brought back from India in the time of Chosroes I. Nûshîrwân, by the physician Barzûya. He also wrote the *Durra al-Yatîma*, on the obedience due to kings, which has been printed at Cairo, and the *Siyar Mulûk al-ʿAjam* — biographies of the Persian kings, translated from a Pehlevi book, *Khudâi-nâma*, which was produced during the reign of the last of the Sâsânians, Yezdegird III. This book was one of the sources whence the Persian poet Firdausî later drew the elements of his *Book of the Kings*. The Arabic translation is lost, but numerous fragments of it occur in Ibn Qutaiba's ʿ*Uyûn al-akhbâr*. Ibn al-Muqaffaʿ's father's name was Dâdawaih. He had been charged, under the rule of the famous and cruel Ḥajjâj, with the duty of collecting the taxes in the Provinces of ʿIrâq and Fârs, and was guilty of extortion. Ḥajjâj had him put to the torture, and as a result one of his hands always remained shrunk and curled up—hence the surname of Muqaffaʿ. ʿAbdallah was in the service of ʿÎsâ ibn ʿAlî, the paternal uncle of the Caliphs Abû'l-ʿAbbâs Saffâḥ and Manṣûr. It was to him that he addressed his abjuration of Zoroastrianism. He has been accused, with other enemies of Islam, of having endeavoured to imitate the style of the Koran, and would in this case have been a predecessor of the contemporary renewer of Islamism in Persia, ʿAlî Muḥammad the Bâb, who also wrote in the Koranic style. Khalîl said of him that he had more learning than judgment; it is true that Ibn al-Muqaffaʿ had said the grammarian had more judgment than learning.

He was asked, one day, to say from whom he had learnt the rules of politeness. "I have been my own teacher," he replied. "Whenever I have seen another

man do a good action, I have followed his example, and whenever I have seen any one do an ill-bred thing, I have avoided doing it."

ANTHOLOGIES

'Amr ibn Baḥr, surnamed AL-JÂḤIẒ (With a wide-open and goggle eye), was a man of extraordinarily varied intelligence, who turned his mind to many subjects, and produced many works, more with a view to amusement than instruction. He lived at Bassora. Theologically speaking, he was a Mu'tazilite, but he nevertheless created a sect which was called after his own name, Jâḥiẓiyya. He was the friend of Ibn al-Zayyât, minister to the Caliph Al-Wâthiq, and very nearly shared his fate when he was put to death by Mutawakkil. However, the Caliph, to whom he had been recommended, sent for him to Bagdâd, to superintend his own son's education. But on seeing how ugly he was he immediately dismissed him, with a gift of ten thousand dirhems. He owed his surname, indeed, to his projecting eyeballs.

He died in 869. Towards the end of his life he was attacked by a kind of paralysis, which inflamed one side of his body, while the other remained so cold and devoid of sensation that he felt nothing, even if it was dragged with pincers. During his illness he often said: "Sicknesses of opposite kinds have conspired against my body. If I eat anything cold, it strikes my feet, and if I touch anything hot, it goes to my head." He was ninety-six years old, "and that is the burden that weighs least upon me," he would say.

Amongst his works, reference must be made to the *Kitâb al-Bayân wa'l-tabayyun* (not *tabyîn*, as it has been

printed), a book on rhetoric, but with no didactic character at all. Its teaching is conveyed through the medium of anecdotes of the most varied description. The text of this work has been published at Cairo. His Book of Animals (*Kitâb al-ḥayawân*) is not precisely a treatise on natural history, but rather an anthology of passages in which animals are mentioned, with what has been said about them. He also wrote a book on the conduct of kings, which is full of interesting details on the rules of etiquette; a book on misers—scenes drawn from the private life and customs of the natives of Bassora, which has lately been published at Leyden by G. van Vloten; another on the virtues of the Turks, a copy of which was at one time in the Schefer collection, and is now in the Bibliothèque Nationale; a parallel between spring and autumn, which has been printed at Constantinople under this author's name, although the proof of its being his work is by no means trustworthy; and a collection of one hundred apophthegms, which were attributed, without any real cause, to ʿAlî, the Prophet's son-in-law, and which attained great popularity. Besides all this, he has been taken to be the author of the *Kitâb al-Maḥâsin* (Book of Beauties and Antitheses), the Arabic text of which has appeared at Leyden, thanks to the care of Van Vloten; this is, at all events, the direct outcome of his school.

Under the title of *Al-Faraj baʿd al-Shidda* (Pleasure after Pain), IBN ABÎ'L-DUNYÂ (Abû Bakr ibn ʿAbdallah) wrote a compilation of anecdotes and short moral tales, on the model, and with the same name, as one of Al-Madâ'inî's works, now lost. He was born in 823, and, though a client of the Omeyyads, was appointed tutor to the Caliph Al-Muktafî, when that

monarch was a child. He died in 894. His *Makârim al-Akhlâq* (Noble Qualities) is a moral treatise on the human ideal, according to the traditions of the Prophet. His *Dhamm al-malâhî* (Blame of Musical Instruments) is a treatise of the same nature, directed against dissipation in general, which, he avers, begins with music and ends in drunkenness and debauchery. He wrote many others which either only exist in manuscript or are merely known to us through quotations.

IBN 'ABD-RABBIHI (Abû 'Umar Aḥmad ibn Muḥammad), born at Cordova in 860, was descended from a freedman of the Omeyyads who ruled in Spain. He was at once a classical and a popular poet, and died in 940, after having suffered, for several years, from paralysis. He was the author of another well-known anthology, *Al-'Iqd al-Farîd* (The Unique Necklace), divided into twenty-five chapters, the pearls forming the necklace, the thirteenth chapter being the central and largest pearl.

AL-TANÛKHÎ (Abû 'Alî Muḥsin) (939–994), son of the *qâḍî* and poet 'Alî ibn al-Ḥusain, who was born at Bassora, wrote a *Faraj ba'd al-Shidda* (Collection of Stories to Drive away Boredom), modelled on works by Madâ'inî and Ibn Abî'l-Dunyâ. This author acted as *qâḍî* in various towns near the Euphrates and in Susiana. He also wrote a *Kitâb al-Mustajâd*, a collection of anecdotes and characteristic traits, in the time of the 'Abbâsids, and the *Nashwân al-muḥâḍara* (Stimulus to Conversation), which is a book of the same kind, now in the Bibliothèque Nationale. When he wrote his *Faraj* (957) he was at the head of the Weighing Office at the Mint of al-Ahwâz, in Susiana.

CHAPTER VIII

THE 'ABBÂSIDS—*Continued*

THE TRADITIONS OF THE PROPHET—JURISPRUDENCE

THE Koran alone did not suffice to provide laws for so great an empire; it became necessary, at a very early period, to cast light on its precepts by means of the explanations furnished by Mahomet himself, transmitted, more or less faithfully, through the medium of human memory, at Medina and elsewhere. By the time an attempt was made to commit these sayings of the Prophet to writing, the mischief was already done—the greater part had been deformed by untrustworthy memories; others, again, had been fabricated from beginning to end, to justify the tendencies of certain groups of dissidents. Then was created the science of the *ḥadîth*, that is to say, of criticism as applied to the sources of tradition, all of them of the same nature, since all necessarily went back to the study of the testimony of the succession of oral witnesses who transmitted the Prophet's sayings by word of mouth, as they had received them from his companions, who had heard them spoken, and learnt them by heart. This science of the *ḥadîth*, as it was understood by the Arabs, really follows the course prescribed for a Moslem judge, who, before he permits any witness to give evidence, must inquire

into his moral character, his manner of life, and his reputation for uprightness. By this system of criticism a sustained chain of evidence has been established as to a certain number of these apophthegms; it can only guarantee the authenticity of the transmission, not that of the original tradition. All we have to vouch for the truth of that is the veracity and good memory of the man who received it, in the first instance, from the Prophet's lips.

The first works devoted to the *ḥadîth*, then, are works on jurisprudence. After those of Mâlik ibn Anas and Aḥmad Ibn Ḥanbal, we must notice the *Musnad*, in which the traditions are arranged in the order of the most recent witnesses, without any regard to the subject matter contained. After these come the books known as *Muṣannaf*, in which the traditions are arranged by their contents, and divided into chapters according to the various subjects, ritual, legal, or moral, whereof they treat. The object of adopting this arrangement was to render inquiry relatively easy to those jurists who favoured adherence to the letter of the *ḥadîth*, in opposition to their opponents, who recognised interpretations founded on the sense accepted by individual judges (*aṣḥâb al-ra'y*). The earliest work of this description, and one which is still looked on as a pattern and a masterpiece, is the *Ṣaḥîḥ* (Sincere Book), by BÛKHÂRÎ. Abû 'Abdallah Muḥammad ibn Ismâ'îl was born at Bukhârâ on 21st July 810, of an Iranian family. His grandfather was called Berdizbeh, or Yezdizbeh. When he was sixteen, he went on pilgrimage to Mecca, and took this opportunity of attending the lessons given by teachers of the tradition at Mecca and Medina. He then went on to Egypt, and travelled with the same

object all over Moslem Asia, spending five whole years at Bassora. After an absence of sixteen years in all, he returned to Bukhârâ, and there wrote his *Ṣaḥîḥ*. He died on 30th August 870. The Governor of Khurâsân had banished him to Kharteng, a village in the neighbourhood of Samarqand. While he was at Medina he wrote his great historical work on the trustworthy traditionists. The manuscript of this work is now in the St. Sophia Library. When he returned to Bukhârâ, he brought back six hundred thousand traditions with him, and out of these he chose seven thousand two hundred and seventy-five, which alone are included in the *Ṣaḥîḥ* and which, according to his view, are the only ones universally admitted to be authentic. He also wrote a commentary on the Koran.

Another *Ṣaḥîḥ* was written at the same period by a contemporary of Bukhârî, MUSLIM (Abû'l-Ḥusain ibn al-Ḥajjâj), who was born at Nîshâpûr in Khurâsân in 817, paid several visits to Bagdâd, and died in the city of his birth on 6th May 875. The matter of Muslim's book, like that contained in Bukhârî's (with which it is identical, save for the addition of more authorities), is arranged in the order adopted for legal subjects, but without any chapter headings. It is also remarkable for its introduction, wherein the author treats of the science of the traditions in a general and complete manner.

He, too, went to the Ḥijâz, to ʿIrâq, Syria, and Egypt, to search out traditions. He is said to have collected more than three hundred thousand, on which his selection is based. The friendship between Muslim and Bukhârî survived even the persecutions which drove the latter author from his native city. Muslim defended his friend's cause against certain theologians who affirmed the

doctrine that not only was the Koran itself eternal, as being the word of God, but that the same rule applied to the pronunciation of the words of which it is composed.

These two *Ṣaḥîḥs*, Bukhârî's and Muslim's, have become two canonical books of Islam. They may be considered to sum up the science of tradition in the third century of the Hegira. Four other works complete the six canonical books to which Moslems pin their faith: they were all produced during the same period. These are the *Sunan* (Customs), by Abû Dâ'ûd (Sulaimân ibn al-Ash‘ath), who belonged to Sijistân, and was born in 817. After long wanderings in foreign countries, like those undertaken by his fellow-authors, he settled at Bassora, and died there in February 889. His work only contains those traditions which are interesting as regards jurisprudence or the rules affecting ritual. This work, at the outset, gained immense popularity, equalling that attained by the *Ṣaḥîḥs*, but it ultimately fell into complete obscurity, whereas the authority of the works of Muslim and Bukhârî has increased steadily until the present day. Abû Dâ'ûd had collected some five hundred thousand traditions, four thousand eight hundred of which he selected for his book. He was not very critical, for he himself acknowledged he had inserted not only the authentic traditions, but others which seemed authentic, and yet others which were nearly authentic: but he added that out of this number, only four were indispensable for the religious guidance of man. Here is his summary of Islamic law: "Actions will be judged according to intentions: the proof of a Moslem's sincerity is that he pays no heed to that which is not his business: no man is a true believer unless he

desires for his brother that which he desires for himself: that which is lawful is clear, and that which is unlawful likewise, but there are certain doubtful things between the two, from which it is well to abstain."

Under the title of *Jâmi'* (Complete Collection), Abû 'Îsâ Muḥammad AL-TIRMIDHÎ has written a kind of encyclopædia of the traditions which throw light upon the law, pointing out those which have served as arguments in such and such legal questions, and indicating the differences between the various schools of jurisprudence. This renders his book, which has been printed at Bûlâq, one of the first importance to the student desirous of keeping the schools distinct from their original beginnings. He was a pupil of Bukhârî, was born at Bûsh near Tirmidh, a small town on the banks of the Oxus in Central Asia, and died at the same place in 892, having, like his fellows, travelled all over the world to seek out traditions. Besides his book on the *ḥadîth*, we have his *Kitâb al-shamâ'il*, on the physiognomy and external qualities of the Prophet Mahomet, a book on which more than ten commentaries have been written, and the text of which has been printed at Calcutta, at Cairo, and at Fez, and also a collection of forty selected traditions, intended to sum up the principles of Moslem law. This is the first known specimen of a work of this nature—they were eventually to swarm.

Another *Sunan* is that of Abû 'Abdal-Raḥmân Aḥmad AL-NASÂ'Î, remarkable for his useful inquiries into the smallest details of ritual. (My readers are aware that the cases of conscience set forth and decided by Moslem casuists, on such points as degrees of bodily impurity, the nature of the water used for ablutions, &c., are exceedingly subtle and far-fetched.) He quotes texts for

every case, even for popular manifestations of religious feeling. In the part dealing with jurisprudence, he provides formulas for every possible case in law. The book is therefore an ample formulary of ritual and legal casuistry; it furnishes very little information as to the history of dogma. The author was born at Nasâ in Khurâsân in 830. He went to Old Cairo, where he lived till 914: he then departed to Damascus, and there stirred up popular opinion by a book of traditions favourable to the family of 'Alî. The mob, which still clung to the memory of the Omeyyads, drove him out of the Mosque, and trampled him under foot. He was taken to Ramla in Palestine, and there died of the effects of the treatment he had received. One author, however, asserts that he was conveyed to Mecca, and was buried there. He has left us another book, on the *weak* traditionists—that is to say, those in whom only a limited confidence can be placed. This work is now to be found, in manuscript, in the British Museum, and also in the Bodleian Library. Nasâ'î was a man of strong passions, and, to keep them under, was in the habit of fasting every second day.

The fourth of these works is the *Sunan* of IBN MÂJA (Abû 'Abdallah Muḥammad ibn Yazîd) (824–887), of Qazvîn in Persia, who travelled over the whole East, from Khurâsân to Egypt. The success of this book was but mediocre, on account of the number of doubtful traditions it contains: it was not included among the canonical books till at a later date. It has been lithographed at Delhi. Ibn Mâja also wrote a history, now lost, of his native town.

Besides these six *corpuses* of Moslem law and traditions, we have the *Musnad* of AL-DÂRIMÎ ('Abdallah ibn

'Abdal-Raḥmân) of Samarqand, who died in 869. This does not contain more than a third of the matter the first six embrace, and is drawn up for practical use. It has been lithographed at Cawnpore. Ibn Ḥibbân (Muḥammad ibn Aḥmad) (885–965), who was born at Bust in Sijistân, between Herât and Ghazna, and may have been of Iranian origin, travelled far and wide, from Central Asia to Alexandria, and, on his return, was appointed *qâḍî* of Samarqand, Nasâ, and Nîshâpûr. He finally went back to his native town, as a teacher of the traditions, and died there. He had built himself a house, in which he arranged his large library. He studied astronomy, medicine, and other sciences. His book bears the title of *Taqâsim wa'l-anwâ'*.

Abû Bakr AL-ÂJURRÎ (Muḥammad ibn al-Ḥusain), who was born at Âjurr (The Bricks), a village near Bagdâd, is the author of a book of forty traditions, which brought him fame, and is now to be found, with other works by the same author—such as a treatise on the question of whether the true believer ought to seek learning, and what qualities those who carry the Koran should possess—in the Berlin Library.

Abû'l - Ḥasan 'Alî ibn 'Umar AL-DÂRAQUṬNÎ, who owes his surname to a large quarter in the town of Bagdâd, called Dâr al-Quṭn (House of Cotton), was born in that city in April 919. He was a celebrated jurisconsult of the Shâfi'ite rite. He learnt the traditions at an early age, at the feet of Abû Bakr, son of Mujâhid, and was his true successor. Towards the end of his life he began to teach the reading of the Koran. He knew the *dîwâns* of several of the desert poets by heart, amongst them that of Sayyid Ḥimyarî. This made many believe he was a follower of this poet's Shî'ite

tenets. He was a man of scrupulous conscience. Once, having been called to bear witness against Ibn Ma'rûf, he repented, after it was done, because his evidence as to the traditions had been accepted by the judge without any demur, and merely on his own authority, whereas as a rule two witnesses are considered necessary. Having heard that Ja'far ibn Ḥinzâba, the vizier of the Ikhshîdite Prince Kâfûr, in Egypt, had made up his mind to prepare a *Corpus* of traditions after the manner of the *Musnad*, he resolved to take the journey into Egypt, to assist him in the work. He remained in that country, where he was liberally rewarded, till it was concluded. He died on his return to his native city (December 995). His *Kitâb al-Sunan* (Book of Customs) is in the St. Sophia Library. In another work (*al-istidrâkât wa'l-tatabbu'*) he proves the uncertainty of two hundred of the traditions accepted in the two *Ṣaḥîḥs* of Bukhârî and Muslim. The book is thus a critical work, dealing with the traditions.

AL-KHAṬṬÂBÎ (Ḥamd ibn Muḥammad), whose name was popularly pronounced Aḥmad, instead of Ḥamd, was born at Bust in Sijistân, in 931, and died in the same town in March 998. His works are commentaries on the great canonical books. Towards the close of his life he inclined to mysticism, and took refuge in a *ribâṭ* or Ṣûfî convent, on the banks of the river Hilmend. He had studied in 'Irâq. He was a poet, and it was he who said: "It is not the pain of absence, but the lack of a sympathetic friend, which is the greatest affliction a man can endure. I am a stranger to Bust and its people, yet here I was born, and here my kinsfolk dwell."

AL-BAYYI' (Muḥammad ibn 'Abdallah), born at Nîshâpûr in 933, was appointed *qâḍî* of his native town in 966,

but he made a long journey through Khurâsân and the Ḥijâz during the following years. Later, although appointed *qâḍî* of Jurjân, he declined the post, and was frequently employed by the Sâmânids on embassies to the Buwaihids, who, through their conquest of Bagdâd, had become masters of the Caliphate. He died on 3rd August 1014. He made a second journey through the East in 971, and held successful disputations with the learned men of the different cities in which he halted. He leant, at that time, towards the doctrines of the Shî'ites. He wrote his *Kitâb al-Mustadrak* as a criticism of the two *Ṣaḥîḥs*, to prove that several traditions overlooked in these two works were perfectly authentic, and had been wrongly passed over.

IBN FÛRAK, of Ispahan (Abû Bakr Muḥammad ibn al-Ḥasan), was educated at Bagdâd, and afterwards proceeded to Rai, where his stay was rendered uncomfortable by certain innovators in religious matters, and thence to Nîshâpûr, where he was exceedingly successful both as a teacher and a writer. He was later summoned to Ghazna in Afghanistan, where he carried on numerous controversies. He was on his way back from this town when he died of poison. He was known as *Ustâd*, the Master *par excellence*. A college and a dwelling-house were built on purpose for him. His body was conveyed to Nîshâpûr, and the funeral chapel erected there became a place of pilgrimage. When rain was wanted for the country, prayers were offered on his tomb, and were always answered. One of his sayings was as follows : "The burden of a family is the result of a lawful passion ; what then can be the result of an unlawful one ?" His book defining the foundations of Ḥanafite law is in the British Museum : the Leyden

Library possesses his treatise on certain traditions: other works of his are in the library of Râghib-Pacha at Constantinople.

Criticism of the Authorities of the Ḥadîth

Alongside of the science of the *ḥadîth*, which is one of codification and criticism, there rises up, in the tenth century, that called *'ilm al-rijâl*—strictly speaking, the science of men, which is specially applied to the criticism of the witnesses and authorities on whom the whole edifice of tradition rests. Among the most important authors who have written on this subject we may mention Ibn Abî Ḥâtim ('Abdal-Raḥmân), born at Rai in 894, died at Ṭûs in Khurâsân in 939, author of the *Kitâb al-jarḥ wa'l-ta'dîl* (Criticism and Correction), in six volumes, the manuscript of which is both at Cairo and at Constantinople: Al-Ṭabarânî (Abû'l-Qâsim Sulaimân) (870–971), born at Tiberias, who spent thirty years in travel, then settled at Ispahan, and died there; his best known work is the *Mu'jam* (Alphabetical Dictionary of the Traditionists), of which he furnished three editions, one complete, one of middle size, and one abridged; the isolated volumes now in Paris, at the British Museum, and the Escurial belong to this last edition: Al-Kalâbâdhî (Abû Naṣr Aḥmad), born in 918, in one of the quarters of Bukhârâ, from which his surname was derived, died in 398 (1008), leaving a work on the names of the *ḥuffâẓ* quoted in Bukhârî's *Ṣaḥîḥ*: also 'Abdal-Ghanî ibn Sa'îd, the Egyptian, born at Cairo in 944, who, with the two philologists Abû Usâma Junâda and Abû 'Alî al-Ḥasan, of Antioch, frequented the library founded by the Caliph Al-Ḥâkim; this friendship was

broken in sad fashion by the execution of the two philologists, on the Caliph's order, and 'Abdal-Ghanî, alarmed for his own life, remained in hiding till he felt he was safe. He died in the night of 25th–26th June 1018, leaving a book on the names of traditionists resembling each other, and those which differ. It is now in the library of Kyüprulu Mehemet-Pacha at Constantinople.

Subsequent Development of the Ḥadîth

The science of the traditions, which reached its highest point in the composition of the six great books, now approaches the period when it became necessary to abridge, commentate, and explain the codes left by the famous authors. Before long the fundamental rules of the Moslem faith were summed up, for the benefit of the general public, into a selection of forty traditions, and these, in their turn, became the subject of endless commentaries. My readers will understand that only those works, out of this very large body, which have earned some lasting success and produced some durable impression, can be mentioned here.

In Egypt, Abû'l-Qâsim al-Ḥusain ibn 'Alî al-Wazîr al-Maghribî was born in 981, of an important family of Persian descent. His great-great-grandfather's name was Bahrâm. When, on 10th July 1010, the Fâṭimid Caliph Al-Ḥâkim caused the chief members of his family to be put to death, he fled to Ramla, and induced the prince who governed that town to rise against his suzerain, but in spite of the support afforded by the Sharîf of Mecca, who was defeated, the undertaking failed, the prince of Ramla made terms with the savage Ḥâkim, and Abû'l-Qâsim departed into Eastern regions,

where he filled high official posts in the service of the princes of those countries. At the time of his death, at Mayyâfâriqîn (in 1027 or 1037), he was acting as minister to Prince Ibn Marwân. Of his literary work nothing now remains. The British Museum possesses the *Kitâb al-inâs*, a dictionary, in alphabetical order, of the names of the Arab tribes, with quotations from the poets, and historical and biographical notices.

Abû Bakr ibn al-Ḥusain AL-BAIHAQÎ (994–1066) was born in the village of Khusraugird, a dependency of Baihaq, near Nîshâpûr in Khurâsân, travelled for a long time, seeking traditions of the Prophet, and taught Shâfiʻite law at Nîshâpûr, where he died. He was the first writer to collect the sentences or legal opinions of Al-Shâfiʻî into ten volumes. One large collection of traditions bears the title of *Kitâb al-sunan wa'l-âthâr*. Of this an autograph manuscript, and also an abridgment, are now preserved at Cairo.

The Amîr Abû Naṣr ʻAlî IBN MÂKÛLA was also of Persian origin. He was born at ʻUkbarâ, not far from Bagdâd, on 9th August 1030. His father, Hibat-Allah, became minister to the Caliph Al-Qâ'im ; he went with him to Bagdâd, where his uncle was *qâḍî*, and then undertook long journeys. During one of these, on Persian territory, he was murdered and stripped by his Turkish slaves. The exact date of this event is not known (towards 1094). He had devoted himself to the study of proper names. We still have his *Ikmâl* (Completion), intended to complete the *Mu'tanif*, by Al-Khaṭîb al-Baghdâdî, on the same subject. It is, according to Ibn Khallikân, an exceedingly useful and practical work, determining the orthography of proper names, more especially in the study of the traditions.

Abû'l-Faḍl Muḥammad ibn Ṭâhir IBN AL-QAISARÂNÎ was born at Jerusalem, of a family belonging to Cesarea in Palestine, on 18th December 1058; but he finished his education at Bagdâd, and did not return to his native town till after a prolonged course of travel. He stayed for some time at Hamadhân, where he taught the science of the traditions. He died in 1113, at Bagdâd, on his return from the Mecca pilgrimage. His *Kitâb al-ansâb al-muttafiqa* has been published by De Jong under the title of *Homonyma inter nomina relativa.* Berlin possesses his manuscript treatise on falsified traditions; his *Aṭrâf al-gharâ'ib* is at Cairo.

Abû Muḥammad al-Ḥusain AL-FARRÂ AL-BAGHAWÎ, born at Baghshûr, between Herât and Merv, died in the last-named town in 1116 or 1122, after having compiled a book of traditions (*Maṣâbîḥ al-Sunna*), according to the seven fundamental works, which has been frequently commentated and abridged, as, for example, in the *Mishkât al-Maṣâbîḥ* of Muḥammad ibn 'Abdallah al-Khaṭîb al-Tabrîzî, which is widely known in the East, and has been reprinted in India and in Russia. Another collection of traditions (*Sharḥ al-Sunna*), an epitome of jurisprudence, and a commentary on the Koran have survived to the present day.

'ABD AL-GHÂFIR ibn Ismâ'îl AL-FÂRISÎ, born at Nîshâpûr in 1059, travelled through the Khânate of Khiva, and proceeded to India by Afghanistan. He had been an infant prodigy. When only five years old he could read the Koran, and recite the Articles of the Faith in Persian. When he came back from his travels, he was appointed preacher in his native town, and died there in 1134. To him we owe one of those *Kitâb al-Arba'în* in which the doctrines of

Islam are summed up in forty selected traditions. A more useful work is his *Majmaʿ al-Gharâʾib* (Collection of Curiosities), a dictionary for the great collections of the *ḥadîth*, and his *Mufhim*, a commentary on Muslim's *Ṣaḥîḥ*.

Another learned traveller born in Persia was Abû Ṭâhir AL-SILAFÎ (1082–1180), who went from Ispahan, where he was born, to Bagdâd and Alexandria. In the last-mentioned town, Ibn al-Sallâr, minister to the Caliph Ẓâfir, the Fâṭimid, built him a *madrasa*, in the year 1151, and in it he taught till his death. In addition to a collection of forty traditions called *al-Buldâniyya*, because every tradition was found in a different town, he compiled a dictionary of the Sheikhs of Bagdâd, the manuscript of which is now at the Escurial.

Majd al-dîn Abû'l-Saʿâdât al-Mubârak, the brother of Ibn al-Athîr, the historian, was born at Jazîrat ibn ʿUmar in 1149. He entered the service of the Amîr Qaimâz, Prince of Mosul, as secretary, and improved his position under his successors. At an advanced age he was attacked by paralysis in his feet and hands, and died in June 1210. The illness which obliged him to quit the public service gave him leisure to dictate and publish the books he has left behind him. His satisfaction in this work, and his delight at being no longer obliged to pay court to great personages, led him to discontinue a course of treatment which might have cured him, and which had been prescribed for him by a bone-setter from the Maghrib. He wrote the *Jâmiʿ al-Uṣûl* (Encyclopædia of Principles), which gives the traditions of the prophets arranged in chapters by alphabetical order, and also biographies of Mahomet

and his contemporaries; the *Nihâya*, a dictionary of rare and curious traditions; the *Muraṣṣaʿ* (Adorned with Brilliants), a lexicon of the surnames in *Ibn* and *Abû;* and the *Mukhtâr*, biographies of celebrated Moslems.

Muḥibb al-dîn Muḥammad IBN AL-NAJJÂR (1183–1245), a Shâfiʿite lawyer, and pupil of Ibn al-Jauzî, born at Bagdâd, devoted twenty-seven years of his life to making long journeys. The learning he thus acquired enabled him to settle in his native town as a teacher and man of letters. While at Medina he wrote the *Nuzha*, on the history of that town; at a later period he wrote the *Kamâl*, a collection of biographies of the witnesses who handed down the traditions. This has served as the basis for other treatises of the same nature. He also composed a supplement (*dhail*) to Al-Khaṭîb's history of Bagdâd, an abridgment of which, by Ibn Aibek al-Dimyâṭî, is now at Cairo.

ABÛ NUʿAIM Aḥmad AL-IṢFAHÂNÎ, a Shâfiʿite lawyer (948–1038), produced the *Ḥilyat al-anbiyâ* (Ornament of the Prophets), a history of holy and pious individuals and of their miracles; and the *Ṭibb al-nabî* (Medicine of the Prophet), a collection of *ḥadîths* touching medicine; and also a history of the learned men of Ispahan, which is now at Leyden, and other works on the traditions.

Taqî al-dîn Abû ʿAmr ʿUthmân IBN AL-ṢALÂḤ (1181–1245), born at Sharakhân, between Irbil (Arbela) and Hamadhân, was of Kurdish descent. He began his studies at Mosul, and travelled through the chief towns in Khurâsân. He was a teacher at Jerusalem, and then went to Damascus, where he finally settled. He taught Shâfiʿite law in several *madrasas*, notably in that just founded by Saladin's sister, and died there. His *Aqṣâ*

'l-amal wa'l-Shauq (The Liveliest Hope and Desire), which treats of the science of the traditions, has been the subject of many commentaries, and has furnished authors with many extracts. He devoted one of his works to the examination of traditions relating to the superiority of Alexandria and Ascalon over other cities; his collection of *fatwâs* and his treatise on the rules of the holy pilgrimage are now at Cairo.

Sharaf al-dîn ABÛ'L-ḤASAN Ibn al-Mufarrij AL-MAQDISÎ (1149–1214) was born on Syro-Arabian territory, near the Egyptian border. He was vice-judge at Alexandria, and afterwards taught at Cairo, where he died. His book of the forty traditions is remarkable for its exact specification of the date of each witness, and for its complete *isnâd*.

Abû Muḥammad 'Abdal-'Aẓîm AL-MUNDHIRÎ (1185–1258), who was born in Egypt, travelled for the purpose of study all through Mecca, Damascus, Edessa, Alexandria, and the surrounding countries. He taught the *ḥadîth* of the Shâfi'ite rite for twenty years, in the Kâmiliyya Madrasa at Cairo, and died in that city. His *Kitâb al-targhîb wa'l-tarhîb* is a collection of traditions arranged in such a fashion that those which guide to what is right appear on one side, and those which lead to the avoidance of evil, on the other. His book of the biographies of remarkable traditionists is in the British Museum.

In Spain, Abû 'Umar Yûsuf IBN 'ABDAL-BARR, who was born at Cordova in 978, studied in that city, and had the reputation of being the greatest authority on the *ḥadîth* in the Maghrib. He travelled for some time in the west of Spain, and then settled at Denia, paying occasional visits to Valencia and Jativa. Under

the rule of Prince Muẓaffar ibn al-Afṭas, King of Badajoz, he was appointed *qâḍî* of Lisbon and Santarem. He died at Jativa on 3rd February 1071. His *Kitâb al-Istî'âb* deals with the biographies of the companions of the Prophet: his *Durar* (The Pearls) is an abridged history of the wars of Mahomet's times: his *Intiqâ* is devoted to the three great founders of the rites, Mâlik, Abû Ḥanîfa, and Shâfi'î: his *Bahjat al-Majâlis* is a collection of proverbs, sayings, tales and poetry, dedicated to Prince Muẓaffar.

Abû 'Abdallah Muḥammad IBN ABÎ'L-KHIṢÂL al-Ghâfiqî, born in 1072 at Burgalet, a village in the district of Segura, near Jaen, a poet and learned man, lived at Cordova and at Grenada. He was appointed to perform the duties of Minister of the Interior and of War, and perished when Cordova was captured by the Moravids, on 27th May 1146. His *Ẓill al-saḥâb* (Shadow of the Clouds) is devoted to the wives and relations of the Prophet Mahomet. His *Minhâj al-manâqib* is a poem in honour of the Prophet and his companions. Documents belonging to his correspondence and literary lectures of his composing are still preserved at the Escurial.

Abû'l-Faḍl 'IYÂḌ ibn Mûsâ, who was born in December 1083, studied at Cordova, and was made *qâḍî* at Ceuta, his native town. He went on to Grenada in the same capacity, then back to Morocco, and there died in 1149. He wrote a book which is celebrated in the East, called *al-Shifâ fî ta'rîf ḥuqûq al-Muṣṭafâ*, a life of Mahomet, printed at Cairo, on which many commentaries have been written: *al-Ilmâ'*, a theory of the traditions, their sources and principles, edited by one of his pupils: the *Mashâriq al-Anwâr*, on the authentic

traditions and the meaning of the obscure expressions occurring in them : *al-I'lâm*, a work on penal law : and the *Tartîb al-mudhâkara*, on the proper names of the Mâlikite rite.

Abû'l-'Abbâs Aḥmad ibn Ma'add AL-IQLÎSHÎ, who was born at Denia, studied both in that town and at Valencia. He took advantage of his pilgrimage into Arabia (1147) to spend several years at Mecca, remaining there until 1152. While on his journey back, he died at Qûṣ, in Upper Egypt, in 1155. His *Kaukab al-Durrî* (Brilliant Star) is a collection of *ḥadîths*, drawn from the great canonical works. His *Najm* (Star), a book on proverbs, Arabic and foreign, has been printed at Cairo.

Abû Isḥâq Ibrâhîm IBN QURQÛL (1111–1173), who was born at Almeria and died at Fez, considered the traditions in his *Maṭâli' al-anwâr* (Dawn of Light).

JURISPRUDENCE

The science of the traditions, through the criticism of those sayings of the Prophet which cast light on the points which the Koran had left obscure, established one of the bases of law. Jurisprudence, on the other hand, was building up a very considerable mass of literature, arising out of the numberless difficulties in the application of the simple rules provided in the sacred book. These two branches of study, indeed, moved on abreast, for it was the necessity for seeking out clear and precise rules, founded on the legislator's authenticated deeds or words, which had led the learned to search out, collect, and select traditions which, as often as not, were contradictory in their bearing, and to explain and interpret them by criticising the witnesses who had

handed them down. When the judge was sure of his authorities, he felt more sure of the legality of the sentence he pronounced, and his conscience, therefore, was more easy. Yet for a long time before the body of opinion divided—the *Aṣḥâb al-ra'y* accepting individual interpretation, while the partisans of the letter of the law insisted on adherence to the traditional text of the *ḥadîth*—the judge's right to decide according to his own lights had been recognised by the law. Probably the intercourse of the Arabs with Syrian Christians, who, as we have seen, played a prominent part at the Omeyyad Court at Damascus, introduced them to the theories of the Roman law of Justinian's period, which, in the Syrian community, had survived the Moslem conquest. As the ancient works on Moslem law are lost, we must begin our study of this branch of literature with the heads of the four great orthodox rites—the Ḥanäfite, the Mâlikite, the Shâfi'ite, and the Ḥanbalite.

The Ḥanafites

The founder of this rite, Abû Ḥanîfa Nu'mân ibn Thâbit (699–767), was the grandson of a Persian slave. He was born at Kûfa, and plied the trade of a cloth merchant. Being a freedman, he proclaimed his sympathy with the movement which, supported by the latent forces concealed in Persia, placed the 'Abbâsids on the throne, but his real feelings were in favour of the so-called legitimate claim of the 'Alids, and the trick by which the 'Abbâsids filched their rights from them must have been abhorrent to this man of Persian blood. He took his share in the 'Alid rising at Medina in 762, and was cast into prison, where he died. In later days, when

men began to wonder how it was that the 'Abbâsid Government had made no effort to attract so great a teacher, known to this day as the Great Imâm, to its own side, a legend was built up, and it was said that Caliph Manṣûr tried to force him to accept a post as *qâḍî*, and that it was the rough treatment he received when he refused this office which brought about his death. He had sat at the feet of Ḥammâd ibn Abî Sulaimân, who died about 737. From him he had learnt the system of the *qiyâs*, the application of analogy in matters of jurisprudence, which has continued to be the rule of this school. The following books are attributed to Abû Ḥanîfa : the *Kitâb al-Fiqh al-Akbar* (Great Book on Dogmatics)—it was at a later date that *fiqh* began to signify jurisprudence—which was printed at Lucknow in 1844, with a Hindustani translation ; a *Musnad*, collected by his pupils ; a *Waṣiyya*, or Last Testament, dealing with the dogmas of Islamism, and addressed to his friends ; and a *Makhârij fî'l-ḥiyal*, devoted to the study of legal quibbles. The greater number of Abû Ḥanîfa's works were probably edited by his grandson, Ismâ'îl ibn Ḥammâd, *qâḍî* of Bassora and Raqqa, who died in 827.

Abû Ḥanîfa left a pupil named Abû Yûsuf (Ya'qûb ibn Ibrâhîm) (731–795), surnamed the Second Imâm, who was born at Kûfa, of an old Arab family. He was appointed *qâḍî* of Bagdâd by Caliph Mahdî, and held that post till he died. Although he had put his master's doctrines into practice, he began to rebel against the use of personal reasoning, and to allow greater weight, in the decision of doubtful cases, to the traditions of the Prophet than to analogy, on which Abû Ḥanîfa very largely relied. His *Kitâb al-Kharâj* (Book on the Land-Tax) has been printed at Bûlâq.

Abû Yûsuf, in his turn, had a pupil, MUḤAMMAD ibn al-Ḥasan AL-SHAIBÂNI, who was born at Wâsiṭ in 749. After having travelled to Medina, to draw knowledge of the traditions on which the study of the law is based at the fountain-head—from the teachings of Mâlik ibn Anas—he was appointed *qâḍî* of Raqqa. He was dismissed in 802, and afterwards lived at Bagdâd, till he went with Hârûn al-Rashîd in 804 to Rai, where he died.

At a later date we find AL-KHAṢṢÂF (Abû Bakr), who lost his library when his house was sacked by the Turkish soldiery after the assassination of the Caliph al-Muhtadî; an Egyptian, Al-Ṭaḥâwî (Abû Ja'far), of Ṭaḥâ (843–933); a Bukhârian, Al-Marwazî, minister to the Sâsânian Prince Ḥamîd, who fell into the hands of Turkomans, and was drawn and quartered by them, in 945; Al-Qudûrî of Bagdâd (Abû'l-Ḥusain) (972–1036), who wrote an abridged manual which bears his name, and is frequently consulted, even in our own days—all of them lights of the Ḥanafite sect.

THE MÂLIKITES

The Mâlikites take their name from their founder, Abû 'Abdallah MÂLIK IBN ANAS, who was born at Medina in 715. He was taught by the traditionist Al-Zuhrî, was a strong partisan of the 'Alids, helped, by a *fatwâ*, Muḥammad ibn 'Abdallah's revolt against the 'Abbâsids in 762, submitted, at a later date, to the Bagdâd Government, and beheld Caliph Hârûn attending his lessons as a student, on the occasion of his pilgrimage in 795. His *Kitâb al-Muwaṭṭa'* is founded on the *ijmâ'* of Medina—in other words, the

unanimous agreement of the dwellers in that town as to the accepted traditions and customs. He settles many doubtful cases, in the absence of any traditional basis, by the decisions of the judges who came before him and the proved custom of Medina. Mâlik took no pains to leave his pupils a revised and co-ordinated text, and this must explain the considerable variations in the different recensions of his book—those, for instance, of the Spaniard Yaḥyâ al-Maṣmûdî, and of Muḥammad al-Shaibânî, whom we have lately mentioned as attending Mâlik's lessons at Medina.

His disciple, ʿAbdal-Raḥmân ibn al-Qâsim (719–806), spread and popularised Mâlik's teaching in the Maghrib, where, as my readers know, it has continued dominant till the present day. The whole of Algeria is Mâlikite. He died in Cairo. Under the title of *Kitâb al-Mudawwana* he left a manual of Mâlikite law, originally drawn up by Asad ibn al-Furât, and consisting of Ibn al-Qâsim's answers to his questions, afterwards revised, corrected, and amended by Saḥnûn Abû Saʿîd al-Tanûkhî, *qâḍî* of Qairawân.

Among the most important Mâlikite doctors of these periods, Ibn Abî Zaid of Qairawân, who was born at Nafza in Spain in 928, lived in Tunis, and died at Fez in Morocco about 980, must be mentioned.

THE SHÂFIʿITES

The Imâm AL-SHÂFIʿÎ (Muḥammad ibn Idrîs) (767–820), founder of the Shâfiʿite rite, was born at Gaza (some say at Ascalon, or even in Yemen), lived till manhood in the Bedouin tribe of the Beni-Hudhail, and thus acquired the pure classic Arabic. To him the

grammarian Al-Aṣma'î applied, at Mecca, to obtain the poems of the Hudhailites and of Shanfarâ. In 786 we see him proceed to Medina and listen to the teachings of Mâlik. Having accompanied his uncle, Abû Muṣ'ab, who had been appointed *qâḍî* in Yemen, he became compromised by the intrigues of the 'Alid party, and was brought before the Caliph Hârûn at Raqqa. He was saved by the intervention of the minister Faḍl ibn Rabî'. He took advantage of this enforced presence at court to attend the teachings of Muḥammad al-Shaibânî. In 804 he went on into Egypt, was well received by the governor of the province, returned at a later date to Bagdâd, and seems to have been successful in teaching his doctrine, which differed in many particulars from that of his predecessors. He started on his way back to Egypt in 813, and died there, after having made a pilgrimage to Mecca, at Fusṭâṭ or Old Cairo, on 20th January 820. His tomb is a favourite place of pilgrimage at the present day. Shâfi'î resumed Abû Ḥanîfa's analogical system, and reduced it to practical rules. Of the hundred and nine works he produced, none now remain, save a few as yet unpublished manuscripts, scattered about the libraries of Cairo and Constantinople, and some poems in those of Leyden and Berlin.

The Shâfi'ite School in Egypt claims Al-Muzanî (Abû Ibrâhîm), who died in 877, the author of an abridged version of the doctrines of the master Al-Mundhirî of Nîshâpûr, who lived at Mecca, and died there in 930; Al-Zubairî (Abû 'Abdallah), who carried the teachings of the Shâfi'ite rite to Bassora and Bagdâd; Ibn al-Qâṣṣ, or the Son of the Story-teller (Abû'l-'Abbâs), who taught at Âmul in Ṭabaristân, and

died at Tarsus in Cilicia, whither he had journeyed (946)—or, as others assert, where he performed the duties of *qâḍî;* Al-Qaṭṭân (Abû'l-Ḥasan), a professor of law at Bagdâd, who died in 970; Al-Maḥâmilî, who studied at Bagdâd under pupils of Al-Shâfiʿî, taught there himself, and died there in 1024; also Al-Lâlakâ'î, the sandal-maker (Abû'l-Qâsim Hibat Allah), who studied and taught in the same town, removing at a later date to Dînawar in Irâq ʿAjamî, where he died in 1027.

The Ḥanbalites

Ibn Ḥanbal (Aḥmad ibn Muḥammad) (780–855) was born at Bagdâd; his parents belonged to Merv, which place they quitted a short time before his birth. Like all the traditionists of his period, he travelled in Syria, Mesopotamia, and in the Arabian Peninsula, where he made some stay. He returned to Bagdâd, where he sat at the feet of Al-Shâfiʿî until that master departed to Egypt. He founded the fourth orthodox sect, which differs from the others more especially in that its founder totally refused to accept the personal elucidation of any lawyer, and would admit no basis for the law save the traditions of the Prophet, to the exclusion of all others. This was a reaction which had little effect either in time or space, for it made but few proselytes beyond the province of its birth, and has now almost completely died out. A few of its adherents still exist at Damascus, where they may be distinguished from their brother-Moslems by the fact that they will not eat the produce of kitchen gardens fertilised by the water which has passed through sewers. The Ḥanbalites were remarkable for their fanaticism, and caused a great deal of disturbance

in Bagdâd when the power of the Caliphs began to wane. When the Caliph Al-Mu'taṣim adopted the Mu'tazilite doctrine of the creation of the Koran, Ibn Ḥanbal was one of the victims of the persecution which ensued. He was cast into prison, and remained there till Mu'taṣim's death in 842; but Wâthiq would not allow him to leave his own house, in which he was shut up; he regained his liberty when, from purely political motives, Al-Mutawakkil returned to orthodoxy. Ibn Ḥanbal died on 31st August 855, leaving a *Musnad* or collection of traditions arranged by his son 'Abdallah, and various works, all of them in manuscript.

Most of the books written by Ibn Ḥanbal's pupils have disappeared. The only ones we can mention are an epitome of jurisprudence by Al-Khiraqî, who died at Damascus in 945, on his way from Bagdâd, which city he had left on account of popular disturbances there—his works were lost in a fire after his departure; and the *Tahdhîb al-ajwiba*, a book written by Abû 'Abdallah al-Ḥasan ibn Ḥumaid al-Baghdâdî, containing answers to questions on legal subjects, which is now preserved at Berlin.

The Ẓâhirites

Other and less important sects sprang from the study of jurisprudence in which so many enlightened intellects were absorbed. The Ẓâhirite School, our knowledge of which we owe to the fine studies of it by Herr I. Goldziher, was founded by Abû Sulaimân Dâ'ûd ibn 'Alî (815–883), whose family belonged to Ispahan, but who was born at Kûfa. He studied under the most famous traditionists of Bagdâd, and knew Isḥâq ibn Râhawaih when he was at Nîshâpûr. He himself taught

with brilliant success at Bagdâd, where he died. The school he founded utterly repudiated any analogy, or quotation on the authority of any imâm, and insisted on the external meaning (hence the name borne by this doctrine, *Ẓâhir*) of the Koran and the traditions. This doctrine spread over Persia, India, and 'Umân, more especially amongst the mystics. Yet it had no lengthy vogue in the East, though at a later date it flourished in the Maghrib and in Spain, and many works on its tenets were produced.

Besides these great leaders of schools, we must also mention Yaḥyâ ibn Sulaimân, born in 818, who gave his attention to legal subjects, without attaching himself to any particular school, and wrote a book on the land-tax, the text of which has been published at Leyden by Juynboll; and the famous historian Ṭabarî, who combined the study of jurisprudence with that of Koranic exegesis, and whose pupil, Abû'l-Faraj al-Mu'âfâ ibn Zakarîyâ of Nahrawân (915–1000), wrote the *Kitâb al-Jalîs* (Book of the Habitual Guest), a summary of explanations as to various sayings of the Prophet and his companions, in the form of a hundred lectures.

THE SHÎ'ITES

Outside the circle formed by the four great orthodox sects, and the other schools of the same nature, the Shî'ites were in process of evolving a jurisprudence we must now consider, though but few ancient vestiges of it remain. In the province of Yemen, the Zaidite sect, which had taken possession of that country in the second century of the Hegira, and is still dominant there, reckoned among its teachers: Al-Qâsim ibn Ibrâhîm

al-Ḥasanî, who died in 860; his grandson, Al-Hâdî Ilâ'l-Ḥaqq (He who guides to the Truth) Abû'l-Ḥusain Yaḥyâ (859–910); another descendant of his, Al-Mahdî Lidînillah (He who is guided towards the Religion of God) al-Ḥusain ibn al-Qâsim, who died in 1013; the Imâm Al-Mu'ayyad-Billah Aḥmad ibn al-Ḥusain (944–1020). The works of these writers, formerly unknown to European students, have been brought back from Yemen by Herr Glaser, and are now in the Berlin Library.

In Persia, where the Shî'ite School of thought was always mixed up with the feeling for national revenge, we may mention: Abû Ja'far al-Qummî (died in 903), author of a collection of Shî'ite traditions; Al-Kulînî (Muḥammad ibn Ya'qûb), died in 939, who wrote a theological treatise under the title of *al-Kâfî fî 'ilm al-dîn* (That which is Adequate in the Knowledge of Religion); Abû Ja'far Ibn Bâbûya of Qum, who came to Bagdâd out of Khurâsân in 966, and died there in 991—several of his many works (over three hundred in number) are in Europe; Al-Nu'mân Ibn Ḥayyân, who forsook the Mâlikite sect to become an Imâmite, went to Egypt with the Fâṭimid conqueror Al-Mu'izz, was appointed *qâḍî*, and died there in 974; and Abû 'Abdallah al-Mufîd of Bagdâd (949–1022).

Further Development of Jurisprudence

Amongst the host of authors who expounded the principles laid down in the preceding centuries, we can only mention the chief.

'Alî ibn Abî Bakr al-Marghînânî, who died in 1197, wrote a manual for scholars beginning the study of

Ḥanafite law, called *Bidâyat al-Mubtadî*, on which he himself produced a commentary under the name of *Hidâya* (The Guidance); the Persian translation of this latter work was rendered into English by Charles Hamilton (1791). The *Hidâya* has been commentated by Persian, Turkish, and Arabic writers, and has had the greatest success that could be desired for any manual of Moslem law.

Sirâj al-dîn Abû Ṭâhir Muḥammad AL-SAJÂWANDÎ, who flourished toward the end of the sixth century of the Hegira, wrote a *Kitâb al-Farâ'iḍ*, or Treatise on the Division of Inheritances, which was surnamed *Sirâjiyya* after its author's own surname. This was translated into English in 1885, by Prasauma Kumar Sen, at Serampore, and in 1890, by A. Rumsey, in London.

The Shâfi'ite rite glories in the possession of Abû'l-Ḥasan 'Alî ibn Muḥammad AL-MÂWARDÎ (974–1058), who was born at Bassora, studied in his native town and at Bagdâd, acted for some time as Grand Qâḍî at Ustuwâ near Nîshâpûr, and finally settled down at Bagdâd, where he was appointed Chief Justice. His works were not published during his own lifetime; they were ultimately given to the world by some pupil of his. His chief work is the *Kitâb al-aḥkâm al-sulṭâniyya*, published at Bonn, in 1853, by Enger. This is a treatise on politics, which defines the ideal of Moslem government as conceived by the lawyers of that day—one which has been but little attained, a kind of model society, such as has never really existed, much like Plato's *Republic* and Xenophon's *Cyropaedeia*. The abstract definition of the Caliphate, the qualities indispensable for the exercise of the supreme power, the study of the various methods of election, the limits of the executive power of viziers and governors of

provinces—these are the most interesting of the points dealt with by the Moslem thinker. A French translation of the book, one volume of which has already appeared, has been made by Count Louis Ostrorog. Besides this famous treatise, Al-Mâwardî wrote a book of advice to sovereigns, another on the rules to be observed by their ministers, a treatise on politics and government called *Tashîl al-Naẓar wa-ta'jîl al-Ẓafar* (The Means of Facilitating Reflection and Gaining Swift Victory), another on the signs of prophecy (*a'lâm al-nubuwwa*), a collection of proverbs and sayings, and a treatise on morals (*âdâb al-dunyâ w'al-dîn*), printed at Constantinople and Cairo, and still used in the schools of the first-named city.

ABÛ ISḤÂQ Ibrâhîm ibn 'Alî AL-SHÎRÂZÎ (1003–1083) was born at Fîrûz-Âbâd, near Shîrâz. He went to Bassora and thence to Bagdâd. He was placed at the head of the Niẓâmiyya University when that establishment was founded by the illustrious Niẓâm al-Mulk, the great minister of the Seljûqids, in 1066. He began by refusing the office, but finally, pressed by his pupils, who threatened to leave him unless he transported the scene of his teaching to the new school, he agreed to accept it. He journeyed to Nîshâpûr as the envoy of the Caliph Al-Muqtadî, and, thanks to his renown as a teacher and writer, his journey was a triumphal march. He died very soon after his return, on 6th November 1083. His *Muhadhdhab* (Corrected Book) is a treatise on Shâfi'ite law, as is also his *Kitâb al-Tanbîh* (Book of Advice), published at Leyden in 1853 by H. Keijzer. Other works by him, on jurisprudence, dialectics, the Moslem catechism, and the history of the learned men of the Shâfi'ite sect, are less well known.

When Abû Isḥâq first refused to act as head of the Niẓâmiyya in 1067, his place was taken, though for a very short time, seeing that Abû Isḥâq reconsidered his refusal within three weeks, by Abû Naṣr 'Abdal-Sayyid IBN AL-ṢABBÂGH. He was born at Bagdâd in 1009. He had a second opportunity of filling the professorial chair which had once slipped through his fingers, but his sight failed, and he was forced to give up all teaching work. He waited on the minister Niẓâm al-Mulk at Ispahan, and obtained his promise that a school should be built expressly for him, but died three days after his return, in 1084. The *Shâmil fî'l furû'* (Complete Treatise on Jurisprudence), the only one of his works we now possess, is at Cairo ; it is, according to native critics, not only one of the best of the treatises on Shâfi'ite law, but one containing the most authentic traditions and the most conclusive arguments.

Abû'l-Ma'âlî 'Abdal-Malik AL-JUWAINÎ IMÂM AL-ḤARAMAIN was born at Bushtanîqân, near Nîshâpûr, on 12th February 1028. On the death of his father, Abû Muḥammed 'Abdallah ibn Yûsuf, who was a teacher in the latter town, he took his place, though barely twenty years of age. Nevertheless, to complete his own studies, and make the sacred pilgrimage, he went to Bagdâd, and thence to the two holy cities, Mecca and Medina, where he taught for four years, hence his surname. When he returned to Nîshâpûr, Niẓâm al-Mulk founded a school for him, in which he gave courses of lessons till his death, which overtook him on 20th August 1085, while on a visit to his native village, whither he had gone in the hope of recovering from an illness. Along with his professorial duties, he had discharged those of a preacher. At Nîshâpûr, he held

gatherings every Friday, at which he preached sermons, and presided over discussions on various doctrinal points : to these occupations he added that of managing the *waqfs*, or landed property devoted to the support of pious undertakings. For more than thirty years he continued in undisputed possession of these various posts. When he died, the mourning was general; the great pulpit of the Mosque from which he had delivered his sermons was broken up, and his pupils, to the number of four hundred and one, destroyed their pens and ink-horns, and gave up all their studies for a year. His masterpiece is his *Nihâyat al-Maṭlab* (Satisfactory Results of Inquiry), a treatise on Shâfi'ite doctrine, of which it was said that Islam had never produced its equal : the manuscript is preserved at Cairo. His *al-Waraqât* (The Leaves), on the principles of law, has been the subject of many commentators : his *Mughîth al-Khalq* is intended to demonstrate the superiority of the Shâfi'ite doctrine over all others.

Abû'l-Maḥâsin Abd al-Wâḥid al-Rûyânî, a Shâfi'ite doctor, who was born in Ṭabaristân in February 1025, was one of the victims of the Assassins, who were then terrifying the Moslem world by their active form of propaganda. The great minister of the Seljûqids honoured him with his special favour, on account of his eminent merits. After having lived for some time at Bukhârâ, the doctor travelled to Ghazna and Nîshâpûr, then returned to his native country, and founded a school in the capital, Âmul. At a later date he taught both at Rai and at Ispahan. His *Baḥr al-Madhhab* (Sea of Doctrine) is the most voluminous treatise on Shâfi'ite jurisprudence in existence : it is now at Cairo. The author was in the habit of saying : "If all the Imâm

Shâfi'î's works were to be burnt, I could dictate them from memory." In 1108, just as he had concluded one of his lessons, he was murdered at Âmul by the fanatics, who were then holding the castle of Alamût, in the neighbouring mountains.

Abû'l-Ḥasan 'ALÎ AL-KIYÂ AL-HARRÂSÎ (1058–1110) was also born in Ṭabaristân. He studied at Nîshâpûr under the Imâm al-Ḥaramain, who made him his assistant, taught himself at Baihaq, and then at Bagdâd, where he entered the Niẓâmiyya School, with which he maintained his connection all the rest of his life. The Seljûqid Sultan, Barkyâruq, son of Malik-Shâh, who highly esteemed him, appointed him chief *qâḍî*. He was a fine-looking man, with a clear voice, and expressed himself in polished language. His surname *Kiyâ* is a Persian word signifying "personage of high rank and great influence." His *Uṣûl al-dîn* (Principles of Religion) and his *Aḥkâm al-Qur'ân* (Judgments of the Koran) are now at Cairo.

ABÛ BAKR Muḥammad AL-SHÂSHÎ, surnamed Fakhr al-Islâm, and generally known under the name of Mustaẓhirî (1037–1114), was born at Mâyyâfâriqîn, of a family belonging to Shâsh, a town in Turkestan, north of the Yaxartes or Sir-Daryâ. After having studied in his native town, he went on to Bagdâd and Nîshâpûr, and then returned to the 'Abbâsid capital, where, in 1110, he was appointed professor at the Niẓâmiyya, a post he held till his death. His *Ḥilyat al-'Ulamâ* (Ornament of the Wise) is a treatise on Shâfi'ite law, dedicated to the Caliph Mustaẓhir.

Abû Shujâ' IBN AL-DAHHÂN was born at Bagdâd, where he acquired a huge mass of information, not only on legal subjects, but in various fields of literature,

and even of mathematics, which last was of service to him for the calculations connected with the division of inheritances. He first of all attached himself, at Mosul, to the service of the minister Jamâl al-dîn al-Iṣfahânî, and afterwards passed over to Saladin, who gave him a Government post at Mayyâfâriqîn. Not being able to work with his superior, the governor of the town, he proceeded to Damascus and to Egypt, seeking a more suitable employment. He made the pilgrimage in 1193. On his way back, close to Ḥilla, on the site of ancient Babylon, his camel fell, and he was killed by the blow he received from its wooden saddle (February 1194). It was said of him that his pen was more eloquent than his tongue. His close acquaintance with the use of astronomical tables led him to draw up legal tables, which he collected into a volume called *Taqwîm al-Naẓar* (The Calendar at a Glance); these tables are divided into ten columns, indicating the different points of view from which the orthodox rites may be considered, and the solutions of them therein provided.

Towards the close of the sixth century of the Hegira, another Abû Shujâ' Aḥmad al-Iṣfahânî wrote an epitome of Shâfi'ite law, entitled *Taqrîb;* it was published at Leyden, by Keijzer, in 1859. The *Fatḥ al-Qarîb* by Muḥammad ibn al-Qâsim al-Ghazzî, published and translated by Van den Berg, under the title of *Revelation of the Omnipresent,* is a commentary on the above work.

In the town of Âmid, now known as Diyârbakr, was born Saif al-dîn 'Alî al-Âmidî (1156–1233), who at first belonged to the Ḥanbalite rite, but joined the Shâfi'ites at Bagdâd. He studied philosophy in Syria, and taught at Cairo. He was accused of heresy, atheism, and immorality, on account of his philosophical learning,

and was obliged to flee to Ḥamât, where his books were written : notwithstanding this, he was recalled to Damascus as a professor, but again dismissed after a time. He wrote the *Abkâr al-Afkâr* (Virgin Thoughts), a treatise on dogmatic philosophy, and the *Iḥkâm al-Ḥukkâm*, dealing with the bases of judicial decisions.

ABÛ ZAKARÎYÂ Yaḥyâ ibn Sharaf AL-NAWAWÎ (1233–1278), who was born at Nawâ near Damascus, in the Ḥaurân, studied theology in the Syrian capital, where he settled as a private individual when he returned from the pilgrimage in 1253. He filled Abû Shâma's place when he died, and was his successor at the Ashrafiyya School of the *ḥadîth*. He died in his native town, whither he had gone to recruit after his heavy labours, on 22nd December 1278. His *Minhâj al-ṭâlibîn* was translated and published in 1884, by Van den Berg, at Batavia, by order of the Netherlands Government, under the title of *Guide to Fervent Believers*, a manual of Moslem jurisprudence according to the Shâfi'ite rite. Many commentaries have been written on this work, an honour also bestowed on the same author's *Collection of Forty Traditions*. His study of jurisprudence led him to draw up, with the object of establishing the orthography of the names of the authors quoted in the texts, the *Tahdhîb al-asmâ* (Correction of Proper Names), published at Göttingen in 1842–1847, by F. Wüstenfeld, under the title of *Biographical Dictionary of Illustrious Men*. His *Taqrîb wa-Taisîr* (Study Facilitated), an introduction to the study of the traditions, printed at Cairo in 1890, with Suyûṭî's commentary (entitled *Tadrîb*), has been translated into French by Marçais. A score of other works by Al-Nawawî are to be found in various European and Eastern libraries.

To balance all these names, the Ḥanbalites can only bring forward that of MUWAFFAQ AL-DÎN 'Abdallah Ibn Qudâma AL-MAQDISÎ (1146–1223), born at Jammâ'îl in Palestine, who studied at Bagdâd, and wrote a treatise on Ḥanbalite law called *al-Muqni'* (That which Satisfies), and other works, of which twelve manuscripts at least still exist. His nephew Abû'l-Faraj 'Abdal-Raḥmân (1200–1283), who was born at Damascus, was his pupil, became a preacher and teacher in the school of the traditions, and was chosen *qâḍî* of the Ḥanbalite rite, when special judges for each of the orthodox rites were appointed, in 1265. He founded a school which bore his name. Ḍiyâ al-dîn Muḥammad ibn 'Abdal-Wâḥid al-Dimashqî, who was born at Dâr al-Mubârak in 1173, studied in Egypt, at Bagdâd, and at Hamadhân. He returned to Damascus in 1203, started again on a long journey which took him as far as Merv, and ended by accomplishing the pilgrimage. He died in 1245, leaving a treatise on the medical science of the Prophet, which is now in Paris, and a *Faḍâ'il al-A'mâl* (Merits of the Works), which specially treats of the merit to be acquired by use of the peculiar litanies of the Dervishes. He built a school to which he left his library, but this was sacked and dispersed at a later date.

In Spain, the Ẓâhirite doctrine had found its great protagonist in the person of Abû Muḥammad 'ALÎ IBN ḤAZM, a man of Persian extraction, son of an important official at Cordova, where he was born on 7th November 994, in the Oriental quarter of the city, called at that time Munyat al-Mughîra. He followed the same Government career as had his father before him, and in spite of his avowed and complete indifference to worldly success, rose to the rank of vizier. He gradually withdrew himself

from the Shâfi'ite School of the traditions, and attended the lessons of Dâ'ûd the Ẓâhirite, from whom he first gathered the "principles according to dogmatism"—that is to say, the adoption, pure and simple, of the exoteric meaning of the text, without any explanation by analogy, nor the authority of a *juris peritus*. He wrote many books, which enlightened but a few pupils. The acrimony of his attacks earned him many enemies, who avenged themselves by accusing him of heresy, thus obtaining his dismissal, and his banishment from several provinces in Spain. He spent the rest of his life on his property near Niebla, where he died on 16th August 1064. The Gotha Library possesses his *Ibṭâl al-qiyâs wa'l-ra'y* (Destruction of Analogy and Speculative Examination), a polemical disquisition, from the Ẓâhirite point of view, against the principles of orthodox law. He also wrote a *Kitâb al-milal wa'l-nihal* (History of the Philosophical and Religious Sects), which has been studied by Steinschneider and Goldziher. Together with several other treatises on jurisprudence, we come upon a purely literary work of his, now in the Leyden Library, called *Ṭauq al-ḥamâma* (The Dove's Necklace), an anthology of love poems.

Abû 'Abdallah Muḥammad Ibn Tûmart (the Berber form of the name 'Umar) was born in the Atlas Mountains, overlooking the province of Sûs in Morocco, on 21st February 1092. While still very young he earned a great reputation for piety. He travelled; his longing to make the Mecca pilgrimage brought him in the first place to Cordova, then to the Ḥijâz, and thence to Bagdâd, where he attended the Niẓâmiyya lectures. His teachers were professors of the Ash'arite doctrine, and he carried it back with him to Tripoli in

Barbary, mingling with its allegorical interpretations the Shî'ite theory of the impeccability of the imâm descended from 'Alî. The disturbances caused by his teaching drove him out of Tripoli and Bijâya, and he took refuge with the Berber tribe of Maṣmûda, from which he was descended, and which espoused his cause; he was prosecuted by the Government, proclaimed himself Mahdî in 1121, and began the struggle against the Moravids. He died in the course of an attempt on the city of Morocco, four months after his troops had been defeated before that fortress, in 1130. His successors disseminated his teaching over Northern Africa and Spain; and his pupil, 'Abd al-Mu'min, founded the Almohad dynasty. The Paris Library possesses a complete set of his works, a collection of small treatises on theology and jurisprudence. Another of his books, the *Kanz al-'Ulûm* (Treasury of Knowledge), a work on religious philosophy, is at Cairo.

The Almohads lead us on to the Shî'ites. The Zaidites of Southern Arabia produced works to explain and defend their doctrines. Abû Ṭâlib Yaḥyâ al-Buṭḥânî, surnamed "the Imâm who speaks according to the Truth (*Nâṭiq bil-ḥaqq*)," who died in 1033, wrote, besides a treatise on jurisprudence (*al-Taḥrîr*), a history of the Zaidite imâms down to 971 (*al-Ifâda*); a collection of traditions was compiled, under the title of *Durar al-aḥâdîth*, by Taqî al-dîn 'Abdallah Ibn Abî Najm, who died towards 1165; 'Abdallah ibn Zaid al-'Ansî wrote the *Fatâwî al-nabawiyya*, against the Muṭarrifites, and the *Manâhij al-bayân*, with a similar tendency—he was alive about 1233; the Imam al-Manṣûr Billah 'Abdallah ibn Ḥamza (1166–1237) left a collection of poetry, a treatise on the mutual duties of parents and their children (*al-*

bayân wa'l-thabât), a defence of the Zaidite party (*risâlat al-Kâfiya*), and other treatises of the same nature. Most of these works are at Berlin; the remainder are in the British Museum.

Amongst the Imâmites, the Sharîf AL-MURTAḌÂ, whose name was Abû'l-Qâsim 'Alî ibn Ṭâhir, the descendant of 'Alî ibn Abî Ṭâlib (966–1044), held the post of inspector of the 'Alid family at Bagdâd, and died there. Under the title of *Al-durar wa'l-ghurar* (Pearls and Stars), he collected the eighty-two discourses he had occasion to deliver before gatherings over which he himself presided. These embrace a great variety of literary subjects, and contain grammatical observations on passages in the Koran or the *ḥadîth*, explained by means of ancient poetry. His *Shihâb fi'l-Shaib wa'l-shabâb*, on white hair and youth, has been printed at Constantinople. He is also the author (unless it be his brother Râḍî) of the *Nahj al-balâgha*, a collection of sayings which he himself ascribed to Alî; the commentator Mustaqîm-Zâdè has even asserted him to be the real author of the *dîwân* attributed to 'Alî, and this is by no means an impossibility.

Abû Ja'far Muḥammad, born at Ṭûs in Khurâsân in 995, spent the greater part of his life at Bagdâd, and died at Najaf (Meshhed 'Alî) in 1067. He wrote the *Fihrist Kutub al-Shî'a* (List of Shî'ite Books), which was published at Calcutta by A. Sprenger and Maulawy 'Abdul-Ḥaqq. Besides divers works on jurisprudence, notably the *Tahdhîb al-Aḥkâm* (Correction of Judgments), in which he endeavours to reconcile the various *ḥadîths*, he has composed a book of prayers (*al-ḥall wa'l-'iqd*), and a treatise on Moslem worship, entitled *Miṣbâḥ al-Mutajahhid.*

Râḍî al-dîn Abû 'Alî al-Ṭabarsî, who died in 1153, wrote a great commentary on the Koran, under the name of *Majma' al-bayân*, and another yet larger, entitled *Jâmi' al-jawâmi'*; he defended the Imâmite doctrine in his *Kitâb al-iḥtijâj* (Book of the Argument).

Najm-al-dîn Ja'far al-Ḥillî, surnamed *al-Muḥaqqiq* (the Examiner), who was born at Ḥilla in 1205, wrote the great Shî'ite code known under the title of *Sharâ'i' al-Islâm* (Laws of Islamism), which has been printed at Calcutta, and the publication of which, with a Russian translation, was begun by Kasem-Beg; it has been translated into French in its entirety, by Monsieur A. Querry. The astronomer Nâṣir-al-dîn Ṭûsî, who travelled with the Mongol Emperor Hulâgû, is said to have been proud to attend this author's lessons. He died in 1277, of a fall from the terrace of his own house.

The Study of the Koran

As a result of the researches necessitated by the study of law, the Koran, on which the whole of Moslem jurisprudence and society was founded, was studied more and more deeply. It was important to be able to read the text well, so as to avoid any wrong reading which might vitiate its meaning; it was yet more important thoroughly to grasp that meaning. These were the two branches of science which sprang up in the East—the science of reading, and the science of exegesis.

When Caliph 'Uthmân laid down a single and only text which was to be absolute, and whereby all discussion as to the real reading of the sacred book was to

be silenced, he had believed himself to be providing an unshakable foundation for the new religion. This was an illusion. In spite of the disappearance of the texts which did not agree with the accepted Vulgate, schools arose in the great cities of the empire—at Mecca and Medina, jealous of their reputation as holy cities; at Bassora and Kûfa, the homes of grammatical knowledge. In these the art of reading the Koran was transmitted by oral tradition, and each of the fashions taught could appeal to the authority of some great name from which its teaching had come down. Yet the multifarious differences growing out of oral tradition soon necessitated the substitution of written tradition. As early as the middle of the second century of the Hegira, Ya'qûb al-Ḥaḍramî compiled a work on the various ways of reading. Of all the books the titles of which are mentioned to us, none, however, now remain—neither the compilation by the famous historian Ṭabarî, nor the summary of the seven schools of readers given by Abû Bakr Ibn Mujâhid; we must come down to the fourth century before we find short works by Ibn Khâqân (died 927) and Ibn Mihrân (died 991), which are now preserved at Berlin, Algiers, and Leyden.

Far more interesting, from our point of view, is the interpretation of the actual text of the Koran. At a very early date, the companions of the Prophet were endlessly questioned as to the meaning of obscure and difficult passages, which are very numerous—sometimes on account of the style, which is intentionally concise and admitting of several explanations, and sometimes owing to the use of words belonging to the Quraishite dialect, which the other Arabs either misunderstood or did

not understand at all. ʿAbdallah Ibn ʿAbbâs, the uncle of Mahomet, to whom is ascribed the origin of many *ḥadîths*, of which he was the first ear-witness, was often obliged to pronounce regular exegetical judgments on the difficulties laid before him, and his authority is frequently quoted by commentators of a later date. From this period commences the development of a considerable body of literature which still crowds the shelves of Eastern libraries. We have already had occasion to mention, amongst the productions of the third century, the works of Ibn Qutaiba, Al-Zajjâj, Ṭabarî, and Nîshâpûrî. Then the mystics begin to add their phantasmagoric explanations and their dreams to their predecessors' investigations; men like Sahl ibn ʿAbdallah al-Tustarî (a disciple of the Moslem saint Dhû'l-Nûn, the Egyptian, who died at Bassora towards 886 in the odour of sanctity, and who performed miracles) introduced a mass of esoteric interpretations into their commentaries on the text, to wrest its sense to the advantage of their own ideas, moral and mystic, drawing complete explanations, intended to serve their own ends, from the simple words they turned aside from their natural signification. With these mystics, of Aryan origin, we do find certain lawyers who practised a healthy form of exegesis, simply taking what the text really contains. Among them we may mention Al-Jassâs al-Râzî, a learned Ḥanafite of the Bagdâd School, who long lived as a teacher at Nîshâpûr, and whose works are to be found at Constantinople and at Cairo; ʿAbdallah ibn ʿAtiyya, of Damascus, who applied his profound knowledge of the Arabic of the pre-Islamic poets to the explanation of the Koran; Ibn Zamanain, a learned Spaniard, belonging to the

Mâlikite rite, who died in 1008, leaving a commentary, an abridgment of which is preserved in the British Museum; Al-Ḥasan al-Nîshâpûrî, originally a disciple of the dogmatic school of the Karrâmiyya, who became a Shâfi'ite, and added to his reputation as a learned exegetist that of a philologist and historian (died 1015); Ibn Salâma, of Bagdâd, in which city he taught at the Mosque of Al-Manṣûr, and wrote the earliest work in our possession on those peculiar passages in the Koran which do away with each other, and which are called *nâsikh* and *mansûkh* (that which abrogates, and that which is abrogated). My readers are aware that although the Koran is reputed to be the Divine word, merely transmitted by the Prophet's mouth, certain of its precepts have been abrogated and annulled by subsequent injunctions; thus will a monarch correct himself under pretext of having been better informed on the second occasion. This is no shock to the Moslem mind, accustomed as it is, through the system of passive obedience which is the very foundation of its faith, to look on the Deity as an autocrat far more mighty than anything known on earth. The Shî'ites themselves, as early as the fourth century, had interpreters of the Koran, such as Abû'l-Ḥasan 'Alî al-Qummî, the author of an abridged commentary which represents the family of 'Alî as the source of all knowledge, and which gives us an insight, so to speak, into the evident and entire fabrication which is the characteristic peculiarity of Shî'ite literature.

The art of reading the Koran has been treated by Abû Muḥammad MAKÎ ibn Ḥammûsh AL-QAISÎ. He was born at Qairawân in 966, went to Egypt at the age of thirteen, to study philosophy and arithmetic, returned to his own country, left it again in 987, to go to Mecca,

and continued his studies in Egypt when he came back. He was an incorrigible traveller, started for the valley of the Nile a third time, with the intention of studying the different methods of reading the Koran, numbering seven, and remained there a year. In 997 he returned to Mecca, where he spent four years, and thence proceeded to Spain, taught in various mosques at Cordova, was appointed imâm and preacher at the Great Mosque, and retained that position till his death in 1045, though he was hardly fitted to fill it efficiently, for he was more proficient in the art of psalmody than in the composition of sermons. The Bodleian possesses his *Riâya li-tajwîd al-qirâ'a* (Observation of Good Reading); the Berlin Library, and those of Gotha and Cairo, have his *Tabṣira*, his *Kashf*, his *I'râb mushkilât al-Qur'ân* (Grammatical Explanation of Certain Difficult Words in the Koran), and his *Sharḥ Kallâ wa-balâ* (Commentary on those two Arabic expressions).

Abû 'Amr 'Uthmân ibn Sa'îd al-Dânî (981–1053), who was born at Denia in Spain, made the pilgrimage in 1006, and remained four months at Qairawân, and a year at Cairo. On his return he settled in his native town, and died there. Under the title of *Taisîr*, he left a treatise on the seven different readings, another of the same nature called *Jâmi' al-Bayân*, a book on the composition of the Koran and the definition of its orthography (*al-Muqni'*), and some other treatises of a similar kind—nine in all, of the hundred and twenty works he produced.

Abû Ṭâhir Ismâ'îl IBN KHALAF AL-SARAQOSṬÎ was born at Saragossa, and died there on 4th January 1063. He was deeply versed in literature, and never ceased tsudying and communicating the information thus ac-

quired to the public till the day of his death. His *Kitâb al-'Unwân* exists in manuscript at Berlin.

Abû'l-Muẓaffar Yaḥyâ IBN HUBAIRA was the son of a soldier belonging to the military colony established on the Dujail in 'Irâq. He was of pure Arab blood. He studied Ḥanbalite law and the Koranic sciences at Bagdâd, and subsequently entered the Government service, and rose to be vizier, being thus rewarded for a well-turned letter whereby he brought about the repudiation of the Abyssinian eunuch Mas'ûd al-Bilâlî, Prefect of the Police at Bagdâd, under the Seljûqids. He died in 1165. His *Ifṣâḥ* deals with those words in the sacred book as to the reading of which the most famous readers disagree : it is now in existence, at Paris. His *Ishrâf* treats of the difference between the four orthodox rites.

Al-Qâsim ibn Firroh al-Shâṭibî (1144–1194), who was born at Jativa in Spain, went to Cairo in 1176, and was a reader of the Koran there. His father's name is the ancient Spanish *fierro* (for *hierro*), iron. His masterpiece, which is entitled *Ḥirz al-Amânî wa-Wajh al-Tahânî* (Wishes Accomplished and Open Felicitations), but which is better known under the name of *Châṭibiyya*, is a didactic poem in one hundred and seventy-three lines, a versification of the *Taisîr*, intended for learning by heart, which gives in rough and not very intelligible language all the rules for reading the Koran. Ibn Khallikân was of opinion that no work of the same nature had been previously produced. Let us admire the conquest of a difficulty, and pass on our way. Al-Dâni's *Muqni'* was also put into verse by the same author, and he likewise left a commentary on the Koran.

He had a pupil, 'Alam al-dîn Abû'l-Ḥasan 'Alî AL-

SAKHÂWÎ, who was born at Sakhâ, in Egypt, in 1163, and exercised the calling of Koran reader at Damascus, where he died in 1245. He wrote a number of works on the religious sciences, amongst them the *Hidâyat al-Murtâb* (Direction in Doubtful Cases), a poem in four hundred and twenty-seven lines, on the homonymous expressions to be found in the Koran, commentaries on the works of his master, al-Châṭibî, seven religious poems, and a correspondence in verse with his contemporary Kamâl al-dîn al-Sharîshî, the commentator of Ḥarîrî's *Lectures*. So successful was his oral teaching, that crowds eager to learn to read the Koran under his guidance might be seen round him in the Great Mosque of the Omeyyads. Each person was allowed near him in turn, but only after a long wait; sometimes two or three read difficult passages to him at one and the same time, and he would give his criticisms of each, one after the other.

The grammarians devoted their leisure moments not only to reading the text of the Koran, but to interpreting its meaning. ABÛ'L-ḤASAN 'Alî ibn Ibrâhîm AL-ḤAUFÎ came from a village near Bilbîs, in Egypt: he died in 1038, after having written the *Burhân* (The Proof), a commentary on the Koran in twenty-eight volumes. Abû'l-Ḥasan 'Alî Ibn Mattûya AL-WÂḤIDÎ, of Nîshâpûr, was descended, as the name of his ancestor (*Mattai*, Matthew) indicates, from an Aramean and Christian family: he was a disciple of Tha'labî, and died, after a long illness, in 1075. His *Asbâb al-Nuzûl* is an historical narrative of the occasions on which the *sûras* and verses of the sacred book were revealed: he also wrote two commentaries, the *Wajîz* and the *Wasîṭ*, and turned his attention to explaining Mutanabbî's verses in a fashion superior to that of his predecessors.

Abû Bakr Muḥammad Ibn al-'Arabî was born at Seville in 1076, accompanied his father on a journey through the East in 1092, and visited Damascus, Bagdâd, and the Ḥijâz. After he had accomplished the ceremonies of the pilgrimage, he returned to Bagdâd, to attend the teachings of Ghazâlî, and then went back to Seville by Alexandria and Cairo. He reached his native city in 1100, and acted for some time as *qâḍî*, teaching there afterwards, till his death in 1151. His commentary on the traditions of Tirmidhî, called *'Âriḍat al-Aḥwadhî*, is lost, but at Cairo his other commentary on the Koran (*Qânûn al-ta'wîl*), his judicial studies of the sacred text, and his treatise on marriage (*farâ'iḍ al-nikâḥ*), may yet be seen. 'Abdal-Raḥmân al-Suhailî al-Khath'-amî, who was born near Malaga, in the village of Suhail, in 1114, studied at Grenada, lived for some time at Seville, and finally returned to Malaga. The Sultan of Morocco, Ya'qûb ibn Manṣûr, summoned him to his court, and he died in Northern Africa some three years later, on 23rd November 1185. His *Ta'rîf wa'l-i'lâm* explains those passages of the Koran which contain proper names: his *Rauḍ al-Unuf* is a commentary on the biography of the Prophet by Ibn Hishâm, which has been closely examined by P. Brönnle.

All the extensive labours of the commentators we have hitherto noticed, most of them grammarians, are summed up in Baiḍâwî's celebrated work, *Anwâr al-tanzîl wa-asrâr al-ta'wîl* (The Light of Revelation and the Mysteries of Interpretation), edited by Fleischer. 'Abdallah ibn 'Umar al-Baiḍâwî, who belonged to Baiḍa, a little town in Fârs, was the son of the Grand Qâḍî of that province, under the *atâbek* Abû Bakr ibn Sa'd, the Mæcenas of Persian poetry. He himself acted as *qâḍî*

at Shîrâz, the capital of the province, and afterwards lived at Tabrîz, where he died about 1286. His commentary is based on Zamakhsharî's *Kashshâf*, to which he has added much matter, drawn from other sources. It is the favourite commentary of the Sunnites: but it is insufficient, because its treatment of the subject matter is too brief, and indeed it has been a good deal criticised, even in the East. His *Minhâj al-Wuṣûl* is a treatise on Shâfi'ite law, like his *Ghâyat al-Quṣwâ*: his *Miṣbâḥ al-arwâḥ* is a theological manual: his *Ṭawâli' al-anwâr* is a metaphysical treatise. He also wrote a history of Persia from the days of Adam till the year 1275, in the Persian language. It is called *Niẓâm al-Tawârîkh*.

ABÛ'L-WALÎD Sulaimân ibn Khalaf AL-BÂJÎ (1012–1081), born at Badajoz, went to the East in 1029, and remained there for thirteen years, three of which were spent at Mecca and three at Medina. On his return he held a post as Mâlikite *qâḍî*, and died at Almeria. He left the world a *Sunan al-Ṣâliḥîn* (Habits of Pious Folk), a collection of traditions touching moral conduct, a *Fuṣûl al-Aḥkâm* on jurisprudence, and a Reply, now preserved at the Escurial, to an Apology for Christianity contained in a letter from a French monk to Muqtadir, Prince of Saragossa.

DOGMATIC THEOLOGY

The Koran had certain inveterate enemies, to whom, indeed, it had assigned an inferior position in the new society, without insisting on their forswearing their religion—these were the Jews and the Christians. The last, especially, did not fail to argue against a religion which claimed to rule them. In Syria, above all, a

country but recently snatched from the hands of the Roman Emperors of the East, the struggle was sharp and the disputations hot. The necessity for replying to these redoubtable adversaries called Moslem dogmatic theology into existence. Soon the sects which sprang up in the very bosom of Islam constrained the orthodox teachers to wrestle against the innovators, with arguments drawn from the ancient texts. The Murjites held the doctrine of absolute predestination too extreme, and softened it down; they had the glory of counting the great jurisconsult Abû Ḥanîfa among their disciples. But the real attack on orthodoxy came from the rationalists, called in Arabic Mu'tazila, that is to say, "those who separate themselves." It was at Bassora that Wâṣil ibn 'Aṭâ founded the Mu'tazilite sect. This school directed its inquiries specially to the existence and attributes of the Deity. The ancient Mu'tazilites are said to have drawn their ideas from the dialectics of the Greeks. This may be, but, in the absence of their writings, proof is impossible, and these are all lost. In the third century much argument was expended on the famous question whether the Koran had been created, or had existed through all eternity. The orthodox party inclined to the second opinion; the Mu'tazilites authoritatively put forward the first. The struggle was a long one, and steeped the Moslem Empire in blood. In 827, the Caliph al-Ma'mûn officially declared the Koran to be created, and commanded that all who controverted this doctrine should be prosecuted. This brilliant triumph of the Mu'tazilite teaching did not last long. In 851, Al-Mutawakkil, who, for political reasons, desired the support of the orthodox party, upset the fragile edifice, and placed the secular arm at the

disposal of the Muʿtazilites' foes. At the same period, Muḥammad ibn Isḥâq of Nîshâpûr wrote a book against them, affirming the unity of, and noting the proofs of the attributes of, the Deity. But the final disappearance of the Muʿtazilite movement, and the establishment of a rigid orthodoxy, cast in a definite mould, and never again to be altered, must be ascribed to a great Moslem doctor, Abû'l-Ḥasan ʿAlî ibn Ismâʿîl AL-ASHʿARÎ. He came of an ancient and noble Arab family, and was born at Bassora in 873. Although he was brought up in a family of orthodox opinions, he became a Muʿtazilite, convinced by the teachings of the great doctor of that sect, Al-Jubbâ'î, and continued in this belief till he had reached his fortieth year. He then awoke to the truth and returned to the orthodox fold. His Muʿtazilite studies made him a dangerous enemy, for he was able to fight the rationalists with their own weapons. His abjuration took place in public, and made a great stir, for it was from the pulpit of the Great Mosque at Bassora that he announced his repudiation of Muʿtazilite opinions and his submission to the faith of his fathers (912). At a later date he went to Bagdâd, and there wrote ninety-nine works, many of which are quite small treatises.

During Al-Ashʿarî's period, Abû Manṣûr Muḥammad ibn Maḥmûd al-Mâturîdî, thus surnamed after the quarter in Samarqand in which he was born, was preaching a reform of the orthodox dogma which met with brilliant success in India, Transoxania, and Turkey. There was but very slight divergence, indeed, between his views and those of Al-Ashʿarî. He died in his native city in 944. Soon after, a most prolific polygraph was born in the same town — Abû'l-Laith al-

Samarqandî, a Ḥanafite doctor, whose studies embraced the various fields of theology, jurisprudence, exegesis, and moral science. He died about 993.

Abû Ḥâmid Muḥammad AL-GHAZÂLÎ (1049–1111), thus surnamed, according to Sam'ânî, after the village of Ghazâla, near Ṭûs, in Khurâsân, where he was born (not al-Ghazzâlî, as it is commonly pronounced), studied theology at Nîshâpûr, where he received instruction from the imâm Al-Ḥaramain. After the death of his master, he attached himself to the famous Vizier Niẓâm al-Mulk, who gathered all the most illustrious men of his time about him; he was victor in the public disputations which took place, and the caravans soon carried his fame far and wide. In 1054 he was appointed to teach at the Niẓâmiyya at Bagdâd, where an audience of three hundred persons crowded to hear him; but at the end of four years he resigned his post, and had it conferred on his brother Aḥmad, so that he himself might be more free to prosecute his philosophical researches. For the space of eleven years, as he tells us, he withdrew from the world, and gave himself up to ascetic practices. He travelled, and Damascus, Jerusalem, Mecca, and Alexandria each welcomed him in turn. Then it was that he endeavoured to reconcile science with faith, and plunged into the pantheistic mysticism of the Ṣûfîs.

While at Alexandria, he heard of the Moravid rising, the leader of which believed himself to have brought forth a reforming movement in Islam, and conceived the idea of entering the service of Yûsuf ibn Tâshifîn. But Yûsuf died in 1106, before Ghazâlî had started on his journey, and the philosopher renounced his plan, and returned to his native town of Ṭûs, where he lived in peace, except for the period during which, in response

to the request of Muḥammad, son of Malik-Shâh, he taught at Nîshâpûr. He died in the Ṭabarân quarter, on 19th December, 1111. He had founded a Ṣûfî monastery there, and also a *madrasa* for theological study. Suyûṭî was able to say of him : "If there was to have been any prophet after Mahomet, Al-Ghazâlî would surely have been that prophet." The admiration of the Moslem world decorated him with the title of *Ḥujjat al-Islâm* (The Decisive Argument of Islamism). He belonged to the Shâfi'ite rite, which was the most general in Persia at that time. This was long before the triumph of Shafi'ism, which was not to become the State religion till the time of the Ṣafavids, in the sixteenth century.

The works we owe to Ghazâlî's pen are very numerous. Brockelmann tells us of sixty-nine which are still in existence. In this place we can only hastily review them. The *Jawâhir al-Qur'ân* (Jewels of the Koran) is a system of theology ; the *'Aqîda* is a statement of the articles of the Moslem faith, which has been published by Pococke in his *Specimen ;* the Precious Pearl (*Al-durra al-fâkhira*) is a treatise on the Last Judgment and the end of the world—what theologians call an *eschatology*—it has been translated and published by L. Gautier. The morality and theology of the mystics are codified in the *Iḥyâ 'ulûm al-dîn* (Revivification of the Religious Sciences). The *Mîzân al-'amal* (Balance of the Works) has been translated into Hebrew by Ibrahim ben Hasdaï of Barcelona, and published by Goldenthal. The *Kîmiyâ al-sa'âda* (Alchemy of Happiness) is a popular lecture founded on mysticism ; this work, which was originally written in Persian, has been translated into English by H. A. Homes, under the above English title. *Ayyuhâ'l-walad* (O Child !) is a celebrated moral

treatise, which has been translated into German and published by Hammer-Purgstall. In the judicial department, his treatises on Shâfi'ite law have earned great success in the Moslem world; his *Basîṭ*, *Wasîṭ*, and *Wajîz* are all abridgments of them. In that of philosophy, the *Tahâfut al-Falâsifa* (Collapse of the Philosophers) is an attack on the adherents of the Greek philosophy; it has been studied by De Boer. The *Maqâṣid al-falâsifa* (Aims of the Philosophers) is a sort of introduction to the above. Its text has been published by G. Beer, and a Latin translation by Gondisalvi is in existence, which was printed at Venice in 1506. The *Munqidh min al-ḍalâl* (Preservative from Error), written after the author recommenced his life as a teacher at Nîshâpûr for the second time, describes the development of his line of philosophic thought. It was translated and published by Schmölders, in his *Essay on the Schools of Philosophy among the Arabs*; a second and greatly improved translation was published in the *Journal Asiatique* for 1877, by that learned savant, Barbier de Meynard.

Together with this great Shâfi'ite doctor we must not forget to mention his brother, Abû'l-Futûḥ Majd al-dîn Aḥmad, who succeeded to his professorial chair at the Niẓâmiyya. Like him, he had mystic leanings, and he disseminated his views by exhortation, as well as by his pen, for he was a fine-looking man, and had the gift of miracles. He had a passion for preaching in public, which led him somewhat to neglect his judicial studies. He died at Qazvîn in 1126. He abridged his brother's *Iḥyâ*, and wrote treatises on Ṣûfism, such as the *Minhâj al-Albâb* (Road for Hearts), a treatise on the advantages of poverty and the assumption of monkish garb among

the mystics; a book (*Bawâriq al-ilmâ'*) in defence of music, which was considered futile and frivolous by strict Moslems, but which the mystics held to be one means of reaching the state of ecstasy. His *Kitâb al-dhakhîra* is a summary of his brother's system.

Najm al-dîn Abû Ḥafṣ 'Umar AL-NASAFÎ (1068–1142), who was born in the town of Nasaf, in Transoxania, was one of the greatest Ḥanafite teachers of his time. His most famous work is his *'Aqâ'id* (Articles of Faith), a Moslem catechism, published by W. Cureton, and translated into French in the *Tableau de l'empire othoman*, by Mouradjea d'Ohsson, and into German by Ziegler. He also wrote a long didactic poem of two thousand seven hundred lines, on the differences which divide the leaders of the orthodox rites, and at least two commentaries on the Koran.

Abû'l-Fatḥ Muḥammad AL-SHAHRASTÂNÎ (1086–1153) was born at Shahrastân, a large village in Khurâsân, and studied at Jurjâniyya (Ourghendj), and at Nîshâpûr, where he specially devoted his attention to the theological system of Al-Ash'arî. He took advantage of his pilgrimage to Mecca (in 1116), to spend three years at Bagdâd, on his way back. He then returned to his own country, and died there. His *Kitâb al-milal wa'l-nihal* is a complete and detailed statement of the various philosophical opinions and religious sects, Moslem and other. It has been published by Cureton, and translated into German by Haarbrücker. He also wrote a history of the philosophers, which was in the possession of Bland—a Persian translation brought to London by Fraser was purchased by a Prince of Oudh, and taken back to India by him. The *Nihâyat al-iqdâm* (Limit of Progress) is a complete treatise on scholastic theology.

The *Muṣâra'at al-falâsifa* is a discussion of seven questions of metaphysics.

Sirâj al-dîn 'Alî AL-ÛSHÎ, who was born at Ûsh in Farghâna, wrote, towards the year 1173, a didactic poem rhyming in *l*, and known by the title of *Amâlî* (Dictations), which deals with the principles of the Moslem faith, and which has been published by P. von Bohlen, and frequently commentated. An extract, consisting of a hundred short traditions, from his *Ghurar al-akhbâr* is preserved in manuscript both at Cairo and at Berlin.

On the occasion of the receipt of a letter from the Roman Emperor of Constantinople by the Egyptian Sultan Malik-Kâmil, Abû'l-Baqâ Ṣâliḥ al-Ja'farî indited, in the year 1221, a refutation of Christianity and Judaism, under the title of *Al-bayân al-waḍîḥ al-mashhûd*, which has been utilised by F. Triebs in his dissertation, published at Bonn in 1897.

'Abdal-'Azîz ibn 'Abdal-Salâm AL-SULAMÎ (1181–1262), surnamed *Sulṭân al-'Ulamâ*, who was born at Damascus, was a preacher there till he was summoned to Egypt, about 1240, by Malik-Shâh. He remained in that country till he died, and wrote a large number of works on Shâfi'ite jurisprudence, eighty-four of which have come down to us, among them the great and the little *Qawâ'id al-Sharî'a* (Rules of the Law), the *Mulḥat al-i'tiqâd*, which is a criticism of Al-Ash'arî's system, and a polemical attack on certain innovators, such as the *ḥashwiyya*.

THE MYSTICS

The same impulse which drew men's minds towards religious orthodoxy carried a great many of them beyond the bounds of reason, and, aided by influences of Persian

origin, developed the theories of mysticism in the Moslem world. The men who have been called the Saints of Islam were all mystics, or, to give them the name under which they were known in the East, they were Ṣûfîs — men clad in wool, or, as we should say, in fustian. Originally they were ascetics, after the fashion of the Christian monks—men who renounced the world and its perishable good, to devote themselves to the contemplative life in desert places ; at a later date we find brotherhoods, religious orders, with certain appointed spots where they met for united prayer—prayers which rapidly became spiritual exercises of a very material description, such as the dance of the whirling dervishes, the juggling tricks of the ʿÎsavîs, and the screams or roarings of the Rifâʿiyya. But at the distant period of which we now speak, all these things were in the future. The question arises whether Moslem mysticism had its origin in India, or among the Greek and Syrian monks. In either case, it is the very antithesis of the Semitic spirit, and must have been the outcome of the most powerful of Aryan influences.

The oldest mystics whose works have come down to us are the following : Abû ʿAbdallah al-Ḥârith ibn Asad al-Muḥâsibî, who belonged to Bassora. He preached the renunciation of worldly things, and set a practical example by refusing his patrimonial inheritance on pretext of a legal scruple, founded on the fact that his father had been a supporter of the doctrine of human free will, which is contrary to the orthodox theory of predestination, and that, in Moslem law, persons of different faiths cannot inherit from each other. He lived in indigence, and died in 857. His contemporary, Dhû'l-Nûn the Egyptian, born at Ikhmîm, seems to have held religious

views which were closely bound up with most fantastic notions on the subject of alchemy. In the person of Al-Junaid (died 910), who came of a family belonging to Nahâwand (his father was a glassworker), Ṣûfism appears to have taken a decided trend in the direction of pantheism. This master gathered a certain number of disciples about him. One, Al-Ḥusain ibn Manṣûr al-Ḥallâj, became famous. He was of Persian birth, performed miracles, and attracted a certain number of proselytes—so many that the sovereign power took umbrage, and on pretext that he had declared the Deity to be incarnate in his own person, he was haled before the judge at Bagdâd, condemned to death, and executed (921).

In Ghazâlî we have seen the theologian with mystical leanings. We are now about to study the impulse imparted to literature by this new branch, inspired by Persian thinkers. Abû'l-Qâsim 'Abdal-Karîm AL-QUSHAIRÎ (986–1072), of a family settled in Khurâsân after the conquest, lost his father at a very early age, and inherited a landed property near Ustuwâ. He went to study at Nîshâpûr, with the object of acquiring sufficient knowledge to enable him to protect himself against the exactions of the public treasury. Abû 'Alî al-Ḥasan al-Daqqâq, the great master of Ṣûfism, whose teachings he attended, incited him to study science and mysticism, and ended by inducing him to devote himself to them entirely. He even, at a later date, gave him his own daughter in marriage. In 1056 he proceeded to Bagdâd, and there taught the traditions according to the Shâfi'ite view; he died at Nîshâpûr. To a profound knowledge of the Ṣûfî tenets, he united great skill in caligraphy, and a remarkable amount of erudition in

literary matters. The *Risâla*, which bears his name, was written with the object of imparting fresh glory to the doctrines of the mystics, which had fallen rather out of fashion in his day. His *Tartîb al-Sulûk fî ṭarîq Allâh* (Method of Progress in the Way of God) is a guide for the Ṣûfî beginner. His *Taḥbîr* is a treatise on the hundred names of God, and their use in prayer.

Abû Ismâ'îl 'Abdallah AL-HARAWÎ, who was born at Quhan-diz in 1005, and died at Herat in 1088, left a *Manâzil al-Sâ'irîn*, which treats of the various stages through which the Ṣûfî must pass before he reaches a knowledge of the truth; a *Dhamm al-Kalâm*, which is an attack on dogmatic and scholastic theology, and a *Ṭabaqât al-Ṣûfiyya* (History of the Mystics), which is the basis of the Persian poet Jâmî's *Nafaḥât al-Uns*.

Tâj al-Islâm al-Ḥusain IBN KHAMÎS al-Mauṣilî, who was born at Juhaina, a village near Mosul, travelled down the banks of the Tigris, to study Shâfi'ite law under Ghazâlî at Bagdâd, and became *qâḍî* of a big village on the Euphrates, between Raqqa and Bagdâd. He ultimately retired to Mosul, and died there in May 1157. His *Manâqib al-abrâr* (Biographies of Pious Men) is an imitation of Qushairî's *Risâla*, combined with a history of the Ṣûfîs.

Sheikh 'Adî ibn Musâfir al-Hakkârî was born in the village of Bait-Qâr, near Baalbek. When still a young man he made long journeys to visit the chief Ṣûfîs of his time. At a later date he retired to the ruins of a Christian convent, in the mountains to the west of Mosul, where he set up his *zâwiya;* and there he died in 1163, after having founded the religious order of the 'Adawiyya. The Yazîdîs, who at that period probably inhabited the mountains of Sinjâr, adopted him as their

patron, rendering him a kind of worship which has hardly anything Moslem about it; down to the present day he continues to be their favourite saint, and his tomb is still a place of pilgrimage. The Berlin Library possesses his catechism, *i'tiqâd ahl al-sunna* (Beliefs of the Sunnites), his counsels to the Caliphs and to his own followers (*Waṣâyâ*), and two odes, both of them mystic in their conception.

Muḥyî al-dîn ABD AL-QÂDIR AL-GÎLÂNÎ (1078–1168), one of the great Islamic saints, traced his origin back to 'Alî. He was born in Gîlân, to the south of the Caspian Sea, and when still young went to Bagdâd, where he commenced the study of Ḥanbalite law in 1095. In 1127 he began to hold edifying gatherings, swiftly acquired a reputation for sanctity, and performed miracles. He used to say: "I would all the goods in the world were in my hands, so that I might feed all who are hungry." The religious order of the Qâdiriyya, which he founded, still maintains its doctrines and its fame all over the East. The great adversary of the power of France in Algeria, the Amîr 'Abdal-Qâdir (Muḥyî al-dîn 'Abdal-Qâdir al-Ḥasanî), with whom, after his retirement to Damascus, the writer of these lines had the honour of a personal acquaintance, was proud to claim descent from the illustrious saint of Bagdâd. He wrote the *Ghunya liṭâlibî ṭarîq al-ḥaqq* (The Work which Suffices those who Seek the True Path), a complete treatise on Ṣûfism; the *Futûḥ al-ghaib* (Opening of the Mysteries), rules for the conduct of his disciples; the *Jalâ al-khâṭir*, a collection of sermons delivered either in the *madrasa*, or in the Ṣûfî Convent at Bagdâd, in 1150 and 1151, which is preserved in the Library of the India Office; another

collection of the same kind, *Al-fatḥ al-rabbânî* (Revelations of the Lord), which has been printed at Cairo; numerous forms of prayer, and some mystic poetry.

Ḍiyâ al-dîn 'Abdal-Qâhir ibn 'Abdallah AL-SUHRAWARDÎ, a descendant of the Caliph Abû Bakr, who was born at Suhraward, a little town near Zenjân in Âdharbaijân, in the year 1097, studied Ḥanafite law at the Niẓâmiyya, became imbued with mysticism, lived a solitary life, and built himself a *zâwiya* to the west of Bagdâd. Between 1131 and 1152 he taught at the Niẓâmiyya; in 1160 he held dervish meetings at Mosul; he afterwards moved towards Jerusalem, but could not get into the city, which was then in the hands of the Crusaders, and so remained at Damascus, where Nûr-al-dîn Maḥmûd ibn Zangî received him with great honour. He afterwards returned to Bagdâd, and died there in 1168. His treatise on mystics bears the title of *Âdâb al-murîdîn* (Morality for Disciples); the Vienna Library also possesses a commentary of his on the hundred names of God.

He must not be confused with another celebrated ascetic, Shihâb al-dîn Yaḥyâ ibn Ḥabash ibn Amîrak AL-SUHRAWARDÎ (1153–1191), who studied law at Marâgha, became a convert to Ṣûfism, and wandered to Ispahan, Bagdâd, and Aleppo. His eclectic doctrine was a mixture of Neo-Platonic ideas and Iranian tradition, modified by Islamism, and by the Shî'ite conception of a hidden and impeccable Imâm. He called it *Ḥikmat al-Ishrâq* (Philosophy of the Illumination, Illuminism), and his disciples have taken the name of *ishrâqîs* (illuminists). In the early part of his residence at Aleppo he seems to have found the prince who ruled that city, Malik-Ẓâhir, the son of Saladin, favourably disposed towards him; but

he was suspected of heresy by the orthodox party, and, in spite of his careful disguising of his teaching under a cloak of obscure terminology, his enemies succeeded in turning the royal mind against him, and he was put to death. His tomb is a place of pilgrimage, and the people call him *Shaikh maqtûl* (the murdered sheikh). Besides the *Ḥikmet*, to which we have already referred, he wrote the *Talwîḥât*, on logic, physic, and metaphysics; the *Hayâkil al-Nûr*, on mysticism; the *Alwâḥ al-'Imâdiyya*, on the infinite, the absolute, and the Divine attributes, dedicated to the Urtuqid prince, 'Imâd al-dîn Qara-Arslân, and other works of less importance.

At the same period there dwelt in the Maghrib ABÛ MADYAN Shu'aib ibn al-Ḥasan, known in Algeria under the surname of Bû-Medin. He died in 1193, leaving a reputation for sanctity as great as that of 'Abdal-Qâdir al-Gîlânî's at Bagdâd. We have several of his collections of sentences, one of which, an abridgment of the *Tuḥfat al-Arîb*, has been published and translated into Latin by Fr. de Dombay. He also wrote mystic poetry.

A Spaniard, who settled at Damascus and practised there as a physician, Abû'l-Faḍl 'Abdal-Mun'im ibn 'Umar AL-JULYÂNÎ (1136–1205), wrote a manual of mysticism under the title of *Adab al-Sulûk*, and an apology for Saladin in rhymed prose and verse, to celebrate the taking of Jerusalem, called the *Manâdiḥ al-mamâdiḥ*. In praise of the same prince he was also led to compose poems to which he gave the external form of trees, columns, circles, and chessboards. These quaint compositions may be seen in the Paris and Upsala Libraries; they are called the *Dîwân al-tadbîj*.

Rukn al-dîn Abû Ḥâmid AL-ÂMIDÎ, of Samarqand, a

learned lawyer, who died at Bukhârâ in 1218, treats the subject of the independence of the microcosm, the human body, in relation to the macrocosm, according to a Persian translation of an Indian book, in a work entitled *Mir'ât al-Ma'ânî* (Mirror of Various Thoughts). De Guignes, Gildemeister, and Pertsch have all devoted attention to this book. He also left two manuals of dialectics and controversy (*al-ṭarîqa al-Âmidiyya* and *al-Irshâd*), and a treatise on talismans (*Ḥauḍ al-ḥayât*).

NAJM AL-DÎN Abû'l-Jamâl al-Khîwaqî, surnamed KUBRÂ, who died in 1221, wrote works on mysticism: the *Fawâtiḥ al-Jamâl;* the *Khâ'if al-hâ'im*, on the ten means whereby a man may attain purity of the body and the soul, and so draw nearer to the Divinity; and two tracts on analogous subjects.

SHIHÂB AL-DÎN Abû Ḥafṣ 'Umar AL-SUHRAWARDÎ, who must not be confused with the sheikh who was murdered at Bagdâd, and whose surnames were similar, was born at Suhraward in 1145. He studied Shâfi'ite law, and felt himself drawn towards mysticism. At a later period we find him settled as a teacher at Bagdâd, where he died in 1234. He was nephew to Ḍiyâ al-dîn (see above); he studied under him, and also under 'Abd-al-Qâdir al-Gîlânî. His '*Awârif al-ma'ârif* (The Divine Gifts of Knowledge), in which he deals with the mysticism of the Ṣûfîs, has been printed at Bûlâq; his *Kashf al-faḍâ'iḥ al-Yûnâniyya* is directed against the study of Greek philosophy, and to the support of the Moslem religion. Others of his treatises are devoted to the praise of poverty and renunciation of this world, to descriptions of the various stages through which the soul must pass before it can attain to the knowledge of God, and to remarks on the assumption of the dress which

marks the dervishes' consecration to the contemplative life.

MUḤYÎ AL-DÎN Abû 'Abdallah IBN AL-'ARABÎ (1165–1240), who was born at Murcia, went to Seville in 1172, and devoted his time to the study of the *ḥadîth* and of jurisprudence. In 1201 he began a series of journeys which brought him to the Ḥijâz, to Bagdâd, to Mosul, and into Asia Minor. He died at Damascus, without having been able to get back to his native land. While following the strict doctrine of the Ẓâhirites in matters of jurisprudence, he indulged in the most disordered fancies as to the mystic training. He wrote an untold number of books, and his inventive facility, together with the great number of his works which have come down to us, has earned him the reputation of being the greatest mystic of the Moslem East. His masterpiece, the *Futûḥât al-Makkiyya* (Revelations of Mecca), is a treatise on mysticism, in twelve volumes; his *Fuṣûṣ al-Ḥikam* (Mosaic of Precepts), on the existence and importance of the twenty-seven chief prophets, was written at Damascus in 1230, after the Prophet Mahomet had appeared to him; his *Mashâhid al-asrâr al-Qudsiyya* (Apparition of the Sacred Mysteries) and his *Anwâr* (Lights) were written at Konia in 1209; his *Inshâ al-dawâ'ir* is devoted to the explanation of man's place in creation and its cosmogony; his *'Uqlat al-mustaufiz* describes the denizens of the upper world, and of this lower one, the spirits, the throne of God, the stars, the earth; his *Tuḥfat al-safara* (Gift Bestowed on Travellers) details the stages of the mystic's journey towards the knowledge of God; his *Ḥilyat al-Abdâl* (Ornament of the Ascetics), a guide to happiness, was written at Ṭâ'if, near Mecca, in 1202. The *Kîmiyâ al-Sa'âda* (Alchemy

of Happiness) treats of the properties and virtues of the formula of the belief in one God; the *Ifâda* (Information) speaks of the three fundamental branches of knowledge—God, the rational world, and the world of sense. A certain number of his treatises deal with the occult sciences, as his studies of the *Jafr*, or cabalistic work ascribed to 'Alî; his *Fâ'ida* (Utility) turns on the subject of divination by means of the letters of the alphabet. His *Tarjumân al-ashwâq* (Interpreter of Love) is a collection of Ṣûfî poetry published at Mecca in 1201; he wrote a commentary on his own work to defend himself against the accusation of having sung the praises of carnal and not Divine love. Many other poems of the same nature have been collected under various titles. Of his two hundred and eighty-nine works, one hundred and fifty have been catalogued by Brockelmann as existing, at the present day, in different European and Eastern libraries.

The founder of the religious order of the Shâdhiliyya, Abû'l-Ḥasan 'Alî AL-SHÂDHILÎ, who was born in a small town to the west of Tunis, died in 1258, after having written *al-Muqaddima al-Ghazziyya* (The Preface of Gaza), on the duties of divine worship; the famous *Ḥizb al-baḥr* (Litany of the Sea), a prayer, the formula of which he believed he had received from Mahomet himself, and which the traveller Ibn Baṭûṭa thought sufficiently interesting to be inserted *in extenso* in the story of his own adventures; and other litanies of the same kind, which are still extant.

ṢADR-AL-DÎN Abû'l-Ma'âlî AL-QÔNAWÎ, of Konia, in Asia Minor, the ancient Iconium, a pupil of Ibn 'Arabî, wrote a commentary on the Fâtiḥa, or first chapter of the Koran, entitled *I'jâz al-bayân* (Miraculous Explana-

tion), on the forty *ḥadîths*, and on the hundred names of God; the *Hâdiya* (The Directress) is a tract on the principles of the Moslem theodicy; the *Nuṣûṣ* is a treatise on Ṣûfî mysticism; the *Miftâḥ al-Ghaib* (Key of the World of Mystery) is a scientific introduction to the knowledge of the Divine personality and mysteries. He died in 1273.

'Izz al-Dîn 'Abdal-salâm Ibn Ghânim al-Maqdisî (or al-Muqaddasî, that is to say, he who belongs to Jerusalem), who died in 1279, put the praise of the Creator into the mouth of birds and flowers, in his *Kashf al-Asrâr* (The Mysteries Unveiled), which has been published and translated by Garcin de Tassy under the title of *Les Oiseaux et les Fleurs*. His *Ḥall al-rumûz* (Solution of the Problems) is a treatise on mysticism; his *Taflîs Iblîs* (The Devil Ruined), an imitation of Ibn Jauzî's *Talbîs*, is intended to combat the opinion that God has nothing to do with evil, whereas, on the contrary, He purposely tolerates it.

'Izz al-dîn 'Abd al-'Azîz al-Dîrînî (1215–1295), born at Dîrîn in Egypt, was the author of a famous poem on the Last Judgment, *Qilâdat al-durr al-manshûr* (The Pearl Necklace Displayed), which is generally placed with Ibn al-Wardî's *Kharîdat al-'Ajâ'ib*, or Cosmography. He also produced other works, such as the *Ṭahârat al-Qulûb* (Purity of Hearts), a collection of edifying anecdotes, counsels, and prayers; the *Taisîr*, a didactic poem numbering over three thousand two hundred lines, on Koranic exegesis; and a refutation of Christianity (*Irshâd al-ḥayârâ*, the Guide for Wanderers), now preserved at the Paris Library.

CHAPTER IX

THE ‘ABBÂSIDS—*Continued.*—SCIENCE

TRANSLATIONS FROM THE GREEK

AFTER Alexander's conquests, the Hellenic spirit swept over the whole of Asia, and in the midst of a population which never gave a thought to intellectual cultivation, the Alexandrian School long remained a centre of erudition and scientific research. In spite of the catastrophes that overtook the libraries, which had been the storehouses of ancient thought, enough written books remained in circulation to make men feel the mind of the ancients was not altogether dead. Syria and Mesopotamia were both influenced by Greek civilisation. For centuries, in the numberless cloisters inhabited by Syrian monks, the Greek works on philosophy and science were translated into the Syriac tongue, and to these Syrian reproductions the Arab translators went for their material. The school founded at Gundêshâpûr, in Susiana, by Chosroes I., in the year 350, had also spread the knowledge of Greek learning, and the taste for philosophical and medical study, in the East. In the very heart of Mesopotamia, the town of Ḥarrân, the ancient Carrhæ, where Crassus was defeated, had retained its pagan faith, and there, by a syncretism which recalls the days of the later Roman Empire, the Greek and Roman

gods were allied with the antique divinities of the Semites. This was another centre of Hellenic civilisation, even in the midst of the Middle Ages. The dwellers in Ḥarrân were particularly addicted to mathematical and astronomical studies.

It was the Caliph Al-Ma'mûn who, by his foundation of a university (*bait al-ḥikma*) at Bagdâd, to which he attached a library and observatory, first gave impetus, in the Moslem world, to a considerable scientific movement, of which the echo was taken up and repeated in distant lands, and ultimately, through the medium of Moslem Spain, stirred up the sleeping intelligence of Europe. This movement it was which called forth a mass of Arab translations of the Syriac manuscripts already translated from the Greek, thus further enriching, with a fresh branch, an already very rich and varied literature.

Thus Al-Ḥajjâj al-Hâsib translated Ptolemy's *Astronomy* under the title by which it is still known, that of the *Almagest*, and also Euclid's *Elements;* Yûḥannâ ibn Baṭrîq (died 815) translated Aristotle's *Politics;* and Abdal-Masîḥ Nâ'ima of Ḥimṣ, Aristotle's *Theology*, after Porphyry, at the request of Caliph Al-Mu'taṣim. Qusṭâ ibn Lûqâ of Baalbek, well known by his original works on medicine, astronomy, and mathematics, turned numbers of Greek works into Arabic; Abû Zaid Ḥunain ibn Isḥâq, the son of a Christian apothecary at Ḥîra, studied medicine under Yaḥyâ ibn Mâsawaih, who flourished under Hârûn al-Rashîd, travelled through Asia Minor, where he had an opportunity of learning Greek, returned to Bagdâd, where he was chosen to be the personal medical attendant of the Caliph Al-Mutawakkil, and wrote books on

medicine and philosophy, at the same time translating the Old Testament out of the Septuagint into Arabic, not to mention Plato's *Timaeus* and his *Republic*, Hippocrates' *Aphorisms*, the works of Galen and Dioscorides, and others. His end was unfortunate. He was mixed up in the quarrel about images which divided the Christian Church, was excommunicated by Bishop Theodosius, and, in his grief, poisoned himself, in November 873. His son and chief disciple, Isḥâq ibn Ḥunain, a close friend of the Vizier Qâsim ibn 'Ubaidallah, was more of a philosopher than of a physician. He translated Aristotle's *Categories*, and died, paralysed, in 910.

After these we hear of Ḥubaish ibn al-Ḥasan, the nephew of Isḥâq, whom he assisted in his labours, who translated Dioscorides and Galen; Abû Bishr Mattâ ibn Yûnus, who died at Bagdâd in 940, and turned his attention to Aristotle's *Art of Poetry;* and Abû Zakariyyâ Yaḥyâ ibn 'Adî, surnamed the Logician, a Jacobite Christian, of whom nothing remains to us beyond his name, as is also the case with regard to the physician Ibn Zer'a, of the same Christian confession, who translated works on medicine and philosophy.

PHILOSOPHY

The perusal of the translations of Aristotle gave birth to a study of philosophy, which remained restricted, in the Moslem world, within the comparatively narrow circle of learned men and thinkers. It never took hold of the common people, but was received with enthusiasm amongst the labourers in the intellectual field. So early as in the days of Caliph Al-Mu'taṣim, towards 840, Shibâb al-dîn Ibn Abî'l-Rabî' composed, at

his sovereign's request, a treatise on politics, preceded by some reflections on psychology, which may perhaps be looked on as the oldest work of the kind in the Arabic tongue. It is now preserved in the Paris Library, and has been printed at Cairo (*Sulûk al-Mâlik fî tadbîr al-Mamâlik*). After him comes Ya'qûb ibn Isḥâq al-Kindî, the son of the Governor of Kûfa, who belonged to an old Arab family. He was born at Kûfa, and studied first at Bassora and then at Bagdâd, where he finally settled. He was included in the prosecutions which were the outcome of the orthodox reaction in the time of Mutawakkil, saw his library confiscated, and was not able to obtain its restoration till a short time before the Caliph's death and his own. He wrote some two hundred works on the most varied subjects.

Aḥmad ibn al-Ṭayyib al-Sarakhsî, who was born at Sarakhs in Khurâsân, is better known under his surname of TILMÎDH AL-KINDÎ, the pupil of Al-Kindî; none of his works are now extant. He was a member of the suite in attendance on the Caliph Al-Mu'taḍid, whose tutor he had been; and, as a punishment for having betrayed a secret entrusted to him, he was thrown into prison and put to death in the year 899.

Abû Naṣr Muḥammad AL-FÂRÂBÎ, who was born at Fârâb, the modern Otrar, belonged to a Turkish family of Transoxania. He studied medicine and philosophy at Bagdâd. Attracted to Aleppo by the glamour of the court of Saif al-daula, a patron of arts and learning, he lived there retired from the world, giving his lessons in the delightful gardens which surround the town, and died at Damascus in 950, while attending his master on a journey. He wrote on logic, morals, politics, mathematics, alchemy, and music. Ibn Khallikân calls

him the greatest philosopher Islâm ever produced. It is to him that Avicenna owed his learning, and so illustrious a pupil must needs have had a great master. When he reached Bagdâd he knew no Arabic, and to acquire it was the first object of his study. When he had mastered the language, he was able to profit by the teachings of Abû Bishr Mattâ ibn Yûnus, who was teaching logic. Al-Fârâbî filled seventy volumes with the notes he took at these lectures, which explained Aristotle's treatise on logic. He read the Greek philosopher's treatise on the soul two hundred times over. "If I had lived in his days," he was fond of saying, "I should have been his chief disciple."

His Utopian ideas of a model city—an adaptation of Plato's *Republic*—are of the most curious description. They are the ideas of a philosopher, not those of a politician or a lawyer. Men, according to him, must have a monarchical government and a religious faith. The most perfect State would be one which should include the whole of the inhabited globe. In such a universal monarchy the governed classes would need to be saints and their rulers sages. Yet the author admits that if one man did not possess all the qualities he would require of the monarch, a second, a third, and even more might be associated with him; this fine system would soon end in an aristocratic republic.

In 966 an Arab from Jerusalem, Muṭahhar ibn Ṭâhir al-Maqdisî, being at Bust in Sijistân, drew up, at the request of the minister of one of the Sâmânid princes, a summary of the learning of his times, under the title of *Kitâb al-bad' wa'l-ta'rîkh* (Book of the Creation and of History), in which he imparts to the public, besides the common stock of Moslem erudition, the fruits of his

own personal investigations, of his conversations with Zoroastrian priests and Jewish Rabbis. This work was later ascribed, nobody can tell why, to the philosopher Abû Zaid Aḥmad ibn Sahl al-Balkhî, and catalogued under his name. A copy of the unique manuscript, now in a library at Constantinople, was brought from the East by the writer of these lines, and is, together with his translation of it, in actual course of publication by the École des Langues Orientales Vivantes, in Paris.

The Buwaihid capture of Bagdâd in 945, and the condition of tutelage to which the ʿAbbâsid Caliph was thereby reduced, leaving him in the position of an automaton with a merely spiritual power, gave some life to free philosophic speculation, which had been shackled by the successful religious reaction under Mutawakkil and his successors. These princes, descended from a poor fisherman in Ṭabaristân, who became a *condottiere* in the service of the chief of that province, were Shîʿites, and cared but little for the progress of orthodoxy. Under the shelter of this comparative liberty a society of philosophers, who called themselves *Ikhwân al-Ṣafâ* (Brothers of Purity), was formed, towards the middle of the fourth century of the Hegira, at Bassora. This body set forth, in fifty-one treatises, the whole sum of Arab philosophy. Its celebrated work has been translated into German, and a study of it has been produced in the same language by F. Dieterici.

Abû ʿAlî al-Ḥusain IBN SÎNÂ, known as AVICENNA, was the son of the governor of a small town near Bukhârâ; he was born in 980, and studied philosophy and medicine simultaneously in the chief town of his native province. When he was barely eighteen,

his wonderful cure of the Sâmânid Prince Nûḥ, son of Manṣûr, opened the palace gates to him. At two-and-twenty, his father having died, he went to the court of the King of Khwârizm (Khiva), 'Alî ibn Manṣûr, travelled in Khurâsân and Jurjân, and remained in the latter country for some time, as a teacher. There he produced his masterpiece in medical science, *Qânûn fi'l-ṭibb* (Canon of Medicine). He proceeded later to Rai and Qazvîn, and as far as Hamadhân, where he became minister in the service of the Buwaihid Prince Shams al-daula, but was forced by the military party to resign his office. Under the son and successor of this prince, Tâj al-daula, he was accused of high treason and shut up in a fortress, from which he contrived to escape, and took refuge with 'Alâ al-daula Abû Ja'far Ibn Dushmanziyâr, at Ispahan. Worn out by excessive labour and by debauchery, he died of an illness contracted in the course of a campaign against Hamadhân.

His works cover the whole field of the learning cultivated in the East of that day. In theology, he wrote *risâlas*, or tracts, on various *sûras* of the Koran, on the Last Judgment, on miracles, dreams, magic, and talismans. But philosophy was his special subject. His *Shifâ* is a treatise on logic, physics, mathematics, and astronomy. When he was accused of having displayed enmity to the doctrines of the Koran in this work, he wrote a letter to his favourite pupil, 'Ubaid Allah, of Jûzajân, to clear himself. His *Ishârât wa'l-tanbîhât*, a manual of logic, has been published and translated by Forget at Leyden under the title of *Livre des theorèmes et des avertissements*. His *'Uyûn al-ḥikma* (Sources of Wisdom) is devoted to logic, physics, and theology.

His *Ḥayy ibn Yaqẓân*, a treatise on mysticism, has been translated by Mehren. Baron Carra de Vaux has published, translated, and commentated his *Ode on the Soul*. His *Khuṭbat al-Gharrâ* (Brilliant Sermon) has been edited by Golius. The Tract of the Birds (*Risâlat al-ṭair*) is a mystic parable on captive birds. His refutation of astrology shows how the great physician had cast off the most tenacious prejudices of his time, which have by no means disappeared from the East even at the present day. Avicenna's didactic poem on logic, in two hundred and ninety-nine lines, has been published by Schmoelders.

In the domain of natural and physical science, besides some half score of tracts on astronomy and physics, we find the code of medicine, the famous *Qânûn*, on which so many commentaries have been written, and some didactic poems, such as the *Manẓûma*, or poem on medicine, in three thousand one hundred and thirteen lines, and another on anatomy.

Abû'l-Wafâ MUBASHSHIR ibn Fâtik, an Egyptian Amîr, wrote, in the year 1053, a book of sayings of all the wise men of the ancient times and the Middle Ages, called *Mukhtâr al-Ḥikam* (Selected Thoughts); the part of this work relating to the legend of Alexander has been published and translated by Meissner.

Abû Bakr al-Ṭurṭûshî IBN ABÎ RANDAQA (1059–1126) was born at Tortosa. He studied Mâlikite law at Saragossa and literature at Seville, made the pilgrimage in 1083, and travelled in the East. He went as far as Bagdâd, halted in Egypt on his return, and settled at Alexandria, where he died. He was then a teacher of the traditions. His *Sirâj al-Mulûk* (Torch of the Kings) is a guide to conduct for royal personages;

it was finished at Old Cairo in 1122, and dedicated to the Vizier Al-Ma'mûn. His life was that of a devout ascetic, who made a practice of mortifying his body, and his existence was that of a poor man, content with very little.

The philosopher Avenpace (Abû Bakr Ibn al-Ṣâ'igh Ibn Bâjja) was born at Saragossa. He lived at Seville and Grenada, and later proceeded to the Moravid court at Fez, where he was poisoned at the instance of the physician Abû'l-ʿAlâ Ibn Zuhr, in 1138. In addition to his philosophical studies, he bestowed his attention on music. We have twenty-four small works of his, on philosophy, medicine, and the natural sciences, a farewell letter, and a poem about hunting, *Ṭardiyya*. His enemies looked on him as a freethinker.

IBN ṬUFAIL, who was born at Cadiz, was Avenpace's pupil in philosophy and medicine. He entered the service of the Governor of Grenada as his secretary, and afterwards became private physician and minister to the Almohad Prince Yûsuf, at whose court, at Morocco, he died in 1185. His *Asrâr al-ḥikmat al-Mashriqiyya* (Secrets of Illuminative Wisdom) has been printed at Bûlâq. His philosophic novel, *Ḥayy ibn Yaqẓân*, which represents the awakening of the intelligence of a child born alone in the desert, has been published at Oxford by E. Pococke, under the title of *Philosophus Autodidactus*. He strove to reconcile the revealed law with philosophy.

Abû'l-Walîd IBN RUSHD, who is known as AVERROES (1126–1198), who belonged to a family of lawyers, was born at Cordova, and received his education there. He went to Morocco in 1153, and was there presented to the Almohad King, Yûsuf, by Ibn Ṭufail. In 1169 he was

appointed *qâḍî* at Seville, and two years later he returned to his native city, whence he was summoned by Yûsuf, who would have appointed him his body physician, but the man of learning was soon back at Cordova as *qâḍî*. Towards the close of his life he was exiled, and interned at Elisâna, not far from Cordova, by Yûsuf's successor, Yaʿqûb al-Manṣûr, who suspected him of heresy on account of his studies in philosophy. Notwithstanding this, he was once more summoned to Morocco, and died there on 10th December 1198. He left us his *Faṣl al-Maqâl* (Decisive Discourse), in which he endeavours to reconcile Moslem law with science; a refutation of Ghazâlî's *Tahâfut*, which he entitled *Tahâfut al-tahâfut* (The Collapse of the Collapse), the Arabic text of which has been printed at Cairo; a work on therapeutics, called *Kulliyyât;* and his commentary on Aristotle's *Poetry* and *Rhetoric*, which has been published and translated into Italian by F. Lasinio. A fragment of the commentary of Alexander of Aphrodisias on the metaphysics of the great Stagyrite philosopher has been translated by Freudenthal.

Burhân al-dîn AL-ZARNÛJÎ wrote, towards 1203, the *Taʿlîm al-mutaʿallim* (Instruction for Him who Desires to Learn), a manual of which many copies are in existence, and which has been published first by Reland, and then by Caspari, under the title of *Enchiridion Studiosi*.

Many books were written to meet the needs of students. Abû ʿAbdallah AL-KHÂWINJÎ, who was born in 1194, of a Persian family, became *qâḍî* at Cairo, and died in 1248, wrote, when at Mecca, in 1227, a summary of this description, called *al-Jumal*, or *al-Mûjiz*, and also a fuller treatise entitled *Kashf al-asrâr*

(The Secrets Unveiled). Athîr al-dîn Mufaḍḍal al-Abharî, who died in 1264, composed a *Hidâyat al-ḥikma* (Guide to Wisdom), which treats, in Arabic, of logic, physics, and metaphysics, and a *Kitâb al-îsâghûjî*, after the *Εἰσαγωγή*, or introduction to the *Categories* of Aristotle, by Porphyry. Najm al-dîn 'Alî AL-KÂTIBÎ, of Qazvîn, who died in 1276, wrote, on the command of Shams al-dîn Muḥammad Juwainî, and in his honour, a treatise called *Al-Risâla al-shamsiyya*, published by Sprenger as an appendix to the *Dictionary of the Technical Terms;* the *Ḥikmat al-'Ain* (Philosophy of the Essence), on physics and metaphysics, and the *Jâmi' al-daqâ'iq*, on the same subjects. Sirâj al-dîn Abû'l-Thanâ AL-URMAWÎ, who died in 1283, wrote the *Maṭâli' al-anwâr*, on logic.

The controversy and dialectics of this period claim the names of Burhân al-dîn AL-NASAFÎ (1209–1288), with his *Fuṣûl*, his *Muqaddima*, and other similar books, and of Shams al-dîn AL-SAMARQANDÎ, who wrote a *Risâla*, the *Qusṭâs*, and the *'Ain al-Naẓar*, on logic, the *Ṣaḥâ'if*, on dogmatics, and the *Ashkâl al-ta'sîs*, on Euclid's geometry.

'Abdal-Ḥaqq IBN SAB'ÎN, who was born at Murcia, and is known as the founder of the mystic sect of the Sab'îniyya, was at Ceuta when the Almohad Sultan Abdal-Wâḥid ordered him to reply to certain philosophical questions set the learned Arabs by the German Emperor Frederick of Hohenstaufen. His correspondence on this subject has been published and commented on in the *Asiatic Journal*, by A. F. Mehren. Ibn Sab'în committed suicide in 1269, at Mecca, by opening the veins of his wrist. He left an introduction to metaphysics, called *Budd al-'ârif;* another work called

Asrâr al-Ḥikmat al-mashriqiyya (Mysteries of Illuminism), and prayers in which every word begins with the letter *q*.

Shams al-dîn AL-SHAHRAZÛRÎ el-Ishrâqî, in the seventh century of the Hegira, wrote, besides his *Rumûz wa'l-amthâl al-lâhûtiyya* (Divine Mysteries and Parables) and his *Shajarat al-ilâhiyya* (The Divine Tree), a history of the philosophers, from Adam down to Galen, entitled *Rauḍat al-afrâḥ* (The Garden of Joys).

MATHEMATICS

Mathematical study, as we have seen, moved abreast with that of philosophy. There is no doubt that geometry was derived solely from Greek sources, and Euclid's *Elements* more particularly. But it may fairly be questioned whether arithmetic owes much to Indian science. According to Brockelmann, it was the adoption of the Indian numerals which permitted the Arabs to make great progress in that science. But this adoption is of recent date, and the Arabs, like the Greeks, made use of the numerical value of the letters in their own alphabet before they passed on to the decimal system of numeration which originated in India, and has since, under the name of Arabic figures, travelled round the world, but which may possibly have been borrowed by the Indians from the system of the *abacus* (the empty compartment representing the zero), probably invented in Alexandria in the earliest centuries of the Christian era. The Arab author of the tenth century, Muṭahhar ibn Ṭâhir, who wrote the *Kitâb al-bad' wa'l-Ta'rîkh* (The Book of Creation and of History), notes, as a curiosity in Indian or *devanagari* numerals, a pretty

high figure ascribed by Indian populations to the length of the duration of this world. In his day, it is evident, Arabic numerals did not as yet exist in the form the Arabs afterwards gave them, and Indian numerals, though known to the learned, were not in current use; otherwise neither this writer nor his readers would have thought there was anything remarkable in the appearance of the numeral he quotes.

The earliest of the Arab mathematicians was Abû ʿAbdallah AL-KHWÂRIZMÎ, who lived under the Caliphate of Ma'mûn, about 820. At the request of this prince, he prepared an extract from the Indian work called *Siddhânta*, and undertook a revision of Ptolemy's *Tables*. His works on algebra and arithmetic, which were early translated into Latin, found their way all over Europe. My readers are aware that the word *algorithm* is derived from his ethnical surname of Al-Khwârizmî (he came from Khwârizm, the ancient Khanate of Khiva). At Ma'mûn's court, too, dwelt the three sons of Mûsâ ibn Shâkir — Muḥammad, Aḥmad, and Al-Ḥasan—who wrote a great many technical treatises. But the most prominent mathematician of that day was a Ṣâbian belonging to Ḥarrân, Thâbit ibn Qurra. He originally followed the trade of a money-changer, but went to Bagdâd to study science, quarrelled over theological matters with his co-religionists, after returning to his native town, and was cast out of their community. He retired to Kafartûthâ, there made the acquaintance of Muḥammad, son of Mûsâ ibn Shâkir, to whom we have just referred, was taken by him to Bagdâd, and presented to the Caliph Al-Muʿtaḍid. At Bagdâd he devoted himself exclusively to writing medical and mathematical works, and specially in-

terested himself in the theory of numerals; he died there on 18th February 901.

Woepcke has given his views on a theory added by Thâbit ibn Qurra to the speculative arithmetic of the Greeks; the Fifth book of the *Conic Sections* of Apollonius of Perga has been published and translated into German by L. Nix; other works in manuscript are preserved in public libraries. His son Sinân was body physician to the Caliphs Muqtadir and Qâhir; he yielded to their threats, and ended by becoming a Moslem; but his concession did not disarm them, and he took fright and fled to Khurâsân, but ultimately returned, and died at Bagdâd in 942. His mathematical and historical works are lost. All now remaining to us are the works on the dimensions of parabolas, written by his son Ibrâhîm, who died in 946. Abû Bakr al-Karkhî, thus surnamed after one of the suburbs of Bagdâd, is known as having dedicated an epitome of arithmetic (an extract from which has been published by Woepcke, and which has been translated into German by Hochheim) to Fakhr al-Mulk, minister to the Buwaihid prince, Bahâ al-daula.

IBN AL-HAITHAM held a Government appointment in his native town, Bassora, with the title of vizier, and had already earned a reputation for mathematical knowledge, when Caliph al-Ḥâkim, hearing he had boasted of his ability to regularise the periodical inundations of the Nile, summoned him to his court. He travelled up the river as far as Assouan, and convinced himself of the impossibility of carrying out his plan. The Caliph, to indemnify him for his trouble, gave him an administrative post at Cairo, the duties of which he was not able to perform. This roused the sovereign's rage against him,

and he hid himself till his master's death in 1020, when he recovered his confiscated property, and turned his whole attention to literary labours. He died in 1038. Sédillot has written a notice of Ibn al-Haitham's treatise on geometrical knowledge. His treatise on optics (*Taḥrîr al-munâẓara*) was published and translated by Fr. Roesner at Basle in 1572 under the title of *Opticæ thesaurus Alhazeni.*

Abû'l-Fatḥ 'UMAR AL-KHAYYÂM, the Persian poet, celebrated for his mystic quatrains in that tongue, and universally known by the paraphrase of FitzGerald, was also a mathematician, and used the Arabic for his scientific works. His treatise on algebra has been published and translated into French by Woepcke. The Leyden Library possesses a commentary on Euclid of his composition, and that of Gotha a treatise on the chemical analysis of minerals, for the purpose of determining the relative quantities of gold and silver in an amalgam of the two metals. He was astronomer, and more especially astrologer, to the Seljûqid Sultan Malik-Shâh. He it was who proceeded to the reform of the Calendar known under the name of the Jalâlian era, after the surname Jalâl al-dîn, which was borne by Malik-Shâh. He died in 1121.

Maḥmûd AL-JAGHMÎNÎ al-Khwârizmî, who died in 1221, wrote an abridged astronomy (*Mulakhkhaṣ fî'l-hai'a*), which was translated into German by Rudloff and Hochheim in the *Journal* of the German Oriental Society.

Abû'l-Ḥasan 'Alî al-Marrâkushî (or, according to the Leyden MS., Abû 'Alî al-Ḥasan) wrote, in 1230, his *Jâmi' al-mabâdi' wa'l-ghâyât* (Meeting of the Beginnings and the Ends), which has been translated into French

by J. S. Sédillot, and published by his son under the title of *Traité des instruments astronomiques des Arabes.*

Yaḥyâ Ibn Abî Shukr, who bore the honorary title of *Muḥyî'l-milla wa'l-dîn* (Revivifier of the People and of Religion), was of Spanish origin. He was a contemporary of the Syriac historian, Bar Hebræus, and lived first of all in Syria, and then at the court of the Mongol Emperor Hulâgû. Besides writing many astrological and astronomical works, he gave his attention to the *Conic Sections* of Apollonius of Perga, and the *Spherics* of Menelaus and Theodosius, and also to the computation of time amongst the Chinese and the Uigurs.

Astronomy and Astrology

The one cannot live without the other. For centuries the astronomer's only means of ensuring himself the necessaries of life and study was by selling astrological formulæ. Who cared for the movements of the stars? But in the casting of horoscopes, the knowledge of the dim and slow-moving future, there lay interest alike for states and for private individuals! At a very early date, in the beginning of the third century of the Hegira, we find a popular treatise on astrology, in twelve chapters, after the twelve Signs of the Zodiac, by Abû Yûsuf Ya‘qûb al-Qarshî, which is now in the Berlin Library. A little later, Aḥmad ibn Muḥammad al-Farghânî, of whom we know nothing more, beyond the fact that in 861 he built a new Nilometer in Egypt, wrote an astronomical treatise, which rendered him famous all over Europe, under the name of *Alfraganus*, and was translated into Latin, and published by Golius at Amsterdam in 1669.

In 885 the great astronomer Abû Ma'shar Ja'far ibn Muḥammad died at Wâsiṭ. He belonged to Balkh, in Central Asia, and was known in the Middle Ages as ALBUMASER. If Europe admires his astronomical attainments, the East marvels at his powers of divination and his astrological performances, whereby he discovered treasures, and recovered objects which had gone astray. Of his compositions we still possess the *Madkhal*, or introduction to astrology, and other astronomical works, preserved in manuscript in various European libraries.

Muḥammad ibn Jâbir al-Battânî, famous in Europe under the name of ALBATEGNIUS, was a Ṣâbian of Ḥarrân. At Raqqa, on the Euphrates, where he lived, he took astronomical observations from 882 to 900, and there drew up his *Tables*, which are now at the Escurial, and which Signor Nallino is translating into Latin, and publishing at Milan. He was going to Bagdâd to prosecute a lawsuit, in 929, when he died in a little town on his road. Towards the end of the eighteenth century his *Tables*, which were translated by Plato Tiburtius under the title of *De Scientiâ Stellarum*, and printed at Nürnberg in 1537, were still valued by Lalande.

Besides these great names, we may also cite those of the following Persians: Kûshyâr ibn Labbân, author of various astrological and astronomical works, *circa* 961; Abû Naṣr al-Qummî, *circa* 968; Abû'l-Ḥusain 'Abdal-Raḥmân al-Ṣûfî, of Rai, an astronomer in the service of the Buwaihid Prince 'Aḍud al-daula, who died in 986, wrote a description of the fixed stars, which has been translated into French by Schelljerup at St. Petersburg in 1874, and a memoir on the astrolabe, of which Bernard Dorn has made use for one of his studies; Abû Sahl Waijân ibn Rustam al-Kûhî, *circa* 990; Abû'l-Wafâ

Muḥammad al-Bûzjânî, who came from a large village near Nîshâpûr in Khurâsân, died in 997, wrote an imitation of Ptolemy's *Almagest*, and, by his deductions of certain previously unknown corollaries, earned the reputation of a great geometrician—it is doubtful whether, as Sédillot believed, he discovered the third inequality on the moon's surface before Tycho Brahé. After these Persians came ʿAlî ibn Abî Saʿîd al-Ṣadafî, who was astronomer to the Fâṭimid Caliph of Egypt, Al-Ḥâkim, to whom he dedicated his great *Ḥâkimite Table*, dealt with by Caussin de Perceval in *Notices et Extraits*—he died in 1008; Abû'l-Ḥasan ʿAlî ibn Abî'l-Rijâl, in Africa, whose book on astrology was translated into Latin, and published at Basle under the title of *Albohazen* in 1551; and Abû'l-Qâsim al-Ghâfiqî, a Spanish physician and mathematician, whose treatise on the astrolabe is preserved in the British Museum.

Geography

The geography of the Arabs is of Greek origin; Al-Kindî had Ptolemy's work on geography translated for him, and this translation was improved at a later date by Thâbit ibn Qurra; it is now lost. The most ancient abridged geography in our possession is the *Ṣûrat al-arḍ* (Face of the Earth), by Muḥammad ibn Mûsâ al-Khwârizmî (1036), which has been studied by W. Spitta and C. Nallino. But the Arabic tongue, in response to the political and economic needs of the huge empire the Caliphs had to rule, was soon able to produce descriptive geographical works of immense interest in their bearing on our knowledge of the East of the Middle Ages, and some of the most eminent Orientalists have

been content to limit their attention to their study and publication. The postmasters of the horse-posts—those functionaries who, both in the capital and in the provincial centres, were responsible for the transmission of the Government correspondence, and at the same time were expected to keep the central authority informed of everything that occurred all over that huge empire—wrote descriptions of the countries ruled by the Koran, to facilitate the performance of their own official duties. Ibn Khurdâdbeh (ʻUbaidallah ibn ʻAbdallah) was of Persian descent; his grandfather, who was a fire-worshipper, had become a convert to Islam, and his father was for some time governor of the province of Ṭabaristân on the Caspian Sea. He himself lived at Bagdâd, and there made the acquaintance of the famous musician Isḥâq, of Mosul, who instructed him in music and *belles-lettres*. He was ultimately sent to ʻIrâq as a director of posts, and was at Sâmarrâ on the Tigris between 844 and 848, when he wrote his *Book of the Roads and Provinces*, which accurately gives the postal stations and the amount of taxation in each province. Barbier de Meynard was the first to translate and publish this work, of which, at a later date, De Goeje issued a corrected text, according to less defective manuscripts, at Leyden.

Ibn Wâḍiḥ al-Yaʻqûbî, properly called Aḥmad ibn Abî Yaʻqûb, belonged to the family of the ʻAbbâsid Caliphs. His great-grandfather, Wâḍiḥ, a freedman of Caliph Manṣûr, who became governor of Armenia, Âdharbaijân, and Egypt, was a Shîʻite; his devotion to the ʻAlid Prince Idrîs, whom he helped to escape towards Morocco, brought him the penalty of death. As for our geographer, he lived at the court of the Ṭâhirid

princes of Khurâsân, and made a journey into India, Egypt, and the Maghrib, where he wrote, under the title of *Book of the Countries*, a description of this latter country, rich in topographical detail, and accounts of the chief towns. He also wrote a history of the 'Abbâsids, which is really a universal history in two volumes, carried down to the year 872, and the interest of which is doubled by the fact that it is the earliest work of the kind produced by a Shî'ite, and marked by Shî'ite tendencies, and that the author has drawn on ancient and valuable sources of information, which have thus become available in the interests of science.

Abû Bakr Ibn al-Faqîh belonged to Hamadhân, in Persia. Very soon after the death of the Caliph Mu'taḍid (902), he wrote a geographical work, of which all we now possess is the extract made in 1022 by 'Alî ibn Ja'far of Shaizar, and which is also remarkable, because no mention is made in it of the capital, Bagdâd, a fact which would lead us to suppose the book was founded on information collected in the days of the Omeyyads, before that famous city was built. Ibn Rosteh (Abû 'Alî), who was at Ispahan towards 903, there compiled an encyclopædia entitled *al-A'lâq al-Nafîsa;* the geographical portion of this work, which forms its seventh volume, has been preserved at the British Museum, and has been published, with the preceding ones, by De Goeje, in his *Bibliotheca Geographorum Arabicorum.* Quite recently Mr. Guy Le Strange has made us acquainted with a certain Ibn Serapion, whose curious name recalls Egypt to our minds, and who, after the taking of Bagdâd by the Buwaihids in 945, wrote an account of that capital, and of Mesopotamia. But nothing is known of this topo-

grapher, whom historical order places here. Ibn Faḍlân, an ambassador sent in 921, by Caliph Al-Muqtadir, to the King of the Bulgarians, whose abode, in those days, was on the banks of the Volga, brought back an account of his mission, which was utilised by Yâqût in his great geographical dictionary; the part dealing with the ancient Russians has been translated into German and published by Frähn.

Qudâma (Abû'l-Faraj), surnamed the Secretary of Bagdâd, left a book on the land-tax, which, before dealing with the questions connected with the levying and yield of the tax, gives an account of the organisation of the postal service, and a summary of the geography of the Arab Empire and the adjoining countries. But Qudâma was only a geographer on occasions; by profession he was a literary man. He wrote a book called *Criticism of Poetry*, which treats of the poetic art amongst the Arabs, and one of his pupils composed a work on rhetoric, founded on his teachings, which is now in the Escurial Library.

The Sâmânid dynasty was then beginning to attract attention in Khurâsân, where it had attained complete independence. It protected literature and learning, and to it geographical science owes the appearance of a work written between 892 and 907 by Al-Jaihânî, who acted as minister to several of the Sâmânid princes—a work which has now completely disappeared, unless, indeed, Idrîsî used it, as has been insinuated, for his description of Asia. This same Al-Jaihânî, taking advantage of the presence of the Indian prince, Kalatli, the son of Chakhbar, at the Bukhârian court, caused the Arab poet, Abû Dulaf Mis'ar ibn Muhalhal, who was born at Yambo, on the Red Sea, to accompany the royal visitor on his return

journey through Thibet. The poet-traveller made his way back from India by Kashmîr, Afghanistan, and Sijistân, and after his return wrote a book called *Marvels of the Countries*, which has been utilised by Yâqût and by Qazwînî, and studied by Schlözer.

In the year 921, the philosopher Abû Zaid ibn Sahl al-Balkhî wrote a book entitled *Ṣuwar al-aqâlîm* (Figures of the Climates), the contents of which consist, for the most part, of geographical maps. A copy of this work is now at Berlin. The author had belonged, in his youth, to the Imâmite sect; to attain a closer acquaintance with it, he went to 'Irâk, sat at the feet of Al-Kindî, and devoted himself to philosophical studies. The Prince of Balkh, who bore the same name as himself, Aḥmad ibn Sahl, loaded him with benefits, and enabled him to buy a landed property. He died in 934. For a very long time, though probably quite incorrectly, the authorship of the *Book of the Creation and of History* (which appears to have really been written by Muṭahhar ibn Ṭâhir al-Maqdisî, who lived in the town of Bust, in Sijistân) was ascribed to him.

The geography of the Arabian Peninsula was the favourite theme of Al-Hamdânî, who belonged to a family of Yemen, and was passionately interested in the antiquities of Arabia Felix, in its historical memories, and the ancient ruined fortresses which recall the past splendours of the kingdom of Sheba. His account of the Peninsula has been published by D. H. Müller, and studied by Sprenger. His book entitled *Iklîl* (The Crown), which is now at Berlin, furnished D. H. Müller with the subject-matter for his study of the strong castles in Southern Arabia.

Abû 'Abdallah al-Maqdisi, still called Al-Muqaddasî

by long-standing habit (this form of his surname is admissible, but very unusual), was born at Jerusalem. He spent a great part of his life in travelling all over the Moslem Empire, with the exception, perhaps, of its eastern and western extremities, India and Spain. His book entitled *Aḥsan al-taqâsîm fî ma'rifat al-aqâlîm* (The Best of Divisions for Knowledge of the Climates) is a very complete work, in which, besides the results of his own personal observation, he gives a summary of all previous information. It was written in 985. This account of the Moslem states has been frequently utilised by subsequent geographers. Abû Raiḥân Muḥammad AL-BÎRÛNÎ derived his surname from the fact that he was born in one of the suburbs of Khwârizm (Khiva), in September 973. His family was of Persian origin. He studied profoundly, history, mathematics, and medicine. He kept up a correspondence with Avicenna. At a later date he proceeded to India, and studied the learning of that country, of which he has left us a very exact description in his *Ta'rîkh al-Hind* (History of India), translated into English and published by E. Sachau. After his return he attached himself to the court of the famous Ghaznavid prince, Maḥmûd ibn Subuktakîn, to whom he dedicated his *Qânûn al-Mas'ûdî*, a complete treatise on astronomy. He died at Ghazna on 13th December 1048. Like most of his compatriots, he was a Shî'ite, and ill-disposed towards the Arabs. His chronology of the Oriental peoples (*al-Âthâr al-bâqiya*, The Existing Monuments of Past Centuries), which is full of the most interesting information as to the populations inhabiting Central Asia, has been translated into English and published by Sachau.

Abû 'Ubaid AL-BAKRÎ (1040–1094), who was born and

died at Cordova, wrote, under the title of *Mu'jam mâ ista'jam*, a geographical dictionary of the names of localities mentioned by the ancient Arab poets, with an introduction dealing with the geographical positions of the various tribes, which has been published by Wüstenfeld, and a general geography, under the title commonly borne by most Arabic treatises on this subject, *al-Masâlik wa'l-mamâlik* (The Roads and the Provinces), from which the Baron MacGuckin de Slane has extracted and translated the *Description de l'Afrique Septentrionale.*

Muḥammad ibn Abî Bakr AL-ZUHRÎ, who lived at Grenada in 1137, has left a geography from which an extract—an account of the *Sûs al-aqṣâ*—has appeared in the *Bulletin de correspondance Africaine.*

Abû 'Abdallah al-Sharîf AL-IDRÎSÎ, who was born at Ceuta in 1099, of an 'Alid family, studied at Cordova, travelled far and wide, and reached the court of the Norman King of Sicily, Roger II., for whom he wrote, in 1154, his great geographical work, *Nuzhat al-Mushtâq*, which has been translated into French—not, indeed, in a very satisfactory manner—by Amédée Jaubert.

Abû 'Abdallah Muḥammad AL-MÂZINÎ (1080–1169), who was born at Grenada, travelled over a great part of the Moslem world—Egypt, where he arrived in 1114; Bagdâd, whither he went in 1161; and Khurâsân, whence he returned to Syria, and settled at Damascus, where he died. He founded his geography, entitled *Tuḥfat al-albâb wa-nukhbat al-A'jâb* (Gift Bestowed on Hearts, and Selection of Wonders), on his own journeys, and on accounts furnished by reliable witnesses. He collected for the library of Abû'l-Muẓaffar Yaḥyâ ibn Hubaira accounts of all his travels, in which many fabulous legends are embodied, under the title of *'Ajâ'ib*

al-Makhlûqât (Wonders of the Creatures); it is now at the Bodleian. The title of this book was frequently used by later writers.

Abû'l-Ḥusain Muḥammad IBN JUBAIR, who was born in 1145, wrote, towards the end of the sixth century of the Hegira, an account of his pilgrimage to Mecca from its starting-point in Spain. The text of this work has been published by Wright, and extracts from it have been translated into French by Amari and Crolla. The author was of Valencian extraction. He settled at Grenada, but left it in 1182, when he started on his journey. When he came back, he went to Malaga, Ceuta, and Fez, where he taught. He died in 1217, having amassed a considerable fortune, which he renounced from motives of piety.

YÂQÛT ibn 'Abdallah al-Rûmî was born of Greek parents, on territory belonging to the Roman Empire of the East, towards the year 1179. He was carried off in a foray, taken to Bagdâd, and sold as a slave to a merchant from Ḥamât, who had settled in the Caliphs' capital. His owner had him carefully educated, and sent him, when still quite young, on journeys connected with his trade. Returning in 1194 from his third voyage on the Persian Gulf, he quarrelled with his master, who was also his benefactor, and, being turned out of his house, began to copy for his livelihood, and studied under the grammarian Al-'Ukbarî. Some years later he made up his difference with his patron, and once more started for the Persian Gulf; but when he got back in the following year, he found the merchant was dead, set up as a bookseller, and began to publish writings. In 1213 he started on his travels again, went first of all to Tabrîz, then left Mosul for Syria and Egypt, and proceeded to Khurâsân in 1215. To console himself for

the loss of a Turkish slave-woman, from whom he had been constrained to part on account of his poverty, he read the books in the libraries of Merv, and conceived the plan of his great geographical dictionary. Having spent some two years at Merv, he proceeded to Khiva and Balkh, and, while in the latter town, heard that Bukhârâ and Samarqand had been taken by the Mongols. Alarmed by this catastrophe he turned back into Khurâsân, and returned, in 1220, to Mosul, where he took up his old occupation of copying. The Vizier Jamâl al-dîn al-Shaibâni, to whom he had recourse, supplied him with the means to join him at Aleppo in 1222. He returned to Mosul and set himself to complete his dictionary, which was finished on 13th March 1224. In 1227 he once more travelled to Alexandria, returned to Aleppo in the following year, and busied himself with correcting the manuscript of his great work. He died there on 20th August 1229.

His *Mu'jam al-buldân* has been published by Wüstenfeld, and so has his *Mushtarik*, a dictionary of geographical homonyms. An abridgment of the first-named work, *Marâṣid al-iṭṭilâ'*, published at Leyden by Juynboll, was for many years the only one of its kind within the reach of Orientalists. He also produced a dictionary of literary men, *Mu'jam al-udabâ*, of which an edition is in course of preparation by Mr. Margoliouth. The *Muqtaḍab min jamharat al-nasab*, the manuscript of which is now at Cairo, is a selection from the genealogies of the Arab tribes.

Muwaffaq al-dîn 'ABDAL-LAṬÎF ibn Yûsuf (1160–1231), a physician, was born and died at Bagdâd. He wrote an account of Egypt, to which J. White, Wahl, and Silvestre de Saçy have all turned their attention.

He also left a collection of sayings of the Prophet and his companions, the *Tajrîd*, and a description of Mahomet's personal appearance, abridged from the *Maqâlat al-Tâj*.

Zakariyyâ AL-QAZWÎNÎ, who was born at Qazwîn in Âdharbaigân towards 1203, was descended from Anas, the son of Mâlik. He left his native town, for what reason we know not, and settled, in 1232, at Damascus, where he made the acquaintance of Ibn al-ʿArabî. We next find him serving as *qâḍî* of the towns of Wâsiṭ and Ḥilla, under Al-Mustaʿṣim, the last ʿAbbâsid Caliph of Bagdâd; he died in 1283. He was the author of the ʿ*Ajâ'ib al-Makhlûqât* (Marvels of the Creatures), a cosmography, published by Wüstenfeld, and of the *Âthâr al-Bilâd* (Monuments of the Countries), an historical geography.

Abû Muḥammad AL-ʿABDARÎ, who belonged to Valencia, wrote, in the year 1289, a *Riḥla* (Journey), which contains accounts of the African towns, and details both of their inhabitants in general, and of the learned men who dwelt in them.

MEDICINE

The Syrians had carried the knowledge of medicine even into the East; the school of Gundêshâpûr kept up its medical traditions until the days of the ʿAbbâsid Caliphs. Thence it was that the Caliph Manṣûr called George Bôkhtyishûʿ to be his body physician. Yet India exercised a certain influence over Arab medicine. We know that Hârûn al-Rashîd had the Indian physician Manka at his court; and A. Müller has proved that Rhazes made use of the Indian *Suçruta* for his *Ḥâwî*.

The body physician to the Caliphs Muʿtaṣim and

Mutawakkil was Abû'l-Ḥasan 'Alî ibn Sahl ibn Rabban, son of a Jewish physician from Ṭabaristân; the first of these two sovereigns never rested till he had converted his medical attendant to the Moslem faith, and his change of religion established him in his position. His claim to glory lies in the fact that he was Rhazes' instructor. His two books, *al-Kunnâsh* (System of Medicine) and *Ḥifẓ al-Ṣiḥḥa* (Preservation of Health), are now at Berlin, at the British Museum, and the Bodleian.

From Gundêshâpûr, too, came Abu Zakariyyâ Yaḥyâ ibn Mâsawaih, the son of an apothecary in that town. At Bagdâd, where he was studying, he met Gabriel, son of Bôkhtyishû', private physician to Hârûn al-Rashîd, who entrusted him with the management of an hospital. At a later date he succeeded to Gabriel's post about Caliph Manṣûr and his successors, down to Wâthiq. He translated many books from the Greek, and himself wrote original works, such as his *Nawâdir al-ṭibb* (Curiosities of Medicine), dedicated to Ḥunain ibn Isḥâq.

Isḥâq ibn 'Imrân, who was summoned to Qairawân by the Aghlabite Prince Ziyâdat-Allah III., who suffered from melancholia, belonged to Bagdâd. He quarrelled with the prince, and died under torture, having been denounced by one of his enemies, a Jew. He left a treatise on melancholia, which is now at Munich.

The great physician of that period was RHAZES, otherwise called Abû Bakr Muḥammad ibn Zakariyyâ al-Râzî—that is to say, born at Rai, the ancient Rhages. Till his twentieth year he gave all his attention to music. He then went to Bagdâd, and studied medicine under 'Alî ibn Sahl ibn Rabban, physician to the Caliph Mu'taṣim. When he had attained the mastery of his profession, he was sent to manage the hospital at Rai,

and later returned to Bagdâd, to hold a similar post there. Then he travelled. The fame of his knowledge had already spread over the East; the Sâmânid prince Manṣûr ibn Isḥâq welcomed him to his court, and to him the physician dedicated the work he entitled *Manṣûrî*. There was no little brutality about this sovereign of Khurâsân. When Râzî presented him with his work on alchemy, he insisted that the learned writer should demonstrate the reality of the facts he put forward, and as he failed in doing anything of the kind, Manṣûr, in a rage, lashed him across the eyes with a whip, and blinded him. The date and place of the great physician's death are alike unknown to us. Some say he died at Rai, some at Bagdâd; the date is variously given as 923 and 932. He had been unable to complete the preparation of his great work, the *Ḥâwî*, during his lifetime. It was finished, after his death, by one of his pupils, according to his manuscript notes, on the order of the minister to the Buwaihid prince Rukn al-daula. His *Manṣûrî*, a treatise on medicine in ten books, his book on smallpox, and many others, were translated into Hebrew and Latin, or published in the original text, at an early date. A great number of them are in the Escurial Library.

In Egypt, again, Isḥâq ibn Sulaimân, whose surname, Isrâ'îlî, denotes his Jewish origin, had come into the world. He went to Qairawân in the days of the Aghlabite prince Ziyâdat-Allah III., and there knew Isḥâq îbn 'Imrân; later, after the Aghlabites had fallen, he passed into the service of the Fâṭimid Caliph Al-Mahdî, and died towards 932, after writing a book on fevers, a treatise on food and medicine, and inquiries into the nature of the elements.

'Îsâ ibn 'Alî, a Christian physician, wrote, when at Bagdâd, a memoir on the diseases of the eye and their treatment, which was known in Europe at an early period, being much consulted by surgeons. It was printed at Venice in 1499. Another author, also well known in Europe during the Renaissance period, was 'Alî ibn 'Abbâs, physician to the Buwaihid prince 'Aḍud al-daula. He was the son of a Magian (hence his surname of Majûsî), and was born at al-Ahwâz, in the heart of Susiana. His principal work, entitled *Kâmil al-Ṣanâ'a al-ṭibbiyya* (Complete Treatise on the Art of Medicine), was translated into Latin by Stephen of Antioch, and published at Leyden in 1523.

Abû Sahl 'Îsâ ibn Yaḥyâ was a Christian from Jurjân, who practised medicine in Khurâsân. He died young, at the age of forty, towards the year 1000, and was the medical instructor of Avicenna. He wrote a Medical Encyclopædia divided into one hundred monographs, a book on general therapeutics, a demonstration of the wisdom of the Deity as seen in the creation of the various members and organs of the human frame, and several other less important works.

To return to the West. We first find a native of the Maghrib, lawyer and physician at once, named Abû 'Abdallah Muḥammad ibn 'Alî ibn Tûmirt, who died in 1001, and is said to have composed five hundred works, some fragments of which still exist in the libraries of the present day; Al-Jazzâr (Abû Ja'far), unlike his contemporaries, preferred attending the private residents in the town of Qairawân to doctoring royal personages, and in his zeal for religion served year after year with the piratical expeditions organised in Tunis under pretext of warring against the infidels,

which did not prevent him from dying at the advanced age of over eighty years, in 1004. His abridged treatise on medicine, entitled *Zâd al-Musâfir wa-Qût al-Ḥâḍir* (The Traveller's Viaticum and Food for the Sedentary Man), a book on the confidence that should be placed in simples, and another on the education of children, are still extant. His treatise on the medicine of the poor and indigent marks him as a predecessor of Raspail. At Cordova, under Caliph ʿAbdal-Raḥmân III., we find Abû'l-Qâsim Khalaf ibn ʿAbbâs al-Zahrâwî, better known under the European corruption of his name, ALBUCASIS, a great surgeon, who frequently resorted to cauterisation, and whose works, translated into Latin, were published in the early days of the art of printing.

Abû'l-Faraj ʿAbdallah IBN AL-ṬAYYIB, a Christian physician, who taught at the hospital in Bagdâd founded by the Buwaihid prince ʿAḍud al-daula, and also acted as secretary to the Catholicos Elias I., died in 1043. He paraphrased Galen's works, and wrote books on Christian theology.

His pupil, Abû'l-Ḥasan al-Mukhtâr IBN BOṬLÂN, likewise a Christian and a physician, travelled to Egypt in 1047, to make the acquaintance of his literary opponent, Ibn Riḍwân. Feeling defeat close upon him, he made his way to the territory of the Greek Empire, went to Constantinople and Antioch, took refuge in a cloister, and died there after the year 1063. His *Taqwîm al-Ṣiḥḥa* (Tables of Health) is a collection of forty tables of mortality, which were translated and published at Strasburg in 1532. His *Daʿwat al-aṭibbâ* is a conversation on medical subjects between the author and a physician of seventy years of age, residing at Mayyâfâriqîn. His *Amrâḍ al-ʿÂriḍa* is a treatise

on therapeutics, for the use of persons living far from a town. He also wrote two tracts, one to point out what defects in a slave may be regarded as redhibitory in cases of sale, and the other to demonstrate that the temperature of the blood of the common fowl is higher than that of any other bird.

Abû Sa'îd 'Ubaidallah IBN BÔKHTYISHÛ' belonged to the famous medical family of that name. He was the friend of Ibn Boṭlân, lived at Mayyâfâriqîn, and died towards 1058. He wrote on love as a disease, and on specifics.

Abû'l-Ḥasan 'Alî IBN RIḌWÂN was an Egyptian, born at Gizeh, at the base of the Great Pyramid. The Caliph Al-Ḥâkim chose him to be his body physician, and this was his stepping-stone to fortune. Unhappily the wealth he amassed was ultimately squandered by an adopted son who betrayed his confidence. He died in 1061 or 1068. Under the title of *Kifâyat al-Ṭabîb* (That which Suffices to the Physician), he left a treatise on the classification of diseases and on diagnosis, in which the examination of the patient's urine is much insisted upon. Of his *Uṣûl fî'l-ṭibb* (Principles of Medicine) nothing but a Hebrew translation now remains to us. His commentary on Galen's *Ars Parva* was translated into Latin, and published at Venice in 1496, and his commentary on Ptolemy's *Quadripartitum* at the same city in 1484.

Abû 'Alî Yaḥyâ Ibn Jazla, a man of Christian origin, became a convert to Islamism in 1074, and was appointed secretary to the Ḥanafite *qâḍî* of Bagdâd. He wrote a letter, which has now disappeared, to refute the doctrines of Christianity. He devoted his attention to medical matters, and practised his art on his friends

and neighbours, without ever demanding a fee, nor even any payment for the drugs he supplied. He died in 1100. Under the title of *Taqwîm al-Abdân*, he drew up tables of diseases on the system followed for astronomical tables. These were translated into Latin at Strasburg, in 1532. He also made out an alphabetical index of remedies, simple and composite, entitled *Minhâj al-bayân*.

Abû'l-Ṣalt Umayya ibn 'Abdal-'Azîz (1068–1134) was born at Denia in Spain. In 1096 he went to Alexandria, and thence to Cairo. As a punishment for having failed in an attempt to float a stranded vessel, he was cast into prison, and there remained till 1111. He left Egypt in consequence of this misadventure, and retired to Mahdiyya in Tunis, where he was received with honour, and ultimately died. He left a book on the simple drugs (*al-Adwiya al-mufrada*), a treatise on the astrolabe, astronomical problems with figures attached, and a treatise on logic called *Taqwîm al-Dhihn* (Tables of the Mind). He also wrote poetry, all of which, except one ode, now at Berlin, has disappeared.

Abû'l-Faraj 'Abdal-Raḥmân ibn Naṣrallah of Shîrâz, who practised medicine at Aleppo towards 1169, wrote, besides his treatise on the mysteries of the science of marriage (*al-Îḍâḥ fî asrâr 'ilm al-nikâḥ*), and his *Rauḍat al-Qulûb* (the Garden of Hearts), on love, a book explaining dreams (*Khulâṣat al-Kalâm*), which has been translated into French by P. Vattier, under the title of *Oneirocrite musulman*.

Abû 'Imrân Mûsâ Ibn Maimûn, known as Maimonides, the great Jewish philosopher of Cordova, was a physician. He was born at Cordova, and studied Jewish theology and medicine. For some time, under the second

Almohad Sultan, 'Abdal-Mu'min, who ordered all the Jews and Christians in his dominions to choose between retractation and banishment, he passed himself off as a Moslem. Then, when he had put his affairs in order, he departed to Egypt, avowed his real faith, and even founded a Talmudic school in Old Cairo. Saladin appointed him his own physician, and he held the same post under Saladin's successor, Malik-'Azîz. Maimonides died in 1204. His *Guide for the Lost*, written in the Arabic language, but in Hebrew characters, belongs to Arabic literature. It is a philosophical treatise on certain terms of the Biblical *théodicée*. It has been published and translated into French by S. Munk. Among his medical works, one dedicated to the *qâḍî* Al-Fâḍil, a treatise on the venom of reptiles, and how to cure their bites, is particularly curious.

Alchemy

There were students of alchemy in the Omeyyad family, for we find that a prince belonging to that dynasty, Khâlid ibn Yazîd, pupil of the monk Marianus, wrote three treatises on the subject. Jâbir ibn Ḥayyân, the great alchemist, whose teaching ruled the Middle Ages, was probably his pupil, and we are also told that the Imâm Ja'far Ṣâdiq, the master of all occult science, was Jâbir's teacher. What was his native country? No man knows. Some say he came from Ṭûs, in Khurâsân. Others declare his home was Antaradus, on the Syrian coast. Brockelmann inclines to the opinion that he was a Ṣâbian from Ḥarrân. All that can be said with certainty is that he was living at Kûfa towards 776. Twenty-seven of his works are known to the world, several of which were translated

into Latin and German, and published at Nuremberg, Frankfurt, and Strasburg, between 1473 and 1710.

At the end of the third century of the Hegira, as Rosen has established, the alchemist Muḥammad ibn Umail wrote an ode on certain winged forms seen on the walls of a temple at Bûṣîr, which popular legend asserted to be the prison in which Joseph was shut up, and added a commentary on his own ode, with observations derived from the science of alchemy.

Together with these reveries, in which the germ of chemistry appears as yet to possess no scientific basis, we note the appearance of a work devoted to the agriculture of the Nabateans, and full of scientific observation preserved by tradition among the toilers on the Mesopotamian plains. My readers are aware that the Arabs gave the name of Nabateans to the aboriginal populations of Chaldea and Babylon, a Semitic race, among whom the Aramaic had supplanted the ancient dialects, and become the national language. Abû Bakr Ibn al-Wahshiyya was of Aramean blood, and was born in ʿIrâq. In the year 904, he wrote a book on Nabatean agriculture, in which Chwolson thought he had discovered the remains of the ancient Babylonian literature, whereas, in reality, the Arab author, in his anxiety to demonstrate the Aramean-Syrian civilisation to be better and more highly developed than that of the Arab conquerors, had not hesitated to fabricate writings wholesale, with the object of strengthening his own theory. The Russian Orientalist never stopped to consider that Ibn al-Waḥshiyya—like the Egyptian Arabs in the matter of the hieroglyphs—knew nothing of the Babylonian literature, the written characters of which were not deciphered till our own time. Another tendency to be

noted in this same work is the author's evident desire to oppose Moslem dogmas by the quotation of alleged texts, and this in spite of the fact that he himself always appears to be a pious disciple of Islam. Another forgery due to the same writer is the *Shauq al-Mustahâm* (The Desire of the Troubled Heart which would know the Secrets of the Writings), devoted to the writings of the various nations, a subject on which the author, like all Orientals, must have been very imperfectly informed. We also owe him several treatises on alchemy, and the *Sidrat al-Muntahâ* (The Bush of the Boundary), a conversation on religious and philosophical topics.

A Spaniard of Madrid, Abû'l-Qâsim Maslama al-Majrîṭî, who died in 1007, was famous, in the days of Al-Ḥakam II., for his knowledge of mathematics and astronomy, and perhaps even more so for his practice of the occult sciences. He wrote on alchemy, and on the fabrication of talismans and amulets.

At about the same period we must place the author of the most ancient known Arabic book on mineralogy. It is called the *Book of Minerals and Precious Stones*, and was written by ʻUṭârid ibn Muḥammad, surnamed Al-Ḥâsib (the Calculator), or Al-Kâtib (the Secretary). Towards the year 900, the Superintendent of the Stables belonging to Caliph Muʻtaḍid wrote a treatise on horses and horsemanship, also the oldest known Arabic work on that particular subject. It is now in the British Museum. This student of horse-flesh was named Abû Yûsuf Yaʻqûb ibn Akhî Ḥizâm. The interpretation of dreams, one of the most ancient of the pseudo-sciences of the East, is represented by the *Kitâb al-Qâdirî*, dedicated to the Caliph Al-Qâdir by Abû Saʻîd Naṣr ibn Yaʻqûb al-Dînawarî, in 1006.

Towards the same period, too, we perceive the first advent of the abridged encyclopædias, which were later to increase in considerable numbers. The oldest of these is the *Mafâtiḥ al-'Ulûm* (Keys of the Sciences), published by G. van Vloten, after the Leyden manuscript, and written by Abû 'Abdallah Muḥammad al-Khwârizmî for Abû'l-Ḥasan 'Ubaidallah al-'Utbî, minister to the Sâmânid prince, Nûḥ II. The *Kitâb al-Muqâbasât*, by 'Alî al-Tauḥîdî (died 1009), divided into a hundred and three sections, and dealing with various sciences, should be classed in the same category.

'Abdallah Ibn Baiṭâr, who was born at Malaga, travelled as a botanist in Egypt, Asia Minor, and Greece. At Damascus, he entered the service of the prince Malik-Kâmil, as his chief botanist. On the death of his protector he returned to Cairo, but in spite of the honourable reception bestowed upon him there by Malik-Ṣâliḥ he soon returned to Damascus, and died in the Syrian capital in 1248. He left two works on simples, the *Mughnî* and the *Jâmi' mufradât*, which last has been translated into German by J. von Sontheimer, and into French by L. Leclerc.

Abû Zakariyyâ Yaḥyâ Ibn al-'Awwâm, of Seville, wrote, during the first half of the sixth century of the Hegira, the *Kitâb al-Falâḥa* (Book of Agriculture), founded on Greek authorities and on the results of his own inquiries. This has been published and translated into Spanish by Banquera, and into French by J.-J. Clément-Mullet.

Shihâb al-dîn Abû'l-'Abbâs al-Tîfâshî, who died in 1253, wrote a book on minerals and precious stones called the *Azhâr al-afkâr* (Flowers of Thought), which was studied by Ravius at Utrecht in 1784, and by Clément-Mullet in 1868.

The occult sciences, too, added their quota to the enrichment of literature, as, for instance, in the case of the *dîwân* called *Shudhûr al-dhahab* (The Parings of Gold), a collection of poems on the philosopher's stone, by Burhân al-dîn IBN ARFAʿ-RAʾSAHU, of Jaen in Spain, who died at Fez in 1197. Zain al-dîn ʿAbdal-Raḥîm AL-JAUBARÎ, was born in the village of Jaubar, near Damascus, was at Ḥarrân in Mesopotamia in 1216, at Konia in Asia Minor in 1219, and, on the order of Masʿûd, the Urtuqid prince of Âmid (Diyârbakr), and Ḥiṣn Kaifâ, wrote the *Mukhtâr fî Kashf al-asrâr* (Select Book for the Revelation of Mysteries), which contains explanations of sleight-of-hand tricks and prestidigitation.

Muḥyîʾ al-dîn ʿAbûʾl-ʿAbbâs AL-BÛNÎ, who died in 1225, wrote a number of tracts on the magic art, such as the *Faḍâʾil al-basmala*, on the use of the formula "*Bismillah*" and its employment in magic operations; the *Qabs al-iqtidâ*, on the mysterious properties of the name of God, and the manner in which it should be used in connection with talismans; the *Mawâqit al-ghâyât*, on the mysteries of the contemplative life of the Ṣûfîs; and the *Sirr al-ḥikam*, on the Kabbala and on divination.

ENCYCLOPÆDIAS

Original composition gradually becomes more and more rare, and its place is taken by compilations, abridgments of such great works as were difficult to come by, and the too concise text of which needed the skill of a commentator to shed light on its obscurities. We also notice a tendency, on the part of authors, to forsake special subjects, and plunge into a constantly

widening field of general knowledge. Some of these universally-minded men we have already mentioned; we now proceed to some others of the same temperament.

Thus it was that, in the year 1135, Jamâl al-dîn Abû 'Abdallah AL-QAZWÎNÎ wrote his *Mufîd al-'ulûm*, a popular encyclopædia, religious, moral, geographical, and historical; that Abû 'Âmir Muḥammad AL-BALAWÎ, who died at Seville in 1164, drew up his *Unmûdhaj al-'Ulûm*, devoted to twenty-four different sciences, and that Abû Bakr Muḥammad AL-ISHBÎLÎ (1108–1179), born at Seville, who, at the age of seventy, became Imâm of the Great Mosque of Cordova, and died there, collected the titles of over fourteen hundred books in his *Fihrist*, which has been published by Codera and Tarrago at Saragossa.

A polygraph gifted with an extraordinary facility for composition was Jamâl al-dîn Abû'l-Faraj Abdal-Raḥmân IBN AL-JAUZÎ (1116–1200), belonging to an ancient Arab family which traced its descent from the Caliph Abû Bakr. He was born at Bagdâd; his father, a wealthy man, gave him a careful and expensive education. He was a great lover of books, and when his money ran short he sold the two houses his father had left him, so as to be able to add to his library. His intelligence was precocious. At seven years old he was following the explanation of the *Musnad* delivered by Ibn Ḥanbal, and throughout his life he preserved a special taste for the study of the traditions of the Prophet. He was a rigid Ḥanbalite, and fought vigorously against the disciples of the other orthodox schools. For fertility of production, no writer except Suyûṭî can be compared with him. His works cover the whole field of

literature, with the exception of grammar, scholastic theology, and the exact sciences. He preached both at Mecca and Bagdâd, not in the Mosques, but in private gatherings. The Sunnites and the Shîʻites, who were eternally at variance, chose him one day to be their arbiter. He got out of the difficulty by pronouncing an ambiguous sentence which satisfied both parties. He boasted that he had converted more than a hundred thousand men to lead a pious life, and had induced over ten thousand young people to think seriously about themselves. To give an idea of his prodigious activity, it was asserted that if the number of quires, or folds of twenty pages, written by Ibn al-Jauzî during his life were to be totted up, and the total divided by that of the days he lived, he would be found to have produced nine for each day. Ibn Khallikân rejects this result, as being inadmissible by any reasonable man.

In the field of linguistic study we find him writing a *Taqwîm al-lugha*, or vocabulary of popular mistakes in language : in that of history the *Muntaẓam*, a universal history ; the *Dhahab al-Masbûk* (Molten Gold), a history of the Moslem sovereigns ; the *Akhbâr al-adhkiyâ* (Annals of Intelligent People) ; the *Kitâb al-Ḥumaqâ* (Book of Fools) ; the *Kitâb al-quṣṣâṣ* (Book of Popular Story-Tellers); the *Wafâ*, on the biography of the Prophet ; the *Manâqib*, or panegyrics of ʻUmar, Ḥasan al-Baṣrî, and Ibn Ḥanbal. As connected with the traditions we may cite his *Jâmiʻ al-Masânid*, drawn up by Muḥibbî al-Ṭabarî ; his *Manṭiq al-Mafhûm*, containing traditions as to animals and inanimate objects miraculously endowed with powers of speech, and his *Mauḍûʻât*, or forged traditions, now at Cairo.

Jurisprudence owes him two works—the *Taḥqîq*, on

the disputed traditions, and the *Bâz al-ashhab al-Munqaḍḍ*, which is a defence of the Ḥanbalite doctrine against the anthropomorphists. Koranic exegesis furnished him with matter for his *'Ajâ'ib 'ulûm al-Qur'ân*, a general introduction to the study of the sacred text; his *Mukhtaṣar* and his *Mujtabâ*, both of them abridgments of the first-named work; his *Zâd al-Masîr* (Provisions for the March), a manual for preachers; and his *'Arîb*, a commentary on passages which are difficult to read.

His interest in practical morality and edification led him to compile many works, amongst which we may mention the *Talbîs Iblîs* (The Devil's Wiles); *al-Ḥadâ'iq* (The Gardens), edifying stories of the Prophet and his companions; the *Maurid al-'Adhb*, a collection of seventy sermons preached by him at Mecca; and a book of lectures, accompanied by a lexicographical commentary, written in the space of thirty-four days, at Bagdâd. Medical science owes him the *Luqaṭ al-manâfi'*, a work on history, nosology and therapeutics, and the *Ṭibb al-Rûḥânî* (Medicine of the Soul). The *Muthîr al-'Azm* and the *Tabṣirat al-akhyâr*, which treats of the Nile, both belong to the geographical department. The *Kitâb al-Mudhish* is not easy to classify, for it deals at once with the Koran, with the science of language, with the traditions, with history, and with morality.

FAKHR AL-DÎN AL-RÂZÎ was the son of a preacher at Rai, the ancient Rhages, near the present city of Teheran, and was born there on 7th February 1149. He studied both in his native town and at Marâgha, travelled along the banks of the Amû-Daryâ and in Transoxania, was driven out of that country, went to Ghazna and Khurâsân, and was there received with much honour. He finally settled at Herât, and died there in 1209. His

writings earned considerable success, and cast those of many of his predecessors into oblivion. He was the first to introduce a systematic arrangement, which no writer before his time had ever attempted. His sermons, which he delivered both in Arabic and in Persian, created a profound impression, and touched himself so much that he would sometimes shed tears. He led a great many disciples of the anthropomorphist sect of the Karrâmiyya back to the orthodox faith.

He belonged to the Shâfi'ite rite, and wrote a panegyric on the Imâm Shâfi'î. For a long time a history (the *Fakhrî*, by Ibn Ṭiqṭaqâ), of which fragments have been published by Jourdain and Henzius, was ascribed to him. He wrote a treatise on jurisprudence entitled *Maḥṣûl;* a great commentary on the Koran, called *Mafâtîḥ al-ghaib* (Keys of the World of Mystery), which has been printed at Cairo and at Constantinople; the *Asrâr al-tanzîl* (Mystery of Revelation), on scholastic theology; the *Maṭâlib al-'âliyya* (Superior Questions), on the nature of the Deity; the *Mabâḥith al-sharqiyya* (Oriental Questions), on physics and metaphysics, a subject also dealt with in the *Muḥaṣṣal*, to which Schmoelders and Schreiner have devoted their attention. The *Sirr al-Maktûm* (Hidden Secret) is a complete treatise on astrology, as is also the *Ikhtiyârât al-'Alâ'iyya*, originally written in Persian for 'Alâ al-dîn, King of Khwârizm, and later translated into Arabic by some unknown hand.

Abû Ja'far NÂṢIR AL-DÎN AL-ṬÛSÎ (1210–1273), a famous astronomer, was born at Ṭûs in Khurâsân, and was highly esteemed by the Mongol Emperor Hulâgû, who valued his astrological powers, and built him an observatory at Marâgha. He accompanied the sovereign on his campaigns, and had the books pillaged

from the libraries of Bagdâd, Syria, and Mesopotamia set apart for himself, thus amassing a considerable library, amounting to over four hundred thousand volumes, and saving the books from utter destruction. His own works are compilations from others existing before his time; yet he deserves credit for having dealt with trigonometry as a separate science. He died at Bagdâd.

In the field of jurisprudence he wrote the *Jawâhir al-farâ'iḍ;* in that of scholastic theology, the *Tajrîd al-'Aqâ'id,* which has been frequently commentated; and the *Qawâ'id al-'Aqâ'id* (Rule of the Articles of Faith), on the nature of the Deity, the character of the prophecies and of the order of the Imâms, and the resurrection. In philosophy, he drew up a system of metaphysics in Persian, entitled *Fuṣûl,* which has been translated into Arabic by Jurjânî, and also a Ṣûfî manual called *Auṣâf al-ashrâf.* In mathematics, he left an Arabic edition of Euclid's *Elements,* which was printed at Rome in 1594; his treatise on the *Quadrilateral* has been translated into French by Alexandre-Pacha Carathéodory from a manuscript at Constantinople. In astronomy, we have his edition of Ptolemy's *Almagest,* the elements of astronomy, under the title of *Tadhkira,* and another book of the same nature called *Zubdat al-Idrâk.* He drew up in Persian the famous astronomical tables known under the name of *Zîj Ilkhânî* (Imperial Tables), which were later translated into Arabic; and he studied various works by Autolycus, Hypsicles, Theodosius, and Aristotle, with which he made acquaintance through the Arabic translations of Thâbit ibn Qurra and Qusṭâ ibn Lûqâ. His *Albâb al-bâhiyya* is a treatise on hygiene, and his *Wâfî* is a comprehensive treatise on geomancy. Herr Brockelmann enumerates fifty-six works from his pen.

CHAPTER X

ARABIC LITERATURE FROM THE CAPTURE OF BAGDÂD DOWN TO THE END OF THE EIGHTEENTH CENTURY

Poetry

THE court poet to the Urtuqids, then reigning at Mâridîn, Ṣafî al-dîn ʿAbdal-ʿAzîz ibn Sarâya al-Ḥillî, who was born on 27th August 1278, paid a visit to Egypt, to the court of Malik-Nâṣir, in 1326, but very soon returned to Mâridîn. He died at Bagdâd towards 1351. His contemporaries held him to be one of their best poets. His *dîwân* has been printed at Damascus and at Beyrout. His poems principally consist in play upon words. Under the title of *Qaṣîda of the Urtuqids* he composed twenty-nine poems, each containing twenty-nine couplets, beginning with the same letter of the alphabet, and ending in the same order. They are devoted to the praise of Malik-Manṣûr the Urtuqid, who reigned from 1294 till 1312. The ode he addressed to the Egyptian prince to whom he paid a visit has been translated both into Latin and German by Bernstein. He also wrote popular poetry, and a book entitled *al-ʿÂṭil al-ḥâlî*, of which the unique manuscript is at Munich.

IBN NUBÂTA Jamâl al-dîn (1287–1366), who was born

at Mayyâfâriqîn, was brought up in Egypt, and went to Damascus in 1316. He had opportunities of frequenting the court of Abû'l-Fidâ, Prince of Ḥamât, historian and geographer, and was afterwards attached to his administration as a secretary. He was past seventy when Sultan Ḥasan summoned him to Cairo to act as his secretary there. His patron unfortunately died in the following year, and the pension assigned him was very irregularly paid. He lived to be seventy-nine years old, and died in hospital. He left a *dîwân*, an anthology (*Saj' al-Muṭawwaq*), a treatise on the conduct of kings (*Sulûk duwal al-mulûk*), and some other works.

Ibn Ḥijja (Abû'l-Maḥâsin Taqî al-dîn) (1366–1434) was born at Ḥamât. He first practised the manual craft of a button-maker, hence his surname of al-Azrârî; at a later period he devoted himself to study, visited Mosul, Damascus, and Cairo, and saw Damascus in flames during the siege of that city by the Sultan Barqûq. He composed a letter to Ibn Makânis on the subject of this disaster. He saw Cairo once more, and held a post as secretary to the administration there. In 1419 we see him in attendance on Prince Ibrâhîm during a campaign in Asia Minor. He returned to his native town in 1427, and died there. His most famous work is an imitation of the poem of "The Cloak," in honour of the Prophet, in which all the flowers of Oriental rhetoric are displayed, and which is known as the *Badî'iyya*. He collected his own poems, some of them written at Cairo and others at Ḥamât, under the title of *Thamarât al-Shâhiyya*. The letters and diplomas drawn up while he was in the service of the Egyptian Mamelukes have been put together in a book called *Qahwat al-inshâ* (The Intoxicating Liquor of Epistolary Style). An anthology

in prose and verse called *Thamarât al-Aurâq* (Fruits of the Leaves) was printed at Bûlâq on the margin of Râghib Iṣfahânî's *Muḥâḍarât.* Other and less important works of his of the same nature are some compilations drawn from the books of Ibn Khallikân, Ibn Hishâm, and Damîrî.

Nâṣir al-dîn Nuṣair al-Ḥammâmî lived at Cairo. He was a man of shrewd and crafty character; he lived by hiring and farming out the public baths (*ḥammâm*), hence his surname. When he grew old he was obliged to relinquish this occupation, and took to begging, offering poems and *muwashshaḥs* of his own composition for sale. He died in 1312.

Sirâj al-dîn 'Umar ibn Mas'ûd, surnamed al-Majjân (the Obscene), was much sought after in society; he was the author of *muwashshaḥs,* and died at Damascus in 1301.

A grammatical critic who discovered mistakes even in the work of the best poets and lexicographers was Sheikh Taqî al-dîn 'Abdallah al-Sarûjî, who was born at Sarûj in 1230, and died at Cairo in 1294. He wrote many poems which singers made known to the public. He rarely left his home, never being seen except on Fridays. He did not like his name to be announced, and was in the habit of saying: "Amongst friends there are three degrees of friendship. At first, I hear myself called Sheikh Taqî al-dîn; later, I hear nothing but plain Taqî al-dîn, and I feel they are getting tired of me; but when they come to calling me al-Sarûjî, I know they have done with me."

Shams al-dîn AL-DAHHÂN (Muḥammad ibn 'Alî) was an oil-maker, hence his surname. His trade in no way harmed his talent. He was a poet and musician, a

virtuoso on the stringed instrument known as the *qânûn* (a harp laid on a sounding board, rather larger than the Austrian *zither*, and smaller than the Hungarian *cymbalum*), and he also composed musical airs. He died in 1321.

Sharaf ibn As'ad al-Miṣrî was a man of the lower class, with a natural gift, who composed comic and obscene poetry, and frequented loose society and public singers of the fair sex. He died in 1337.

'Uthmân Abû'l-Fatḥ al-Balaṭî was born at Balaṭ, a small town near Mosul. He was tall and fat, with a long beard. Even in the height of summer he wore a huge turban, and garments piled one on top of the other. He had studied for some time at Damascus. When Saladin seized Egypt, he proceeded to that country and was appointed reader and teacher of grammar in the Great Mosque. He was addicted to drink and pleasure. One day, when a musician had come to sing him an air, he began to weep, and the singer followed his example. Abû'l-Fatḥ, in surprise, asked why the other wept. "Because my father used to weep when he heard that air, and you reminded me of him," quoth the singer. "Then you must be my brother's son!" said Abû'l-Fatḥ, and from that time he never called the musician anything but "my nephew," and made him his only legatee. He wrote a *muwashshaḥ* in praise of the *qâḍî* Al-Fâḍil.

IBN FAḌL-ALLAH AL-'UMARÎ (Ṣhihâb al-dîn Abû'l-'Abbâs) (1301–1348) was descended from the Caliph 'Umar, and came of a family of Shâfi'ite magistrates. The facility with which he could write sudden improvisations was much extolled. He was, according to Ṣafadî's expression, a finished man of letters; that is to

say, that in his verse and in his prose, theory and practice, science and action, were equally balanced. He possessed a wide knowledge of biography, history, and geography. He was born at Damascus, studied law and prosody in his native city, and then travelled in the countries under Egyptian rule. He accompanied his father when Malik-Nâṣir appointed him Secretary of State; was himself appointed *qâḍî* in Cairo, and Secretary of State as well, when his father died in that office. He finally returned to Damascus, and died there of the plague. His *Masâlik al-abṣâr* is a geographical, historical, and biographical work in over twenty volumes, of which studies by Guignes (1758) and Quatremère (1838) appeared in *Notices et Extraits*. Pococke made use of it for his history of the Arabs. His *Ta'rîf bil-muṣṭalaḥ al-sharîf* is a collection of models for letters addressed by the Mameluke Sultans to foreign powers. The *Shatawiyyât* (Hibernals) are letters sent to several learned men from Damascus during the winter of 1343–1344, when the city was deep in snow. The manuscript of this book is now at Leyden. A large work in four volumes, *Fawâḍil al-samar*, is devoted to the praise of the virtues of his own family. He composed many odes and poems in the classic metres, besides popular poetry in strophes, *muwashshaḥs*, and *dû-baits*.

IBN AL-THARADA ('Alî ibn Ibrâhîm), a preacher at Wâsiṭ, was born in June 1298. He studied at Bagdâd, and paid several visits to Damascus, where he preached in the Great Mosque of the Omeyyads. He then fell ill of melancholia, and died in Ibn Suwaid's lunatic hospital, at Damascus, in 1349. His harmless mania consisted in carrying a bag under his arm, to which he fastened all the threads and strings he came across, and with which

he would never part. His malady did not prevent him from composing excellent poetry. He fancied himself the possessor of a library of two thousand volumes, which he had left behind him at Bagdâd, and of which the merchants had taken possession, and sold it, book by book, in the Damascus bazaars. When he died, his bag was opened, and its only contents were found to be scattered sheets, on which verses and sermons were inscribed. He also composed poems in strophes *muwashshaḥs*, and *mawâliyâs*.

IBN AL-MURAḤḤAL (Ṣadr al-dîn Muḥammad) (1267–1316), who is better known in Syria by his surname of Ibn al-Wakîl, was of Egyptian origin. He was born at Damietta, and died at Cairo. It was at Damascus that he studied jurisprudence—the basis of all other knowledge in that country, as theology was elsewhere. He knew a great many books by heart, such as the *Mufaṣṣal*, which he committed to memory in a hundred and one days; Ḥarîrî's *Lectures*, which he learned in fifty; and Mutanabbî's *dîwân*, which, we are assured, he acquired in a single week. He had a gift for controversy, and was the only person among the Shâfi'ites capable of holding his ground in discussion with Sheikh Taqî al-dîn Ibn Taimiyya. For seven years he performed the duties of Sheikh of the Ashrafiyya School of the traditions. He was a discreet and a very reserved man, a friend of great folks, and a lover of society. He wrote verses in every style, including such popular forms as the *muwashshaḥ*, *dû-bait*, *mukhammas*, *zajal*, and *billîq*. He collected his principal poetical compositions into an anthology entitled *Al-ashbâh wa'l-Naẓâ'ir*.

Yûsuf IBN ZAILAQ was killed by the Mongols at

the taking of Mosul in 1262. Some of his poems—several of them *muwashshaḥs*, intended to be sung, and of an erotic tendency—are preserved in al-Kutubî's *Fawât al-Wafayât*. Shams al-dîn Muḥammad, the preacher of Wâsiṭ, who died in 1344, when nearly seventy years of age, also wrote popular poetry.

AL-KAIWÂNÎ was descended from Kaiwân, a former slave belonging to Riḍwân-Pâshâ, Governor of Gaza, who became a soldier in the Syrian troops, and reached high military rank. These Syrian troops were well known for the violence and injustice of their conduct. Kaiwân was killed at Baalbek in 1623. When 'Uthmân Khaliṣa, *kiaya* to the Grand Vizier, reached Damascus, al-Kaiwânî attached himself to his service, and followed him on the campaign in which he took part and was killed. After his patron's death he returned to Constantinople, and thence to Syria. Here it was that his character assumed the sad and melancholy tone which marks his poetry. He addressed panegyrics to Abdallah-Pacha Chetejî, when that functionary, as Governor of Damascus, put down the riots which were filling the city with blood. The quality of his rhymed prose was also remarkable.

'ABDAL-GHANÎ of Nâbulus (1641–1731), who was affiliated to the religious orders of the Naqshbandîs and the Qâdirîs, was born at Damascus, of a family belonging to Nâbulus. He lost his father while still very young, studied jurisprudence, and began to write when he was only twenty. For seven years he stayed within the house he occupied, close to the Mosque of the Omeyyads, and spiteful tongues asserted that he no longer performed his devotions five times a day, and that he satirised his neighbours in his poems. The mob rose, and handled him

roughly, for which cause he wrote satires against it; but in later years he was looked on as a saint, and people crowded to see him. He went to Constantinople in 1664, but did not remain there long. In 1688 he went to the Beqʿa and to Lebanon; in 1689, to Jerusalem and Hebron. In 1693 he travelled to Egypt, and thence to the Ḥijâz. In 1700 he spent some forty days at Tripoli in Syria. In April 1707 he left the house hitherto occupied by his masters in the centre of the town, and settled at Ṣâliḥiyya, on the slopes of Mount Qâsyûn, a sort of suburb of the Syrian capital. His principal prose works are an unfinished commentary on Baiḍâwî's *Tafsîr*, a commentary on the *dîwân* of ʿUmar Ibn al-Fâriḍ, and innumerable stanzas of poetry. It is said that Abdal-Ghanî could perform miracles, but disliked any reference to this gift. He was always ready to intercede with the authorities in favour of any unfortunate person who applied to him. His poetry became known all over the Arab world. He died, aged over ninety, after a very short illness, on 24th Shaʿbân 1143 (4th March 1731). The bazaars of the city were all closed on the day of his funeral, and the populace crowded to Ṣâlihiyya to be present at the last rites.

The Amîr MANJAK ibn Muḥammad al-Yûsufî (1596–1669) was descended from the chief of the same name, who ruled Damascus about the year 1370. On his father's death, he spent his fortune freely, completely dissipated it by his extravagance, and then retired from general society. He left Arab territory and went to Turkish countries, and even presented a poem to the Sultan Ibrâhîm, receiving, however, nothing in exchange. To record his days of poverty and suffering at Constantinople, he wrote his *Rûmiyyât;* other poems are

devoted to the praise of wine and of asceticism. A year before he died, he returned to his dissipated habits.

Sheikh Muṣṭafâ Efendî Âl-Bâbî derived his surname from a village in the neighbourhood of Aleppo called al-Bâb. After beginning his legal studies at Aleppo, he proceeded in 1641 to Damascus, for the purpose of completing them there. Later, as the result of a journey to Constantinople, in the course of which he wrote a poem on that city, in which he conjures up the memory of his own fatherland, he entered the Ottoman magistracy. He also addressed praises to the Sheikh al-Islâm, Yaḥyâ Efendî, and to the Grand Vizier, Aḥmad-Pâshâ Kyüprülü. He held the post of *qâḍî* at Tripoli in Syria, at Magnesia in Asia Minor, at Bagdâd, and last of all at Medina (1680). He made the pilgrimage that year, and died at Mecca in January 1681. His *dîwân*, which was printed at Beyrout in 1872, contains a funeral oration on one of his molar teeth, which had been pulled out. It is a very amusing piece of verse.

The daughter of Aḥmad ibn Nâṣir al-dîn al-Bâ'ûnî, 'Â'isha al-Bâ'ûniyya, wrote the *Fatḥ al-Mubîn*, an ode, rhymed in *m*, in praise of the Prophet. This work is accompanied by a commentary of the author's own composition, which was completed in 1516. Witty verses from her pen are also quoted, in which she has contrived, in the space of five stanzas, to express the opinions of the doctors of the four orthodox rites on some legal controversy. To this same family of Al-Bâ'ûnî also belonged Bahâ al-dîn Muḥammad ibn Yûsuf (1446–1505), who was born in the suburb of Ṣâliḥiyya, which spreads over the lower slopes of Mount Qâsyûn, near Damascus. He was a lover of history, and was fond of reducing its annals within the limits

of short mnemonic poems. Thus he wrote a *rajaz*, the *Tuḥfat al-Ẓurafâ*, on general history down to the enthronement of the Mameluke Sultan Qâït-Bâï, and another on the rule of the two Egyptian sovereigns Bârs-Bâï and Qâït-Bâï. He likewise did not fail to follow ancient custom, by devoting a panegyric, for which he was doubtless well rewarded, to the glory of the latter of these two sovereigns, and also wrote a poem called *Bahja al-Khalad*, a treatise on the education of children.

The *dîwân* of Ibn Maʿtûq (1614–1676), which was collected and published by his son, is full of panegyrics on various Persian governors under the reign of the Ṣafavid prince, Shâh Ṣafî. It was lithographed, probably at Cairo, in 1861.

Aḥmad al-Kurdî ibn Ilyâs, surnamed al-Arrajânî al-Ṣaghîr, and the "strolling Qâmûs," a man of Kurdish origin, was a poet and lexicographer. His father, who came from Shahrizûr, had settled at Damascus, and been appointed preacher in the caravanserai of the small town of Nebk, where he had married. He was born in the twelfth century of the Hegira (from 1689 onwards), went to Damascus to study at the Sumaisât Madrasa, and became cook in that school. His fickle nature, and his perpetual quarrelling, made his life difficult, and he departed to Constantinople, fearing legal proceedings might be taken against him on account of some misbehaviour. His own thoughtless conduct forced him, at last, to leave the capital of the Empire, although he had found a protector there, and he went to Tripoli in Syria, where he married and obtained various posts. Thence he passed on into Egypt, where the governor, Muḥammad-Pâshâ Râghib, took him under

his protection. He attended him to Aleppo when he was appointed governor of that city, and died there in April 1756.

History

Muḥammad ibn ʿAlî Ibn Ṭabâṭabâ, surnamed IBN AL-ṬIQṬAQÂ, who was born towards 1262, was the guest of the Governor of Mosul, Fakhr al-dîn ʿÎsâ ibn Ibrâhîm, in the year 1302, when he dedicated his history of the Moslem Empire, from its foundation down to the Caliphate of Bagdâd, to him. It was entitled *al-Fakhrî*, and has been published first by Ahlwardt, and afterwards by H. Derenbourg.

The author of this work has applied himself to writing a clear style, which all may comprehend, having remarked that many writers have limited the utility of their productions by indulging in affected language, and employing unusual terms. His great desire is to make himself understood, for his book is a treatise on politics for the use of sovereigns who desire to rule themselves, and not to continue mere toys in their ministers' hands. His precepts on government are supported by instances drawn from the history of the Oriental dynasties.

Aḥmad AL-GHABRÎNÎ (1246–1314), of the Berber tribe of Ghabrâ, was born at Bijâya, acted as *qâḍî* of that place, and died there. Under the title of *ʿUnwân al-dirâya,* he has left us a gallery of the men of letters of his native town during the seventh century of the Hegira, which has been introduced to European readers by Cherbonneau.

Abû'l-Ḥasan ʿAlî IBN ABÎ ZARʿ, who was born at Grenada, and settled in Morocco, relates the history of the kings of the Maghrib and of the town of Fez in

his *Rauḍ al-Qarṭâs* (The Paper Garden, the name of a favourite spot outside the gates of Fez), which has been published by Tornberg at Upsala, translated into German at Agram, in 1794, by F. von Dombay, into Portuguese at Lisbon, in 1828, by Brother Jozé de Santo Antonio Moura, and into French by Beaumier, in 1860.

The *qâḍî* Ibn Taimiyya (Taqî al-dîn Abû'l-ʿAbbâs) (1263–1328) was born at Ḥarrân. He was descended from a famous preacher who bore the same surname. His father, with his whole family, fled before the Mongols. Not being able to procure beasts of burden, he loaded his books upon a cart, which, so hot was the enemy's pursuit, he was obliged to abandon in order to save himself. They took refuge at Damascus, where young Ibn Taimiyya studied Ḥanbalite law, and, when his father died, taught in his place. He was then only twenty-one years old. He enjoyed the favour of Sultan Malik-Nâṣir, who had ascended the throne in 1294, but his strong polemics made him many enemies, and his reply to a question put forward at Ḥamât as to the attributes of the Deity stirred public opinion against him, and led to his dismissal. This persecution never ceased, though he was occasionally recalled to his post, as, for instance, when his preaching was needed to stir up the populace to war against the Mongols. In 1305 he went to Cairo with the Shâfiʿite *qâḍî*. After a sitting of the council and leading men he was shut up, with his two brothers, in the well of the citadel, and remained there for two years. He was then brought back with post-horses to Damascus, and spent as long a time in prison there. He employed the period of his imprisonment in edifying his fellow-prisoners on religious subjects. He was sent back to

Cairo, and Sultan Baibars had him detained in the fortress of Alexandria, where he only remained for eight months, Malik-Nâṣir's return to power having brought him his liberty. Instead of taking vengeance on his enemies, he forgave them. Ibn Taimiyya was appointed professor at the school founded by the Sultan, and continued to be his counsellor. He took advantage of the departure of the army for Syria to accompany it, went to Jerusalem, and returned to Damascus after an absence of more than seven years. He assumed his former functions as teacher and judge, but the hatred of his enemies, which now broke out afresh, procured a decree forbidding him to hold any public employment. He refused to obey, and was imprisoned for nearly six months. On recovering his liberty he recommenced his former mode of life, until the publication of his work on a visit to the tombs of the prophets and saints resulted in his imprisonment in the citadel. He was assigned a separate cell, in which he was able to carry on his literary work, and wrote several books on subjects connected with the cause of his incarceration. But when these works became matters of public knowledge, his books, paper, and ink were taken from him, and this was the most cruel blow he ever received. He very soon fell ill, and died within three weeks, in September 1328. His funeral obsequies were attended by an extraordinary concourse of people. Of Ibn Taimiyya's many works, that most utilised in European science has been the *fatwâ* issued by him against the Nuṣairîs or Anṣârîs of the Syrian mountains, which has been studied by E. Salisbury and Stanislas Guyard. Maracci made use of one of his works against the Christians (*Takhjîl ahl al-Injîl*)

in the preface to the refutation of the Koran. Forty-five works from the pen of this original writer are now in various European libraries.

It was from the Ḥanbalite teachings of Ibn Taimiyya and his disciples that ʿAbdal-Wahhâb drew the Sunnite fanaticism and hatred of innovation which are the distinguishing features of the movement for the reform of Islam known under the name of Wahhabeeism. This has been demonstrated by Snouck Hurgronje, and Goldziher. The *qâḍî* was an anthropomorphist, and insisted on the literal interpretation of the passages in the Koran relating to the personality of the Deity. In jurisprudence he accepted logical deductions drawn by himself from the *corpus* of the traditions, and practised the *qiyâs* or use of analogy. Ibn Baṭûṭa, the traveller, relates that he was greatly respected at Damascus, that he discoursed on the various sciences, but that there was something unhinged in his brain. When brought before Malik-Nâṣir at Cairo, his only answer to the Grand Qâḍî's questions as to the accusations put forward against him was: "There is no God but God." His favourite disciple was Ibn Qayyim al-Jauziyya (Shams al-dîn Muḥammad), who probably helped him to revise the style of his compositions, and himself wrote books, some thirty of which are now preserved in various libraries. He was born in Damascus in 1292, the son of the curator of the Al-Jauziyya Madrasa. He shared his master's tribulations, and was imprisoned with him at Cairo. His persecutions did not end with Ibn Taimiyya's death, but continued for some time afterwards. Shams al-dîn died on 17th September 1350.

Scarcely anything is known of the life of Ḥâfiẓ

al-dîn Abû'l-Barakât al-Nasafî, who died in 1310, and whose works have enjoyed the signal honour of tempting a swarm of commentators. Of his *Manâr al-anwâr* (The Beacon of Lights), a work on law, the bibliographer Ḥâjî Khalfa mentions nearly fifty commentaries. His *Wâfî*, and its commentary the *Kâfî*, were finished at Bukhârâ in 1275. An abridgment by the author himself, at a later date, is the *Kanz al-daqâ'iq*. His *Umda*, a Moslem catechism, has been published in London, by W. Cureton, under the title of *Pillar of the Sunnite Creed.* A commentary on this work, by its own author, is called *al-I'timâd fi'l-i'tiqâd.*

Rashîd al-dîn (Faḍl-Allah ibn Abî'l-Khair), the Persian historian of the Mongols, was born at Hamadhân in 1247, and executed at Tâbrîz in 1318, having been accused of poisoning the Sultan Uljâitû. He was a physician, of Jewish origin. He was physician to Abaqa, and afterwards minister to Ghâzân and to his brother Uljâitû. He wrote four Arabic works, now preserved in the Bibliothèque Nationale—*Mafâtîḥ al-tafâsîr, Laṭâ'if al-ḥaqâ'iq, Tauḍîḥât,* and *Sulṭâniyya.*

ABÛ'L - FIDÂ Ismâ'îl ibn 'Alî belonged to that Ayyûbite family which the fortunes of Saladin raised to various thrones. His ancestors had ruled at Ḥamât. His father, Al-Malik al-Afḍal, brother of Prince Al-Malik al-Manṣûr, had been forced, with all his family, to flee before the Mongols, and had taken refuge in the house of Ibn al-Zanjabîlî, at Damascus. There Abû'l - Fidâ was born, in the year 1273. He was brought up both as a warrior and as a man of letters. He was hardly twelve years old when he accompanied his father to the siege of the fortress of Markab, which

was wrested from the Knights Hospitallers in 1285. He was at the taking of Tripoli, and at the siege of St. Jean d'Arc, on which occasion he commanded a squad of ten men. In 1310, as a reward for his services to the Egyptian Sultan Malik-Nâṣir, he was made Prince of Ḥamât, after that State had been confiscated because his cousin had died childless. The title of honour of Malik-Ṣâliḥ, and subsequently that of Malik-Mu'ayyad, rewarded the attention with which he yearly journeyed to Cairo to renew the bonds of vassalage between himself and the Sultan. In 1313 he assisted the Egyptian troops to re-establish the Sharîf Abû'l-Ghaith in power at Mecca. He died of intermittent fever, in his sixtieth year, in October 1331. His *Universal History*, which made his reputation, is a mere abridgment of that of Ibn al-Athîr, itself abridged from Ṭabarî's, and carried down to the year 1329, but it had the advantage of attracting the notice of Orientalists at a time when the world was not, as yet, in possession of the two older works.

This text, part of which was published by Reiske at Copenhagen, under the title of *Annales Muslemici*, has furnished subject-matter for other inquirers. Thus Fleischer has translated into Latin and published the portion devoted to pre-Islamic history, from which Albert Schultens and Silvestre de Saçy had already given extracts. The life of Mahomet, translated into Latin by Gagnier, has been translated into French and published by Noél des Vergers, and into English by W. Murray. His general geography, with tables, has been published by Reinaud and MacGuckin de Slane, and translated into French by Reinaud and Stanislas Guyard. The first of these Orientalists has written, as a preface to his translation, a

general introduction to the geography of the Orientals, which is one of his best works.

Abû'l-Abbâs Aḥmad AL-NUWAIRÎ (1282–1332) was born in Egypt, in the little town of Nuwaira. He was famous both as a lawyer and a historian. So highly was his penmanship esteemed that he was paid a thousand dirhems for each of his eight copies of Bukhârî's *Ṣaḥîḥ*. His encyclopædia, *Nihâyat al-arab* (The Extreme Need), is a general review of human knowledge, in five great divisions—Heaven, Earth, Man, Animals, Plants, and History; from this work Albert Schultens drew his history of the Yoqṭânids in the Yemen. His history of Sicily has been translated into French by the elder Caussin; his *Conquest of Northern Africa by the Arabs* has been studied by Otter; his history of the same country has been translated by De Slane. Silvestre de Saçy has made an extract of the part relating to the Druses, Hammer-Purgstall one of that dealing with the Egyptian decrees as to the dress of Christians and Jews, and Defrémery has quoted the anecdotes connected with the life of the Sultan Baibars.

Abû'l-Fatḥ Muḥammad IBN SAYYID AL-NÂS (1263–1334), whose parents were of Sevillian origin, was born at Cairo, and went to Damascus in 1291, to complete his studies. He is said to have taken lessons from almost one thousand professors. On his return, he taught in his native town. He loved books, and collected a fine library, in which, besides his own manuscripts, autographs of famous works were to be found. He compiled a biography of Mahomet called *'Uyûn al-âthâr* (Sources of the Monuments), and, under the title of *Bushrâ al-labîb* (Message of the Man of Sense), collected his own verses in praise of the Prophet. It is from this collec-

tion that Kosegarten extracted the ode included in his *Carminum Orientalium Triga.*

SHAMS AL-DÎN Abû 'Abdallah al-Ṣûfî AL-DIMASHQÎ (1254–1327) was imâm of the little village of Rabwa, near Damascus, whereof Ibn Baṭûṭa has written "it is one of the prettiest views in the world, and one of the most beautiful pleasure spots; there are tall palaces, noble buildings, and exquisite gardens." It was a place of pilgrimage, on account of a little grotto, opposite which was the supposed oratory of Khiḍr, who was likened to the prophet Elias. A large proportion of the cultivated fields, orchards, and houses were legacies from pious persons, and what they brought in served to support the imâm, the muezzin, and the pilgrims. Here Shams al-dîn wrote his cosmography, *Nukhbat al-dahr*, which has been published by Mehren, at St. Petersburg, and translated by him at Copenhagen. This work has quite recently (1898) served as the basis of a dissertation by H. Dehérain. Shams al-dîn, who was a mystic, retired, at a later date, to Ṣafad in Palestine, and there died. He also cultivated poetry, and some lines of his, inspired by the beauty of the neighbourhood of Damascus, are often quoted. From the critic's point of view, according to Reinaud, his cosmography leaves much to be desired, but it has been most useful to students of the geography of the Middle Ages, for it contains information as to facts which are not mentioned elsewhere.

ABÛ ḤAYYÂN Muḥammad ibn Yûsuf, of the Berber tribe of Nafza, surnamed al-Jayyânî, because his forebears lived in the Spanish town of Jaen, was born in Grenada in November 1256; completed his studies at Malaga, Velez, and Almeria; left Spain in 1280, in consequence of a difference with his master, Ibn al-Zubair;

travelled through Northern Africa and Egypt; made the pilgrimage, and returned to Egypt by Syria. He was a polyglot—knew Persian, Turkish, and Ethiopian, and wrote books in those languages. In 1298 he succeeded his master, Ibn al-Naḥḥâs, as teacher of grammar, and then of the traditions, and gained the friendship of the Amîr Saif al-dîn Arghûn, who became Governor of Egypt in 1312. He was very frugal, and lived on a few copper coins. He never bought books, not feeling any need of them, but borrowed those he desired to read from the public libraries. He was originally a Ẓâhirite, but came over completely to the Shâfi'ite view, and never relinquished it again. He died in July 1345, five years after his daughter Nudhâr, herself a literary character, on whom he wrote a tract, which is a kind of autobiography. His *Idrâk*, which describes the Turkish tongue as it was spoken in Cairo by the colonists from Central Asia in the fourteenth century, has been published at Constantinople. He also wrote the kind of popular poetry known as *muwashshaḥât*.

SHAMS AL-DÎN Abû 'Abdallah Muḥammad AL-DHAHABÎ (1274–1348), a man of Turkoman blood, was born at Damascus, began his studies when he was eighteen years of age, and undertook journeys which brought him the acquaintance of more than twelve hundred learned men. He was a teacher of the traditions at Damascus, but was unable to enter the Ashrafiyya in that capacity, because the founder of that school had laid down conditions, as to the religious beliefs of those employed to teach in it, which he could not fulfil. Of the many works he left behind him, the best known are his *Mushtabih*, published by P. de Jong at Leyden, and a *Medicine of the Prophet*, translated into French by Perron. His

Ṭabaqât al-Ḥuffâz (Classes of those who know the Traditions by Heart), abridged and continued by Suyûṭî, has been published by Wüstenfeld under the title of *Liber Classium.* His great history of Islamism (*Ta'rîkh al-islâm*) is scattered in odd volumes through various European libraries.

Zain al-dîn Abû Ḥafṣ ʿUmar IBN AL-WARDÎ was born in 1290, at Maʿarrat al-Nuʿmân, in Upper Syria. He studied law at Ḥamât, and was appointed assistant to the *qâḍî* Ibn al-Naqîb at Aleppo. In consequence of a dream, he resigned this post, and devoted himself entirely to literary composition. He died of the plague, in the town of Aleppo, in March 1349. His history is an abridgment of that of Abû'l-Fidâ, with a continuation carried down to the year of his own death. Others of his works are devoted to grammar, jurisprudence, mysticism, and even to pure literature, as, for example, the *Lecture* on the plague, preserved by Suyûṭî in the book he wrote on that hideous epidemic. The authorship of the *Kharîdat al-ʿAjâ'ib*, a treatise on geography and natural history, containing all sorts of wondrous and fantastic tales, has been ascribed, probably incorrectly, to him. This work, indeed, is no more than an almost literal transcription of the *Jâmiʿ al-funûn* (Encyclopædia) composed by Najm al-dîn Aḥmad al-Ḥarrânî, a learned Ḥanbalite, who was in Egypt in 1332. It is a curious book, and has been printed at Cairo, and studied by De Guignes, Fraehn, Hylander, Tornberg, Freund, Wüstenfeld, and Mehren.

ʿAḌUD AL-DÎN AL-ÎJÎ of Shîrâz, a Shâfiʿite lawyer, *qâḍî*, and Ṣûfî, who died in 1355, wrote a history of the patriarchs, of Mahomet, and some of his companions. Under the title of *Mawâqif* (The Stations) he has given

us a treatise on metaphysics and Moslem theology, of which the fifth and sixth parts, together with the appendix, dealing with the Moslem sects and Jurjânî's commentary, have been published by Soerensen.

IBN SHÂKIR AL-KUTUBÎ (the Bookseller), who was of Aleppan origin, and died in 1363, studied in his native city and at Damascus. He entered the book trade as a means of making a livelihood, and grew rich in it. Under the name of *'Uyûn al-tawârîkh*, he drew up a chronicle of the Caliphs and learned men, with special particulars as to Damascus, and he also prepared a continuation or supplement to Ibn Khallikân's great biographical dictionary, *Fawât al-Wafayât*, which has been printed at Bûlâq.

KHALÎL IBN AIBAK AL-ṢAFADÎ, who was born at Ṣafad, in Palestine, was a Government secretary at Damascus, Cairo, and Aleppo, and Director of the Treasury at Damascus. He died in 1363. His chief work is his *Wâfî bil-Wafayât*, a complete dictionary of biography, the twenty-six volumes of which are scattered among various European libraries. Another of his books is specially devoted to the famous men and women of the eighth century of the Hegira—his own contemporaries, in fact (*A'yân al-'aṣr*). A very curious anthology is that dedicated by him to poems in which mention is made of tears, *Ladhdhat al-Sam'*. His *Lau'at al-shâkî wa-dam'at al-bâkî* is an immoral story, intermingled with verse. His *Jinân al-jinâs*, on Flowers of Rhetoric, has been printed at Constantinople. Other collections of verse and compilations were produced by his fertile pen.

SIDI KHALÎL al-Jundî, a Mâlikite lawyer, studied at Cairo, where he was both professor and mufti, and where he died in November 1365. He was the author of the

Mukhtaṣar, a summary of Mâlikite jurisprudence used in the native courts in Algeria, which has been frequently reprinted by the Société Asiatique in Paris, translated into French by Dr. Perron in his *Exploration scientifique de l'Algérie*, and concordance tables of which have been drawn up by E. Fagnan. This concise and practical manual has found many commentators. Sidi Khalîl also wrote a biography of Sheikh ʿAbdallah al-Manûfî, his own teacher, and some other works, which, like this last, are still in manuscript.

Ismâʿîl ibn ʿUmar IBN KATHÎR (1302–1372), a traditionist and historian, succeeded al-Dhahabî in his professorial chair at Damascus, and taught for some time in the Ashrafiyya, but was dismissed from these latter functions. His *Bidâya wa'l-Nihâya* (The Beginning and the End) is a great universal history, beginning with the Creation and ending in 1337; the most perfect copy now in existence is at Vienna. The part relating to the government of the Ethiopians in Yemen has been published by J.-F.-L. George at Berlin. Ibn Kathîr also dealt with the Imâm Shâfiʿî, and the traditionists of his school.

Shihâb al-dîn Abû'l-ʿAbbâs Aḥmad IBN ABÎ ḤAJALA, a philologist and poet, and a Ḥanbalite, belonging to Tilimsân, where he was born in 1325, travelled, went to Mecca to accomplish the rites of the pilgrimage, returned by Damascus and Syria, and settled in Cairo, where he was appointed sheikh of a dervish convent. He died at Cairo, of the plague, in 1375. His grandfather had been given the surname of *Abû Ḥajala*, or "the Man with the Partridge," because a partridge had laid its egg one day in his cloak. He wrote the *Sukkardân* (The Sugar-bowl), an historical and geographical work

on Egypt, which includes a biography of Sultan Malik-Nâṣir, to whom the book is dedicated. It is an anthology, on the subject of the importance of the number seven in everything concerning the land of Egypt. This idea of connecting everything with the fateful number seven deprives the work of any historical value. It has been printed at Bûlâq. Ibn Abî Ḥajala's *Dîwân al-Ṣabâba* deals with the history of celebrated lovers; it has been published at Cairo, on the margins of Dâ'ûd al-Anṭâkî's *Tazyîn al-aswâq*.

LISÂN AL-DÎN Abû 'Abdallah Muḥammad IBN AL-KHAṬÎB came of a Syrian family which had emigrated to Spain. He was born at Grenada in November 1313. His father's property, which had been confiscated, was restored to him, and he became the friend of the seventh prince of the Beni'l-Aḥmar dynasty of Grenada, Abû'l-Ḥajjâj Yûsuf, who confided the management of his kingdom to his hands. He was continued in this post by the monarch's successor, Muḥammad V., and attended him when he was forced to flee to Africa from his brother Ismâ'îl in 1359. Muḥammad V. returned from Africa three years later, retook Grenada, and reappointed Ibn al-Khaṭîb to his former post. Nevertheless, within a very short time, he was accused of treason by his enemies, cast into prison, and executed (1374). His history of the Caliphs of Spain, the East, and Africa, furnished Casiri with a long excerpt relating to the Aghlabite Sultans, and the Fâṭimid Caliphs who reigned in Sicily and Africa, for his Hispano-Arab Library. This has been reprinted in Rosario Gregorio's collection of historical documents relating to Sicily. He studied the history of Grenada, and left annals of its sovereigns down to the year 1363. He wrote biographies of the

famous men belonging to that capital, including his own. From these Casiri drew the matter for two hundred and eighty notices. An account of his travels contains descriptions of the Spanish towns, the learned men to be found in them, and the most frequented libraries.

Badr al-dîn Abû Muḥammad al-Ḥasan Ibn Ḥabîb, a learned Shâfi'ite, was born at Damascus in 1310. So well did he profit by the instruction bestowed upon him, that at the age of thirteen, having been present at prayers in the Great Mosque, he wrote a poem on the incident. He went to Aleppo with his father, who had been appointed professor of the *ḥadîth* in that town, and for some time performed the duties of chief of the municipal police. The Mecca pilgrimage afforded him an opportunity of visiting Cairo, Alexandria, Jerusalem, and Hebron. In the following year he made a second pilgrimage to Mecca (1338). He was then given a post in the public service at Aleppo, and accompanied the Amîr Sharaf al-dîn on his tax-collecting rounds, thus making acquaintance with the chief Syrian towns. From 1344 onwards, he devoted himself to editorial work. In 1354 he made a pleasure trip to Tripoli, and there made the acquaintance of the governor, Saif al-dîn Manjak. Being well received, he spent two years in that town. When the governor was appointed in the same capacity at Damascus, he joined him there, remained three years, and was honourably welcomed by the learned men of the Syrian capital. He spent the closing years of his life at Aleppo, and died there in August 1377. To him we owe a history of the Mameluke Sultans of Egypt, entitled *Durrat al-Aslâk* (The Pearl of the Threads), which covers the period between 1250 and 1375, with references to contemporary events in neigh-

bouring countries, and very valuable obituary notices of the great dignitaries and learned men of that epoch. But, as the whole of the text is in rhymed prose, it may be objected that historical accuracy has been sacrificed to rhyme. His son, Zain al-dîn Ṭâhir, carried his father's annals down to the year 1398. This work proved useful to Maqrîzî, who drew information for his history of the Mameluke Sultans from it. He also wrote a history of the Sultan Qilâwûn and his sons. His *Nasîm al-Ṣabâ* (Breath of the Breeze), a representation of scenes from nature and from human life, is a mixture of rhymed prose and verse.

Muḥammad ibn ʿAbdal-Raḥîm IBN AL-FURÂT belonged to an important Cairene family. He made a special study of the traditions and of jurisprudence. Yet it is as regards history that he is most interesting to us, for he is one of the sources of the history of the Crusades. He was born in 1334, and died on 2nd April 1405. His History of Dynasties and Kings is a Moslem chronology, down to the year 1396, only a certain portion of which has been clearly set forth by the author. Nine volumes of it are in the Vienna Library, and are believed to be the autograph manuscript. They run from 1107 to 1396, but with many gaps. These volumes were conveyed to Paris after the campaign of 1809, and remained there till 1814. During this period, Jourdain, a most hard-working Orientalist, made a long extract from them, which has been utilised by Michaud in his *Histoire des Croisades*, and by Reinaud in the fourth volume of the *Bibliothèque des Croisades*.

Towards the same epoch, a learned *qâḍî* of Constantine, Abû'l-ʿAbbâs Aḥmad Ibn al-Khaṭîb al-Qsamṭînî, compiled a series of very short biographical notices of

five hundred famous personages, arranged in chronological order, from Mahomet's time down to the year 1404, and also wrote, in honour of the Marînid prince Abû Fâris 'Abdal-'Azîz, his *Fârisiyya,* a history of the Ḥafṣid dynasty, extracts from which have been published by Cherbonneau in the *Journal Asiatique,* after a manuscript actually discovered by him at Constantine.

Arabia had then produced a mystic writer, 'Afîf al-dîn 'Abdallah al-Yâfi'î, who was born in Yemen in 1298, studied at Aden, and, after the year 1318, settled partly at Mecca and partly at Medina. He never again left these two towns, except to make a journey to Jerusalem, Damascus, and Cairo, in 1324, and a short excursion into the Yemen in 1337. He died at Mecca in 1367. His work on the mystical interpretation of the Koran, *Mukhtaṣar al-durr al-naẓîm,* extracted from a work by Ibn al-Khashshâb, an author who died about 1252, has been printed at Cairo, and so has his *Rauḍ al-rayâḥîn* (Flower-plots of Basil), containing five hundred edifying stories of saints and pious persons. Another of his books contains no less than two hundred little tales of the same nature, touching a saintly individual called 'Abd al-Qâdir al-Gîlânî, and other illustrious Ṣûfîs.

With him must be mentioned Abû Madyan Shu'aib al-Huraifîsh, who was born in Egypt, and died at Mecca in 1308. His *Rauḍ al-fâ'iq* (The Excellent Flower-plot), a collection of moral and pious anecdotes, and of traditions relating to the Last Judgment, has also been reprinted at Cairo several times over. The *Nuzhat al-Majâlis* (Recreations of the Gatherings), by 'Abdal-Raḥmân al-Ṣaffûrî, written at Mecca in 1479, is another of the successful publications of the Egyptian printing presses.

Yemen was the home of Sharaf al-dîn Ismâ'îl Ibn

al-Muqrî, the author of a strange work. He was born in 1354, at Abyât-Ḥusain, in the district of Surdad, and taught at Ta'izz and at Zabîd. He acted for some time as judge in the latter town, and died there in 1433. His principal work, the '*Unwân al-Sharaf al-wâfî*, is divided into three broad columns, separated from each other by four narrow ones. The centre columns contain a treatise on law, and the narrow ones between, which must be read separately, are treatises on history and grammar, while the two columns on the outer edges, composed of single letters which form the beginnings and endings of the columns next them, present, when read from the top downwards, an intelligible meaning of their own. This extraordinary arrangement, which makes the work a masterpiece in the overcoming of a difficulty, has been imitated by Suyûṭî in his *Nafḥat al-Miskiyya.*

We now come to the great historian and philosopher Abû Zaid 'Abdal-Raḥmân IBN KHALDÛN (1332–1406). He was descended from the tribe of Kinda in the Haḍramaut; his ancestor, Khâlid, who came with an army into Spain, in the third century of the Hegira, had given his name to the family of the Benû-Khaldûn, altering the termination of his appellation in a manner frequently adopted in Yemen. This family first resided at Carmona, near Seville, then at Seville, and finally settled at Tunis, where Ibn Khaldûn was born on 27th May 1332. Having finished his education, he entered the service of the Ḥafṣid Sultan, Abû Isḥâq Ibrâhîm, as a caligraphist. He was in attendance on this prince in 1352, when he was defeated in battle, and obliged to take refuge at Ceuta, and when his protector recovered his power, and set up his capital at Fez, the young caligraphist was

summoned and appointed his master's secretary. The favour shown him stirred up envy; his intimacy with the Amîr of Bijâya, who was interned at Fez, furnished a pretext for accusing him of treason, and he was cast into prison, and remained there till the death of the Sultan Abû 'Inân, in 1358. The regent of the kingdom, Al-Ḥasan ibn 'Umar, who governed in the name of the youthful Abû Sâlim, a boy of five, set him free, and gave him back his post. From that time his position improved. When Sultan Abû 'Abdallah Ibn al-Aḥmar reconquered the kingdom of Grenada from his brother Ismâ'îl, Ibn Khaldûn was charged by him to conclude peace with Don Pedro, the tyrant of Castile. He made up his mind to remain in Spain, and sent for his family, but finding himself surrounded by jealousy, he took advantage, in 1364, of the fact that Abû Abdallah Muḥammad, his fellow-prisoner at Fez, had recovered possession of Bijâya, to proceed to that town, and there became chamberlain to the prince, and regent of the State.

This prosperity was not of long duration. In the following year, his protector lost his life in an expedition against Abû'l-'Abbâs, Prince of Constantine, and Ibn Khaldûn, instead of holding out and defending the town of Bijâya, as its inhabitants would have had him do, delivered it over to the victor. Then, feeling that the new sovereign treated him with suspicion, he departed by stealth. In spite of Ibn Khaldûn's assertion that he preferred study to public functions, he certainly had a ruling passion for politics, to which his knowledge and acute judgment naturally predisposed him. Thus he attached himself to the service of 'Abd al-'Azîz, who had driven Abû Ḥammû out of Tilim-

sân, and after his death, to that of ʻAbdal-Raḥmân and Abû'l-ʻAbbâs, who had divided the power between them. He fell under suspicion of favouring the first of these duumvirs, and was imprisoned by the second, in 1374, but after a few days he was granted his freedom, and permission to depart to Spain. He was at first well received at Grenada by Ibn al-Aḥmar, but he soon fell into disgrace, and returned to Tilimsân just in time to see Abû Ḥammû restored to the throne.

Abû Ḥammû invited him to serve him, as he had served him previously, by undertaking a mission to the Bedouins, to bring them over to his side. On this mission Ibn Khaldûn duly started, but he tarried four years in Qalʻat Ibn Salâma, the castle of a petty prince, writing his Prolegomena and his great historical work. As he lacked the books necessary for their completion, he proceeded to Tunis, in 1378; was received with great honour by the Sultan, Abû'l-ʻAbbâs, and there wrote his history of the Berbers. His former fellow-disciple, Ibn ʻArafa, who by this time had become a mufti, represented him to be a dangerous character, and the Sultan would have taken him away with him, on an expedition which he was then preparing. But Ibn Khaldûn begged to be allowed to go on pilgrimage to Mecca, and with this object, departed by sea, in 1382. When he passed through Cairo, whither his fame had already spread, students came to his house in crowds, beseeching him to stay in Egypt, and give them lessons. To this he agreed, as no caravan was going to Mecca that year. Against his will, he was appointed Mâlikite *qâḍî* by Sultan Barqûq. His impartiality, and the severity with which he put down abuses, brought him many enemies. Meanwhile, his family had at last obtained permission to

join him, but all perished in a shipwreck. Touched by this misfortune, the Sultan relieved him of his duties as *qâḍî*, and he sought consolation in teaching and in literary labours. Three years later, he performed his interrupted pilgrimage.

On his return, he wrote the history of his own life, but Sultan Barqûq had him carried off from a property in the Fayyûm, which he himself had bestowed upon him, and obliged him once more to accept the post of *qâḍî*, in which he remained till 1400, when, under Barqûq's successor, Malik Nâṣir Faraj, he was accused and imprisoned on account of his excessive severity. Notwithstanding this, he obtained a post as professor. He attended the Sultan on his campaign against Tamerlane in Syria, but when the faithless behaviour of the Egyptian officers forced his master to beat a precipitate retreat, the historian left Damascus by stealth, and went over to the Tartar conqueror, who received him with great honour, and allowed him to return to Cairo and go back to his post as *qâḍî*, which he lost and recovered again more than once. He was still holding it when he died, on 20th March 1406.

Ibn Khaldûn is one of the greatest historians of Arabic literature, because he formulated, in his Prolegomena, a whole philosophy of Moslem history as conceived by a statesman and magistrate of the close of the fourteenth century. He also lays down sound principles for the writing of history. It is a pity, as Wüstenfeld has pointed out, that he did not follow them himself, for his annals are a compilation, too concise, occasionally, to be comprehensible, and the sources of his information are not always correctly

given. His style is not classic, yet it is quoted as a model because of the clear fashion in which he has dealt with the philosophy of history. His work is called the *Book of Examples* (Kitâb al-ʿIbar); it is divided into three parts — the Prolegomena, translated into French in the *Notices et Extraits*, by MacGuckin de Slane, after Étienne Quatremère had published the text in the same periodical; the main history of the Arabs and neighbouring peoples; and the history of the Berbers and of the Moslem dynasties of Northern Africa, published and translated into French, at Algiers, by De Slane. The history of the Aghlabites and of the Sicilian Arabs, which is included in this work, had already been published and translated by Noël des Vergers.

He begins his Prolegomena by laying down rules for the composition of critical history, which ensure thorough accuracy as to facts. He opens his subject by dividing the populations into two great classes—the nomad tribes and the sedentary tribes; he describes the formation of the towns, the influence exerted by them, the birth of all power springing from the family feeling, the foundation of the empires and causes of their decadence; the nature of the various forms of royalty, of the Caliphate and the Imâmate—in other words, of the temporal and spiritual power of the Caliphs. All this is set forth in uneven fashion by a man who is carried away by his own ideas, who repeats himself in his desire to press them, and who is perpetually breaking off to put forward historical proofs of his theories. His steady and sagacious intelligence and his great power of generalisation are everywhere noticeable, and I know no book so worthy of study by any one desirous of understanding the

history of the Moslem empires. From the general point of view the author's utter ignorance of the history of the free Republics of Greece, and of the formation of the Roman Empire, largely detracts from the value of his observations, but this in no way diminishes their weight as regards the history of the Moslem peoples.

The little town of Beyrout, which owes its name to the wells by which it was supplied (for it stands on a rocky cape at some distance from any river, and never had any drinking water carried into it till about thirty years ago), received the honour of being commemorated in a special history of its own, written by a member of the Buḥtur family, who ruled the mountainous country called al-Gharb in the Lebanon, with the title of Emîr. His name was Ṣâliḥ ibn Yaḥyâ, and he is known to have died after the year 1436. His book, which deals with the history of his own family and of the town of Beyrout under Egyptian and Frankish rule, and which exists in manuscript in the Bibliothèque Nationale, has been published by L. Chéïkho in the *Mashriq*, a Beyrout journal.

A *qâḍî* of the little town of 'Aintâb, north of Aleppo, was the father of the historian Al-'Ainî (Badr al-dîn Maḥmûd), abbreviated to 'AIN-TÂBÎ. He was born in July 1360, and began to study law under his father, with so much success that he was able to take his parent's place on the bench, even before he had completed his education. To perfect this he went to Aleppo, to which locality his family originally belonged, and, after his father's death, visited several Syrian towns, made the pilgrimage, returned from it, in 1386, by Damascus and Jerusalem, and there made

the acquaintance of the Ṣûfî 'Alâ al-dîn Aḥmad al-Sîrâfî, who took him to Cairo, and obtained him a position in the newly-founded Barqûqiyya convent. The influence of one of his protectors, the Emîr Ḥakam, procured him, in 1399, the post of Commissary of the municipal police in Cairo, from which Maqrîzî had just been dismissed. The uncertainty attending all such municipal employments led to his losing and recovering this one several times over. He fell into disgrace and was put to the torture, under Sultan Malik Mu'ayyad Shaikh, in 1412. He was recalled to favour, and appointed professor of a school founded by the same sovereign, and even sent as his ambassador to the Roman Emperor of the East at Constantinople. He rose to the highest favour under the Sultan's successors, Malik Ẓâhir Tatar and Malik Ashraf Bârsbâï—the latter especially delighted in his company, because he could talk over religious questions with him in the Turkish tongue. The accession of Malik 'Azîz Yûsuf restored him to his professorial chair (1438), and he then took advantage of a wave of favour to unite in his own person the posts of Grand Qâḍî of the Ḥanafites, head of the police, and curator of the pious foundations, which had never previously been held by the same individual. He lost the last of these three positions through some intrigue, and then turned his back on public life. He died on 29th December 1451. His *'Iqd al-jumân* (Necklace of Pearls) is a universal history from the Creation down to the year 1446. His *Jauhara* is a versified biography of Sultan Malik Mu'ayyad. His many commentaries on works of theology and jurisprudence have earned him a celebrity which has no special interest for us.

Abû'l-Ṭayyib Aḥmad al-Ḥijâzî (1388–1470) studied the traditions under the direction of Ibn Ḥajar al-'Asqalânî. His over-indulgence in the use of the marsh-nut or anacardium ruined his health, and obliged him to give up his legal studies and confine himself to literature. In addition to his own poems, which may be seen in manuscript at the Escurial, he made a collection of poetry in which appear such popular forms as *muwashshaḥ* and *zajal*, and which is entitled *Raud al-âdâb* (Flower-beds of Literature); this work has been printed at Bombay. The Bibliothèque Nationale and the British Museum both possess his *Nail al-râ'id*, a tract giving the height of the annual rise of the Nile from the Hegira onwards.

Abû'l-Khair IBN AL-JAZARÎ (1350–1429) was born at Damascus. On his way back from the Mecca pilgrimage, he went to Cairo. Returning to his native town, he became *qâḍî* of Damascus; saw his Egyptian properties confiscated in 1395; and then moved into Asia Minor, to the court of the Ottoman Sultan, Bâyezîd I. After the battle of Ancyra, Tamerlane sent him as a prisoner to Samarqand. When the Tartar conqueror died, he returned to Persia and settled at Shîrâz, where he was appointed *qâḍî*, and where he died, having spent the closing years of his life in travels which took him from Bassora to Mecca and Medina. His works, notably a didactic poem which has been lithographed at Cairo, and on which many commentaries have been written, deal with the art of reading the Koran. His *Dhât al-shifâ* is a poem which includes a short survey of the history of the Prophet and the four orthodox Caliphs, followed by a very succinct summary of Moslem history, down to the time of Bâyezîd I. It was written at Shîrâz

in 1396, at the request of Sultan Muḥammad, who then ruled that city.

A Ṣûfî named Jamâl al-dîn 'Abdal-Razzâq of Qâshân, who died in 1330, left a dictionary of technical terms (*iṣṭilâḥât*), used by the mystics, which has been published by Sprenger at Calcutta (1845). His *Laṭâ'if al-i'lâm*, which deals with a similar subject, has been utilised by Tholuck in his study of the speculative doctrine of the Trinity in the modern East; his treatise on Predestination and Free-will has been translated by Stanislas Guyard.

A descendant of the famous ascetic 'Abdal-Qâdir al-Gîlânî, Qutb al-dîn 'Abd al-Karîm, who was born in 1365, and was still alive in 1423, wrote a book called *Insân al-Kâmil* (The Perfect Man), on human destiny, which has been printed at Cairo, and nineteen other works on various points in mysticism.

Even the Persian poet Jâmî (1414–1492) wrote thirteen Arabic works on theological questions.

Ṣârim al-dîn Ibrâhîm Ibn Duqmâq, a zealous disciple of Abû Ḥanîfa, who was born in Egypt towards 1350, was haled before the *qâḍî* Jalâl al-dîn al-Bulqînî in 1401, for having written that Abû Ḥanîfa was superior to Shâfi'î. Though he excused himself by saying he had drawn this judgment from the works of other men, he was condemned to be whipped and cast into prison. He died in 1406. His *Nuzhat al-ânâm* (Pleasure of Humanity) is a history of Islam, in twelve volumes, arranged in chronological order, and dealing principally with Egypt. A portion of the autograph manuscript is at Gotha. He also wrote, at the request of Barqûq, his *Jauhar al-thamîn*, a history of Egypt, down to 1402—continued, at a later date, and by an anonymous author, to the year

1500. Other works of his have sung the wonders of Cairo and Alexandria, and the praises of Sultan Barqûq, and recalled the lives of the great Imâm Abû Ḥanîfa and his famous disciples. His description of Egypt (*al-Durra al-Muḍî'a*) has been published at Cairo by C. Vollers (1893), after the autograph manuscript in the Khedive's library.

A Ḥanafite *qâḍî* at Aleppo, who was received by Tamerlane when he conquered that town, and has left an account of his interview, which has been utilised by Ibn 'Arabshâh in his life of Tîmûr, Abû'l-Walîd IBN SHIḤNA, drew up an abridgment of Abû'l-Fidâ's work, and carried it down to the year 1403, under the name of *Rauḍat al-Manâẓir* (Flower-bed of the Sights). Gottwaldt wrote a notice of this in the *Journal Asiatique*, and the text has been printed at Bûlâq, on the margins of Ibn al-Athîr's works. This writer was born in 1348, and died in 1412. He left a mass of short didactic poems on theology, logic, and law. His son, MUHIBB AL-DÎN Abû'l-Faḍl IBN SHIḤNA, was likewise a magistrate. He lived at Cairo; was Grand Qâḍî of the Ḥanafites, with a few intervals, from 1461 to 1471; and afterwards Shaikh al-Islam. He died in 1485. He rehabilitated the text of his father's book, which had been corrupted by the copyists, and wrote a commentary on it. He himself left a history of Aleppo, extracts from which have been published by Alfred von Kremer.

Abû'l-'Abbâs SHIHÂB AL-DÎN AL-QALQÂSHANDÎ drew his surname from a small town near Cairo, in the district of Qalyûb, where his family had settled. He died in 1418. He wrote on the more or less legendary history and genealogy of the pre-Islamic Arab tribes, and a manual on the art of graceful composition, intended for the use of

candidates for administrative posts in Egypt, which contains interesting details on the history, geography, and civilisation of that country, and of the Syrian provinces. These have been utilised by Wüstenfeld, and extracts from the work have been published by H. Sauvaire.

Abû'l-Ṭayyib TAQÎ AL-DÎN AL-FÂSÎ, who was born at Fez, on 31st August 1373, went to Medina with his mother in 1377, and returned with her to Mecca in 1386. He afterwards travelled, going to Cairo, Damascus, Jerusalem, Alexandria, and Yemen. He returned to Mecca in 1405, and was appointed *qâḍî* and professor of Mâlikite law. He lost these posts in 1414, and was reappointed to them within a month. In 1425 he became blind, was obliged to resign his judicial position, and went to Cairo, to consult the Mâlikite mufti as to whether, in spite of his infirmity, it would be possible for him to continue to judge causes. The matter was decided in his favour, and he returned to his post at Mecca, but was dismissed from it in 1427, and died two years afterwards. He wrote a topographical and historical description of Mecca, under the title of *al-'Iqd al-Thamîn* (The Precious Necklace), which he himself epitomised in two other works, and of which he also furnished a second edition in his *Shifâ al-Gharâm*, from which Wüstenfeld has made extracts which have appeared in his *Chronicles of Mecca*.

Ibn Kathîr's chronicles were carried on by Abû'l-Abbâs Aḥmad AL-ṬABARÂNÎ, who was born at Tiberias, and died in 1432. His labours cover the period between 1220 and 1337. There is a French manuscript translation of his work, which we owe to Cl. Bérault, who succeeded D'Herbelot at the Collège de France, and which is now in the Bibliothèque Nationale.

TAQÎ AL-DÎN Abû'l-'Abbâs Aḥmad AL-MAQRÎZÎ (1365–1442) took the surname by which he is known from a suburb of the town of Baalbek in Syria, in which his grandfather, a Ḥanafite traditionist, had lived before emigrating to Damascus. His father, 'Alâ al-dîn, settled at Cairo, where Maqrîzî was born in 1365. The teachings of the Shâfi'ites made a profound impression upon him, and he became an opponent of the Ḥanafites. In 1385, after his return from the Mecca pilgrimage, he became assistant *qâḍî*, as his father had been before him, and was employed in the administrative department. In 1399 he was head of the police, and was afterwards preacher in the Mosque, and taught the traditions. In 1408 he moved to Damascus, where he was employed in the management of the *waqfs* belonging to the Qalânisiyya and the Nûriyya Hospital, and taught in the *madrasas*, but he refused the post of *qâḍî*. When he returned to Cairo, he devoted himself to literary composition, and became the historian of Moslem Egypt. In 1431 he started with his family on the Mecca pilgrimage, and, with all his caravan, was attacked by Bedouins on the road. He returned to Egypt in 1435, and died there. His *Mawâ'iẓ wa'l-i'tibâr* (Exhortations and Considerations), better known under the name of *Khiṭaṭ* (The Survey), is a geography and history of Egypt, dealing more especially with the topography of Cairo, in which he has appropriated work done by his predecessors, without making any acknowledgment. Extracts from this book have been published by Langlès, Silvestre de Saçy, and Hamaker. Wetzer has published his history of the Copts, which Wüstenfeld has translated into German. The complete text has been published at Bûlâq, and

Monsieur U. Bouriant has given a French translation of it, in the *Mémoires de l'École du Caire.*

The Gotha Library possesses the autograph manuscript of his history of the Fâṭimid Caliphs. From this Kosegarten has taken the account of the entry of Al-Muʿizz into Egypt, which figures in his *Arab Chrestomathy.* He wrote a history of the Mameluke Sultans under the title of *Sulûk li-maʿrifat duwal al-muluk* (The March towards the Knowledge of the Royal Dynasties), the substance of two volumes of which has been translated by Étienne Quatremère. He began an alphabetical biographical dictionary of all the princes and famous men of Egypt. The complete work was to have consisted of eighty volumes. Of these only sixteen reached the state of fair copies; three are at Leyden, and one at Paris, all autographic. A collection of his tracts, also to be seen at Leyden and in Paris, furnished Silvestre de Sacy with the substance of the *Traité des monnaies Musulmanes,* the text of which had already been published by Tychsen after a manuscript in the Escurial. Tychsen has also published the text of his treatise on the legal weights and measures. Paul Noskowyj has published, at Bonn, his history of the province of the Ḥaḍramaut, written at Mecca on information furnished by pilgrims who were natives of that country. Wüstenfeld has given the public his explanations as to the Arab families which immigrated into Egypt. His history of the Moslem sovereigns of Abyssinia was printed at Leyden by Rink as early as 1790; that of the fall of the Omeyyads and the accession of the ʿAbbâsids to the Caliphate has been translated by S. de Sacy in the *Magasin encyclopédique,* and published by G. Vos, in 1888, at Leyden.

Abû Bakr TAQÎ AL-DÎN IBN QÂḌÎ SHUHBA (1377–1448), a doctor of Shâfi'ite law at Damascus, was Grand Qâḍî of his native town, professor at various *madrasas*, and inspector of the Nûriyya Hospital. He employed himself in completing Dhahabî's chronicle by the addition of an alphabetical list of celebrated men, arranged in decades. He wrote the biographies of the Shâfi'ites down to the year 1433, and this work has been utilised by Wüstenfeld for his inquiries into the educational institutions of the Arabs.

Shihâb al-dîn Abû'l-Faḍl IBN ḤAJAR AL-'ASQALÂNÎ (1372–1449) also belonged to the Shâfi'ite rite. He was born at Ascalon, lost his father at an early age, and was brought up by a relative. Before he was eleven years old, he went on pilgrimage to Mecca, remained there for several years and engaged in trade, studying literature at the same time, and writing very good poetry. He then travelled, to study the traditions, went to Cairo, paid one visit to Palestine, and two to Yemen, and in 1403 reached Cairo, where he taught the *ḥadîth* and jurisprudence with great success. He trained the young generation of law students, who were all able to call themselves his pupils, and thus built himself up a high reputation. He later, and several times over, became Grand Qâḍî, made the holy pilgrimage again in 1421, took a journey to Aleppo in 1432, and taught in public there. He died at Cairo. His *Inbâ al-Ghumr* (Instruction of the Ignorant) gives us the political and literary history of his period (1371–1446) both in Egypt and Syria, with his own autobiography and details as to the traditionists of that epoch, a subject near his heart, for he devoted a great number of his works—as many as thirty-six, in Herr Brockel-

mann's list—to matters connected with traditionists and jurisconsults. His *Durar al-Kâmina* (The Hidden Pearls) contains the biographies of famous personages of the eighth century of the Hegira. His *dîwân* has gained so much appreciation among the moderns that it has been thought worthy to be reprinted.

Abû'l-'Abbâs Aḥmad Ibn 'Arabshâh (1389–1450), who was born at Damascus, was carried captive with his mother and brothers to Samarqand when the Syrian city was captured by Tamerlane in 1400. He found means, in that distant land, of completing his education, with the addition of a thorough knowledge of Persian and Turkish. In 1408 he went to Khaṭâ (the Chinese Turkestan of the present day), to Khwârizm, and to the Dasht-Qyptchaq (the Great Tartary Steppe), and spent several years in the town of Ḥâjî Tarkhân (the present Astrachan) to prosecute his legal studies; he was still there in the year 1411. Having travelled in the Crimea, and held intercourse with the learned men of that country, he proceeded to Adrianople, where the Ottoman Sultan Muḥammad I., son of Bâyezîd I., had just made himself sole master, in spite of his brothers' opposition. The Sultan received him with great honour, took him into his own service, and refused to allow him to go to Damascus, when the Emîr Jaqmaq summoned him thither. He commissioned him to translate Persian and Arabic books into Turkish, made him his private secretary, and employed him to keep up Arabic, Persian, and Turkish correspondence with foreign courts. On the death of Muḥammad I. in 1421, Ibn 'Arabshâh, desirous of seeing his native country once more, went to Damascus, where he was surnamed 'Ajamî (the Stranger). Here he gave himself up entirely to a life

of contemplation, and to the editing of his works. This peaceful time was interrupted by his departure for Mecca in 1428. When he returned, he settled at Cairo, there to continue his existence as a philosopher, and won the consideration and friendship of the learned. The Emîr Jaqmaq, who had become Sultan in 1438, with the title of Malik Ẓâhir, already displeased with Ibn 'Arabshâh for not having responded to his former invitation, lent a ready ear to calumny and denunciation, and had him cast into prison. The unhappy writer fell sick, and, in spite of his immediate liberation, died, after twelve days' illness, on 25th August 1450.

His *'Ajâ'ib al-maqdûr* (Marvels of Predestination) is the story of the life and conquests of Tamerlane, written in a pretentious, difficult style, full of affected expressions, and in rhymed prose. The text was published by Golius from the Elzevir Press in 1636; and by Manger, with a Latin translation (1767–1772), at Calcutta and Cairo; and Pierre Vattier has issued a French translation entitled *L'Histoire du grand Tamerlan, traduite de l'arabe d'Ahmed, fils de Gueraspe* (1658). His *Fâkihat al-Khulafâ* (The Sweetmeat of the Caliphs) is a political work, disguised under the form of fables and rhymed prose, imitated from the Persian *Marzubân-nâma.* It was edited by Freytag in 1832, and has been printed at Mosul and at Cairo.

Two of this author's sons attained minor celebrity in the field of literature. Tâj al-dîn 'Abdal-Wahhâb (1411–1495), who was born at Astrachan, accompanied his father to Damascus, and returned, at a later date, to Cairo, where he died, wrote didactic poems on exegesis and genealogy. Al-Ḥasan wrote, towards the

year 1494, and under the title of *Îḍâḥ al-Ẓulm*, a history in rhymed prose of the tyrant Ibrâhîm of Nâbulus, who was in command at Damascus in 1446, and whose exactions earned him the hatred of the inhabitants. This manuscript is at Berlin.

ABÛ'L-MAḤÂSIN Jamâl al-dîn IBN TAGHRÎ-BIRDÎ was the son of a Turkish slave, owned by a merchant of the name of Bashboghâ, who was bought by the Sultan Barqûq early in his reign (1382), educated by him, and whom he later employed as Governor of Aleppo. Under this Sultan's successor, Malik-Nâṣir Faraj, he was *atâbek* (commander of the troops) and Governor of Damascus three times over. He was still holding this office when he died in 1412. Abû'l-Maḥâsin was born at Cairo in 1411. Either on account of his rank, or because a post which carried this dignity with it was conferred on him, he bore the title of Grand Emîr. He was at Mecca in the early days of 1459, when Shihâb al-dîn Aḥmad al-Tatârî was appointed *qâḍî* there. He died in 1469. His *Nujûm al-Zâhira* (The Shining Stars) is a history of Egypt from the Arab conquest under 'Amr ibn al-'Âṣ down to the year 1453, and gives the names of the prominent personages who died in each successive year. Juynboll's edition of this work goes down to the year 975. The author's own abridgment is carried on down to 1460. His *Maurid al-laṭâfat* (Drinking Fountain of Sweetness) contains, after a short history of the Prophet, a list of some of his companions, of the rulers of Egypt, and their ministers, down to the author's own days. An edition of this work was published by J. E. Carlyle in 1792. The *Manhal al-Ṣâfî* is a biographical dictionary, a continuation of Ṣafadî's *Wâfî*, just as the *Ḥawâdith al-duhûr* carries Maqrîzî's *Sulûk* down to the year 1456. The *Baḥr al-*

Zâkhir was a great historical work, of which one volume only, covering the period between 652 and 690, is now preserved, in Paris.

Abû'l-Faḍl Qâsim IBN QUṬLÛBUGHÂ (1399–1474) was the author of a dictionary of the Ḥanafite writers and jurisconsults, entitled *Tâj al-tarâjim* (Crown of Biographies), which is important as a means of acquaintance with historic names. An edition of this book has been published by G. Flügel. Very little is known about the man who wrote it. He was born and died at Cairo, studied Arabic, logic, and Ḥanafite law there, completed his studies at Damascus and other towns, and was a prolific writer.

SOYOÛTI (1445–1505)

SUYÛṬÎ, the Egyptian (Jalâl al-dîn Abû'l-Faḍl 'Abdal-Raḥmân), was a man whose encyclopædic works were destined to incarnate the Moslem learning of the fifteenth century. He belonged to a Persian family, which had been settled for three hundred years at Suyûṭ or Usyûṭ, in Upper Egypt, but he was born at Cairo. His ancestors had held public employments—one had been a judge, another head of the municipal police, a third had become a rich merchant. His father had been *qâḍî* at Cairo, and afterwards retired from the world, so as to devote his time to reading the Sacred Book. When he died, in March 1451, young 'Abdal-Raḥmân was only five years and a half old. He was brought up by a man of ascetic habits, who made him learn the Koran by heart before he was eight years old. After visits to the Fayyûm and Damietta, he went on pilgrimage to Mecca in December 1464. On his

return he taught the science of the traditions, and his master, ʿAlam al-dîn al-Bulqînî, obtained him the senior professorial chair of jurisprudence at the Shaikhûniyya Madrasa, a post formerly held by his father.

His arrogance, and lack even of loyalty, earned him the hatred of the other learned men of the city, and this feeling was fed by his love of controversy. His covetousness led him to cut down the pensions allotted to the Ṣûfîs belonging to his school, or give them to other persons, and they rose against him, in February 1501. After a judicial inquiry, he was dismissed by the Sultan Tûmân-Bâï, and retired to his house on the island of Rauḍa. On the death of Ibn Ballân, the successor to his professorial chair, an offer was made to restore him to it, but he refused, and died in retirement on 17th October 1505. He himself gives us the names of three hundred of his books; Herr Brockelmann's list contains three hundred and fifteen; and Flügel has drawn up another, mentioning five hundred and sixty-one. But many of these compositions, the majority of which are not original, consist of only a few sheets. A single volume, now at Leyden, contains fourteen of these little treatises. He has been accused of taking the works of his predecessors, touching them up and transforming them, and then sending them forth as his own. They have, nevertheless, gained considerable popularity, like every compilation which brought works kept in the libraries of remote countries within the reach of the younger generation, at a period when there was no printing press to multiply and disseminate copies. It was not till the end of the eighteenth century that printing in Arabic characters made its first appearance in Constantinople. Up to that date the only printed works known to the Orientals were

the Eastern *incunabula* of Leyden and Rome. Be that as it may, Suyûṭî, as far as we are concerned, deserves the credit of having preserved ancient writings, which would have been utterly lost to us, but for his labours as an epitomiser and compiler.

His *History of the Caliphs* has been praised, because it is a summary, which, though convenient, perhaps, for the use of schools in the East, is quite insufficient for our needs. It covers the period between Abû Bakr and the year 1497, when Al-Mustamsik became the 'Abbâsid Caliph at Cairo. It has been published at Calcutta by Nassau Lees, and translated into English by Jarrett. It is followed by a didactic poem intended to be learnt by heart, and in which the names of all the Caliphs are arranged in order. His history of Egypt and of Cairo, *Ḥusn al-Muḥâḍara*, is a compilation from twenty-eight historical works. He also wrote the abridgment, and the continuation, of Dhahabî's *Ṭabaqât al-Ḥuffâẓ*, which has been published by Wüstenfeld. His book on the interpreters of the Koran has been published by Meursinge. His abridgment of 'Izz al-dîn Ibn al-Athîr's *Lubâb*, extracted from Sam'ânî's great work, has appeared at Leyden under the auspices of Veth. His *Kitâb al-Awâ'il* (Book of Primordial Knowledge) is an abridgment from Al-'Askarî, which has been studied by Gosche. His *Itqân*, on Koranic exegesis, has been edited at Calcutta, and reprinted at Cairo. A commentary on the Koran, which is famous in Eastern countries, is the *Tafsîr* of the two Jalâls, of which the first part, down to and including the seventeenth chapter, was written by Jalâl al-dîn Muḥammad al-Maḥallî (born 1389, died 1459), a Cairene teacher of jurisprudence and a persevering commentator, and the second half by his pupil,

Jalâl al-dîn Suyûṭî, who completed the work in forty days. Kosegarten and Grangeret de Lagrange have published extracts from the anthology entitled *Al-Marj al-nâḍir* (The Flowery Meadow). His *Shamârîkh*, on the science of history, was published by C. F. Seybold in 1896, and so was his treatise on *Kunyas* or surnames.

Ghars al-dîn Khalîl ibn Shâhîn al-Ẓâhirî (1410–1468) was given a robe of honour when he was Governor of Alexandria in 1435. In the following year he was appointed to conduct the Sacred Caravan from Cairo to Mecca, and the title of vizier was bestowed on him for the occasion. In 1437 we find him governor of the fortress of Karak, and in the two following years at Ṣafad and Damascus. He left, in his *Zubdat kashf al-mamâlik*, a description, political and administrative, of the states ruled by the Mamelukes from the thirteenth to the fifteenth century—in other words, of Egypt, Syria, and the Ḥijâz. The text of this work has been published by Monsieur P. Ravaisse. He also composed an oneirocritical treatise entitled *al-Ishârât* (The Signs), which has been studied by N. Bland, and printed at Cairo on the margins of 'Abdal-Ghanî al-Nâbulusî's *Ta'ṭîr al-anâm*.

A learned man of Suyûṭ in Egypt, not to be confounded with the famous polygraph Suyûṭî, was Shams al-dîn Abû 'Abdallah, also surnamed Suyûṭî, who, in his pious longing to behold the sacred spots of Islam, went to Mecca, with his whole family, in 1444. He remained there for nine years, living on public charity. He then returned to Cairo (1453), and entered the service of a high functionary, who took him with him to Syria, which gave the zealous pilgrim the opportunity of going to Jerusalem, in 1469, and there writing

his *Itḥâf al-akhiṣṣâ*, a history and description of the Temple, which was studied by P. Lemming at Copenhagen in 1817, translated into English by J. Reynolds in 1836, and extracts from which have been lately retranslated by Guy Le Strange.

In Egypt, too, dwelt the veterinary surgeon to Sultan Malik-Nâṣir, son of Qalâ'ûn, Abû Bakr ibn al-Mundhir, who died in 1340, and wrote the *Nâṣirî*—the name usually given to the *Kâmil al-Ṣinâʿatain* (The Perfection of the Two Arts)—a complete treatise on Hippopathology and veterinary science, which has been translated by Perron. A Cairene physician, born at Sinjâr, who died of the plague in 1348, Ibn al-Akfânî, wrote an encyclopædia of sixty different sciences, called *Irshâd al-qâṣid* (The Direction of Him who Searches out the Highest Questions), published by Sprenger in the *Bibliotheca Indica*, and added to it treatises on ophthalmology (*Kashf al-rain*), domestic medicine (*Ghunyat al-labîb*), and the practice of bleeding (*Nihâyat al-qaṣd*), and works on precious stones (*Nukhab al-Dhakhâ'ir*), and on the purchase of slaves (*al-Naẓar wa'l-taḥqîq*), which have never been printed. At the same period, Kamal al-dîn Muḥammad ibn Mûsâ AL-DAMÎRÎ, who was born in 1344, and died in Cairo in 1405, wrote his *Ḥayât al-ḥaiwân* (The Life of Animals), a dictionary of zoology which also touches on questions of grammar and etymology as connected with the names of animals, with quotations from the traditions, fragments of poetry, and proverbs, bearing on the subject. He revised this work three times, and the largest edition, finished in 1371, has been printed at Cairo six times.

Izzʿ al-dîn AIDAMIR ibn ʿAlî ibn Aidamir AL-JILDAKÎ, who died at Cairo in 1342, was an alchemist, who wrote

many books upon his favourite science, the mother of modern chemistry, which he calls the science of the scales (*'ilm al-mîzân*), and of the key (*'ilm al-miftâḥ*). Several of his works, of course, are devoted to the search for the philosopher's stone (*ṭalab al-iksîr*), the elixir of life *par excellence.* Ḥâjî Khalfa enumerates eighty-four books of his, dealing with the *arcana* of the mysterious science.

The Beni-Ziyân of Tilimsân found their historian in the person of Abû 'Abdallah Muḥammad îbn 'Abdal-Jalîl, Imâm of Tanas, who flourished at Tilimsân under Sultan Al-Mutawakkil, to whom he dedicated his book, *Naẓm al-durr wa'l-'iqyân* (Necklace of Pearls and Native Gold), of which the first part has been translated by the Abbé Bargès. He died in 1494.

Abû'l-Ḥasan 'Alî NÛR AL-DÎN AL-SAMHÛDÎ, the historian of the city of Medina, was born on the banks of the Upper Nile, at Samhûd, a large village in Upper Egypt. He went to Cairo for his education, left it to go on pilgrimage, and never returned, for in 1465 he made his home at Medina, and taught in one of the chief schools of that place. He undertook to clear the great Mosque, which had been destroyed in the conflagration of 1256, of rubbish and ashes, and never ceased to keep up active correspondence with the Princes of Bagdâd and Cairo, and beg their financial assistance, till, in 1474, he persuaded the Egyptian Sultan Qâïtbâï to provide him with means to reconstruct the ruined building. This Sultan himself paid a visit to Medina in 1479, and Samhûdî had an interview with him, the principal outcome of which was that the natives of the city were forbidden to trade in spurious relics of the Prophet. During his absence at Mecca in

1481, the Mosque at Medina once more caught fire, and this time its ruin included that of the historian's own house, and his library of three hundred volumes. While the rebuilding was in progress, he took the opportunity of going to Samhûd to see his aged mother, after a separation of sixteen years. She died ten days after her son's return, and he took his way back to Medina, carrying with him a large quantity of books presented to him by the Sultan, to re-form his library. He was appointed Shaikh al-Islâm in the city of the Prophet, and died there in 1505. In the fire which consumed his house, he lost the unfinished manuscript of a great history of Medina which he had planned, and which was to have included everything hitherto written on that subject. But, at the request of a great personage, he had made a carefully arranged extract (*Wafâ al-Wafâ*), which he had taken with him to Mecca, intending to make a fair copy of it. From this work Wüstenfeld drew the documents on the history of Medina which he published at Göttingen. A still more abridged edition, entitled *Khulâṣat al-Wafâ*, has been printed at Bûlâq.

A Persian, Ikhtiyâr al-dîn ibn Ghiyâth al-dîn al-Ḥusainî, who had studied at Herat, became *qâḍî* there, and retired, after the town was taken by Muḥammad Khân Shaibânî, to his native village, where he devoted himself to agriculture, dying at Turbat in 1522, wrote the *Asâs al-iqtibâs* (Basis of Plagiarism), in 1492, at the request of the Tîmûrid Sultan, Ḥusain Baiqarâ. This work, which has been printed at Constantinople, is a collection of verses from the Koran, traditions, proverbs, and selected pieces in poetry and prose—a regular editor's manual.

A compatriot of his, Abû'l-Qâsim al-Laithî al-Samar-

qandî, wrote, towards the year 1483, a treatise on metaphors, called *Farâ'id al-fawâ'id*, and better known under the name of *Risâlat al-Samarqandiyya*, which, even within quite recent times, has been the subject of many commentaries.

Suyûṭî, whom we have seen accused of plagiarism, and, worse than that, of downright theft, brought the same charge against Shihâb al-dîn AL-QASṬALLÂNÎ (1448–1517), a learned Shâfi'ite, who was born at Cairo, was a preacher in that city, and died there. He had him summoned before the Shaikh-al-Islâm, declaring he had copied many of his works without mentioning his name. Qasṭallânî, desiring to make up the quarrel, afterwards went to Suyûṭî's house, on the island of Rauḍa, but was not admitted. The dispute arose over his *Mawâhib al-Laduniyya* (The Mysterious Gifts), a work on the biography of the Prophet. The book has attained great popularity, has been translated into Turkish, and a commentary in the same language has been written on it. It has also been frequently reprinted. A commentary on Bukhârî's *Ṣaḥîḥ*, *Irshâd al-Sârî* (Guide for the Nocturnal Traveller), in ten volumes, has been printed at Bûlâq and at Lucknow. The same author produced other works on the merits of 'Abdal-Qâdir al-Gîlânî, of Shaikh Abû'l-Qâsim Shâṭibî, and of Shaikh Abû'l-'Abbâs Aḥmad al-Harrâr, prior of the al-Zâhidî cloister, near Cairo. But, with the exception of the second, these books have not come down to us.

Abû'l-Yumn 'Abdal-Raḥmân MUJÎR AL-DÎN al-'Ulaimî, Grand Qâḍî of the Ḥanbalites at Jerusalem, who died in 1521, wrote a chronicle of Jerusalem and Hebron, called *Anîs al-Jalîl* (The Comrade of the Glorious Man), extracts from which Von Hammer has published in the

Mines de l'Orient, and fragments of which have been translated by Henry Sauvaire. This chronicle was composed, or rather compiled, with marvellous rapidity. It was finished in less than four months, and during one of these circumstances prevented the author from writing at all.

A pupil of Suyûṭî, Abû'l-Barakât Muḥammad IBN IYÂS, a Ḥanbalite of humble birth, who was born on 9th June 1448, and died towards 1524, turned his attention to the general history of the world, and to the history of Egypt down to the year 1522, which he arranged according to the years and months, and entitled *Badâ'i' al-Zuhûr*. We also owe him a book on cosmography, dealing more especially with Egypt, called *Nashaq al-Azhâr* (The Perfume of Flowers), which was completed in 1516, and has been analysed by Langlès in the *Notices et Extraits*.

Abû 'Abdallah 'Abdal-Raḥmân of Yemen, surnamed IBN AL-DAIBA' (which means, apparently, the Son of the White Man), who was born at Zabîd on 7th October 1461, was brought up by his maternal grandfather, Ismâ'îl, while his father was travelling on the Indian coasts. In the course of this journey he died, leaving his son in poverty. The youth had a taste for mathematics and legal studies. He travelled for educational purposes, then returned to Zabîd, made the pilgrimage in 1491, attended the teachings of Sakhâwî at Mecca, and, when back in his native town, conceived the idea of writing its history. His *Bughyat al-Mustafîd*, which goes down to the year 1495, attracted the attention of the Sultan Malik-Muẓaffar 'Âmir ibn Ṭâhir, who commissioned him to write his history of the Beni-Ṭâhir dynasty (*Al-'iqd al-bâhir*, The Shining Necklace), rewarded him

generously for his labour, and appointed him to teach the traditions in the great Mosque at Zabîd, a position which he worthily filled until his death in 1537. From the *Bughyat* Th. Johannsen has made fragmentary extracts which appear in his *Historia Jemanæ*. Previously, Abû 'Abdallah Muḥammad al-Janadî, who died in 1332, had written the political and literary history of Yemen, in a book entitled *Sulûk*, from which Mr. H. C. Kay has drawn facts as to the Carmathians of that country.

The Ottoman Empire was then carrying on that great series of Asiatic conquests which followed on its establishment in Europe. The battle of Marj-Dâbak, near Aleppo, and the death of the Mameluke Sultan Qânṣûh al-Ghûrî had delivered Syria into Ottoman hands, and Egypt was conquered by Selîm I. in 1517. IBN ZUNBUL, surnamed *al-Rammâl* (the Geomancer), because he earned his livelihood by drawing out horoscopes on the sand, had an opportunity of watching the movements of the Turkish troops, probably in some position connected with the military arrangements. He was even shut up, with the body of troops to which he was attached, in the fortress of Aboukir. He drew up a history of the Ottoman conquest of Egypt, a general geography, and a treatise on geomancy.

The Turks, like the Persians in bygone days, were beginning to write in Arabic. Muṣṭafâ, a teacher who was born at Tâshköpri, in the year of Muḥammad II.'s conquest of Constantinople (1453), and who was chosen by Bâyezîd II. to be tutor to his son Selîm, dreamt, the night before he left Broussa for Angora, that a handsome old man appeared to him, and forewarned him of the birth of a son, whom he would call Aḥmad. The dream

came true. Within a month, on 2nd December 1495, Aḥmad was born, and was surnamed Tâshköpri-Zâdè (the Son of Tâshköpri), after his father's local appellation. Having studied every kind of learning known to the Orientals of the Middle Ages, he himself began to teach, at Dimétoka, at Constantinople, at Uskiup in Macedonia, and at Adrianople, where he was *qâḍî* in 1551. In 1554 he was attacked by an inflammation of the eyes, became almost totally blind, and was obliged to dictate his works. He died in 1560. His *Nawâdir al-akhbâr* (Curiosities of History), is a dictionary, in alphabetical order, of the illustrious men of Islam, after Abû Muḥammad's life of the Companions of the Prophet, Ibn Khallikân's biographical dictionary, and Shahrastânî's history of the philosophers. His *Shaqâ'iq al-Nu'mâniyya* (The Anemones) is a work devoted to the biographies of five hundred and twenty-two illustrious men, 'Ulemâ and Ṣûfîs, of the Ottoman Empire, divided into ten classes, according to the ten reigns, beginning with that of 'Osman, son of Ertoghrul, and ending with that of Sulaimân. At the end of the book we find the author's own autobiography, dictated in 1558. His *Miftâḥ al-Sa'âdat wa-Miṣbâḥ al-siyâdat* (Key of Happiness, and Lantern of Mastery) is an encyclopædia on the objects of the various branches of learning, dictated to his pupils, and concluded in 1560. It has been utilised by Ḥâjî Khalfa for his bibliographical dictionary, and translated into German by Von Hammer. The author's son, Kamal al-dîn Muḥammad, translated the work into Turkish, and made additions to it. This version has been printed at Constantinople.

Al-Ḥusain ibn Muḥammad AL-DIYÂRBAKRÎ, who was born at Diyârbakr, settled at Mecca, where he was *qâḍî*,

and died there in 1558. His *Khamîs fî Aḥwâl al-nafs al-nafîs* (Book divided into Five Parts, dealing with the Precious Soul) is a biography of the Prophet, compiled from over a hundred different works, and is followed by a general review of all the Caliphs down to Sultan Sulaimân I. (1520). Certain copies of this work, which was finished in 1533, carry it down to Murâd III. (1574). It has been printed at Cairo. The story of the assassination of the Caliph ʻUmar has been extracted from it, and published, with a German translation, by O. von Platen. A shorter extract appears in Petermann's Arabic grammar.

In India, Shaikh Zain al-dîn al-Maʻbarî was writing an Arabic history of the development of Islam in Malabar, of the Portuguese establishment there, and of the persecution inflicted by that nation on the Moslems, between 1498 and 1577. His *Tuḥfat al-Mujâhidîn* has been translated into English by Rowlandson, and a fragment of it has been inserted into J. Briggs' translation of Ferishta's history of India.

Muḥammad QUṬB AL-DÎN al-Nahrawâli (1511–1582) came of a family which at one time dwelt at Nahrawâla, the capital of Gujerat, in India. Here his great-grandfather, Qâḍî Khân Maḥmûd of Delhi, had lived. His father emigrated to Mecca, where he held a professorial chair, and there Muḥammad was born. Having concluded his studies in his native city, the young man proceeded to Egypt, and attended the lectures of the professors there, who were Suyûṭî's pupils. Thence he went to Constantinople. He was presented to Sultan Sulaimân by Ayâs Pacha, the vizier, a robe of honour was bestowed upon him, and he was appointed professor at the Ashrafiyya, a school at Mecca, the library of which he set in order. He has left an account of a

second journey from Medina to Constantinople, in the course of which he passed through Asia Minor (1558). The Vizier 'Alî Pacha was telling him the story of his campaigns, when Quṭb al-dîn observed that, when ocular witnesses die out, history is apt to fade away, unless the facts are committed to paper, and cited, as a model for this purpose, Abû Shâma's history of Nûr-al-dîn and Saladin. 'Alî Pacha then desired a secretary, 'Alî Chelebi, to write an account of the Ottoman campaigns, a duty he seems to have left unperformed. Quṭb al-dîn went back to Mecca, and was appointed professor of the Ḥanbalite rite when the Sulaimâniyya University was established there in 1567. He was mufti of the Holy City when he died. His *I'lâm bi-a'lâm Balad al-Ḥarâm* (Instruction as to the Notable Peculiarities of the Sacred Dwelling-place) is a history of the city of Mecca and of the Ka'ba, which has been published by Wüstenfeld. His *Barq al-Yamânî* (Lightning Flash of Yemen) contains the history of Arabia Felix from the year 1495, that of the first Ottoman conquest, under the Vizier Sulaimân Pacha, of the return of the Zaidites, and of the second conquest, under the Grand Vizier Sinân Pacha, to whom the whole work is dedicated.

Muṣṭafâ Efendi AL-JANNÂBÎ belonged to the little town of Jannâba, on the Persian Gulf. He was at one time *qâḍî* of Aleppo, but was dismissed, and died in 1591. He wrote in Arabic, and afterwards translated into Turkish, a history of eighty-two Moslem dynasties, in eighty-two chapters, down to the year 1589. From it J. B. Podestà took the history of Tamerlane, which he translated into Latin and published at Vienna in 1680. The same author also left a treatise on the building

of the Mosque of St. Sophia, and on the walls of Constantinople.

'ÂMIR AL-RU'ÂMÎ, secretary to the princes Shams al-dîn and 'Izz al-dîn, who held the fortress of Kaukabân, near Ṣan'â, in the days of the Turkish conquest, was in both personal and epistolary intercourse with the commanders of the Ottoman troops, and especially with Ḥasan Pacha, who was appointed in 1580. He enshrined his recollections in two volumes, one of which, now in the Leyden Library, has been published by Rutgers, under the title of *Historia Jemanæ sub Hasano Pascha*, while the other deals exclusively with the history of the Emîr 'Izz al-dîn.

Abû'l-'Abbâs Aḥmad AL-QARÂMÂNÎ (1552–1610) was born at Damascus. His father, who was inspector of the Mosque of the Omeyyads, sold the prayer-carpets for his own benefit, caused a Mâlikite school to be pulled down, and was punished by being strangled in 1559. Aḥmad, the son, entered the Government service; acted first as secretary, and then as president, of the board of management of the two women's hospitals at Damascus, which depended on Egypt, and was a prominent personage, who specially frequented legal circles. He wrote a summary of the history of Jannâbî, with the addition of some supplementary information and certain inaccuracies, which he entitled *Akhbâr al-duwal wa-Âthâr al-Uwal* (History of the Dynasties and Monuments of the Ancients). The text of this work has been printed at Bûlâq on the margins of Ibn al-Athîr.

Abû'l - Mawâhib 'Abdal - Wahhâb AL - SHA'RÂNÎ was a mystic, belonging to Old Cairo, who gained celebrity, at an early age, by his writings, which his opponents declared to be opposed to the orthodox dogma. An attempt was made to convict him of impiety by falsify-

ing one of his books, but he never rested till he had succeeded in convincing the chief doctors of his innocence. He died in 1565, leaving his name to a sect which he had founded. He believed himself to have received the most wonderful gifts from God, amongst them the power of working miracles. His *Scales of the Moslem Law*, in which he endeavours to elucidate the spirit of Islamic law, and reduce the divergent doctrines of the four orthodox rites to an agreement, has been translated by Dr. Perron. Sha'rânî explains and weighs the reasons for the disagreement between the various lawyers, and accounts for them by the uncertainty as to the meaning of certain *ḥadîths*, thus clearly showing that, in the eyes of Moslem doctors, the great edifice of Moslem law is a purely human work, notwithstanding the religious authority on which it rests. His *Lawâqiḥ al-Anwâr* (The Fecundating Lights), containing the lives of the most famous mystics, from the earliest days of Ṣûfism, has been printed at Cairo, and so has his *Laṭâ'if al-minan*.

Al-Maqqarî of Tilimsân

At the other end of the Moslem world, in the town of Tilimsân, in the heart of the Maghrib, Shihâb al-dîn Abû'l-'Abbâs al-Maqqarî, thus called after the village of Maqqara, to which his family originally belonged, was born about the year 1591. He was educated in the town of his birth, where his uncle Sa'îd was mufti for sixty years, and later went to complete his studies at Fez and Morocco. Here he remained till 1618, when he decided to make the pilgrimage, so as to escape the political disturbances which had just broken out. Returning the following year, he halted at Cairo, and

there took him a wife. Notwithstanding the honour shown him, life in that city struck him as too inhospitable to be pleasant, and, bitten once more with his love of travel, he went to Jerusalem in 1620, made five more journeys to Mecca, and remained some time at Medina, where he gave a course of lectures on the *ḥadîth.* He returned to Cairo in 1627, but did not stay there; paid another visit to Jerusalem, and then went on to Damascus, where his compatriots from the Maghrib had prepared him a residence which did not take his fancy. Aḥmad ibn Shâhîn, the head of the Jaqmaqiyya School, sent him the keys of that establishment with an invitation in verse, to which Maqqarî replied in like fashion. He was delighted with the manner in which the school was housed, and desired no other habitation. During his stay there, he gave lessons in the great Mosque. The success of this course left a most pleasing impression upon him, to which reference is made in his poems, and he returned to Damascus in 1631. He had gone back to Cairo, and was preparing to leave that city for good, when he was attacked by a fever, and carried off, in January 1632. The *Nafḥ al-Ṭîb* (Breath of the Perfumes), his principal work, is divided into two parts, the first devoted to the political history of Moslem Spain, and that of the learned men born there; and the second, to the life of the Vizier Lisân al-dîn Ibn al-Khaṭîb. This bulky work, printed at Bûlâq in four volumes, was written in the space of one year, during his stay at Cairo, after his first journey to Damascus. The book was compiled at the request of Aḥmad Ibn Shâhîn, out of materials brought together long before. The rapidity with which it was produced is evidenced by a certain lack of order in the construction. The first

part of the *Nafḥ al-Ṭîb* has been published, under the title of *Analectes sur l'Histoire et la Littérature des Arabes d'Espagne*, by R. Dozy, G. Dugat, L. Krehl, and W. Wright. The political part of the book has been extracted, and arranged in a different order, by Pascual de Gayangos, and translated by him into English, under the title of *The History of the Mohammedan Dynasties in Spain*.

Ḥâjî Khalfa

Muṣṭafâ Ḥâjî Khalfa, surnamed *Kâtib Chelebi*, was a Constantinopolitan Turk, whose father was employed in the War Office. He himself entered the military bureaux, and accompanied the army on the Bagdâd campaign. The following year he was present at the siege of Erzeroum. When he returned to Constantinople, in 1628, his father was dead, and had left him a request that he would never give up his studies. The young man was not, however, at once able to carry out his parent's last behest, for he was obliged to go with the army to Bagdâd and Hamadhân, in 1629, and to Aleppo, in 1633. But he took advantage of the winter season of the latter campaign to make the pilgrimage to Mecca, whence his honorary title of *Ḥâjî* (Pilgrim). After the Erivan campaign, he left the public service, and devoted himself altogether to learning. The recommendation of the friend of his youth, the mufti 'Abdal-Raḥîm Efendi, procured him the post of Khalîfa (pronounced by the Turks "Khalfa") or lieutenant at the War Office, which left him leisure to choose his own occupations. In this quality he was present at the great council held in the presence of Sultan Muḥammad IV., on 18th February 1653, to remedy the disordered condition of the finances.

He died before he was sixty, in September 1658. Besides his Turkish works, such as his *Jihân-Numâ*, and his history of the naval wars, with which we have nothing to do in this place, he left a great encyclopædic and bibliographic treatise, the basis of all inquiry into Arabic, Persian, and Turkish literature, called the *Kashf al-Ẓunûn* (Doubts Cleared up), the text of which, and a Latin translation, have been given to the world by Gustav Flügel, under the title of *Lexicon Bibliographicum.* His *Fadhlaka* is a summary of Jannâbî's general history, in which the number of dynasties dealt with is carried from eighty-two to one hundred and fifty.

Shaikh Muḥammad ibn ʿAbdal-Muʿṭî AL-ISḤÂQÎ was born at Manûf, in Egypt, and received his education there. At a later date he went to Cairo, where he made his name as a poet. He died in his native town, soon after the year 1650. He had dedicated his *Akhbâr al-Uwal*, an anecdotic history of Egypt from the days of the Arab conquest, to the Ottoman Sultan, Muṣṭafâ I.

Aḥmad AL-KHAFÂJÎ was descended from an old Arab family, settled in a village near Cairo. Having studied philosophy under his own uncle, Abû Bakr al-Shanawânî, surnamed the Sîbawaih of his century, he made the Mecca pilgrimage with his father, and pushed on to Constantinople, where he studied mathematics. He was appointed *qâḍî* in Roumelia, at Uskiup, and at Salonika, where he made his fortune, and was sent to Egypt as Qâḍî ʿAsker. On his return to Constantinople he was so slandered, and such accusations were brought against him, that he was banished, and sent back to Cairo to occupy a post as *qâḍî*, the emoluments of which were expected to suffice for his support. He then turned his attention to literary work, had a pupil, Faḍlallah, who

was father of the famous biographer Muḥibbî, and died on 4th June, 1659. His *Khabâyâ al-Zawâyâ* (Secrets Hidden in Corners) is a history of the literary men of his time, divided into five sections—Syria, the Ḥijâz, Egypt, the Maghrib, and Rûm (in other words, Turkey), with the addition of an appendix devoted to the author's own sermons in verse and prose. His pupil Faḍlallah took a copy of this work at Damascus, and on it Khafâjî's renown rests. His *Raiḥâna* is a second edition of the same work, in which the most prominent place is given to the poets, and it contains several lectures, one of them against Yaḥyâ ibn Zakarîyâ, Shaikh al-Islâm at Constantinople. Both these works were useful to Muḥibbî, to whom we shall later refer. His *Ṭirâz al-Majâlis* (Fringe of the Lectures) is a collection of fifty-one small pieces, dealing with points in grammar, exegesis, and rhetoric.

FAḌLALLAH ibn Muḥibb-Allah (1621–1671), who was born at Damascus, learnt Persian and Turkish, and attracted notice by his precocity. When he was sixteen, having lost his father, he entered the service of the mufti 'Abdal-Raḥmân al-'Imâdî as his secretary. In 1638 he journeyed to Aleppo, whither the Shaikh al-Islâm, Yaḥyâ, had come from Constantinople, and by him was invested with the prebend of the Derwîshiyya Mosque, which had been held by his father. He then went to Constantinople and Cairo, assisted the *qâḍî* Muḥammad al-Bursawî in the latter city, made acquaintance with Khafâjî, and attended his teachings. Sickness drove him back to Damascus, and induced him to peruse medical books and study medical science, but his health was not restored. He was appointed *qâḍî* at Diyârbakr, felt better there, was able to travel to Constantinople, and remained

there four years. In 1666 he was appointed *qâḍî* at Beyrout, and lived there about a year, the usual duration of such posts under the Ottoman rule. He went back to Damascus, where he died. His supplement to the biographies written by Ḥasan al-Bûrînî formed the basis of his son Muḥibbî's great work.

Ibrâhîm ibn 'Abdal-Raḥmân AL-KHIYÂRÎ (1628–1671), who came of an old family settled in Egypt, was born at Medina, where his father, who had come from Cairo on pilgrimage, had remained to preach and teach the *ḥadîth*. Ibrâhîm followed in his footsteps. He became preacher in the Mosque of the Prophet, saw himself ousted from this position by a stranger, and resolved to journey to Constantinople, where his petition was granted by the Shaikh-al-Islâm and the Grand Vizier. On his way back, he travelled across Syria and Palestine, and so reached Cairo, where he sojourned some days before joining the Medina caravan (1670). He did not remain long in possession of his post, for the Shaikh of the Mosque insisted that the Shâfi'ite preachers should pronounce the *Bismillah* according to the Ḥanafite rite—that is to say, in an undertone. Al-Khiyârî refused to obey this order, and died suddenly, of poison, on 4th November 1671. He wrote an account of his journey, the manuscript of which is at Gotha, and which has been studied by Fr. Tuch.

During the same period, IBN ABÎ DÎNÂR al-Ruainî of Qairawân wrote (1689) a history of Northern Africa and Tunis, while in Egypt, in the same year, Muḥammad DIYÂB AL-ITLÎDÎ concluded his romance of the Barmekides, composed almost entirely of fables, which has been printed several times at Cairo and Bûlâq. Muḥammad AL-MUḤIBBÎ, the son of Faḍlallah, was born at Damascus

in 1651. During his father's absence, and when he himself was only twelve years old, he kept up a correspondence with him both in verse and in rhymed prose. He went, when older, to complete his studies at Constantinople. His patron there was Ibn Bairâm, who had been *qâḍî* at Damascus for some time, and who took him with him when he was appointed Qâḍî 'Asker at Adrianople. He followed Ibn Bairâm's fortunes when he was replaced in 1676, and returned to Damascus after his death. There he gave himself up to literary labours, went on pilgrimage to Mecca, acted for some time as assistant *qâḍî* in that city, and then took up the post of professor in the Amîniyya School at Damascus. He died there on 11th November 1699. His principal work, which has been printed in four volumes at Cairo, contains one thousand two hundred and eighty-nine biographies of famous men who died in the course of the eleventh century of the Hegira.

Philology

At the beginning of the eighth century of the Hegira, Aḥmad ibn 'Alî ibn Mas'ûd wrote a grammatical treatise for the use of schools, entitled *Marâḥ al-arwâḥ*, which has been frequently lithographed and printed in the East.

In 1311 Jamâl al-dîn Muḥammad Ibn Mukarram died at Cairo. He was a compiler, gifted with the most astonishing facility of production, for he is said to have left five hundred volumes behind him, and to his zeal we owe a work of very great value as regards our knowledge of the Arabic tongue—the *Lisân al-'Arab*, a huge dictionary, containing the substance of Jauharî's *Ṣaḥâḥ*, of Ibn Duraid's *Jamhara*, and of the *Muḥkam*, written by

Ibn Sîda, the Spanish philologist of Murcia. Ibn Mukarram was born in 1232 in Northern Africa. Compared with his great work, Ibn 'Asâkir's summary of the history of Damascus, and Sam'ânî's abridgment of that of Bagdâd, have very little value.

A surname known all over the Moslem world is that of IBN ÂJURRÛM, borne by Abû 'Abdallah Muḥammad ibn Dâ'ûd al-Ṣanhâjî, of whose history nothing is known, beyond the fact that he died in 1324, and that he wrote, for the benefit of his own son, Abû Muḥammad, a very elementary grammar, which has become famous under the name of *Âjurrûmiyya*, and which is said to have been composed at Mecca. So general has been the popularity of this little book that it has become the basis of all grammatical study in the East. The chief reason for the favour it enjoys is its brevity, but so exceedingly concise is it, that it needs a commentary. There have been many reprints of the work, from the Roman edition of 1592, and the Latin translation given to the world by Thomas Erpenius at Leyden in 1617, down to Bresnier's translation (1846–1866), Perowne's (1852), and Trumpp's (1876).

'Abdallah ibn Yûsuf IBN HISHÂM, who was born in 1308, was a disciple of the Spanish grammarian Abû Ḥayyân. He was a Shâfi'ite doctor, and as such became a teacher of Koranic exegesis at Cairo. Five years before his death, with the object of obtaining a post in a *madrasa* belonging to that order, he went over to the Ḥanbalite rite. He died in 1360, having written, under the title of *Qaṭr al-Nadâ* (The Rain of Dew), a grammar which has been translated into French by Monsieur Goguyer. His *Mughnî al-labîb*, a treatise on syntax in general, written at Mecca between 1348 and 1353, has been printed both at Teheran and at Cairo. His *I'râb*,

on the rules of inflection, published and translated into French by Silvestre de Sacy in his *Anthologie Grammaticale Arabe*, has been printed at Cairo with a commentary, and so have his grammar known as *Shudhûr al-dhahab* (Shreds of Gold), and his "Enigmas" (*Alghâz*) on grammatical difficulties. Fifteen of his works, all dealing with grammar, are preserved in European libraries.

Abû'l-Ṭâhir Majd al-dîn AL-FÎRÛZ-ÂBÂDÎ (1329–1414) came of a family belonging to Fîrûz-Âbâd in Fârsistan. He was born in Kârizîn, a small town near Shîrâz. He studied the traditions and philology at Wâsiṭ, Bagdâd, and Damascus. In 1349 he accompanied his master, Taqî al-dîn 'Alî al-Subkî, to Jerusalem, remained there ten years, occupied with literary undertakings, and then departed for Cairo, and paid visits to Asia Minor and India. He was invited to Bagdâd by the Sultan Aḥmad ibn Uwais. In 1393 he met Tamerlane at Shîrâz, and was well received and richly rewarded by the conqueror. He then departed once more to India. As he was making his way back to Mecca, the Sultan of Yemen, Ismâ'îl ibn 'Abbâs, gave him his daughter in marriage, and, in 1393, appointed him Grand Qâḍî of Yemen, with a residence at Zabîd. There he died, having expressed a desire, which the Sultan would not permit him to gratify, to end his days at Mecca.

He had built houses at Mecca and Medina, in which professors selected by himself taught during his own absences. Fîrûz-Âbâdî is well known to all Arabic students, even to beginners, by his great lexicographical work, the *Qâmûs al-muḥîṭ* (The Ocean that Surrounds the Earth), on which all the European dictionaries of the classic tongue are based, either directly or through

the various commentaries written upon it, amongst which we may mention Sayyid Murtaḍâ al-Zabîdî's *Tâj-al-ʿarûs* (The Bride's Tiara), which has been printed in ten volumes at Bûlâq. He also wrote in Persian, as is proved by the existence of his *Sifr al-saʿâda*, a history of the life of the Prophet, now at Gotha, which was translated into Arabic by Abû'l-Jûd al-Makhzûmî in 1401.

Jabrîl ibn Farḥât, a Christian, belonged to the family of Maṭar. He was born at Aleppo on 20th November 1660, and studied first Syriac, and afterwards Arabic, under Shaikh Sulaimân al-Naḥwî. He also acquired Italian. He retired from the world before he was twenty, took religious vows at the age of twenty-three, and, with several other young men, left his native town to retire into the monasteries of the Lebanon. The community was constituted by the authority of the Maronite patriarch of Ehden, Istifân al-Duwaihî, in 1694. This primate, who bore the title of Patriarch of Antioch, and wrote a well-known history of the Maronites, gave the convent of St. Maura at Ehden, in the region of the cedars, to be its dwelling-place. In 1711 our monk betook himself to Rome, was kindly received by the Pope, returned to the Lebanon, and proceeded in 1721 to Aleppo, at the request of the Melchite bishop there, to correct the Arabic translation of the works of St. John Chrysostom. In 1725 he was appointed Bishop of Aleppo, and received the name of Germanos. He died on 9th July 1732, and Nîqûlâûs al-Ṣâ'igh, a priest and poet, Superior of the Basilian Monks of St. John at Shuair, whose poems were printed at Beyrout in 1859, and who had been the friend of his youth, wrote an elegy on his departure. His *dîwân*, which includes

poems on sacred and edifying subjects, was abridged by his own hand, under the title *Tadhkira*, in 1720. It was printed for the first time at Beyrout in 1866; and a second edition, annotated by Sa'îd al-Khûrî, appeared at the same place in 1894. His Arabic grammar, *Baḥth al-maṭâlib*, has run through three editions; the first appeared at Malta in 1836, the last at Beyrout in 1891. His dictionary (*Aḥkâm bâb al-i'râb*), abridged from the *Qâmûs*, was published, with additions, by Rushaid Daḥdâḥ, at Marseilles, in 1849.

Morocco

Abû'l-Abbâs Aḥmad ibn Muḥammad, surnamed Ibn al-Qâḍî, who lived under the rule of Muley Abû'l-'Abbâs Aḥmad al-Manṣûr (1578–1603), wrote a number of historical and biographical works. His *Jadhwat al-Iqtibâs*, which deals with the men of mark born in Fez, or domiciled there, was lithographed in that town, in 1892. His biography of his sovereign and patron, *al-Muntaqâ al-Maqṣûr*, has been quoted by the author of the *Nuzhat al-Hâdî;* and his *Durrat al-ḥijâl*, a biographical dictionary, is preserved in manuscript in the library of the University at Algiers.

Towards the close of the sixteenth century, there died in the battle of Wâdî'l-Makhâzin (Alcazar el-Kebîr), in which the Moors defeated the Portuguese (4th August 1578), and at the side of King Don Sebastian, and of Muley Muḥammad, a man who had collected the biographies of the most prominent men of the Maghrib during the tenth century of the Hegira into a dictionary, entitled *Dauḥat al-Nâshir*, which was lithographed at Fez in 1891. His name was Muḥammad ibn 'Alî ibn

Miṣbâḥ, better known under the surname of IBN 'ASKAR, and he was born at Hibth, in the district of Alcazar el-Ṣaghîr. His work was carried on by Abû 'Abdallah Muḥammad ibn al-Ṭayyib, who collected the materials for a biographical dictionary for Morocco during the eleventh and twelfth centuries of the Hegira, called the *Nashr al-Mathânî*. This, too, was lithographed at Fez, in 1892.

In 1661, Abû Sâlim 'Abdallah ibn Muḥammad al-'Ayyâshî was accomplishing a journey in Southern Algeria and the Barbary States, his account of which (*Riḥla*) was translated into French by Adrien Berbrugger in 1846.

Early in the eighteenth century, Muḥammad al-Ṣaghîr ibn al-Ḥâjj al-Wafrânî (of the Chelha tribe of the Wafrân), who lived in the city of Morocco, and held an official position at the court of Sultan Muley Ismâ'îl (1672–1727), fell into disgrace at the end of his life, and died, in all probability, before Oran was taken by the Spaniards in 1732. Under the title of *Nuzhat al-Hâdî* he wrote a history of the Sa'dian dynasty (1511–1670), which has been utilised by José de Santo Antonio Moura (1824), by Gräberg af Hemsö (1834), by MacGuckin de Slane, Muḥammad ibn Raḥḥâl, and General Dastugue, and which has been published in its entirety, and translated into French, by O. Houdas.

THE SOUDAN

At the beginning of the fourteenth century, influenced by the Arab learning propagated by the Berber tribes of the Sahara, the northern portions of the negro countries round Timbuctoo opened their portals to

civilisation, and ebony-skinned doctors dilated on the deep subjects a knowledge of which they had attained by journeying to Cairo. The dwellers in the Melli country had been Moslems from the days of the Moravids. Ibn Baṭûṭa, the traveller, has left us very curious details as to this part of the world, which he visited in the course of his tour in Africa. Aḥmad ibn Aḥmad ibn 'Abdal-Raḥmân, who was born in 1357, went to Egypt for his education. He even taught there, and made an abridgment of the commentary written by his master, Ibn Marzûq, the younger, on the *Jumal*. He is known to have been alive after the year 1427. 'Abdal-'Azîz, the Takhûrian, whose learning was very remarkable, was able to quote, in the presence of the learned men of Cairo, and without a single fault, the sources whence Sidi-Khalîl had drawn the matter of the questions dealt with in his *Summary*. Another lawyer, "who knew tales of travel by heart," was Makhlûf ibn 'Alî al-Bilbâlî, who began his education at a very advanced age. So successful were his first efforts in this line that he went to Fez to sit at the feet of 'Alî ibn Ghâzî, and from that time his powers won him a great reputation, which followed him when he went back to the Soudan, and began to teach there himself. He pined for the land in which he had acquired his learning, and returned to Morocco, but was poisoned there, and made his way back to Timbuctoo, where he died towards the year 1534.

Al-Ḥâjj Aḥmad ibn 'Umar ibn Muḥammad Aqîṭ, who belonged to the Berber tribe of the Ṣanhâja, and was born at Timbuctoo, left the reputation of a saint behind him in his own country. It was even asserted that, when he went on pilgrimage in 1485, he saw the

doors of the Prophet's tomb at Medina open wide before him, after he had failed to obtain access to that building. In the course of his journey to Mecca, he made the acquaintance of Suyûṭî. On his return, which coincided with the revolt of the negro tyrant Sonni-'Alî, he settled at Kano, and afterwards at other Soudanese towns, and taught there. The Sultan of the country would have made him an Imâm, but he refused that post, and all public functions, so as to devote his whole time to teaching. He had copied a considerable number of books with his own hand, and when he died, in 1536, seven hundred volumes were found in his house.

His brother, Shaikh Maḥmûd ibn 'Umar (1463–1548), who was born at Timbuctoo, was the most venerated Marabout in the Soudan. He was gifted with a calm nature and a surprising memory, and was universally esteemed. The king of the country was in the habit of going to see him, and requesting his blessing, but the gifts showered from every quarter upon the saintly man made no impression upon him. In 1498, when he was *qâḍî*, he reformed the administration of justice by curbing the corruption rampant on the judges' bench. His judicial duties did not prevent him from continuing to teach, and expound Sidi-Khalîl's *Summary*, which he had introduced into the Soudan, together with Saḥnûn's *Mudawwana*. He made the sacred pilgrimage in 1510.

Muḥammad ibn 'Abdal-Karîm al-Mughîlî belonged to Tilimsân. He was a man of bold and enterprising character, and, by his uncompromising fanaticism, stirred up massacres of the Jews which drenched the Touat, where he was a preacher, in blood. He celebrated this event by composing a poem to the glory of the Prophet, and then left that country, and passed far into the Soudan,

where he taught Koranic learning and jurisprudence at Takeda, Kachena, and Kano. Hearing his son had been murdered, probably in revenge, by the Jews of the Touat, he started on his way back to the Sahara, but died just as he reached the end of his journey. He wrote some twenty books on law and theology, and also left a correspondence on logic, in verse and prose, with Jalâl al-dîn Suyûṭî.

Al-ʿAqib ibn 'Abdallah al-Ansammanî was born at Takeda, a Berber village on the Soudanese frontier. He was the pupil of Al-Marîli, and also attended the teachings of Suyûṭî at Cairo. His facility in expressing himself was especially admired. He died after the year 1543, leaving some legal treatises behind him.

Aḥmad ibn Aḥmad ibn 'Umar (1522–1583), son of the Marabout Aḥmad ibn 'Umar lately referred to, studied theology, logic, and diction, and his erudition gained him a high place among the learned men of his period. His virtue and his popularity enabled him to address sharp remonstrances to persons of all classes, and even to the princes of the country. He was seized with serious illness one day, while on his road to Kaghou. The Sultan, Ashkar Dâ'ûd, went every evening to spend several hours with him, and never slackened in his attentions till the sick man had completely recovered his health. He collected a considerable library, which he never hesitated to place at the disposal of students. In 1549 he performed the journey to Mecca, and passed through Cairo, where he entered into relations with all the learned men of the day, but more especially with Muḥammad al-Bakrî, the Ṣûfî, who caused him to write down, from his dictation, the litanies and orisons used by the religious confraternities of the

mystics. He began works on various legal and theological points, but most of his books were left unfinished.

The most singular figure of this period is that of Muḥammad ibn Maḥmûd ibn Abû Bakr (1524–1593), surnamed Baghyo'o, a lawyer of Timbuctoo, coming of a family belonging to Wankoro, whose whole life was devoted to teaching. He loved all lovers of knowledge, and showed them every sort of kindness. He would willingly lend his most precious manuscripts, and never asked for them back, however rare they might be. He never refused a book to a student, even when the individual was quite a stranger to him. The most astonishing thing about this man, who handed about the books in his library so freely, was that he loved them passionately, and spent a great deal of trouble and money in buying them, or having copies made. His patience as a teacher was unfailing, even when the most difficult subjects had to be communicated to the slowest intelligence. He would spend whole days in this occupation. His modesty was remarkable, and he won the affection of all who knew him. He died very shortly after the capture of Timbuctoo by the Moroccan army, under the Pacha Jaudar. His works are for the most part marginal comments on legal books.

Abû'l-'Abbâs Aḥmad-Bâbâ (1556–1627) of Timbuctoo was descended from Aḥmad ibn 'Umar. He was born in the village of Arawân, refused to submit to the Moorish occupation of the Soudan, and was carried to Morocco, where he lay four years in prison. His liberation, at the command of the new Sultan, Muley Zîdân, enabled him to go back to his own country, and to his career as a teacher of jurisprudence. He was fifty

years old when he wrote his *Takmilat al-dîbâj* (a completion of Ibn Farḥûn's Brocade), a biographical dictionary of the Mâlikite savants, which Cherbonneau has made known to the European world, and from which he has published extracts. His other works deal with law and grammar. "He was rigorously just," writes the Soudanese historian translated by Monsieur O. Houdas, "even towards the humblest of men. Even in his dealings with sultans and emirs, he never dissembled as to justice. The name of Mahomet was to be seen written in natural white characters on the skin of his right forearm."

'Abdal-Raḥmân ibn 'Abdallah al-Sa'dî (1596–1655 ?), who was born at Timbuctoo, was a notary at Jenna, and, from 1627, acted as Imâm of the mosque at Sankora. He was dismissed some ten years later, and returned to his native town, where he occupied a similar post. He ultimately received the title of secretary to the Government, and was entrusted with missions to several Soudanese chiefs. He had attained his sixty-first lunar year when he completed his *Ta'rîkh al-Sûdân* (History of the Soudan), which has been translated by O. Houdas.

The *Tadhkirat al-Nisyân*, also translated by Houdas, is a biographical dictionary of the Pachas of Timbuctoo, from 1590 down to 1750. It was written by the grandson of Muḥammad ibn al-Amîn ibn Muḥammad Sûd, in 1751. The author, whose proper name is not known, was born in the Soudanese capital in 1700. The care with which he quotes exact dates from the year 1716 onwards, leads us to suppose that when he was sixteen he began to keep a journal of some kind. The biographies are of varying lengths. Some give nothing

but a few dates, others are very much worked out, full of detail and of information. Those of contemporary personages are particularly lively and animated.

Anthologies and Popular Works

Jamâl al-dîn AL-WAṬWÂṬ (Muḥammad ibn Ibrâhîm) (1235–1318), surnamed *al-Kutubî* (the Bookseller), and *al-Warrâq* (the Paper-seller), wrote the *Ghurar al-khaṣâ'iṣ al-wâḍiḥa*, an anthology in sixteen chapters, on eight virtues and eight vices, which has been printed at Cairo, and the *Mabâhij al-fikar*, an encyclopædia of natural science and geography. From the printing presses of the Egyptian capital has also issued the *Ḥusn al-tawaṣṣul* (The Good Means), a treatise on the art of letter-writing, by Ibn Fahd (Shihâb al-dîn Maḥmûd), of Aleppo, a secretary in the Mameluke Chancery (1246–1325), in the days of Baibars; he wrote a book on chaste love, called the *Manâzil al-aḥbâb*, some manuscript copies of which exist in Europe. Muḥammad al-Bilbaisî was the author of a work, intermingled with verse, in which he starts on the supposition that thirty guests, belonging to different crafts, are sitting round a table and exchanging jokes. This little book, which is called *al-Mulaḥ wa'l-Ṭuraf* (Pleasantries and Curiosities), and in the language of which the current corruptions of the Egyptian dialect of the present day are already evident, was written in 1345. Towards the same period, 'Alâ al-dîn 'Alî al-Bahâ'î, a man of Berber blood, but of Damascene birth, who died in 1412, was compiling his *Maṭâli' al-budûr* (Rise of the Full Moon), while Shihâb al-dîn Muḥammad ibn Aḥmad AL-ABSHÎHÎ, who was born towards 1388, in a village in the Fayyûm, and died about 1446, was

collecting the materials for his *Mustaṭraf fî kull fann Mustaẓraf*, a book of stories, poems, and maxims, which has been frequently reprinted at Cairo, and which has just been translated into French by G. Rat.

Shams al-dîn Muḥammad al-Nawâjî (1383?–1455), a teacher of the traditions in the Shâfi'ite schools of Cairo, and himself a poet, left a collection of Bacchanalian poetry, entitled *Ḥalbat al-kumait*, which has been frequently reprinted. Scattered through the various European libraries other manuscript works of his are to be found, such as his *Kitâb al-Ṣabûḥ* (The Book of the Morning Beverage), anecdotes and verses of the period of the 'Abbâsid Caliphs, his *Ta'hîl al-Gharîb*, a collection of Arabic poetry belonging to the Moslem epoch, and arranged according to the alphabetical order of the rhymes, his *Marâbi' al-ghizlân* (The Gazelles' Pasturage), which deals with erotic poetry, as does his *Khal' al-'idhâr*, and others, besides a study of the plagiarisms committed by the author's friend, Ibn Ḥijja of Ḥamât.

Dâ'ûd ibn 'Umar al-Anṭâkî was a physician. He lived at Cairo, although, by origin, he belonged to Antioch. His father lived in the village which contains the tomb of the famous Ḥabîb the Carpenter. He himself was cured of congenital rheumatism by a Greek physician, who taught him his own tongue. When questioned on any scientific subject, he would immediately dictate sufficient matter to cover ten or twenty pages. Besides works devoted to medical subjects, he wrote the *Tazyîn al-aswâq*, an anthology, in prose and verse, on the subject of love. He died blind, at Mecca, in 1599.

'Abdal-Qâdir al-Baghdâdi, who died in 1682, left, under

the title of *Khizânat al-adab* (Treasure of Literature), a commentary on the quotations to be met with in Raḍî al-dîn al-Astarâbâdî's (*obiit* 1287) explanation of Ibn Ḥâjib's grammar, the *Kâfiya*, which contains a mass of precious information as to the early days of literature, drawn from sources no longer attainable by us.

Al-'Abbâs ibn 'Alî ibn Nûr al-dîn, a Meccan, wrote, when at Mecca, and on his return, in 1735, from a long journey which had covered twelve years, his *Nuzhat al-Jalîs wa-Munyat al-adîb al-anîs* (Delight of the Comrade and Pleasure of the Man of Letters who Cares for Society), a book of travels, with details, literary and biographical, which carries the reader from Mecca through Egypt, Palestine, Persia, India, and Southern Arabia. This work is a remarkably erudite compilation—a real anthology. It is dedicated to Aḥmad ibn Yaḥyâ Khâzindâr, a jurisconsult, who had advised the author to travel, so as to rid himself of the worry caused him by his relations and friends in his native town.

The Arabian Nights

If there be one book, the fame of which overshadows all others, the delight both of childhood and of ripe age, it is the anonymous work universally known under the title of *Kitâb Alf laila wa-laila* (The Thousand and One Nights). My readers are acquainted with the somewhat flimsy construction whereby a mass of tales of varying nature are gathered into the limits of one story. A fictitious monarch in Central Asia, determined to protect himself against the craft and infidelity of women, resolves that the wife he chooses him every day shall be put to death before the next. The two daughters of his Prime

Minister devote their lives to save their country, and the eldest, a clever woman, versed in the literature of fairies and genii, amuses the king each day with a story, the end of which she prudently holds over till the following night, thus keeping his curiosity in suspense till he finally relinquishes his dark design. The names of the personages mentioned in the prologue are all Persian, and this sufficiently indicates the source from which the work is drawn. The *Hazâr Afsâna* (The Thousand Tales) was, in fact, a Persian book, translated, as the historian Mas'ûdî relates, from the Pehlevi into Arabic as early as the third century of the Hegira. "This book," he says, "is known to the public under the name of the Thousand and One Nights: it is the story of a king, his vizier, his daughter and his slave, Shîrâzâd and Dînâzâd." The remarkable point about this passage from the worthy chronicler is the very ancient and purely Persian form of the names of the two female characters, who were ultimately to become Sheherazade and Dinarzade. For Shîrâzâd (the Arabicised form of Chihr-âzâd) signifies, in the Persian, "noble by race," and Dînâzâd signifies "noble by law." As the names became corrupted, their meaning disappeared. The plan of the work was possibly taken by the Persians from India, with which country they had been in contact ever since the great Sâsânian conquests had renewed the exploits of the empire of the Achæmenians, founded by Cyrus and Darius, and overthrown by Alexander.

Into this evidently artificial framework have been introduced a variety of tales, inserted at diverse periods, which critics have found it possible to determine. To begin with, there is an ancient ground-work, probably of Indian origin, marked by much indulgence in phantas-

magoric description, as the tale of the *Fisherman and the Genius.* Then, at Bagdâd, we have love stories, and adventures in the bazaars, which end in the appearance on the scene of Caliph Hârûn al-Rashîd, his vizier Ja'far the Barmakide, and his eunuch Masrûr, keeping order in the streets of his capital by night. Into this cycle of popular tales some literary excerpts have slipped, such as the story of the Omeyyad Caliph 'Umar ibn 'Abdal-'Azîz and the poets. A third and more recent group is formed by the adventures in Cairo, grouped about the characters called Aḥmad al-Danaf and Dalîla. These are fantastic and supernatural stories, some of which would appear to be a survival from ancient Egyptian days. Others, such as the story of Bulûqiyâ, inserted into that of Ḥâsib Karîm al-dîn, on which Horovitz has recently written, are decidedly Jewish in their origin. The presence of these latter tales has even inspired Chauvin with the idea that one of the editors of the Egyptian arrangement of the work must have been a converted Jew. A further and, as might almost be said, a forcible introduction into this collection of popular tales (necessitated by an adherence to the number of one thousand and one, to which the prologue bound the compilers) is that of certain romances of chivalry, such as the story of 'Umar al-Nu'mân, and even of a romance of adventure by sea, the story of Sindbad the Sailor, the origin of which goes back to the palmy days of trade in the Persian Gulf and the Indian Ocean, and which was probably composed at Bassora during the tenth century. The book, as we now possess it, must have been drawn up in comparatively recent times, for it contains the stories of Qamar al-Zamân and the jeweller's wife, of Ma'rûf and his wife Fâṭima,

both of them belonging to the sixteenth century, and also the tale of Abû Qîr the Dyer and Abû Sîr the Barber, the most modern of all.

The merit of having introduced European readers to the *Arabian Nights* is the chief claim to glory of Antoine Galland, the French Orientalist, who accompanied the Marquis de Nointel on his embassy to Constantinople, and made two subsequent journeys in the East. His translation, which appeared between 1704 and 1708, was an event in literature. His translating labours were carried on by Pétis de la Croix (1710), by Caussin de Perceval (1806), by Edouard Gaultier (1824), Destains (1825), and Trébutien de Caen (1828). Nearer our own times, after Lane (1841), John Payne (1882–1884) and Richard Burton (1885–1888) have given two complete English versions, the first in thirteen, and the second in sixteen volumes. A complete French translation, which will not curtail any of the longwindedness of the original text, is now in course of publication in Paris, by Dr. Mardrus. The editions published in the East, at Bûlâq and Calcutta, have only furnished the matter of the first nine volumes of Payne's edition, and the first ten of Burton's. The text of these works was completed from other manuscripts, such as that at Tunis, edited by Habicht at Breslau in 1835–1839, and continued after his death by Fleischer (1842–1843), and that brought back to England by Wortley-Montague, which was utilised by Burton. In 1886, H. Zotenberg, the curator of the manuscripts at the Bibliothèque Nationale, discovered the Arabic text of the tales of Aladdin and the Wonderful Lamp, and of Zain al-Aṣnâm, which do not appear in the Oriental editions of the *Arabian Nights*. A doubt had even been expressed as to whether Galland

had not wholly invented them. Zotenberg's discovery, and the critical and historical researches he consequently made, with the object of proving that the text he had brought to light was not an Arabic translation of Galland's French version, have demonstrated that this latter Orientalist had consulted a version in the Syriac dialect, and that from it his two delightful stories had been drawn. The sixth supplementary volume of Burton's translation contains the tales published by Dom Denis Chavis, a Syrian priest, and Jacques Cazotte, in 1788–1789, which were translated into German in 1790 and 1810, and into English in 1792.

The style of the *Arabian Nights* is absolutely popular and local. It contains a mass of expressions which have no place in the classic Arabic, and which vary according to the provinces. The whole text of the story of Aladdin is in the Syrian dialect. The source of the stories of Arab origin is easily detected. They came from the *maddâḥ*, the popular story-teller, who wanders, on feast-days, from one café to another, and is the anonymous author of the greater part of the tales of which the collection is composed.

The Romance of ʿAntar

To Al-Aṣmaʿî, the grammarian of the close of the second century of the Hegira (739–831), is ascribed the authorship of the great romance of chivalry, a partial translation of which was issued in English by Terrick Hamilton in 1820, while the full text was brought back to Paris from Constantinople by Cardin de Cardonne. Caussin de Perceval, the younger, wrote a dissertation upon it in the *Journal Asiatique*, and gave extracts from

it in the *Chrestomathies Orientales* (1841). Both these Orientalists, and Cherbonneau, Dugat, and Devic, after them, translated fragments of the work, and it was published in full at Cairo, in 1893. It is quite evident that the popular tales do not date from such remote times, and, in any case, so many centuries have elapsed since those days, that the name of Al-Aṣma'î can be no more than a label placed by the professional *râwî* on the stories, to give them some appearance of authenticity. In its present form, the romance goes back to the days of the Crusades. The Orientals place little value on so unpretentious a literary style, but Westerns recognise in it, with pleasure, the spirit of the people, freed from such ready-made trammels of formulas learnt at school as appear much more frequently, indeed, than may be imagined, in certain passages of the *Romance of 'Antar* (those in rhymed prose and poetical quotations).

In the *Romance of 'Antar*, Caussin de Perceval declares, "may be found a faithful picture of the life of those desert Arabs on whose manners and customs the lapse of time appears to have had scarcely any effect. Their hospitality, their vengeances, their loves, their generosity, their thirst for pillage, their inherent taste for poetry, are all closely described. There are accounts, Homeric in their way, of the ancient Arab wars, the chief events in Arab history before the advent of Mahomet, and the deeds of the antique heroes. The style, varied and elegant, occasionally rising to the sublime, and the characters, powerfully drawn and worked out with art, combine to render the work exceedingly remarkable. It is, so to speak, the Arab *Iliad*." If we allow for his natural enthusiasm about the discovery he had made in Syria, and accept the *Romance of Antar* as a popular work, in which we must not expect any

historical qualities, we may take Caussin de Perceval's flaming description to be fairly accurate. The book is interesting to read, and considerable pleasure may be found in following the knightly adventures therein described. Take it all in all, it is much after the same fashion that Alexandre Dumas the elder wrote the history of France. Now and again, the story-teller gives us treasures of beauty, as in the famous episode of the death of ʿAntar, so greatly admired by Lamartine. The desert hero, stricken to death by a poisoned shaft sped by the hand of a treacherous and implacable foe, remounts his horse, to ensure the safe retreat of his tribe, and dies, leaning on his lance. His enemies, smitten with terror by the memory of his prowess, dare not advance, till one cunning warrior devises a stratagem which startles the horse out of its marble stillness. The creature gives a bound, and ʿAntar's corpse, left unsupported, falls upon the ground.

The Romance of the Beni-Hilâl

In that charming and now classic work, known as the *Modern Egyptians*, the great Arabic scholar, Edward William Lane, has given a very lifelike picture of the public story-teller, sitting on a bench outside the café, with all the neighbouring townsmen gathered around him, smoking their long chibouks, after the general habit in the East. He also gives an analysis of several of the romances related by these men, among them the *Romance of ʿAntar*. Since then others have been published, amongst them the *Romance of the Beni-Hilâl*. The subject is identical with that of the *Romance of Abû Zaid*, so popular in Egypt. In spite of his being

the possessor of ten wives, the Emîr Rizq had only two daughters, and one son, born without arms, when the Princess Al-Khaḍrâ, daughter of the Sharîf of Mecca, became his eleventh wife, and presented him with a negro son, because, having noticed, while on a journey, a jet black bird defending itself victoriously against a crowd of others, she had wished her son might resemble the brave bird, even if he were to be as black as its plumage. Her prayer was granted, but the father, prevented by pressure on his comrades' part from acknowledging his paternity, repudiated Khaḍrâ, and sent her home to her father, the Sharîf. On her journey back to that city, she met the Emîr Faḍl, chief of the tribe of Zaḥlan, who took her under his protection, and adopted her son, the youthful Barakât, later surnamed Abû Zaid, who grew up a hero, the glory of his adopted tribe. Meanwhile his father, who still loved Khaḍrâ, had withdrawn himself from his people, and was living in a tent, attended by a single slave. At a later date, the tribe of which he had been chief, defeated by Barakât, and reduced to a state of misery, appealed to his powers, and besought him to undertake the leadership once more. Thus father and son were brought face to face, neither knowing the other. The Emîr Rizq was thrown from his horse, and would have been slain by his own son, if the mother had not interfered, and revealed the real tie between Rizq and Abû Zaid. Father and son recognised each other, and the Emîr Abû Zaid forgave the injury done him by his tribe. In the great Persian epic, the *Shâh-nâma*, Firdausi introduces Rustam and his son Suhrâb. Here the father kills the son in single combat, and does not recognise him till he is dead. This striking episode is more dramatic than the

corresponding one in the Arabic work. The anonymous author of *Abû Zaid* has recoiled from the conception of a parricide, which indeed would have obliged him to bring his story to a sudden termination, instead of continuing to dilate on the feats of his hero, as is now the case.

Martin Hartmann has shown that the stories of the Beni-Hilâl, and their invasion of Northern Africa (*taghrîbât*), form one complete cycle of legends, connected with the modulated chants still to be heard among the Bedouins of the Libyan Desert. This cycle comprises eight and thirty romances, that of Abû Zaid being merely the last of the series. First of all comes the story of Jâbir and Jubair, the ancestors of the Beni-Hilâl, dating from the days of the Prophet. Four hundred years later, we come to that of Al-Khaḍrâ, mother of Abû Zaid, as we have just related it, and then to the adventures of Shammâ and of Zahr al-Bân, in which we see the Emîr Sirhân made prisoner by Christian corsairs, on his way back to his own country by sea, and becoming chief swineherd in the land of his captors. His wife, Shammâ, goes to join him in the country of the Franks. His son, Sultan Ḥasan, betakes himself to Yemen, to make war on the fire-worshippers—here we have a memory of the historic times when the Sâsânian Persians had garrisons in Southern Arabia—and is aided there by the never-failing Abû Zaid. He proceeds to vanquish the monarch of India, Jarâd, conquers his country, and leads the Beni-Hilâl back to Africa. The continuation of the story relates how Sultan Ḥasan and Abû Zaid remove into the province of Najd, because there is nothing left to eat in their own country. For the same reason the Beni-Hilâl are

constrained to quit Najd, and move westwards; this is what is properly called the *taghrîba* (Emigration to the West). They proceed to Tunis, where the power is held by Al-Zanâtî Khalîfa—a name in which we easily recognise the Berber tribe of the Zanâta. Accounts of fantastic fights with the Persians and with Tamerlane, full of names recalling distant memories of the Crusades (such as Bardewil and Baldwin), of the taking of Tangiers and of Morocco, complete this cycle of adventures, all more or less connected with the invasion of Northern Africa by the Beni-Hilâl, during the eleventh century of the Christian era.

Romance of Saif Dhû'l-Yazan

Saif is the son of a King of Yemen. His mother, a slave, causes him to be exposed in the desert. Here he is miraculously fed by a gazelle which has lost her young, is found by a hunter, and is carried away to Abyssinia. When he grows up, he fights with the giant Mukhtaṭif, and slays him. As a reward, the king would give him his daughter Shâma to wife, but the Prime Minister opposes the plan, and insists that the young man shall first bring him the head of Sa'dûn al-Zanjî, the terror of Abyssinia, and find the book of the history of the Nile, which lies in an inaccessible country, protected by talismans. He is presently recognised by his mother, who desires to kill him, so that she may reign alone. After every kind of wonderful adventure, full of genii and sorceresses, Saif returns to his own country, abdicates in favour of his son, and lives like a patriarch; but undeserved misfortunes soon bring his life to a close.

A French translation from the Arabic of this story, adorned with five lithographs by Ali-Bey, has appeared at Constantinople, under the title of *Sultan Saif-Zuliazan* (J.-J. Wick, 1847, 368 pp. 8vo).

The *Saif al-Tîjân* (Sword of the Crowns) is the story, divided into parts, of the adventures of a fabulous prince, who goes from one country to another, conquering the world, fighting fairies and magicians with mighty sword-thrusts, and warring against multitudinous armies, which are all converted to the Moslem faith, by the intervention of the prophets Abraham and Ismâ'îl. It has been translated into French by Dr. Perron.

The Fables of Luqmân

The matter of the ancient fables known to us as Æsop's, with their axioms of practical morality put into the mouths of animals, has passed into the Arabic tongue, and is ascribed by Arabs to the sage Luqmân. Who was this sage? In the chapter of the *Koran* entitled *Luqmân*, we read: "We have given wisdom to Luqmân, saying to him, 'Be grateful to God,'" and again: "Luqmân said one day to his son, by way of admonition, 'O my child, associate no other divinities with God, for idolatry is a tremendous sin!'"

The Sacred Book of the Moslems contained two allusions to this legendary personage, whose name occurs twice over in the ancient Arab traditions. The first occasion is that of the destruction of the first population of 'Âd, in the south of the Peninsula. He had been sent as ambassador to Mecca, to crave help against the drought, when the people's refusal to accept the prophet Hûd was avenged by the appearance of a black cloud

which ruined the whole country. His piety was rewarded by the gift of a long life, equal to those of seven generations of vultures. The second time, we hear of him in connection with the game called *Maisir*, which consisted in drawing lots with arrows for the parts of a camel killed at the general expense. His passion for this pastime had become a proverb. We also hear of his cunning and cleverness. Nothing more appears in the pre-Islamic traditions concerning him. Yet in the days of Mahomet, as we have just seen, he was accepted as the incarnation of wisdom. The prophet must have taken this idea from the belief of the populations round him, for the scoffers about him would have had a fine opportunity if he had ventured to be the first to attribute the wisdom of the learned to an individual whose celebrity rested principally on his perspicacity. Luqmân was said, indeed, to be the author of some proverbs, but this honour he shared with many others of both sexes. These fables, like other works which passed from the Greek into the Arabic, were translated not directly, but through the medium of a Syriac version, from the pen of a Christian, Barsûma, who died in 1316, and whose work is dated 1299. There is another collection of the same kind, which bears the Syriac title of *Matlé de Soufos* (Æsop's Fables). From these is drawn the Arabic version ascribed to the ancient sage Luqmân, of whose wisdom we find proof in the very pages of the Koran.

CHAPTER XI

THE NINETEENTH CENTURY

IN Egypt, Syria, Tunis, Algeria, and Morocco, among Arabic-speaking countries, there is a more or less active stir in literary matters, denoted by the publication of a number of newspapers, and evidenced also by the production of various works in book form. This is not confined to the countries in which Arabic is the current language, but is also noticeable in certain large cities, where it is familiar only to the learned, as in Constantinople, and in others, such as Paris, where it is utterly unknown, except to a few scholars, but where, thanks to the incessant circulation due to our present facilities for communication, certain Oriental writers, whose works have been published in the city, occasionally meet.

MÎKHÂ'ÎL ibn Niqûlâ ibn Ibrâhîm ṢABBÂGH, who was born at St. Jean d'Acre about 1784, spent his youth at Damascus, served the French during the expedition into Egypt, and accompanied the army when it retired from that country. When the Turks re-entered Cairo, his house was sacked, his goods confiscated, and his fortune engulfed. He was appointed copyist, or rather repairer of manuscripts, at the Imperial Library in Paris. He had formed the acquaintance of Silvestre de Sacy, who made a French translation of his treatise on the pigeon-post, entitled *Musâbaqat al-barq wa'l-ghamâm*, and be-

stowed on it the poetic title of *La colombe messagère, plus rapide que l'éclair, plus prompte que la nue.* At a later period, this little treatise was still further popularised by a German translation due to Arnold, and an Italian rendering, the work of Cataneo. A hymn, addressed by him to Napoleon I. on the occasion of the birth of the King of Rome, was also translated by Silvestre de Sacy in 1811. When, at a later date, the aspect of politics underwent a change, Ṣabbâgh wrote a congratulatory hymn to Louis XVIII. (*Nashîd tahânî*), which was done into French by Grangeret de Lagrange in 1814. He drew up some notes on the modern forms of Arabic poetry (*mawâliya, zajal*), which were in the possession of Grangeret de Lagrange, and utilised by G. W. Freytag in the composition of his work on Arabic metres. He died in June 1816, leaving the manuscripts of a history of the Arab tribes and of a history of Syria and Egypt, and a grammar of the Arabic vulgarly spoken in Egypt and Syria (*Risâla al-tâmma*), which was published at Strasburg by Thorbecke in 1886. The manuscript of this work, at one time in the collection of Etienne Quatremère, has passed, with all other papers belonging to the famous French Orientalist, into the possession of the Munich Library.

Ṣabbâgh's friend, ELYÛS BOQTOR (Bocthor), who was born, of Copt parents, at Suyûṭ, in Upper Egypt, on 12th April 1784, was attached to the headquarters staff of the French army as interpreter, when only fifteen years of age. In 1812 he was employed to translate Arabic works in the archives of the Ministry of War, and was afterwards attached to the general depôt of the army as interpreter. This post was done away with in 1814. In 1817 he was given leave to deliver a course of

lectures on colloquial Arabic at the École des Langues Orientales vivantes (1816), was appointed professor in that establishment (1821), and died, when barely seven and thirty, on 26th September of the same year. He left an Arabic-French dictionary, published in 1828–1829 under the auspices of Caussin de Perceval the younger, who succeeded to his professorial chair.

Nakoula (Niqûlâ) al-Turk, the son of Yûsuf al-Turk, was a member of the Greek-Catholic (Melchite) Church. He was born in 1763 at Dair al-Qamar, where dwelt the Emir Bashîr, chief of the Druses, and now the seat of the Lebanon Government. His family was of Constantinopolitan origin. He entered the service of the Druse prince, with the title of *mu'allim* or professor, and was highly esteemed as a poet, at the little court. His patron sent him into Egypt to obtain information as to the plans of the French, and he remained there during the whole period of the French ascendency. At the close of his life he became blind, and his daughter, Warda, wrote the poems he composed at his dictation. He died at Dair al-Qamar in 1828. His *Summary of the French Occupation* was translated by Alexandre Cardin, and added to his *Journal d'Abdurrahman Gabarti* (1838); the full text was published and translated by the elder Desgranges in 1839. The ode expressing his feelings as to the conquest of Egypt has been translated into French by J.-J. Marcel.

SHAIKH RIFÂ'A al-Ṭahṭâwî, son of the Shâfi'ite Râfi', and descendant of the famous Santon of Ṭahṭâ, Aḥmad al-Badawî, who fought at the Battle of Manṣûra, began his career as a pupil in the al-Azhar Mosque at Cairo, acted as chaplain in the Egyptian army, with the title of preacher, and was afterwards sent to Paris with the

pupils of the Egyptian School just established there, under the direction of 'Abdi-Efendi Muhurdâr. He ultimately returned to Cairo, and spent the closing years of his life as head of the Translating Office. He translated a number of works from the French, among them *La Lyre brisée*, by Agoub, which he put into Arabic verse, under the title of *Naẓm al-'uqûd* (1827). His original works consist of his account of his journey to France, and his residence there, which he entitled *Takhlîṣ al-Ibrîz* (Purification of Gold), and some patriotic Egyptian odes (*manẓûma miṣriyya*). He had planned a history of Egypt from the most remote period, after Arab authors and others; of his *Anwâr taufîq al-jalîl*, only the first volume, carrying the story down to Mahomet, ever appeared.

Shaikh NÂṢÎF ibn 'Abdallah AL-YÂZIJÎ (1800–1871), of the Lebanon, who was born at Kafr-Shîmâ, was attached in a professorial capacity to the American mission at Beyrout, and wrote an imitation of the famous *Lectures* of Ḥarîrî, under the title of *Majma' al-baḥrain* (Confluence of the Two Seas), which was printed at Beyrout in 1856. This work had been preceded by an anthology, *Majmû' al-adab*. A treatise on logic, called *Quṭb al-Ṣinâ'a* (The Pole of Art); an Arabic grammar, called *Faṣl al-Khiṭâb;* a commentary on the works of Mutanabbi, entitled *al-'Arf al-Ṭayyib;* a treatise on Arabic prosody, *'Iqd al-jumân;* a commentary on the *Jâmi'a*, dealing with the art of versification, called *al-Lâmi'a* (1869); the *Nâr al-qirâ*, a commentary on verses quoted in the *Mukhtaṣar;* the *'Uqûd al-durar*, a commentary on the *Khizâna*, and *al-Jumâna*, are his principal productions. He wrote a letter of criticisms to Silvestre de Sacy, relative to his edition of Ḥarîrî's

Lectures, which has been translated into Latin by A. F. Mehren. A selection from his poems, drawn from his unpublished *dîwân*, was printed at Beyrout in 1853, under the title of *Nubdha*, and within two years a selection of chronograms, from the same source (*tawârîkh*), likewise appeared in the same place. Yet another collection of his poetry, entitled *Thâlith al-qamarain* (The Third Crescent), was published at Beyrout in 1883.

Ilyâs Faraj Bâsîl, a Maronite from Kasrawân, in the Lebanon, collected his own verses into a volume at Aleppo, and called it *Majmû' al-azhâr* (Collection of Flowers, an anthology). This was printed at Jerusalem in 1879.

Aḥmad Fâris ibn Yûsuf ibn Manṣûr al-Shidyâq, a Maronite converted to Islam, who died about 1890, was the type of a many-sided and prolific writer, with the inner lining of the journalist. His family name signifies "chorister-boy," although, etymologically speaking, it is closely allied to the French "archidiacre." His fancy was attracted, in the first instance, by lexicographical questions, and his inquiries into this subject, proving the ingenuity of a mind quite devoid of any critical power, were carried on till the end of his life. His *Lafîf fî kull ma'nâ ṭarîf* is a dictionary of Arabic synonyms, preceded by an abridged grammar, which appeared at Malta in 1839. Subsequently came his *Sirr al-layâl* (Mystery of the Nights), on the *qalb* and the *ibdâl*, that is to say, on metathesis, and the alteration of consonants in the Arabic roots; his *Jâsûs 'alâ 'l-Qâmûs* (The Spy on the *Qâmûs*), a criticism of Fîrûz-Âbâdî's dictionary, and his *al-Wâsiṭa fî ma'rifat Aḥwâl Mâlṭa*, a means for gaining acquaintance with the condition of Malta, and the discovery of the secret of European science (Tunis, 1866;

Constantinople, 1881). A poem in honour of the Bey of Tunis was translated into French by Monsieur G. Dugat. But his caustic wit had free play in the work entitled *al-Sâq 'alâ'l-sâq* (Leg over Leg), or the life and adventures of Fariac, an account of his travels, with critical remarks on the Arab nations, and on others. This was published in Paris in 1855. His *Sharḥ ṭabâ'i' al-ḥaiwân* (Commentary on the Nature of Animals), which deals with the habits of birds and quadrupeds (Malta, 1841), is more or less borrowed from Buffon. His son, Salîm Fârîs, has collected into a book, called the *Kanz al-raghâ'ib*, his own and his father's various literary and scientific contributions to an Arabic newspaper, the *Jawâ'ib*, founded by the latter at Constantinople, and subsequently transferred to Cairo.

Another inhabitant of the Lebanon, BUṬRUS BISTÂNÎ (1819–1883), a Maronite who went over to the Protestant Communion, and was dragoman to the United States Consulate at Beyrout, left, in his *Muḥîṭ al-muḥîṭ* (That which Surrounds the Ocean), a supplement to the *Qâmûs*, which was found very useful by R. Dozy, in the composition of his *Supplément aux Dictionnaires Arabes.* The work is full of expressions and meanings peculiar to the various Syrian dialects. His *Miṣbâḥ al-Ṭâlib* (The Student's Lamp) deals with Arabic grammar; his *Kashf al-ḥijâb* (The Lifted Veil) is on arithmetic; and another great work is an Arabic Encyclopædia, still unfinished, which is entitled *Dâ'irat al-ma'ârif.* He also published a life of As'ad al-Shidyâq, and in a speech delivered at Beyrout in 1859, he dealt with the condition of Arabic literature at that date.

The Maronite Shaikh RUSHAID DAḤDÂḤ, son of Ghâlib, subsequently decorated with the title of Count, has made

his name by the publication of certain Arabic texts, such as that of the *Fiqh al-lugha*, by Abû Manṣûr al-Tha'âlibî (Paris, 1861); the *dîwân* of Ibn al-Fâriḍ, with commentaries by Ḥasan al-Bûrînî and 'Abdal-Ghanî al-Nâbulusî (Marseilles, 1853; Paris, 1855; Bûlâq, 1872); a selection of remarkable poems, which may be used as proverbs, collected by him under the title of *Ṭarab al-masâmi'* (Delight of the Ears; Paris, 1861); and a miscellany (*Jamharat tawâmîr*), published at Paris in 1880.

To convey some idea of the literary movement at Beyrout during the course of the nineteenth century, we must also quote the names of Khalîl-Efendi AL-KHÛRÎ, whose collection of poems—occasional verses, written on various political occasions (*Zahr al-rubâ*)—appeared at Beyrout in 1857; Salîm BISTERIS, who published a journal of his travels in Europe, *al-Nuzhat al-Shahiyya* (Beyrout, 1859); Iskandar-Âghâ ABKÂRIYÛS, an Armenian, whose *Rauḍat al-adab* (Flower-bed of Literature; Beyrout, 1858) contains biographical notices of the pre-Islamic Arab poets, contemporary with Mahomet, arranged in alphabetical order, and who had already published, at Marseilles, in 1852, the *Nihâyat-al-arab*, a series of notices of the poets and prominent personages of pre-Islamic times; Jirjîs-Efendi Tannûs 'Aun, who published a technological dictionary at Constantinople in 1884, under the title of *Durr al-Maknûn* (The Hidden Pearl); SA'ÎD AL-KHÛRÎ al-Shartûnî, author of the *Aqrab al-mawârid*, an Arabic dictionary with a supplement (Beyrout, 1894), and of the *Shihâb al-Thâqib*, a manual of epistolary style (1884); Yûsuf Ilyâs DIBS, who taught Arabic grammar without a master, by means of his *Mughnî' l-muta'allim* (1869); and ARSÂNIYÛS al-Fakhâ'irî,

a priest, who wrote a study of rhetoric, entitled *Rauḍ al-jinân* (1868 ?).

In 1865 a Syrian priest, named Joseph David, printed an elementary French grammar in the Arabic tongue, under the auspices of the Dominicans at Mosul, and also a collection of moral subjects treated in prose and verse, called *Tanzîh al-Albâb* (Recreation for the Mind). After he became Monsignor Clement Joseph David, he published, in the same town, his *Tamrina*, an Arabic grammar (1886), which had been preceded, in 1877, by grammatical exercises entitled *Tamrîn*. His *Tarwîḍ al-ṭullâb* (1867) was intended to imbue the minds of the youthful neo-Assyrian dwellers on the banks of the Tigris with the elements of the science of arithmetic. He died in 1891.

Father Louis Cheikho, of the University of St. Joseph, at Beyrout, has helped to spread the knowledge of the Arabic classics by various publications. His *Mukhtaṣar al-ṣarf*, as its title indicates, is a short grammar (Beyrout, 1886); his *Tarqiyat al-Qâri'*, a collection of readings; his *Majânî' l-Adab* is a huge literary anthology in six volumes, with a commentary or notes, in four more, to which is added a preparatory study entitled *Mirqât*, the stepping-stone to the *Majânî*. The *'Ilm al-Adab*, in which he collaborated with G. Eddé, is a course of lectures on *belles-lettres*, and on literary and oratorical composition. The *Shu'arâ al-Naṣrâniyya* is an anthology of ancient Arabic poets, most of them pre-Islamic, and the editor endeavours to demonstrate that they were also Christians.

The mysteries of the faith of the Nuṣairîs or Anṣârîs have been unveiled by Sulaimân-Efendi of Adana, in his *al-Bâkhûra al-Sulaimâniyya*, a little volume translated into English, almost in its entirety, by E. Salisbury.

History, and notably the history specially connected with that mountainous province, has been much cultivated in the Lebanon. Monsignor Istifân al-Duwaihî of Ehden, in the region of the Cedars, above Tripoli, wrote in the course of the seventeenth century, as we have already remarked, a history of the Maronites, which was published at Beyrout, in 1890, by Rashîd al-Khûrî al-Shartûnî, to whom the public was already indebted for a manual of epistolary style, the *Nahj al-murâsala* (1877). Yet another Maronite, Shaikh TANNÛS ibn Yûsuf al-Shidyâq, collected the annals of the Christian families of the mountains, in his *Akhbâr al-A'yân* (1859). Khalîl SARKÎS wrote a history of Jerusalem (1874). At Mosul, a Syrian priest, Louis Raḥmânî, wrote, in 1876, an epitome of ancient history, another of the history of the Middle Ages, in 1877, and one of Sacred History, in 1883. Monsignor Cyril Behnâm Bennî, Archbishop of Mosul, wrote a book there, on the truths of the Catholic Church, called the *Durra al-nafîsa* (1867).

Amongst the poets, mention must be made of Buṭrus Karâma, a Christian, who died about 1850, and wrote *muwashshaḥât*: of Rizq-Allah ḤASSÛN, a free-thinker, who died about 1880, having lived for many years in England, where, for some time, he published an Arabic newspaper; his *Nafathât*, which largely consist of translations from Kryloff's Fables, and were dedicated to the Emîr 'Abdal-Qâdir, were printed in London in 1867: of Yûsuf al-Asîr, born at Saida about 1815, and died at Beyrout in 1890, who studied in the Al-Azhar Mosque, and who, in spite of his deep knowledge of the Arabic tongue, was neglected, all his life, by learned men bent on amassing wealth and honours; he was the author of

muwashshaḥât, and of a controversy on grammar, entitled *Radd al-Shahm li'l-sahm*, which was printed at Constantinople in 1874: of Yûsuf Dibs, appointed Maronite Archbishop at Beyrout in 1870, who was still alive in 1897, and has written popular poetry, as also did Nicolas Naqqâsh, who was born at Saida in 1817, and died at Tarsus in 1855, having written a play called *Arzat Lubnân* (The Cedar of Lebanon): and finally, of Amîn al-Jundî, a poet belonging to the town of Ḥimṣ, who was educated at Damascus, and died in his native town, in the year 1840, leaving a collection of poems, printed at Beyrout, in 1883, in a volume also containing verses by other authors.

At Damascus we note Salîm-Efendi 'ANḤÛRÎ, whose *Badâ'i' Mârût*, pieces of verse which form the third part of his complete poems, appeared at Beyrout in 1886. Under the title of *Kanz al-Nâẓim* (The Poet's Treasure and the Lost Man's Torch), he has sent forth a collection of classic expressions arranged in subjects. At Aleppo we must not overlook FARANSÎS MARRÂSH al-Ḥalabî, whose poems bear the name of *Al-Mir'ât al-ḥusnâ*. Another poet of Aleppo, Philip Basil Bennâ, lived at Constantinople. Three odes with which various incidents inspired him—one written in gratitude for the Prince de Joinville's assistance in putting out the conflagration at Pera in 1839, another in honour of Frederick William, King of Prussia, and a third rendering homage to 'Abdal-Majîd—have been translated into German by Otto Röhrig.

Sulaimân ibn Ibrâhîm Ṣûla, of Aleppo, sang, in lyric numbers, the generous deeds of the Emîr 'Abdal-Qâdir, whose bold resolution saved numbers of Christians during the Syrian massacres, in 1860. His *dîwân* was printed at Constantinople in 1895.

Christian literature is represented by the *Mawâ'iẓ*, or Collected Sermons, of Monsignor Yûsuf Ilyâs Dibs, Archbishop of Beyrout (1874), and controversy by *al-Durr al-manẓûm*, refutations of questions, and answers, bearing the signature of Monsignor Maximus Maẓlûm, and printed in a convent on the Lebanon, in 1863. The department of legal study claims the *Sharḥ râ'iḍ al-farâ'iḍ*, dealing with the division of inheritances, by Yûsuf al-Asîr (1873).

Damascus, like Beyrout, has had a flourishing period of literary activity. Maḥmûd Efendi Ḥamza has published a series of works on legal subjects: the *Qawâ'id al-auqâf*, rules in force as to property in mortmain (1871), *al-Farâ'id al-bahiyya*, on jurisprudence (1881), *al-Ṭarîqat al-wâḍiḥa*, on the establishment of the preferable proof (1883), and *Taḥbîr al-maqâla*, a study on delay and caution (1884). 'Alâ al-dîn Efendi 'Âbidîn wrote a treatise on jurisprudence, entitled *Hadiyya al-'alâ'iyya*, in 1882. In the department of philosophy, Aḥmad al-Barbîr produced an imaginary dialogue between Air and Water, which he entitled *Maqâma*, or Lecture, in 1883. Muḥammad-Efendi al-Qalbaqjî wrote a book on the knowledge of man's inner nature as mirrored in his eyes, called *Kashf al-Akhlâq*, in 1883; and 'Umar-Efendi al-'Aṭṭâr, who had published his *Risâla*, on the object of logic, in 1870, followed it, in 1884, by his *Farâ'id fawâ'id*, on the meaning of the Unity; his *Risâla bahiyya*, on the origin of the world; and his *Taḥqîqât bahiyya*, on the signification of existence.

Muḥammad ibn Aḥmad-Efendi al-Iskandarânî published his study of Natural Science in the same city in 1883, under the title of *Asrâr al-rabbâniyya*, and Dâ'ûd-Efendi Abû Sha'r wrote a treatise on hygiene, which

he called *Tuḥfat al-ikhwân*. The funeral oration of the Emîr ʿAbdal-Qâdir was pronounced there by Muḥammad ibn Muḥammad al-Mubârak al-Jazâʾirî (*Lauʿat al-Ḍamâʾir*, 1883); and Muḥammad-Efendi ʿÂbidîn published a bio-bibliographical work entitled ʿ*Uqûd al-laʾâlî* (1885).

Spiridion Ṣarrûf, a member of the Orthodox Church, and a Damascene by origin, besides issuing a number of liturgical books published from the Greek texts, compiled a Sacred History from the Creation down to the first century after the birth of our Lord (Jerusalem, 1855), and wrote an abridgment of the Catechism (1860). Yaʿqûb Jirjîs ʿAwwâd, a Maronite priest, wrote an epitome of dogmatic theology (*Khulâṣat al-barâhîn al-lâhûtiyya*, 1873); and Simʿân Isḥâq al-Qudsî, a book on the pontificate of St. Peter and his successors, called *Riyâsat Buṭrus* (1870).

Under the impulse of the reforms initiated by the successors of Muḥammad ʿAlî, Egypt, like Syria, has been the scene of most remarkable activity in the matter of literary production. The knowledge of European science imparted in the schools of the country has induced a considerable amount of industry among translators, which we will not follow here, limiting our attention to original work. The activity noticeable in this country, far from being purely scientific, has perhaps been more literary than anything else. For during this period the official printing presses at Bûlâq, and private enterprise in the city of Cairo, have been placing the classics of Moslem learning within the reach of all men. Beside the great names of former days, we come on those of poets of our own, who have communicated the fruits of their inspiration to the public. ʿAlî-Efendi

Darvîsh (1867), with his *Ish'âr;* Ibrâhîm-bey Marzûq, who wrote *al-durr al-bahî al-mansûq* (1880), and died at Khartum in the Soudan in 1866; Maḥmûd ibn Muḥammad al-Qûsî (1892), Shaikh of the Sa'diyya at Dongola, who wrote the praises of the Prophet in the vulgar tongue; Muḥammad ibn Ismâ'îl ibn 'Umar Shihâb al-dîn al-Ḥijâzî, who was of Meccan origin, and was corrector at the Government printing works from 1836 to 1849—he was the author of a *dîwân* which appeared in 1861, and of the *Safînat-al-Mulk* (1865). He himself died in 1857; Amîn ibn Ibrâhîm Shamîl, whose *al-Mubtakar* comprises five lectures and twenty-six odes composed at Liverpool in 1868, and devoted to the description of man; and 'Alî Abû'l-Naṣr (died 1880), complete this pleiad of neo-Egyptian poets. The art of writing popular songs, so despised by the literary men of bygone days, has excited the fancy of Muḥammad 'Uthmân Jalâl (died 16th January 1898), who also translated La Fontaine's Fables into Arabic verse; and that of Ḥasan Ḥusnî, whose *dîwân* bears the title of *Thamarât al-Ḥayât* (Fruits of Life); and of Ibn al-Fahhâm.

The history of Egypt has been written by 'Abdal Raḥman al-Jabartî al-'Aqîlî (1756–1825), whose *'Ajâ'ib al-âthâr* was printed at Bûlâq in 1880, and translated out of the Arabic into French by four Egyptian savants in collaboration. His journal, kept during the French occupation, *Maẓhar al-taqdîs* (an autograph copy is now at Cambridge), was translated into French in 1835, by Alexandre Cardin, Dragoman and Chancellor of the Consulate-General of France at Alexandria. This learned man was born at Cairo, of a family belonging to Zaila, on the Somali coast. He was the son of a learned and

highly venerated man, Shaikh Ḥasan, and was sent to study at the Al-Azhar Mosque. When he was eleven years old he knew the Koran by heart, and before he was twenty he had lost his father. He was a man of handsome physique, and of noble and serious character. General Bonaparte summoned him from his property at Abyâr, to which he had withdrawn; he was appointed a member of the Divan, and earned much respect from the Military Chiefs. After the evacuation he devoted himself entirely to learning. One of his sons was murdered in 1823, on the road to Shubra, near Cairo, and 'Abd al-Raḥmân wept him so inconsolably that he lost his sight, and survived him only a very short time.

Al-Jabartî's history was put into mnemotechnic verse by Abû'l-Su'ûd Efendi (1877), under the title of *Minḥat ahl al-'aṣr;* the same author had undertaken a universal history, the prolegomena and first part of which appeared at Cairo in 1872. Besides this, and preparatory to his historical labours, he translated the history of the Kings of France out of the French (*Naẓm al-la'âlî*), and also translated the history of Egypt under Muḥammad 'Alî. The foundation of the reigning Khedivial family, and the events of the reign of Muḥammad 'Alî, inspired Muḥammad-bey Farîd with the idea of his *Bahjat al-Taufîqiyya,* dedicated to Tewfik-Pacha (1891); the elementary history of Eastern countries has been given an Arabic form by Sayyid-Efendi 'Azmî (*al-masâlik al-ibtidâ'iyya,* 1894).

Jurjî Zaidân (1834 – 1890), a Syrian Christian, has attracted attention by his historical novels (*Riwâyât, Fatât Ghassân*), and has written a history of Egypt during the period of the Mahdi's power in the Soudan. 'Abdallah Fikrî-pacha, who was Minister of Education,

and whose posthumous works in prose and verse were published by his son in 1898, was born at Mecca, where his father was in command of the Egyptian troops occupying that city. In 1882 he was accused of treason, but proved his innocence, and retired into private life. He was a delegate to the Congress of Orientalists at Stockholm in 1889. He left a collection of sentences and proverbs, arranged in alphabetical order (*Naẓm al-la'âlî*); his various works have been collected and published by his son.

The French Orientalist, Jean-Joseph Marcel, who was with General Bonaparte in Egypt, where he rendered valuable service to the expedition, and acted, on his return to Paris, as director of the imperial printing works, unhesitatingly attributes to Shaikh Muḥammad al-Mahdî al-Ḥafnâwî (1737–1815) the authorship of a collection of tales, the title of which—that of the first volume, at all events—is *Tuḥfat al-mustaiqiẓ al-'ânis fî nuzhat al-mustanîm al-nâ'is* (The Present to the Awakened Bachelor for the Delight of the Somnolent Sleeper), which Marcel translated under the title of *Contes du Cheykh el-Mohdy*. This Shaikh was born at Cairo. His original appellation was Hibatallah. His father, Epiphanios Faḍlallah, was steward to the *kâshif* (provincial governor) Sulaimân, at whose entreaty he became a Moslem, studied at the Al-Azhar Mosque, became secretary to the Divan, and held that post during the French occupation. He was fond of coming to taste the strong waters offered him by the young member of the Institute of France, and confided the manuscript of the tales to him, without consenting to admit he had written them. At a later date he accompanied Tossoun-Pacha, the son of Muḥammad 'Alî, on his campaign against the Wahhâbîs,

but after the defeat in the Defiles of Ṣafrâ, promptly betook himself back to Cairo. He was appointed Shaikh al-Islâm in 1812. These tales are imitations of the *Arabian Nights*. The hero of the stories, ʿAbdal-Raḥmân, finds himself a rich man at his father's death. Having no taste for pleasure, he gives himself up to study, and desires, when three years have elapsed, to enjoy the fruits of his learning, and let others enjoy them also. He calls his slaves, friends, and relations together, each in their turn, and relates short stories to them. But he has the fatal gift of sending his hearers to sleep, and bringing misadventure on himself, on every occasion. After a series of unlucky incidents, he is even taken for a madman, and shut up in the Mâristân, the lunatic asylum at Cairo. But, still ruled by his mania, he continues to gather a circle of good-natured listeners about him, and to delight them by his stories. Of these latter tales the two last volumes, presumably finished in 1783, consist. Doubt has been expressed as to whether J.-J. Marcel did not add something of his own composition to the canvas originally furnished him by Shaikh al-Mahdî, but as the same insinuation was made against Galland, who has been completely cleared of it, there is no reason why any further attention should be paid to this imputation.

The historical topography of Cairo, on which the French school kept up in the Egyptian capital by the Republic zealously labours, owes the *Khiṭaṭ Taufîqiyya*, a renewed form of Maqrîzî's classic work, to ʿAlî-pacha Mubârak, Minister of Public Instruction, who died in 1893. He also brought the metric system within the reach of the populace (*al-Mîzân*, 1892). ʿAlî-pacha Mubârak was an interesting type of the savant of his day. He was born at Birinbâl in 1823, and began life

in the army. He studied in Paris, and took part in the Crimean War, with the Egyptian contingent attached to the Turkish army. In 1870 he founded the Viceregal Library at Cairo, and thus rendered a mass of most interesting old manuscripts accessible to the public. Accounts of European travel have been published by Ḥasan-Efendi Taufîq, who made a tour in Germany and Switzerland (*Rasâ'il al-bushrâ*, 1891); by Aḥmad Zakî, secretary to the Khedive, who was delegated to the Congress of Orientalists held at Geneva (*al-Safar ilâ'l-Mu'tamar*, 1894); and by Muḥammad Amîn Fikrî-bey (*Irshâd al-alibbâ*, 1892). Geography claims the names of Maḥmûd Rashâd (*al-durûs el-jagrâfiyya*, 1889); Muṣṭafâ 'Alawî-bey (*al-thamarât al-wâfiya*, 1873); Sayyid-Efendi Taufîq (*al-nafaḥât al-'Abbâsiyya*, 1894); and Shaikh Muḥammad ibn 'Umar al-Tûnisî, who was born in 1789, studied at the Mosque of Al-Azhar, took a journey to Wadai and Darfur, and wrote an account of it, which has been translated into French by Dr. Perron. He died at Cairo, where he held a post in the School of Medicine, in 1857.

In addition to numerous translations from European languages, which do not fall within the province of this work, the exact sciences have been cultivated, as regards arithmetic, by 'Alî 'Izzat-Efendi (1869), Shafîq-bey Manṣûr (1887), Muḥammad-Efendi Ḥâmid (1894), and Maḥmûd-Efendi Mujîr (1870); Muṣṭafâ-Efendi Shauqî (1871) has written on the metric system; Ismâ'îl-Efendi Mar'î (1887), and the above-mentioned Muḥammad-Efendi Ḥâmid, on algebra; Ibrâhîm al-Dasûqî 'Abdal-Ghaffâr, who died in 1883, directed the publication of a treatise on trigonometry in 1853; and Ḥasan-Efendi Ḥusnî has published a work on cosmography (*al-uṣûl al-*

wâfiya, 1890). Maḥmûd-pacha al-Falakî, the Minister (*d.* 1885), to whom the impulse given to these studies is specially due, wrote a memorandum on the Arabic calendar in pre-Islamic times, which was translated by Aḥmad Zakî (Bûlâq, 1888). The Turkish marshal, Ghâzî Muḥammad Mukhtâr-pacha, Commissioner-Extraordinary in Egypt, has sought repose after his struggle with the Russians in Armenia, in the publication of his *Taufîqât al-ilhâmiyya*, a concordance of the Moslem, Gregorian, and Coptic calendars, down to the year 1500 of the Hegira, with historical ephemerides, down to the year 1309 of the same era, and of his *Riyâḍ al-Mukhtâr* (Flower-garden of the Elect), a treatise on the assessment of time.

As regards the subject of grammar, Muḥammad 'Ayyâd al-Ṭanṭâwî, whose fate led him to St. Petersburg, where he taught Arabic, and where he died in 1871, left a treatise on the vulgar tongue, which was published at Leipsic in 1848.

To Physics, Chemistry, and Natural Science, Dr. Muḥammad-Efendi Kâmil al-Kafrâwî, and Muḥammad ibn Sulaimân al-Tûnisî, have devoted their powers. The former wrote *al-jawâhir al-badî'a* (1888), and *Qalâ'id al-ḥisân* (1892), and the latter was the author of the *Tahlîl* (1843). Maḥmûd Anîs wrote on the culture of cotton (1892), and we note a succession of physician authors, attended by a train of chemists. Dr. Ḥasan-pacha Maḥmûd treated the subject of internal pathology in his *Khulâṣat al-Ṭibbiyya* (1892); Dr. Muḥammad 'Alawî-bey deals with ophthalmology in his *Nukhbat al-'Abbâsiyya* (1893); Dr. Aḥmad Ḥamdî-bey imparts teaching as to the nature of simulated diseases in his *Tuḥfat al-'Abbâsiyya* (1895); while the *Durar al-badriyya*, by

Muḥammad Badr-bey al-Baqlî (1893), describes the modern remedies, and serves to complete the *ʿIqd al-jumân*, Muṣṭafâ Ḥasan Kassâb's Pharmacopœia, printed in 1834, and as a continuation of the *Nafaḥât al-riyâḍiyya*, a treatise on pharmaceutical compositions, followed by a Franco-Arabic dictionary of medical and pharmaceutical terms, by ʿAlî-Efendi Riyâḍ (1872).

The *Qudwat al-farʿ bi-aṣlihi*, a treatise on love of the fatherland, by ʿAlî Fahmî (1873), may be classed as a philosophical work; and Ḥamza Fatḥallah's *Al-ʿUqûd al-durriyya* (1891), on the Unity of the Godhead, as also his *Bâkûrat al-Kalâm*, on the rights and duties of Moslem women, which was written for the Congress of Orientalists at Stockholm (1889), under the head of biographies of the Prophet and works on the Moslem faith. To these may be added Sayyid-Efendi Muḥammad's *Durra al-ʿAbbâsiyya*, on the articles of the faith and pious practices of the Moslem religion (1894); and the *Ta'rîkh al-Khulafâ al-râshidîn*, a genealogy of the Prophet, and of his descendant Sultan ʿAbdal-Majîd, by Aḥmad Ḥijâzî Ismâʿîl (1862). The works bearing the name of Muḥammad Qadrî-pacha, who died on 21st November 1888 (*Murshid al-ḥaîrân*, a treatise on obligations and contracts, according to the Ḥanafite rite, 1891), and of Muḥammad Rifʿat (*al-Durra al-yatîma*, Lessons on the Egyptian Penal Code, 1894), must be ranged under the category of Moslem law.

Christian literature, as cultivated by the Copts, justly claims the *ʿIqd al-Anfas*, a sacred story, by Wahbî-Efendi Tâdurus (1881). A monk of the Convent of St. Barmûs has written an ecclesiastical history of Egypt, *al-Kharîda al-Nafîsa*, the first volume of which appeared in 1883.

In the Moslem West, Tunis and Algiers can boast a

few Arabic publications. In the first-named city, Shaikh Abû'l-thanâ Maḥmûd Qâbâdu has composed a poem in honour of the Prophet and his family, the *Kharîdat 'iqd al-la'âlî* (1871), and written other poetry, which has been collected by his pupil, Shaikh Abû 'Abdallah Muḥammad al-Sanûsî (1876–1878). In 1868, General Khair al-dîn al-Tûnisî, Minister to the Bey of Tunis, and subsequently Grand Vizier of the Ottoman Empire, published his *Aqwam al-masâlik*, a description—historical, political, and administrative—of the European States, with geographical notices of various parts of the earth. Muḥammad al-Sanûsî, to whom we have referred above, published, in 1892, his *Istiṭlâ'ât al-bârisiyya*, scenes in Paris during the year 1889, and has written, under the title of *Maṭla' al-darârî* (Rising of the Planets), some inquiries into the conformity of Moslem jurisprudence with the law of real estate (1888).

At Algiers, Abraham Daninos published, in 1848, an Arabic drama, *Nuzhat al-Mushtâq wa-ghuṣṣat al-'Ushshâq*; in the same year, Shaikh Muḥammad ibn Aḥmad al-Tijânî wrote his *Tuḥfat al-'arûs*, three chapters dealing with the subject of women and marriage; Muḥammad Qabîḥ produced a comic poem, the *Risâlat al-abrâr*, which relates the adventures of two Arab students in the negro village of Oran—this has been translated and published by Delphin (1887); Sî Aḥmad walad Qâḍî, Bach-aga of Frenda, has imparted his impressions of a journey to Paris in a volume entitled *al-Riḥlat el-qâḍiyya*—praises of France, and warnings addressed to the desert nomads (1878). In 1852, Sayyid Sulaimân ibn Siyâm had told the story of his journey to France in his *Riḥla*. To conclude, it would be impossible to speak of the Arabic literature of Algiers without noticing the

name of our great and doughty adversary, the Emîr Muḥyî al-dîn ʿAbdal-Qâdîr al-Ḥasanî, whose *Dhikrâ 'l-ʿÂqil* (Reminder to the Intelligent) has been translated into French by G. Dugat, and whose Military Regulations, *Wishâḥ al-Katâ'ib*, were published and translated by F. Patorni in 1890. The *Iktirâth*, which deals with the respect of the Moslem faith for the rights of women, and is the work of Muḥammad ibn Muṣṭafâ ibn al-Khoja Kamâl, an Algerian, was translated by Arnaud in 1895.

Shaikh Muḥammad Abû Ra's al-Nâṣirî (1751–1823), of Mascara, was a learned man who produced several historical works, among them a description of the Island of Jarba, which was translated and published at Tunis in 1884, by Exiga (Kayzer). He lost his parents at an early age, and had a most unhappy childhood. Notwithstanding this, he learnt the alphabet without any instructor, and amassed sufficient knowledge to enable him to give reading and writing lessons to law students. He taught at Mascara, and gathered many pupils about him, to whom he always dictated from memory. In 1790 he went on the pilgrimage, and paid visits to Cairo and Tunis. On his return he acted as *qâḍî* and preacher until 1796. In 1800 he was at Algiers, went on to Fez, and departed again, in 1811, to Mecca, where he met some learned men of the sect of the Wahhâbîs. He recognised their principles as being similar to those of the Ḥanbalites, with rules of practice differing from those adopted by the four orthodox rites. His *Voyages Extraordinaires* (ʿAjâ'ib al-Asfâr), translated by Arnaud, are a commentary on his own poem on the capture of Oran by Muḥammad ibn ʿUthmân (1792).

In Morocco, Abû'l-Qâsim ibn Aḥmad al-Ziyânî has

given the history of that country from 1631 to 1812, in his *Tarjumân al-Muʿrib*, published and translated by Monsieur O. Houdas. The work was written at Tilimsân, where the author, then Governor of Oudjda, had been constrained to take refuge, after having been defeated by the Bedouins. This history was carried down to a later date by Aḥmad al-Nâṣirî al-Salâwî, born 1834, died 1897, who was Custom House employé in various ports along the coast, and made use, in composing his work, of various official documents (*Al-Istiqṣâ*). Muḥammad ibn al-Ṭayyib al-Qâdirî wrote and printed his *Nashr al-Mathânî*, a biographical dictionary of the eleventh and twelfth centuries of the Hegira, at Fez.

At Mecca, Aḥmad ibn Zainî Daḥlân, who performed the functions of *Shaikh al-ʿUlamâ* in the Holy City, and died there in 1886, printed, in 1885, a political history of Islamism, entitled *al-futûḥât al-islâmiyya*.

In the Moslem East, far away in Hindustan, Muḥammad Ṣiddîq Ḥasan-Khân Bahâdur (al-Qânûjî al-Bukhârî) (1833–1889), Nabob of Bhopal by his marriage with the Begum of that State, a vassal of England, who had inherited the throne, caused the following works to be printed at Constantinople: *al-Bulgha*, an Arabic lexicography, followed by a bibliography of Arabic, Turkish, Persian, and Hindu dictionaries (1879); *al-ʿAlam al-Khaffâq*, on the formation and derivation of Arabic words; the *Luqṭat al-ʿAjlân*, an historical miscellany; followed by the *Khabî'at al-Akwân*, a history of the various religions; *al-Iqlîd li-adillat al-ijtihâd wa'l-taqlîd*, a treatise on jurisprudence; *al-Ṭarîqa al-Muthlâ*, advice for finding out the principles of law without assistance; and the *Nuzl al-Abrâr*, on religious morality (1884); and, at Bûlâq, the *Nashwat al-Sakrân* (The Drunkard's

Awakening, 1879); the *Ghuṣn al-bân*, on rhetoric (1879); the *Ḥuṣûl al-ma'mûl* (Obtaining of what one Desires), on the principles of law; the *Fatḥ al-bayân*, a commentary on the Koran, in ten volumes (1884); the *Ḥusn al-Uswa* (The Fair Support), devoted to the authentic words of God and His Prophet touching woman (1884); *al-Rauḍat al-nadiyya*, a commentary on a legal work, entitled *al-Durar al-bahiyya*, by Muḥammad al-Yamanî al-Shauqânî (Bûlâq, 1879); and *Fatḥ al-'allâm*, a commentary on Ibn Ḥajar's *Bulûgh al-marâm* (Bûlâq, 1885). At Bombay, Muḥammad Karâma al-'Alî al-Dihlawî, who died in 1832, printed a life of the Prophet Mahomet.

Far northwards, at Kazan, a learned man, named Mîrzâ Muḥammad 'Alî ibn Muḥammad Kâzhem-beg, published, in 1833, an essay on Arabic literature, entitled *al-Tuḥfat al-ḥaqîra;* and Shihâb al-dîn ibn Bahâ al-dîn al-Ghazzânî al-Marjânî wrote the history of the Khans of Transoxania, which appeared in 1864.

In Paris, Abû Rabî' Sulaimân al-Ḥarâi'rî, who was assistant Arabic master at the École des Langues Orientales Vivantes, published Shaikh Aḥmad ibn al-Mu'aẓẓam al-Râzî's twelve *Lectures* (1865); wrote a treatise on meteorology, physics, and electro-plating (*Risâla fî ḥawâdith al-jaww*, 1862); and delivered a *Fatwâ*, or judicial decision as to whether Moslems may eat the flesh of animals killed by Christians—this with the object of making it easier for his co-religionists to travel in European countries. He wrote a treatise on coffee in 1860, and described the Universal Exhibition of 1867 to his fellow-countrymen in his *'arḍ al-baḍâ'i' al-'âmm*. In Paris, too, the Lebanon Shaikh, Yûsuf Buṭrus Karam, published

his reply to attacks levelled at himself and other Christians of the Lebanon, and another response to further objections (1863). In Constantinople, the capital of the Turkish Empire, where Arabic is a classic tongue, of which the influence on the Turkish language constantly increases because of the scientific terms borrowed from it, concurrently with those of French origin, which are formed from the Greek, Arabic works appear, but they are necessarily fewer and less important than those published in countries where the language is popularly spoken. Muḥammad ibn Muḥammad Ḥasan Ẓâfir, whose birthplace is Tripoli in Barbary, has printed his *Anwâr al-Qudsiyya* (Sacred Lights), on the rules and precepts of the religious order of the Shâdhiliyya, in the city of the Sultan (1885). Shaikh Muḥammad Abû'l-Hudâ Efendi al-Ṣiyâdî, a man of Aleppan origin, affiliated to the religious order of the Rifâ'iyya, is a mystic poet. He published, in 1881, *Al-faiḍ al-Muḥammadî* (The Grace of Mahomet and the Succour of the Prophet), a collection of his own literary compositions, and has devoted his *Qilâdat al-jauhar* (Necklace of Jewels, 1885) to the life and praises of his master, Shaikh Aḥmad al-Rifâ'î. Texts are sent from the most distant corners of the Moslem East to be printed at Constantinople. Most of the works of the Nabob of Bhopal, Muḥammad Ṣiddîq Ḥasan Khân, appeared there; and there, too, Shaikh 'Abd al-Shakûr Raḥmân 'Alî-Khân, of Bendelkend in Hindustan, has laid his *Abniyat al-Islâm* (Edifice of Islamism), based on the traditions of the Prophet (1882), before the public. Sayyid 'Abd al-Ghaffâr ibn 'Abd al-Wâḥid al-Akhras, who was born at Mosul after the year 1805, and died at Bassora in 1874, left a *dîwân* entitled

al-Ṭirâz al-anfas (The Most precious Embroidery), which was printed in 1888. He was dumb. Dâ'ûd-pacha, the last of the independent governors of Bagdâd, sent him to India to undergo an operation; but when the doctors told him he would have to risk his life, he replied: "I will not sell my all for the sake of a part of myself," and took his way back to Bagdâd. Dâ'ûd-pacha found a historian of his own in the person of Amîn ibn Ḥasan al-Ḥulwânî, a professor at the Mausoleum of the Prophet at Medina, whose *Maṭâli' al-su'ûd*, lithographed at Bombay in 1887, carries us through the last victorious struggles of the Porte with the Mameluke masters of the ancient capital of the 'Abbâsid Caliphs. The Imâm of the Shâfi'ites at Medina, Al-Ḥâjj Aḥmad-Efendi, published his *Al-Khuṭab al-wa'ẓiyya* (Sermons and Driblets of Gold from the Pulpit), a collection of sermons for Fridays and Moslem feast-days, and his *Hidâyat al-murtâb* (Guide for Doubtful Passages), a treatise on Koranic exegesis, dealing with obscure passages in the sacred book, in the year 1889. From Tripoli, in Syria, Shaikh Ḥusain-Efendi Jisrî-Zâdê sends his *Risâla Ḥamîdiyya*, on the truths of the Moslem faith, a controversial work directed against the disciples of modern philosophers, for publication (1890). From Yaman comes the *Maqâma adabiyya* (Literary Lecture), under which title the 'Ulemâ Muḥammad Hilâl-Efendi, President of the Court of Appeal in that country, has collected the judicial correspondence between himself and the judges of the inferior courts within his jurisdiction, and his correspondence with the various Attorneys-General (1889), followed by a Turkish translation; and his *'Iqd al-jumân* (Necklace of Pearls), a panegyric

of the family of Osman, with the predictions of the ancient sages of Islam concerning it. A Moor, Shaikh ʿAbdal-Qâdir ibn ʿAbdal-Karîm al-Wardîfî, has written and published, also at Constantinople, an elegy on the death of Sharîf Muley Aḥmad, uncle of Muley Ḥasan, Emperor of Morocco, who found a refuge at Constantinople, and died there in 1889.

CHAPTER XII

THE PERIODICAL PRESS

A VERY flourishing branch of contemporary literature is that consisting of the newspapers and reviews published in the Arabic tongue, which appear not only in the countries in which that tongue is spoken, but even in lands where Arabic is studied and known only as a learned language, and in some where it is utterly unknown, save to the masters and students in a few schools specially devoted to the study of Oriental languages, but which do harbour a certain number of Arabic-speaking emigrants, and possess printing works, the compositors of which are able to use the *naskhî* character. In Egypt, where the brief French occupation had given birth to two newspapers in the French language, the *Courrier d'Égypte* and the *Décade Égyptienne*, Muḥammad 'Alî founded the official organ of his Government, the *Waqâ'i' al-miṣriyya* (Egyptian Events), on 20th November 1828. It appeared at Cairo two or three times a week in Arabic and Turkish. After seventy-three years of a most chequered existence, this sheet, the first newspaper printed in the East, after General Bonaparte's original attempts, and concerning which Reinaud wrote in 1831, that it was "an undertaking of which no other specimen exists, so far, in any Moslem country," is still published three times a week in Arabic. Thirty

years later, Khalîl al-Khûrî, a Syrian *littérateur*, founded the *Ḥadîqat al-Akhbâr* (Garden of News), a bi-weekly journal, the first issue of which appeared on 1st January 1858, at Beyrout.

Towards the year 1860, the official organ of the Regency of Tunis was founded, under the title of *al-Râ'id al-Tûnisî.* In Paris, about the same time, Sulaimân al-Ḥarâ'irî was publishing a paper called *al-Barjîs*, in which the romance of ʿAntar began to appear as a *feuilleton.* In July of that same year, Aḥmad Fâris al-Shidyâq began to publish the *Jawâ'ib*, a weekly paper, at Constantinople. After a long and brilliant career there, this journal was removed, about ten years ago, to Cairo. Any spare time at the printing offices of the *Jawâ'ib* was utilised for the publication of various Arabic classics, drawn from Constantinopolitan libraries.

At Damascus, the chief city of the province of Syria, for which country the Ottoman authorities have revived the ancient name of *Sûriyâ*, an official journal, written in Turkish and Arabic, has been appearing since 1865; and since 1866 the Governor-General of the province of Aleppo, in the southern districts of which Arabic is spoken, has caused an official organ to be published there, under the name of *al-Furât* (The Euphrates).

In 1869, the Jesuit Fathers, who had then just added a branch at Beyrout, soon to become the Catholic University of St. Joseph, to their college at Ghazîr on the Lebanon, began to publish a weekly review called *al-Bashîr.* To this they added, in 1898, a bi-monthly scientific review, *al-Mashriq* (The Orient). To compete with this publication, Buṭrus al-Bistânî founded, in the middle of 1870, a bi-monthly review called the *Janna* (The Garden)—this disappeared in 1886; the *Junaina*

(Little Garden), which only lasted for three years; and a bi-monthly review called *al-Jinân;* while the Moslems of Beyrout, desirous of possessing an organ of their own, founded the *Thamarât al-funûn* (Fruits of Science), a weekly journal, in 1874. About the same time the publication of the *Taqaddum* (Progress) was commenced. To this paper the most active young writers in Syria contributed, among them Iskandar al-ʿAzâr and Adîb Isḥâq, who died very young, and carried to his tomb the brilliant hopes his first literary efforts had raised. The *Thamarât al-funûn* represented the reactionary, or stationary—the attitudes are identical—spirit of the Moslem population. The *Taqaddum*, true to its title, opened its columns to all the modern ideas. On 18th October 1877 Khalîl Sarkîs, son-in-law of Buṭrus Bistânî, founded the *Lisân al-ḥâl* (Tongue of the Situation), which began by being a bi-weekly journal, but has been published daily since 1894. As this paper, which was obliged to guide its political utterances so as to be agreeable to the Ottoman Government, also maintained a due reserve as to the numberless religious confessions which flourish on Syrian soil, the independent Maronites felt the need of a newspaper of their own, and founded one, the *Miṣbâḥ*, in 1880. The Protestants published the *Kaukab al-ṣubḥ al-munîr* (Brilliant Star of the Morning), which has ceased to appear, and the *Nashra al-usbuʿiyya* (Weekly Publication), which is still in existence. For a short time the Orthodox Greek community possessed an organ, called the *Hadiyya* (The Gift), which has now disappeared. To counterbalance the reactionary influence of the *Thamarât al-funûn*, the Government published, on and after 22nd March 1886, a bi-weekly sheet bearing the name of the

city in which it appeared, *Beyrout*. This became the official organ of the new province established in 1888, of which Beyrout is the capital.

The development of industrial and commercial wealth which coincided with the reign of Ismâ'îl-pacha gave a fresh impetus to journalism, and during that period the following journals appeared :—

Al-'Adâla (Justice), a daily paper, founded in 1897, and edited by Muḥammad al-Khayyâmî, noted for its unwavering fanaticism, and its attacks on all foreign elements. It was printed in three columns and on only one side of the sheet. The same editor published, from 1896 onwards, and assisted by Muḥammad Sharbatli, a weekly review, entitled *al-Nahj al-qawîm* (The Straight Path). *Al-Islâm* (Islamism) is the organ of the old Moslem party, which centres in the Mosque of Al-Azhar. It is a journal devoted to science, history, and literature, founded in 1893 by Aḥmad 'Alî al-Shâdhilî, and which used only to appear on the first day of each lunar month. It now appears once a week.

The paper published by Salîm Fâris was called *al-Qâhira*. It has ceased publication.

Al-Salṭana (The Sultanate), a weekly journal, founded in 1857, represents Ottoman interests, and is edited by Iskandar Efendi Shalhûb. *Al-Maḥrûsa* (The Capital) has been in existence since 1877, and was edited by Azîz-bey Zind, who has now been succeeded by Rafâ'îl-Efendi Zind. The chief writers on this paper are Yûsuf-Efendi Âṣaf and Khalîl-Efendi Naqqâsh.

Al-Hilâl (The Crescent), a literary and scientific journal, appearing once a month, edited by Jurjî-Efendi Zaidân, and founded in 1892, is devoted to the dissemination of European ideas.

A certain number of papers and reviews are more especially intended for ladies; among them we may note:—

Al-Fatât (The Young Girl), a monthly publication which has been appearing since 1892, and is edited by Mme. Hind bint Naufal; the *Mir'ât al-ḥasnâ* (Mirror of Beauty), edited by Maryam Mizhir since 1896; *al-Firdaus* (Paradise), by Louise Habbâlin; and *Anîs al-Jalîs* (The Faithful Companion), by Alexandra Avierino and Labîba Hâshim.

The Copts, too, possess an Arabic press, which is entirely devoted to the intestinal quarrels which divide the Coptic nation, and the struggles between the clergy and the people. The *Waṭan* (The Fatherland), founded in 1878 by Mîkhâ'îl 'Abdal-Sayyid, a bi-weekly paper, supports the Patriarch's party, while the *Taufîq* (Success), a scientific and progressive weekly publication, represents the opposition.

In 1876, a journalist of the Lebanon, who found he had not sufficient freedom of action in Syria, Salîm Taqlâ by name, founded at Alexandria, with the help of his brother Bishâra, the *Ahrâm* (The Pyramids), the first Arabic daily paper, which then defended, and still defends, French interests in Egypt. Shortly afterwards, another Syrian founded a weekly review, *al-Maḥrûsa*, at Cairo. A bi-monthly review, the *Muqtaṭif*, founded in 1877 by the pupils of the American College, at Beyrout, was removed to Cairo, where the editors, Fâris Nimr, Ya'qûb Ṣarrûf, and Shâhîn Makârios, established, in 1889, a newspaper called *al-Muqaṭṭam* (after the mountain overlooking the city), which is devoted to the development of British influence. The Moslems had no organ until Shaikh Aḥmad Mâdhî (died 1893) published a

political paper, *al-Mu'ayyad* (1890), which has a large circulation all over the Moslem world, from Morocco to the Dutch Indies, and which has been managed, since the founder's death, by 'Alî ibn Yûsuf, who calls himself Shaikh 'Alî Yûsuf.

To these publications, and many others, such as the *Miṣr*, which favours the English occupation, the *Baṣîr*, the *Salâm*, and the *Akhbâr*, all of them Turko-Egyptian in their leanings, two weekly journals and one daily paper have recently been added. These are the *Murṣad* and the *Musnad*, and the *Liwâ* (The Flag), which last (a daily paper) is edited by Muṣṭafâ Kâmil.

In the provinces of the Ottoman Empire, a certain number of official journals appear in the Turkish language, and, in places where Arabic is spoken, a portion of the sheet is printed in that tongue. Thus, in the province of Bassora, we have *al-Baṣra*, *al-Zaurâ* in that of Bagdâd, *Ṣan'â* in the Yemen, and *Ṭarâbulus al-gharb* in Tripoli of Barbary, where we may also notice the *Taraqqî* (Progress). Turning westward, we find at Tunis, besides the *Official Gazette*, to which we have already referred, *al-Ḥâḍira*, which has been in existence since 1890, *al-Zahra*, *al-Baṣîra*, and two Arabic journals printed in the Hebrew character, the literary style of which lies midway between the Arabic of the classics and the popular form of speech — the *Bustân* and the *Mukhayyir*. In Algeria the Arabic press is represented by the *Mubashshir* and the *Tilimsân* (Tlemcen). A political sheet known as *al-Maghrib* has appeared at Morocco.

At Constantinople, besides the *Jawâ'ib*, which was ultimately transferred to Cairo, various Arabic journals, most of them shortlived, have appeared. Among them we may mention the *I'tidâl*, the *Ḥawâdith*, the *Salâm*, the

Ḥaqâ'iq, and the *Munabbih*, all of them political organs; and the *Insân* and *Kaukab*, scientific journals. The legal paper, *al-Ḥuqûq*, continues to appear in Turkish and Arabic. In the Island of Cyprus, now under English rule, a political journal in Arabic, the *Dîk al-Sharq* (Cock of the East), is published; and in India there is the *Nukhbat al-Akhbâr* (Selection of News), which would appear to be the only Arabic newspaper published in the huge area of Hindustan.

In Italy, the *Mustaqill* (The Independent); in France, the *Anbâ*, the *Abû'l-Haul*, the *Ittiḥâd*, the *Baṣîr*, the *Sadâ*, the *Ḥuqûq*, the *Shuhra*, the *'Urwa al-Wuthqâ*, and the *Rajâ* (all of which, like the *Barjîs*, to which reference has already been made, have discontinued publication); in London, the *Ittiḥâd al-'Arabî*, the *Khilâfa*, and the *Mir' ât al-Aḥwâl*, edited by Rizq-Allah Ḥasûn, represent the journals which have died out on foreign soil. Still green and flourishing are the *Abû Naẓẓâra* (The Old Man in Spectacles), a satirical illustrated paper edited by Shaikh Sanû'a, and the *Tawaddud* and *Munṣif*, in Paris; the *Kashkûl*, which contains Persian and Tartar sheets, at Tiflis; the *Ḍiyâ al-Khâfiqain*, partly printed in English, in London; the *Kaukab Amîrikâ* and *al-Ayyâm*, in New York; the *Marṣad*, in Marseilles; the *Hâdî*, in Philadelphia; and the *Barâzîl*, *Raqîb*, and *Asmaï*, in Brazil.

The Future of Arabic Literature

The foregoing pages have given a picture of the blossoming, the maturity, and the decline of a literature which has lasted for thirteen centuries, from the earliest period of the Middle Ages down to our own days; and

we have watched the second growth, induced by the fecundating influence of modern thought, of the original stock, several branches of which—not to mention that offshoot of circumstance engrafted on it, the periodical press—have brought forth flowers. What future lies before this second growth ? Will it be an imitation of the classic centuries ? Or will the language, forced into modification by the necessity for interpreting fresh ideas, enrich itself with new and youthful forms which shall revivify the ancient groundwork ? It would seem, at the first glance, as though such centres of literary activity as Cairo and Beyrout were destined to produce men who, following the movement initiated by their predecessors of the nineteenth century, will, so to speak, serve as the link between Europe—and in Europe I include the colonies scattered all over the face of the globe, and everywhere continuing the work begun on this continent by the sons of Japhet—and the East, still wrapt in the semi-darkness of a dying twilight. They should be aided in this enterprise by the powerful support of the periodical press, which reaches the greater part of the Moslem world, reckoned at two hundred million souls, and which should be able to do an enormous amount of good in this direction.

But how does all this affect the language ? Will it be transformed, developed ? Will it grow clearer, more accessible to the mass of half-taught people educated in the primary schools ? Any man who has studied the question must answer, No ! Nowhere do we see a movement like that which, in the course of the last thirty years, has altered the old Osmanli-Turkish tongue, by clearing all its ancient rhetorical forms away. Arabic s still swathed about with classic formations, and conse-

quently employs a quantity of expressions which can only be understood by literary men; thus closing the way of comprehension to the majority, in matters which would be of the deepest interest to it. No self-respecting writer would publish a political article in anything but rhymed prose, and the empty and futile rhetoric, the alliterations after the manner of Ḥarîrî's *Lectures*, therein displayed, entertain the educated reader. There it ends. Yet, along with these clap-trap harangues, serious articles on special subjects, which make no attempt at shining by the use of a display of empty words, and appeal direct to the intelligence, without permitting their argument to be disturbed by extraneous trifling, are also published. To tell the truth, one obstacle lies always between the editor and his readers—the uncertainty which attends the reading of a language in which the vowels are very seldom marked. This drawback it will be very hard to remedy. But it would be less difficult to read Arabic, and there would be less uncertainty about it, if the editor or the printer would consent to mark the *ḥarakât* in the case of words which may bear a double meaning, in that of the passive tenses of verbs, and in that of the substantives of which the sense changes according to the spelling. This would render a huge service to that part of the Eastern public which has not worn out its youth on the flags of the universities—for I do not, of course, speak here of the very small circle of Europeans who may, either as a study or a pastime, cast their eyes over an Arabic journal, though they have far better and more practical literature at their command, in their own tongue.

Should Arabic writers, instead of producing their work in literal Arabic, write in the dialect of the various coun-

tries in which Arabic is spoken, and in which a native press exists? That is not to be desired, for a newspaper established on such principles would find no readers beyond the inhabitants of the country in which it appears. A newspaper in Algerian Arabic is not likely to appeal to a man from Damascus, or Bagdâd, or Muscat. The poor fellow's *Qâmûs* would be wasted on it! The use of the literal Arabic ensures each newspaper a circle of readers ranging far beyond Arabic-speaking countries, and comprising all those in which it is the language of the learned, as Latin was amongst ourselves in the Middle Ages. This means every country inhabited by Moslems, from the Caucasus to China, from the Steppes of Tartary to the mouths of the Niger.

Already, indeed, many neologisms have found their way into the language, and it has become possible to render the modern expressions which the needs of modern times have created in Europe. The Arabic tongue, with its skilfully composed grammar, is sufficiently malleable to enable it to express modern thought, and at the same time to supply the whole of the Moslem East with the new technical terms in chemistry, medicine, and most sciences. The path one would fain see the writer of the future tread is that of the search for limpidity and simplicity of expression. Once these are attained, a brilliant career may be predicted for Arabic Literature, which, like Islam itself, will endure for many an age to come.

BIBLIOGRAPHY

GENERAL STUDIES

German

Hammer-Purgstall, *Litteraturgeschichte der Araber.* 7 vols. Vienna, 1850–1856.—Alfred von Kremer, *Kulturgeschichte des Orients unter den Khalifen.* Vol. ii. (Vienna, 1877), chaps. viii. (Poesie) and ix. (Wissenschaft und Litteratur).—Carl Brockelmann, *Geschichte der Arabischen Litteratur.* Vol. i., Weimar, 1898 (in two parts); vol. ii., Berlin, 1899–1902 (also in two parts).—Carl Brockelmann, *Geschichte der Arabischen Litteratur*, second part of vol. vi. of the *Litteraturen des Ostens in Einzeldarstellungen.* Leipzig, 1901 (drawn up with a view to the general public).

Latin

Ḥâjî-Khalfa, *Lexicon bibliographicum et encyclopædicum*, edited in Arabic, with a Latin translation, by G. Fluegel. 7 vols., quarto. Leipzig and London, 1835–1858.

PRE-ISLAMIC PERIOD

Arabic

Septem Muʿallakât carmina antiquissima Arabum. Ed. F. A. Arnold, Lipsiæ, 1850. Abû'l-Faraj al-Iṣfahânî, *Kitâb al-Aghânî* (Book of Songs). 20 vols. Bûlâq, 1868.—Brünnow, *The twenty-first volume of the Kitâb al-Aghânî, being a collection of biographies not contained in the Bûlâq edition.* Leyden, 1888.—Rev. Father Salhani, S.J., published a collection of narratives drawn from the same work at Beyrout in 1888.—Kosegarten began to publish the text of this work, with a Latin translation and notes, at Greifenwald, but only the first volume appeared (1840).

ENGLISH

Sir C. J. Lyall, *Translations of Ancient Arabian Poetry*, with an introduction and notes. London, 1885.—W. F. Prideaux, *The Lay of the Himyarites.* Sehore, 1879.—W. A. Clouston, *Arabian Poetry for English Readers.* Glasgow, 1881.—J. L. Burckhardt, *Arabic Proverbs.* London, 1830.—E. W. Lane's *Arabic-English Lexicon.* 8 vols., 1863–1893 (full of extracts and explanations of early Arabic poetry).

FRENCH

Silvestre de Saçy, *Chrestomathie Arabe.* 2me. edit. 3 vols. Paris, 1826, 3 vols.—F. Fresnel, *Lettres sur l'Histoire des Arabes avant l'Islamisme.* Paris, 1836.—R. Basset, *La poésie Arabe anté-islamique* (Leçon d'ouverture). Paris, 1880.—St. Guyard, *Théorie nouvelle de la métrique Arabe* (*Journal Asiatique*, 1876, and also published separately).

GERMAN

Ahlwardt, *Ueber Poesie und Poetik der Araber.* Gotha, 1856. *Bemerkungen über die Echtheit der alten Arabischen Gedichte.* Greifswald, 1872.— I. Goldziher, *Abhandlungen zur Arabischen Philologie.* Leyden, 1876.—G. Jacob, *Studien in Arabischen Dichtern.* Heft II., *Noten zum Verständniss der Muallaqât*, 1894. Heft III., *Altarabisches Beduinenleben*, 1897.— Martin Hartmann, *Metrum und Rhythmus: der Ursprung der Arabischen Metra.* Giessen, 1896.—Th. Noeldeke, *Beiträge zur Kentniss der Poesie der alten Araber.* Hanover, 1864.

THE KORAN

ENGLISH

Translations by George Sale, London, 1734, 1764, 1821, 1824, 1857.—Rodwell, 1861, 1876, arranged according to the presumed historical order of the chapters.—E. H. Palmer, 2 vols., Oxford, 1880.—E. W. Lane, *Selections from the Kur'án.* London, 1879.—Stanley Lane-Poole, *Speeches of Mohammad.* London, 1882.

FRENCH

Translations by Du Ryer, Paris, 1649, 1672 ; The Hague, 1683, 1685 ; Antwerp, 1719 ; Amsterdam, 1756, 1770, 1775 ; Geneva, 1751.—Savary, Paris, 1783 (An vii., 1798), 1822 ; Amsterdam, 1786.—Kasimirski, Paris, 1840, 1852.

German

Translations by Solomon Schweiggern, Nüremberg, 1616, 1623.—Megerlin, 1772.—Friedrich Eberhardt Boysen, Halle, 1773, 1775.—Wahl, Halle, 1828.—Ullmann, Crefeld, 1840, 1877.—F. Rückert, in extracts, published by A. Müller at Frankfort, 1888.

Latin

Translations by Louis Maracci, Padua, 1698.—Abraham Hinckelmann, Hamburg, 1694.—Chr. Reinecke, Leipzig, 1721.

Italian

Andrea Arrivabene's anonymous translation, Venice, 1547.

There are Dutch translations by Swigger, Hamburg, 1641 ; Glasemaker, Amsterdam, 1698 ; Tollens, Batavia, 1859 ; Keyzer, Haarlem, 1860 ; and a Russian translation by Sabloukov, Kazan, 1877 ; also Swedish translations by Crusenstolpe, Stockholm, 1843, and Tornberg, Lund, 1874.

History of the Koran—Th. Noeldeke, *Geschichte des Korans.* Göttingen, 1863.—E. M. Wherry, *A Comprehensive Commentary on the Qurán.* 4 vols., London, 1882-6.—La Beaume, Analysis of the Koran according to Kasimirski's translation. Paris, 1878.—H. Hirschfeld, *New Researches into the Composition and Exegesis of the Qoran.* London, 1902.

Life of Mahomet.—Ibn Hisham, *Das Leben Muhammed's*, tr. Weil. Stuttgart, 1864.—A. Sprenger, *Das Leben und die Lehre des Mohammed.* Berlin, 1861, 1869.—W. Muir, *The Life of Mahomet and History of Islam.* London, 1858–1861 ; 3rd ed., 1895.—L. Krehl, *Das Leben des Muhammed.* Leipzig, 1884.—Syed Ameer Ali, *The Life and Teachings of Muhammad.* London, 1891.—E. Sell, *The Faith of Islam.* London, 1880.

PERIOD OF THE CALIPHS

Al-Nadîm, *Kitab al-Fihrist*, ed. G. Fluegel, 2 vols., Leipzig, 1871, 1872.—Ibn-Khaldûn, *Prolégomènes*, traduites et commentés par MacGuckin de Slane, 3 vols., Paris, 1858.—*Ḥamâsa,* uebersetzt von Fr. Rückert, 2 vols., Stuttgart, 1846.—*Divan* de Ferazdaq, trad. par. E. Boucher, 2 vols., Paris, 1870, 1875.—*Mutanabbii Carmina,* ed. F. Dieterici, Berlin, 1861.—T. Chenery and F. Steingass,

The Assemblies of Al-Harîrî, trans., 2 vols., London, 1867, 1898.—D. S. Margoliouth, *The Letters of Abu'l-'Alâ of Ma'arra*, text and trans., Oxford, 1898.—E. H. Palmer, *The Poetical Works of Behâ-ed-din Zoheir*, text and trans., 2 vols., Cambridge, 1876, 1877.—F. Dieterici, *Die Philosophie der Araber*, 16 parts, Berlin, 1858–1894.—T. W. Arnold, *The Preaching of Islam*, London, 1896.—E. G. Browne, *Literary History of Persia*, London, 1901 (half of this volume is occupied with Arabic literature under the Caliphate).—R. Dozy, *Recherches sur l'histoire et la literature de l'Espagne*, 2 vols., Leyden, 1881.—S. Lane-Poole, *Cairo*, London, 1902 (with account of Arabic literature of Egypt).—Sir W. Muir, *The Apology of Al-Kindy*, London, 2nd ed., 1887.—Renan, *Averroes et l'Averroïsme*, Paris, 1852.—Ibn-Khallikan, *Wafayât al-A'yân*, in Arabic; autographed by F. Wüstenfeld, Göttingen, 2 vols., 1835–1840; printed at Bûlâq, 1882; translated into English by MacGuckin de Slane, *Biographical Dictionary*, 4 vols., Paris–London, 1843–1871. The Supplement to this work, Ibn Shâkir Al-Kutubî's *Fawât al-Wafayât*, printed at Bûlâq in 1866, has never been translated out of the Arabic. The *Kitâb al-Aghânî* (see *ante*) also covers a part of this period (the three first centuries of the Hegira).—F. Wüstenfeld, *Die Geschichtschreiber der Araber und ihre Werke*. Göttingen, 1882. *Geschichte der Arabischen Aerzte und Naturforscher*. Göttingen, 1840. *Die Academien der Araber und ihre Lehrer*, after the Shâfi'ite school book, written by Ibn Qâḍî Shuhba. Göttingen, 1837.

MODERN PERIOD

Arabic

Muḥammad al-Muḥibbî, *Khulâṣat al-âthâr*, a biographical dictionary of the prominent persons of the eleventh century of the Hegira. 4 vols. Cairo, 1868.—Abû'l-Faḍl Muḥammad Khalîl Efendi al-Murâdî, *Silk al-durar*, biographies of the prominent men of the twelfth century of the Hegira. 4 books in 2 vols. Bûlâq, 1874.

German and English

Martin Hartmann, *Die Zeitungen und Zeitschriften in Arabischen Sprachen*, an article which appeared in the *Spécimen d'une encyclopédie Musulmane*, published by Monsieur Th. Houtsma at Leyden, 1899, pp. 11 and onward.—*The Arabic Press of Egypt*. London, 1899.

INDEX

In arranging the proper names no account has been taken of the Arabic article, al.

THE END